D1453839

Pogromchik

Pogromchik

THE ASSASSINATION OF SIMON PETLURA

Saul S. Friedman

HART PUBLISHING COMPANY, INC. NEW YORK CITY

Contents

List of Photographs

Acknowledgments

M<small>Y</small> <small>RESEARCH HAS</small> benefited tremendously from assistance provided by the staff of the <small>YIVO</small> Institute for Jewish Research in New York. I am especially grateful to Zosa Szajkowski, who opened the Tcherikover Archives to me in 1973, not out of any special preference, but because some of the materials were accessible in Yiddish as well as French and Ukrainian. The records preserved there are unique, the most complete collection of documents relating to the massacres in the Ukraine in 1919. Their importance is evident, because there are no other major sources available since the destruction of the Simon Petlura Library in Paris by the Nazis in World War II. Spirited out of Europe at great personal risk by Szajkowski after the fall of France in 1940, the Tcherikover Archives are presented here for the first time in English translation. Elias Tcherikover's monumental study, *Di ukrainer pogromen in yor 1919*, also used extensively in this work, draws from the same materials. But Tcherikover's book, published by <small>YIVO</small> in 1965, has never been translated from the Yiddish.

I wish to express my gratitude to those persons who have contributed to the completion of this manuscript:

Miriam Leikind, librarian of Rabbi Silver's Temple in Cleveland, who secured materials from Hebrew Union College for me while I was a social worker in the Hough district ten years ago.

Morris Herman, a wonderful friend to four generations of my family, a Yiddishist who introduced me to the beauties of the *mame-loshen*.

Hyman Sisman, Sarah Markowska and Joseph Hill of Youngstown, all of whom assisted with translations of difficult calligraphy and offered insight from personal experience.

Professor Agnes Smith and Susan Forgaras of the History Department of Youngstown State University who assisted with technical aspects of composition.

My brother Earl and his wife Liesel who proofread the early manuscripts and offered many helpful suggestions.

Victor Baras who labored over the final editing.

And my brother Norm, a bright and sparkling young man who helped me understand the meaning of the concept of the just man.

SAUL S. FRIEDMAN
Youngstown, Ohio
May, 1975

*To my wife Nancy
and our little ones,
Jonathan and Molly,
without whom
there is nothing.*

THE UKRAINE

EAST

• Chernigov

• Bakhmach

• Romny
• Priluki
• Piryatin

• Lubny

• Mirgorod

• Poltava

KHARKOV

• Kremenchug
• Znamenka
ka

EKATERINOSLAV

• Zaporozhe

Dnieper R.

Taganrog •

IEA

PARIS

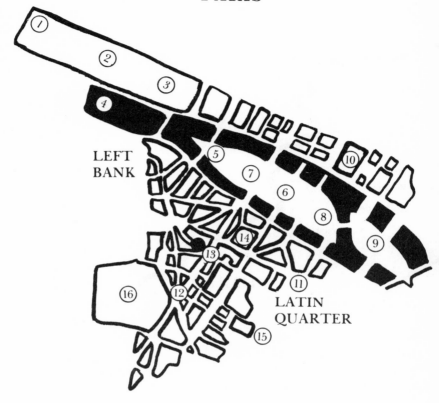

1-Jeu de Paume
2-Tuileries Garden
3-Louvre
4-Seine River
5-Pont Neuf
6-Cité
7-Palais de Justice
8-Notre Dame
9-Ile St. Louis

10-Hôtel De Ville
11-Boulevard Saint Germain
12-Boulevard Saint Michel
13-Rue Racine
● Site of Assassination
14-Cluny Museum
15-Panthéon
16-Luxembourg Garden

Chronology of Major Events

March, 1917   Under the strain of World War I, the Tsarist regime in Russia collapses and is replaced by the parliamentary-democratic *Provisional Government*. In the Ukraine, formerly part of the Russian Empire, an autonomous government, the *Rada* [council], is established.

November, 1917   The Russian Provisional Government is overthrown by the Bolsheviks.

March, 1918   Russia concludes a separate peace (the Treaty of Brest-Litovsk) on German terms. In the Ukraine, the Germans establish a puppet government, the *Hetmanate*, under Hetman [chief] Skoropadsky.

November, 1918   World War I ends in German defeat. In the Ukraine, the Hetmanate is replaced by a government known as the *Directory*. Simon Petlura becomes *Holovni Ataman* [commander-in-chief] of the armed forces of the Directory. He subsequently becomes President of the Directory.

1919   Civil war rages throughout the former Russian Empire, including the Ukraine. There are now three kinds of armies in the Ukraine—*White* (anti-Bolshevik) and *Red* (pro-Bolshevik) armies, both desiring to restore the Ukraine to Russian control, and the Ukrainian separatist forces of the Directory, commanded by Petlura. In many parts of the Ukraine, Jews are massacred in pogroms.

April, 1920   The newly created state of Poland, with the support of the Ukrainian Directory, invades Russia. The Bolsheviks repel the Polish attack and regain control of the Ukraine. Petlura and other nationalist leaders flee into exile.

A Note on Transliteration

Ukrainian, Yiddish, Russian, and Hebrew words and names are transliterated in the simplest way consistent with English usage, unless there is already an accepted Latinized spelling (for example, "Tcherikover" rather than "Cherikover"). In footnotes and bibliographic citations, the spelling of the original author is always used. In quotations, however, all spellings are modified for the sake of consistency. Thus, the title of a work may refer to "Petliura," but quotations from that work will contain the transliteration "Petlura."

Pogromchik

1.

In the Slaughter Town

FOR MOST READERS of the *New York Times* of April 7, 1919, it was merely another of those items telling of foreigners dying in some forgotten corner of the world:

> Cable dispatches received yesterday by the *Jewish Morning Journal* of this city tell of the massacres of Jews in the Ukraine even more horrible than the massacres under Czarism. The dispatches assert that a systematic effort is being made to annihilate the Jewish population in the Ukraine, and that in the city of Felshtin alone, soldiers killed 800 Jews and wounded 400, while the killed and wounded in Proskurov numbered more than 4,000. The surviving Jews in both these cities, according to the dispatches, have been pillaged and robbed of all they possess, and their plight is pitiable.[1]

Ghastly news, and yet not surprising considering the history of the Ukraine. For eight centuries prior to World War I, sacrificial pyres had illuminated the night skies in that part of Eastern Europe. The victims of this cult of inhumanity were aged Chasidic scholars, babes at the breast, women who shaved their heads bald as a sign of conjugal fidelity, and fools from the legendary town of Chelm. They were guilty of a common crime. They were Jews.

The history of the Ukraine has been blood-stained since 1096, when the first medieval charge of ritual murder was brought against Jews of the region by monks of the Pechera monastery. Subsequently, one of the oldest Ukrainian sources, the Ipatiev Chronicle, relates how in 1113 hundreds of Jews were killed in Kiev, a result of exuberance generated by the Crusades. In the time of Ivan the Terrible, many more "Judaizers," Jews and sympathizers who apparently threatened the true faith of Christianity, were ducked under the ice of the Lena, the Volga and the Dnieper Rivers. During the nationalistic uprising of Zaporoghian Cossacks in 1648-54, the *Chern* or "Black Earth" minions of Bogdan Chmielnicki slaughtered more than 200,000 Ukrainian and Polish Jews. Backs were broken, women raped, and children skewered in what Jewish historians refer to as "The Deluge."[2] A century later, 70,000 more were beheaded, disemboweled, and buried alive by the "Haidamaks," the irregular soldiers of Ukrainian nationalism.

After that time, mass killing gave way to more subtle forms of persecution. Expulsion of the Jews, practiced by every West European country since the thirteenth century, was introduced in the Ukraine by the semi-independent Hetman [chief] Ivan Skoropadsky in 1721. Fifty years later, the Empress Catherine II, avowedly more receptive to Muslims within the realm than to Jews, decreed the expulsion of the Jews from the fertile Russian heartland. Her own greed, however, soon frustrated this policy. When Poland was dismembered by Prussia, Austria, and Russia between 1772 and 1795, Catherine was enriched first by Lithuanian lands east of the Dvina-Dnieper line, then by much of the provinces of Minsk, Volhynia and Podolia, and finally by territories extending along the Nieman to Kovno down to Brest-Litbtically the current Russo-Polish border. The result was that a Tsarist state which had wanted no part of the Jews now possessed nearly one millioM. Her n such subjects.

The ultra-orthodox Russian regime applied every manner of pressure against the Jews, either to force their conversion or hasten their departure from the country. In 1794, Jewish habitation was restricted to specific communities in Lithuania, Podolia, Volhynia and Galicia. These areas came to be called the Pale of Settlement.[3]

Within the Pale, Jewish land ownership was practically forbidden. The Jews were forced to survive as peddlers, merchants, tailors, shoemakers, bakers. Conscription for Jewish youths began at age twelve and not eighteen as with other Russian boys. As the dreaded *khappers* passed through towns, dragging boys off to thirty-one years of military service and conversionist catechism, knowing parents wept and said *Kaddish,*the Jewish prayer for the dead.[4]

After a comparatively short enlightened period, during which Jews were even admitted into the officer class of the Tsarist army, pogroms again broke out in the Crimea in 1871. With the assassination of Tsar Alexander II in March, 1881, Russian Jews braced for the worst. One of the "People's Will" revolutionaries responsible for the murder was Jessie Helfman, a Jewess, and the government determined to divert the genuine grievances of the masses against the most convenient scapegoats, the Jews. In the next year, perhaps as many as 50,000 persons perished, chiefly in the Ukraine.

The anti-Jewish violence was directed by such organizations as the Union of the Archangel Michael, the Union of the Two-Headed Eagle, and the Union of the Russian Nation (the infamous "Black Hundreds"). But Jews maintained that much of the trouble stemmed from an anti-Semitism which was endemic to the Ukraine, a pathological hatred which Jews claimed illiterate peasants "suckled with their mother's milk." Without the consent and cooperation of the native Ukrainian populace, the pogroms would have been impossible.

Reacting to such "spontaneous" demonstrations against the Jews, the government of Alexander III issued a set of decrees in May, 1882, the effect of which was to wipe away all gains won by Jews during the previous decades. Those few

Jews who had been permitted to vote were now dis-franchised. The right of residence outside the Pale, till now cherished by a precious few, was summarily revoked. Barred totally from entry into medicine and law for a decade, Jewish students had to compete for a meager 3 percent of all university positions. A Jewish girl attending a university in one of the larger cities might receive a special exemption from residence restrictions if she applied for a license as a prostitute and supplied proof that she was actually pursu-ing this profession.

Many Jews within the Pale, including some veterans who thought they had earned immunity by fighting for the Tsar, lost their homes and possessions. Artisans or craftsmen were declassed for the flimsiest of excuses—trading on the Chris-tian Sabbath, selling coffee at a bakery or watch fobs at a watchmaker's shop. A massive Russification program de-stroyed Jewish schools, newspapers, literature, and arts.[5]

Although the government restricted freedom of move-ment within its boundaries, it continued to encourage the emigration of "undesirables." As a result, between 1884 and 1918 more than 1,300,000 Jews fled Russia. Those who remained suffered through new atrocities at Kishinev, Gomel, and Balta in 1903 and at more than three hundred other localities in 1905. The Black Hundreds, blessed in their work by Nicholas II, continued to arouse the passions of the masses with tales of ritual murder.[6]

Locked in dingy little villages no more than 150 meters by 300 meters on a side, Jews were scorned as Christ-killers, atheists, speculators, socialists, communists, "the interior enemy."[7] Still, after eight hundred years of hatred and abuse, by 1919 there were three and one-half million Jews living in the Ukraine, people who wished to live in peace and who were to feel the impact of the *Kureni Smerti*, the Clans of Death, once more.[8]

Long before the *New York Times* took cognizance of the situation in southern Russia, disturbing reports had been

filtering to the West. Through the winter of 1918-19, the
Jewish National Council of Lemberg, the Zionist Organization
in London, the *Yiddishe Morgenpost* of Vienna, the
Jewish Press Bureau in Stockholm, and the Polish National
Committee in Paris had been warning of special dangers for
the Jews in Galicia. As German, Ukrainian, Bolshevik,
anarchist, Polish, and Tsarist forces struggled with one
another for control of the region, entire communities of
Jews faced extinction.[9]

More than fifty-five separate pogroms were perpetrated
against Jews in the Ukraine between December 14, 1918, and
the middle of February, 1919, but it was not until the spring
of 1919, one of the most severe periods of anti-Jewish persecution, that a clear assessment could be made.

The first victims of the Proskurov pogrom; February 15, 1919.

To some extent, the troubles followed a time-tested pattern of "good-natured" drinking, punching, lechery, and tearing of feather quilts. Packs of soldiers returning from a front (of which there were several at any given moment) would accost Jews, yank at their beards, kick them to the floor of a railway coach, or make them dance in a train station. In some cases, they might even pitch a Jew from a moving train.[10] When passing through a town, the pogromchiks would first loot the Jewish taverns, then proceed on to warehouses and granaries.

Where there existed a Jewish self-defense militia, as at Pogrebishche, the local constabulary intervened, not to aid the Jews but their attackers. After disarming the Jews, allegedly to preserve the peace, the authorities detained all Jewish males over the age of seventeen in the local jailhouse. Emboldened by official police and church collaboration, the pogromchiks would demand a sum of money (35,000 rubles in Dombrovitsy, 85,000 in Gornostaipol, 200,000 in Barychevka, 600,000 in Korostychov) from the Jewish community as atonement for some imagined offense.[11] The fatalistic compliance of Jewish delegations who offered tribute in bread, salt, and money so flabbergasted one Ukrainian officer in Makarev that he remarked, "Who are these dummies?"[12] No bribe was sufficient to stave off massacre once the financial resources of the community were depleted or the vandals' taste for blood sufficiently whetted by alcohol.

The sufferings of Jews through the year 1919 served as a source of some amusement. According to one popular Ukrainian anecdote, when the Bolshevik armies entered a city, they collared a Jew and asked him to divulge his political sympathies. "I'm for the Central Rada [Ukrainian nationalists]," the Jew replied innocently. Thereupon, the Bolsheviks stripped him and gave him thirty lashes on his backside. The next day, the Reds departed and the White Army under General Anton Denikin entered the town. Once more the Jew was apprehended and his loyalties scrutinized.

"I'm for the Bolsheviks," he announced hopefully. Once more he was commanded to drop his trousers to receive thirty strokes. The following day when the Whites fled and the forces of anarchist leader Nestor Makhno entered the city, again the Jew was asked, "Who are you for?" Immediately, the story goes, the Jew dropped his pants, leaned over and said, "Beat me, but don't ask me who I'm for." The tale supposedly demonstrates the shifting fortunes in the Ukraine during the period of civil turmoil, but its real significance lies in demonstrating how the impotent Jew served once more as a scapegoat for all armies.

Women and girls, deprived of the protection of their husbands and fathers who had been locked up, begged civil authorities for help and were driven away. Cases of multiple rape were not uncommon, as young girls became the property of marauding units.[13] In Smotrich, for example, Jewesses were assaulted by ten or more Cossacks at a time. In Potapovichi, two girls who resisted were beaten until their faces were bloody pulps. The same thing happened to a pair of fourteen-year-olds at Vasilkov. At Stepantzy, where fifty women were raped on February 14, nine were so badly mauled they did not survive the day. On June 9, 1919, a peasant brought the last two surviving Jews from Ladyzhenka to the Jewish Hospital in Kiev. Before the pogroms, there had been 1,600 Jews in the town. The two young girls were terribly mutilated, one with her nose broken, the other with both hands smashed. Both were suffering from venereal diseases contracted from their violators.[14]

Often girls leaped from windows, preferring to kill themselves than be dishonored. Others attempted guile against the slavering hooligans, telling them, "No, no, *galupchik*. I'm not Jewish."[15] Thus the story of Etta Soschin, an eighteen-year-old girl in Felshtin when the pogromchiks arrived on February 16:

> The first intimation that I had that anything was amiss was that [*sic*] three soldiers burst into our home at

about 9:30 A.M. on a Monday morning. At the time, our family, with the exception of my father, who had not come home the previous night, were all at home. I distinctly remember this because the samovar was prepared for tea at the time. On the entry of soldiers, the family dispersed in fright, running in different directions. I ran into the room of our tenant and hid in a wardrobe in his room. I heard a voice calling to me to come out, and stepping out I was seized by a soldier who dragged me into the dining room and began questioning me roughly. This soldier I remember as being tall and red-haired, with a forage-cap with a red center piece extending down one side of the head. The soldier then asked me whether I was Christian or Jewish. I replied that I was a Christian and was the tenant's daughter. This the tenant denied. Thereupon the soldier demanded that I make the sign of the cross, saying that he would release me if I were a Christian child but would kill me if I were Jewish. In terror, I kissed his hand and called him "brother" and begged him to release me, but the soldier replied using the Russian slang term "that a goose and a pig have no relationship" (*gus svinye nye tovarishch*.) He then shouted "lozhish [lie down]!"[16]

Etta Soschin survived the massacre at Felshtin with sabre wounds to her head, neck, and body. One arm, which had been badly slashed, had to be amputated below the elbow. Less fortunate were her father, mother, two brothers, and two sisters, all of whom were included in the little community's death toll of 485.

There seemed to be no limit to the depravity of the pogromchiks. At Chernobyl in Western Galicia, Jews were driven into streams. Those who tried to come out of the water were shot. The rest were drowned. A similar occurrence took place at Gornostaipol on May 3, 1919, where thirteen Jews of various ages were told that they would be drinking uncooked tea that same day—in the river.[17] At Ziadkovtzy, fifteen Jews were thrown into a well to perish. Near Kiev, more than 103 were pitched from an excursion

Cadavers in the snow at Felshtin; February 17, 1919.

boat into the Dnieper.[18] In the trees along the road to Ovruch, troops lynched two old Jews. They rotted in the winter air while a sign posted nearby warned: "Whoever takes them down has not more than two minutes to live."[19]

In Bratzlav and Kamenetz-Podolsk, each of which saw more than two hundred Jews murdered, some Jews were hanged by their hands while their tormentors chopped off various limbs. Others were roasted alive over bonfires or had lit cigarettes applied to their wounds. At Brailov (twenty-five recorded deaths), several refugees from an earlier pogrom were tortured anew. Their tongues were plucked out, their eyes gouged, and their noses cut off.[20]

One of the towns which suffered most was Uman, a cantonal capital near the Bug River in the gubernia of Kiev. Before May, 1919, two-thirds of the 65,000 residents had been Jews. In that month, however, following accusations that they were Bolsheviks, the Jews were attacked by Cossacks, Gypsies, and other Christians. Whole families were murdered. There were numerous cases of deliberate barbarism—the cutting off of hands and fingers (to obtain gold wedding bands), mutilation of feet, ears, noses, breasts. Naked and half-naked bodies lay where they had fallen, until the rotting stench compelled authorities to bury them in massive lime pits. One old Jew was shot down as he attempted to flee across an open field. He did not die immediately. His cries attracted Ukrainian schoolchildren who proceeded to stone him to death. A compatriot was shot by soldiers who then tied his body to a tree and used it for target practice.[21]

When murdering families, the pogromchiks first killed the children, torturing them in the sight of their parents, whom they slew afterward. With the same primordial perversity that had moved Turkish *bashi-bazouks* to ravage innocent Armenians, the hooligans split the heads of infants against stone walls or ripped open the bellies of pregnant women to gawk at blackened fetuses.[22] One of 168 deaths at Pechanka was an infant who was taken from its mother's breast. The child was beheaded. The youngest of 119 victims at Belaya Tserkov was a child of one and one-half. Elsewhere victims were fourteen months, four months, three weeks old.

Seventy-two persons died in Kopai-Gorod, where a father was knocked to the pavement and forced to gag on the blood of his dead son. In Kitai-Gorod, the bandits jeered when mothers begged for their children to be spared. The commander of the Ukrainian guards replied with a laugh, "The Jews must be done to death with all their progeny." In the same town, a young woman, carrying her child, was grabbed by the hair, tied to a horse, and dragged through the streets. Both mother and child were then put up against a wall and shot.[23]

Such killing was at once messy and expensive, and cartridges cost fifty rubles each. At Zhitomir (1,500 dead), Koziatyn (600), Fastov, Radomyshyl, and Berdichev (2,000), the pogromchiks emulated their Turkish counterparts once more. "A favorite game," noted the *London Times*, "appears to have been to place a number of Jews in a line and see how many could be killed with one bullet. Six or seven is stated to be the record."[24] At Obodin, the killers preferred bayonets. And in Dubovo on June 17, 1919, troops established a veritable slaughterhouse in the cellar of D. Feldman's home. One by one the victims were brought to the doors of the basement where two executioners, a Moldavian and a Russian, stood with sabres in hand. As the Jews started downstairs, the two lashed out, decapitating them. Within a short time, the cellar was filled with fragments of corpses. Eight hundred of Dubovo's nine hundred Jews perished at this assembly line.[25]

Any convenient building might serve as a killing center. In the Podolian town of Trostianetz, hundreds of Jews who sought refuge in the community house were slaughtered. According to one survivor of the three-hour-long pogrom: "A bloody dance of death began. Knives flashed, axes whizzed, special weapons were improvised for the occasion, pickaxes and boot heels were employed. A river of blood was formed with the victims swimming in it. There were tortures and abuses such as the world never knew."[26]

At Rotmistrovka, more than 1,200 persons were herded into their fortress synagogue by Cossacks who threatened to blow them up unless a ransom were paid. With the exception of a few villagers fleeing on the roads (including an aged woman, her daughter and five children, found with their heads crushed), that particular town survived this extortion attempt in May, 1919.[27]

Less fortunate were 2,000 Jews in Tetiev, who crowded their house of worship on March 25 seeking sanctuary. The old, almost oriental-looking wooden structure had always provided refuge from the Cossacks. Troops under the command of Colonels Averko Kurovsky, Elias Chekovsky, and Michael Shliatoshenko burned the building down. Another eye witness recounted the scene three days later: "Of the synagogue nothing remained except walls blackened by fire and a few charred bodies which it was no longer possible to identify. All around the place, hands, feet and other human remnants were seen." In one cellar, seventy persons were put to death. Small children wandered about blind, their eyes put out. "Infants were tossed up into the air and their bodies dashing against the pavement squirted blood on the murderers." When a group of peasants tried to intercede on behalf of one kindly Jew, Kurovsky proclaimed, "He may be the best of them, but since he is a Jew he must be killed." It is estimated that 4,000 of Tetiev's 6,000 Jews were killed in these pogroms in 1919.[28]

In some instances where the murders were fixed in advance, huge trenches for the expected corpses had been dug by civil authorities the day before the pogrom occurred. Thus, at Novo Mirgorod (population 12,000 with 1,500 Jews), lime was prepared for disinfection before a massacre which left more than one hundred dead in February, 1919. Even then, the grave was no deterrent to the pogromchiks. At Severinevka, eight corpses were exhumed, their shrouds torn off, and the mutilated bodies left to exposure while photo-crazy Ukrainians posed for pictures beside the cadavers.[29]

Generally, the Jews were denied the right to bury their dead, and so they putrefied where they had fallen. Hannah Gozmann, who survived the pogrom at Slovechno in July, 1919, remembered, "On all the streets the bodies of our innocent brothers and sisters were lying strewn about. Among the slain lay the wife of the *shammes* [beadle] Irka, wounded, and a peasant was kicking her in the head. Oh, my God, can it be that Thou dost not see this?"[30]

The eminent barrister A. I. Hillerson, who conducted an inquiry into the February massacre at Felshtin, added:

> They cut the Jews up into pieces and threw them to the dogs. Vovrik Lisse, the father of the town commissar, said: "Turn the swine loose and let them drink Jewish blood." That was done. Shloma Heicher and his wife

were killed; they were both very fat; their bones only were found; their bodies were eaten up by dogs.[31]

Another survivor of five days of mass murder in Cherkassy, where 800 Jews died in May, 1919, recalled:

Dead bodies lay near me. I rose, my underwear was all soiled with blood and near me I heard the groans of a dying man. I summoned all my strength to get to the dying person. All around there was no one, it was quiet, and the groaning was distinctly audible, but I could not find the man. Again, I lost consciousness. How long I lay there unconscious I do not know. But when I woke up, I realized I was lying next to Kanevsky and it was he who was groaning. "Kanevsky," I said, "maybe you can get up and we will try to go home." "No," he replied, "I am dying. I beg you. Find my son and put him next to me. I should like to embrace him before I die." I found his son. He was dead. I moved the father near the son. He embraced him, burst into tears, heaved a deep sigh and died.[32]

Late in the summer of 1919, the pogrom fever finally spread to the ancient capital of the Ukraine, Kiev, the city which Sholom Aleichem had immortalized as "Yehupetz." According to reports reaching Constantinople, the murderers attacked in orderly fashion, cordoning off streets, then houses, then bludgeoning, spearing, or shooting the Jews. They allowed the victims to select their own form of death. Each wave of massacre lasted half an hour. When it was done, many leading Jewish intellectuals lay among the slain.

Even such a notorious anti-Semite as V. V. Shulgin was moved to express his disgust in the pages of *Kievlianin* in October, 1919:

A dreadful medieval spirit moves in the streets of Kiev at night. In the general stillness and emptiness of the streets, a heartrending cry suddenly breaks out. It is the cry of the Jews, a cry of fear. In the darkness of the street

appears a group of "men with bayonets." At this sight,
large five and six story houses begin to shriek from top
to bottom. Whole streets, seized with mortal anguish,
scream with inhuman voices.[33]

Another observer, Charles Jacobowitz, Secretary to the
Belgian Consulate in Kiev, noted:

> At number 55 in our street, I saw an act of pure
> vandalism. The furniture in every room was damaged
> or broken by sword cuts or blows from an axe. In one of
> the rooms, a whole family, father, mother, and little
> girl were lying in a pool of blood, their bodies terribly
> mutilated, their hands torn and cut away from the
> bodies by sword cuts. The faces of those martyrs were
> covered with wounds. Is it necessary to add that the
> poor little girl had been violated before she was
> killed?[34]

Jacobowitz would not soon forget the shrieks of horror
which permeated the Kiev night. "The cries lasted for about
an hour and then they stopped," he wrote. "Only the voice
of a woman which sounded more like the barking of a dog
could be heard. The unfortunate creature wailed, or rather
raved, piteously; she had gone mad."[35]

The exact number of victims who died in 1,400 incidents
recorded at 688 spots in the Ukraine between 1917 and 1921 is
not known. Estimates range from N. Gergel's cautious low
of fifty to sixty thousand (with an equal number of
wounded), a figure accepted by the prestigious *Encyclopedia Judaica*, to Howard Sachar's conjecture that
more than two hundred fifty thousand were slain or permitted to starve to death between 1915 and 1921.[36] In August,
1920, Jewish representatives of twenty-nine nations meeting
at Karlsbad, Czechoslovakia, were informed that more than
138,000 Jews had been massacred and 130,000 children orphaned as a result of the pogroms.[37]

Because of the generally unstable conditions which prevailed in the Ukraine, loss of records and the exaggerations of survivors, the task of ascertaining a reliable figure has been made extremely difficult. Gergel, a longtime expert in Jewish welfare problems in the Ukraine, prided himself on utilizing "the only collection that can serve as a basis for a scientific and objective study of the pogroms." Yet he too was compelled to seek out and apply a variety of questionable statistical techniques. By accepting only the lowest figures available for a community and admittedly guessing at the number of Jews killed along highways or between towns, Gergel concluded that there were 45.5 deaths per pogrom.

The use of low body counts was no guarantee of accuracy, as subsequent information established that more than eight hundred persons died in Fastov (where Gergel listed 366 deaths) and another five hundred perished in Krivoie Ozero (where Gergel counted four hundred dead).[38] Accountings were practically impossible at Khasschevata where the pogromists raided Jews twelve times, or Stavich, hit fourteen times, or Bar, where the Jews were victimized on twenty-three separate occasions. In all, more than half of the Ukrainian sites listed in various reports were pogromized more than once.[39]

The most reliable figures seem to be those of the Kiev Central Committee for Aid of Jews who Suffered from the Massacres. This was, after all, a body whose specific function was to investigate the pogroms. Moreover, it operated in the Ukraine during the height of anti-Jewish activity. The Committee's statistics, supported by the findings of the Russian Red Cross, indicate that more than one hundred fifty thousand Jews were killed or wounded in pogroms prior to December, 1919. There is no accounting for any subsequent period. How many more were murdered in disorders in 1920 no one can say, but some estimates place the number left homeless or starving at more than a million.[40] Their agonies were outlined by the Pogrom Relief

Committee of the Russian Red Cross in its report of September, 1919, to the Information and Statistical Department at Kiev:

> The bare recital of the numbers of victims in no way shows the misery and affliction of the Jewish population and the position of those who survived seems to exceed any imaginable depth of horrors. There are hundreds of thousands who have looked into the eyes of death at any moment. These people, deprived of every possible means of subsistence, physically and morally ruined, are faced with the problem of finding asylum, of saving themselves and their children from starvation, from exposure during the coming winter, from infectious diseases and demoralization.[41]

When the pogromists moved away, the people came out with sleds to drag away their dead. But there were no formal burials for the *bezenches,* the refugees whose corpses lined the railroad tracks from Sarny to Kiev down to Vinnitza and Odessa. So many thousands tried to elude the marauding bands of Cossacks that entire towns were depopulated of Jews, while others, considered safer, overflowed with panicked refugees. It was, said one observer describing the exodus of Jews from Ovruch (which had been pillaged) to Slovechno (which was about to be ravaged), as if "a big barrel were trying to get into a pail."[42]

Well into the 1920s, the Ukraine would be plagued with *bezprizorniki,* dirty, half-frozen waifs who begged or stole to remain alive.[43] Dazed old Jews in soiled caftans sat beside the walls of charred synagogues, selling chalk, wicks, bluing, anything for a few pennies. In unheated Jewish hovels, shirtless innocents slept on floors amidst the scurrying of rats.

Typhus afflicted every third person, including the combatants in the civil war, and thousands died from the disease every day. While thousands of square miles of grain were left to moulder and blacken, and fruit rotted on trees and livestock strayed untended, families were identified as "cat," "dog," or "horse" families depending on the nature of their regular diet. Furniture was bartered and *shiddochs* [marriage contracts] arranged for a sack of salt or a container of kerosene, as Jews scrambled desperately for a potato, onions, a pitcher of milk, a sack of corn meal. In the Ukrainian land of honey, there were not even any bees left alive.[44]

Just to clothe the naked survivors of the pogroms required 2 billion rubles. An additional 20 million was needed to feed the starving each day. Henry Alsburg, commenting on the misery of the Ukraine in 1920, wrote: "All that one can say is that Ukraine is perhaps one of the nearest places imaginable . . . to Hell."[45]

Belaya Tserkov. Oleevka. Balta. Novomoskovsk. Gota. Bogopol. Gaisin. Ananev. Birzula. Bygoda. Tulchin. Yanov. Bakhmach. Sarny. Chodorkov. Vapniarka. Kremenchug. Priluky. Rossovo. Kamenny Brod. Pecheri. Litin. Shargorod. Golovachevsk. Kotelnya. Vasilkov. Novo Ukrainka. Kadima. Habidievka. Anopol. Yelizavetgrad. Piriatin. Smela. Derashna. Olshanka. Vessyolaya Kuta. Tzvetkovo. Medvedovka. Zlatopol. Borshchagovka. Dzunkov. Geshovo. Proshna. Stiepantsy. Belashits. Fundukleevka. Rzhischev. Teophipol. Skvira. Samgorodok. Ishokorost. Emilchino. Vornovitsy. Ushomir. Starye Siniavka. Novo Konstantinov. Ramodan. Bobrinsky. Khmelnik. Strishany. Sablino-Znamenk. Ryshanovka. Brusilov. Kagarlyk. Vasyolaya Podol. Sokolov-Roshevo. Sabrunitzy. Yasnogrodka. Zolotnosha. Orlovetz. Proskurov.[46]

Strange names. Far away names. And yet the world was not completely oblivious to these places or the tragic significance which they held for Jews. As early as February, 1916, Pope Benedict XV had issued a statement on behalf of the Jews who were then suffering special torment in the Ukraine. Speaking for the Pope, Cardinal Gasparri informed Louis Marshall of the American Jewish Committee,

"Natural rights, the Pontiff has said, should be observed and respected with regard to the Children of Israel as with all men." His sentiments were echoed by Msgr. Lavelle, representing Archbishop Hayes at a protest rally attended by 500,000 workmen and veterans in New York City on November 24, 1919. Said Father Lavelle: "I come to speak my own heart and to bear a message from the Catholics of New York, of the United States, and of the world, who sympathize with their Jewish brethren in their terrible afflictions, mourn over their dead, and call upon the Powers to trample down those who are guilty of these dreadful acts against the Jews."[47]

Apparently helpless to influence the Tsarist regime while the war raged, the "Powers" remained equally apathetic afterward. Georges Clemenceau did demand from Jan Paderewski the cessation of expressions of "popular wrath," as pogroms were known in Poland, as a pre-condition to recognition of a new Polish state. But for the most part, the conferees at Versailles and after contented themselves with platitudinous minority guarantees from the newly created Slavic states.[48]

As the Ukraine was a special situation, President Wilson and Secretary of State Lansing attempted to mollify an increasingly surly Congress with an inquiry headed by Brigadier General Jadwin in the fall of 1919. The report of Jadwin's committee concluded: "The situation of the Jews is evidently precarious but will naturally improve greatly when order is established, the population disarmed, a gendarmerie established, the land question improved, and education becomes more general."

Obviously embarrassed by this messianic treatise, Lansing commissioned Evan Young, the American Consul General in Odessa, and Rear Admiral McCully to make a further investigation. Their findings, equally innocuous, failed to recommend any concrete proposals for the relief or rescue of the millions, Jew and Gentile alike, suffering in the Ukraine.[49]

Thousands marched in New York, London, Winnipeg, Paris, Buenos Aires, and Johannesburg to protest the Ukrainian pogroms, but they marched in vain. The Versailles diplomats, still reeling under the impact of Flanders and Gallipoli, Ypres and Verdun, and occupied with the Armenian tragedy, the Greek imbroglio, Middle East mandates, the dissolution and distribution of German colonies, massacres in India, disarmament, and intervention against Soviet Russia, could pay scant attention to the lengthy memorandum prepared by the major Jewish relief organizations on December 8, 1919, which tried to pinpoint responsibility for each pogrom in the Ukraine.

An equally cavalier attitude had been adopted by the peacemakers some months earlier toward a report submitted by Ukrainian Minister Plenipotentiary Josef Buraczynki and Foreign Minister Volodymyr Temnitzky: Seventeen pages in length, it documented atrocities committed by "Polish chauvinists" against Ukrainian children, Ukrainian women, and the Ukrainian Orthodox Church. The only reference to pogroms against Jews was a single line telling of the role which Polish officers and soldiers had played in Eastern Galicia, slaughtering Jews at Leopol, Kolomea, and in several other small towns.[50]

Arnold Margolin, onetime deputy foreign minister of the short-lived Ukrainian Republic and the leading Jewish delegate to the peace conference from the "independent" Ukraine, explained the lack of interest in Jewish suffering in the following manner:

> When, after a prolonged period, a fire breaks out in a city or town and consumes a considerable number of homes belonging to the poor, a committee for the relief of the victims is at once organized, well-to-do people and society ladies display great energy, and impressive sums are collected. But if this is soon followed by even a greater conflagration, or if an earthquake or flood destroys three-quarters of the town, the impression produced by the later disaster is no longer so deep, and the same persons who in the first instance dis-

played so much energy are now non-responsive and apathetic.[51]

Thus the world which had reacted with such indignation to Count Plehve's orchestrated brutality at Kishinev in 1903 was affected less by the bloodier and more extensive pogroms of 1919. A world which believed that the Huns had manufactured soap from women's bodies, which could see its amputees coming home on rollers to peddle pencils for the rest of their lives, a world which would remain apathetic through an even greater Holocaust in the not too distant future, showed little concern about pogroms at Proskurov or Kiev in 1919. No international tribunal of justice was convened. No pogromchiks were punished.

Notes

1. *New York Times,* April 7, 1919, p.2.

2. For a discussion of the Chmielnicki pogroms see Heinrich Graetz, *History of the Jews* (Philadelphia: Jewish Publication Society of America, 1895), Vol. V, pp.1-18; and Simon Dubnow, *History of the Jews in Russia and Poland* (New York: T. Yoseloff, 1972), Vol. IV, pp.25-82.

3. Solomon Grayzel, *A History of the Jews* (Philadelphia: Jewish Publication Society of America, 1974), p.602.

4. Isaac Levitats, *The Jewish Community in Russia, 1772-1844* (New York: Octagon Books, 1970), pp. 61-66.

5. See Michael Florinsky, *Russia: A History and an Interpretation* (New York: MacMillan, 1953), Vol. II, pp.1086-1141; and Louis Greenberg, *The Jews in Russia* (New Haven: Yale University Press, 1951), Vol. II, *passim.*

6. A Jewish bricklayer, Mendel Beiliss, was accused of killing a young Gentile boy in Kiev for ritual purposes in 1911. In the trial which followed, Beiliss was exonerated, but the jury decided that "ritual murder had been committed." See Alexander Tager, *The Decay of Czarism: The Beiliss Trial* (Philadelphia: Jewish Publication Society of America, 1935); Maurice Samuel, *Blood Accusation: The Strange History of the Beiliss Case* (New York: Alfred A. Knopf, 1956); and Bernard Malamud, *The Fixer* (New York: Farrar, Straus and Giroux, 1966.)

7. See Topelberg-Ovcharenko, *A Personal History,* pp.34-35,

unpublished memoir, File 461, Elia Tcherikover Archive, YIVO Institute for Jewish Research, New York.

8. According to Ivan Mirchuk in *Ukraine and Its People* (Munich:Ukrainian Free University, 1949), before World War I there were 3,795,760 Jews in the Ukraine, comprising 8.2 percent of the total population.

9. *New York Times*, March 1, 1919, p.4; March 28, 1919, p.4; March 8, 1919, p. 11; and April 19, 1919, p.3. See also File 411, 35729-31, Tcherikover Archive, for Jewish press reports from Stockholm.

10. Concerning the desperate situation of Jews in the initial pogroms at Bobrinskaya and Bakhmach Stations, see wire of Jewish community of Romny to the Jewish Ministry and Vinnichenko, January 7, 1919, File 406, 35307 and 35310, Tcherikover Archive. Typical of appeals from Kostichev, Volochek, Khemlnik, and a dozen other towns was the wire of the Jews of Trokinitz to the rabbi of Kaminski. Undated, it read:

> The misfortunes which fall upon the Jews of our town of Trokinitz are indescribable. Savage bandits have murdered, massacred and torn to pieces four-fifths of the Jewish population. It is a real wonder that some of them have been able to escape the massacre. The money, the beds, the clothes, the furniture, the wares, everything has been robbed and plundered. Houses have been demolished. Windows and stores broken and hacked to pieces. Here are now several hundred Jewish widows and thousands of Jewish orphans . . .

File 412, Tcherikover Archive.

11. For a discussion of extortion tactics implemented by Haidamak bands, see *Di geshehenisn in Zibuliavo, Lipaviatzer, Poviat, Kiever Gub. fun 19 April, 1919, biz 27 April, 1920,* published by the All-Ukrainian Yiddish Central Committee for Aid to the Victims of Pogroms in the War, File 190, Tcherikover Archive.

12. *A Brief Sketch of Anti-Jewish Pogroms That Took Place in Kiev Territory from the Date of Its Occupation by the Volunteer Army,* File 63, Tcherikover Archive.

13. *New York Times*, January 2, 1920, p.3.

14. While some pogromchiks sifted through samovars, sewing machines, underwear and gramophones, others, in Bersna, Kashdan, and Tagancha concentrated on rape. See *A Brief Sketch of Anti-Jewish Pogroms*, File 63, Tcherikover Archive. See also reports on Stepantzy, File 411, 35693, and Vasilkov, File 416, 36051-36066, *loc. cit.*

15. Interview with Sarah Markowska, a survivor of pogroms, Youngstown, June 24, 1971.

16. Undated Deposition of Etta Soschin, File 362, 32995-6, Tcherikover Archive.

17. Elia Tcherikover, *Di ukrainer pogromen in yor 1919* (New York: YIVO, 1965), p.229.

18. *The Massacres and Other Atrocities Committed Against the Jews in South Russia* (New York: American Jewish Congress, in cooperation with the Committee on Protest Against Massacres of Jews in Ukrainia and Other Lands, 1920), pp.58-71.

19. Elias Haifetz, *The Slaughter of the Jews in the Ukraine in 1919* (New York: Thomas Seltzer, 1921), pp.185-200.

20. I.B.Schechtman, E.Tcherikover, N.Tsatkis, and L.Motzkin (eds.), *The Pogroms in the Ukraine under the Ukrainian Governments 1917-1920* (London: Comité des Délégations Juives, 1927), p.89. For additional information on the Bar pogrom, see reports and depositions of survivors, File 426, Tcherikover Archive.

21. Haifetz, *The Slaughter of the Jews*, pp.310-341.

22. Henri Barbusse, "One Hundred Thousand Murderers," *American Hebrew*, CXXI (October 7,1927), pp.1743 and 1790.

23. Schechtman, *et al, The Pogroms in the Ukraine*, pp.88-89. On the Belaya Tserkov pogrom, see File 416, 36069-36099, Tcherikover Archive. See also alphabetic list of 877 victims at Proskurov compiled by A. Resutzki, File 398, 35046-63, Tcherikover Archive. Regarding the pogrom at Kitai-Gorod, see File 362, 32988-32997.

24. *London Times*, August 5, 1919, p.2.

25. Haifetz, *The Slaughter of the Jews*, pp.341-350.

26. *Ibid.*, p.172.

27. *Ibid.*, pp.143-45.

28. Schechtman, *et al, The Pogroms in the Ukraine,* pp.240-42.

29. *Massacres and Atrocities,* p.71.

30. Haifetz, *The Slaughter of the Jews,* p.379.

31. Schechtman, *et al, The Pogroms in the Ukraine,* p.194.

32. Haifetz, *The Slaughter of the Jews,* pp.248, 272.

33. V.V. Shulgin, "Torture by Fear,"*Kievlianin,* October 21, 1919, File 529, Tcherikover Archive.

34. *Massacres and Atrocities,* p.44.

35. *Ibid.*

36. N.Gergel, "The Pogroms in the Ukraine in 1918-21," originally in *YIVO shriften fun ekonomik un statistik,* I, 1928, reprinted in *YIVO Annual of Jewish Social Sciences,* VI (1951), p. 249. A onetime member of the Central Committee of the Jewish Bund, Gergel served in the Jewish Ministry as Secretary General for Jewish Relief until the end of 1918. For the next three years, he was President of the Committee for Relief of the Russian Red Cross until his departure for Berlin. Gergel's figures have not always been accepted. In his *Jewish Nationality and Soviet Politics: The Jewish Sections of the CPSU, 1917-1930* (Princeton University Press, 1972), p.162, Zvi Gitelman estimates the number of deaths at one hundred fifty thousand, almost 10 percent of the total Jewish population. Lionel Kochan in *The Jews in Soviet Russia Since 1917* (Oxford University Press, 1970), p.298, places the figure at one hundred eighty to two hundred thousand slain, plus another sixty to seventy thousand killed in White Russia. Elias Haifetz estimates seventy thousand deaths due to Ukrainian forces under Simon Petlura and another fifty thousand as a result of pogroms committed by troops of White Russian General Anton Denikin. This figure seems to jibe with that "sworn to with certitude"—one hundred twenty thousand deaths—by the rabbis of Khotin. See *Der pogrom in Kamenetz-Podolsk,* File 412, 35780-35786, Tcherikover Archive. For additional information see *Encyclopedia Judaica* (1971), Vol.XIV, Col.1027; Howard M.Sachar, *The Course of Modern Jewish History* (New York and Cleveland: World Publishing, 1958), p.303; E.D. Rosenthal, *Megilat habetah,* I-III (Jerusalem,

1927-30); L.Zhazanovich, *Der yiddisher khurbn in Ukraine: Materyaln un dokumentn* (Berlin, 1920); J. Lestchinsky, "Der shrek far tisfern," *Tsukunft*, XXVII (1922), pp.328-32, and XXVII (1923), pp.546-50; and J.Koralnik, "Pogrom-materyaln," *Bleter far Yiddisher demografye, statistik un ekonomik*, I (1923), pp.24-27.

37. *New York Times*, VIII, August 8, 1920, p.20.

38. Gergel, "The Pogroms in the Ukraine," pp.241-42

39. *Ibid.*, p.243. In his book, *The Russian Jew under Tsars and Soviets* (New York and London: MacMillan, 1964), Salo Baron notes the confusion over body count but nonetheless agrees with Gergel's basic contention that about fifty thousand persons were slain in the pogroms.

40. *Massacres and Atrocities*, p.62. For a confirmation of the extent and suffering of the pogroms see *The Pogroms in Ukraine in 1919: A Report by the Information Manager of the Danish Red Cross*, File 60, Tcherikover Archive.

41. *Ibid.*, p.15.

42. I. Kipnis, *Hadushim un teg* (Kiev, 1926), pp.43-54.

43. According to one observer, "You see them [the children] all over the cities and towns, in the villages, in the railroad stations, hungry, sick, naked, shoeless . . . with a hand stretched forth for a donation . . . and finally in a camp of little criminals . . . embittered, degenerate." Gitelman, *Jewish Nationality and Soviet Politics*, p.163.

44. See "The Road to Brody," in Isaac Babel's *Red Cavalry: The Collected Stories of Babel*, ed. and trans. by Walter Morrison (New York: Criterion Books, 1955), pp.80-82. Babel's stories, beginning with tales of pogroms in Galicia, demonstrate a contempt for his fellow Jews in the *shtetl*. On the other hand, he has supplied Jewish folklore with the admirable rogue Benya Krik who supposedly exemplified the courage and fortitude of the urban, proletarian Jew.

45. Henry Alsburg, "Situation in the Ukraine," *Nation*, CIX (November 1, 1919), pp.569-70.

46. A preliminary accounting of pogroms committed by Petlurists, Whites, Bolsheviks, Poles and "bandits" was attempted

by F. Rosenblum of the East European Historical Archives in 1920. For a list of pogromed cities, see "A reshimeh fun di pogromirte shtedt in di yoren 1919 un 1920," File 49, Tcherikover Archive.

47. Schechtman, *et al*, *The Pogroms in the Ukraine*, p.256.

48. French Foreign Minister S. Pichon was eloquent in preaching how France would defend minorities and persecuted nationalities. See statement of Pichon, July 4, 1919, File 426, 37017-37014, Tcherikover Archive. It need hardly be emphasized that oppression did not cease with the oratory at Versailles. For an analysis of pogroms in regions under Polish control, see *Pogromen in Poylin*, File 93, and *Poliakh in Veiss-russland*, File 111, Tcherikover Archive. For the activities of Polish bands in White Russia and Galicia, consult Files 105 and 132 respectively. See also Oscar Janowsky, *The Jews and Minority Rights, 1898-1919* (New York: AMS Press, 1966), pp.231-40.

49. *Massacres and Atrocities*, p.38.

50. *Ereignisse in der Ukraine, 1914-1922: deren Bedeutung und historische Hintergründe* (Philadelphia: Druck and Verlag Ferdinand Berger und Söhne, Horn, Österreich, Publikationen des W.K.Lypynsky Ost-Europaischen Forschungs-Instituts, 1969), pp. 67-84.

51. Arnold Margolin, *The Jews of Eastern Europe* (New York: Thomas Seltzer, 1926), p.132.

2.

For the Pogroms

PARIS IN THE SPRING of 1926 was a city of contrasts. Students in Left Bank cafes debated the merits of Picasso and Chagall; yet they still trekked nearly two miles to marvel at the canvases of Monet in the Jeu de Paume. At the Opera, the harsh discords of Stravinsky coexisted restlessly with the rich melodies of Debussy. Monarchists and radicals, chauvinists and expatriates, the brilliant and the merely ambitious—all were at home in Paris.

For many refugees from the Russian Civil War, however, Paris was a city of exile and squalor. The Bolshevik coup of November, 1917, and the ensuing chaos had set in motion nearly one and one-half million anti-communist or "White" émigrés. Of these, perhaps four hundred thousand thronged to France, responding to Clause 120 of the old Jacobin Constitution: "The French people grant asylum to foreigners exiled from their fatherland for the cause of liberty."

Fully half the cab drivers who squired young lovers about the French capital were rumored to be former soldiers in some Russian army. Onetime generals, clad in the vestiges of splendid uniforms, peddled newspapers or polished shoes. Officers, aristocrats, and noblemen directed small choirs and balalaika orchestras. Their wives, banishing all pride, sold petit-point or waited on tables in run-down cafes. Many turned to lives of crime and vice.[1]

27

In the Ukraine, the Bolsheviks were consolidating their control under the direction of Lazar Kaganovich, a bright young Jewish Party Secretary. Some of the exiles were beginning to trickle back to their homeland. The Ukrainian Social Revolutionaries Michael Hrushevsky, Pavlo Khristiuk, Mykola Chechel, and Mykola Shrah, unable to endure the degradation of exile, hoped to survive tyranny in the land of their birth. They could not know that within a decade they would all be dead, victims of Soviet purges.[2]

The more cautious remained in France. Paris in 1926 was home to Bulak Balakhovich, the White military officer whose troops were charged with eight massacres of Jews in pogroms near Mozir.[3] General Anton Ivanovich Denikin, supreme commander of the White forces in the Ukraine, also lived in the French capital.[4] Denikin's troops were charged with at least 213 pogroms. It was this General who once wrote:

> Reader, if ever you come across a Russian White war-rior with toil-worn hands and wearing shabby clothes, but with the open gaze of a man who has the right to look you straight in the eyes, remember that in shed-ding his blood for his own country, he was also saving your home from the Red Terror.[5]

Neither Balakhovich nor Denikin felt responsible for the fate of the Jews; the pogroms were a minor incident com-pared with the greater tragedy of Mother Russia. Apparently French officials concurred, for otherwise they would not have permitted the two pogromchiks to settle in Paris; the very clause in the Constitution which guaranteed sanctuary to freedom fighters continued: "The French people refuse asylum to tyrants."

Just after 1:00 P.M. on Tuesday, May 25, 1926, a short, stocky man in his late forties approached his favorite restau-rant, the Chartier, in the Rue Racine. The street was dingy, shaded from the sky by ugly gray garrets and buttresses jutting from eight-story buildings. Behind the storefronts of the tenements, student cafes offered cut-rate menus to the courageous.

Less than five minutes from the isle called La Cité, where tourists gawked at Notre Dame and the Palace of Justice, the Rue Racine twisted a single treeless block from the Boulevard St. Michel to Rue Monsieur le Prince. This was the heart of the Latin Quarter, the mecca for the misfits of society, the traditional haven of pseudo-intellectuals, self-proclaimed geniuses, and papier-maché revolutionaries.

To the man on his way to lunch at the Chartier, the scene was familiar. He passed by the overpriced shops pandering to the young, the bohemians, the artists, Frenchmen and foreigners, Arabs and blacks. He hardly noticed the clanking of wine glasses, the babel of tongues, the noise, the crowding, the pickpockets and their outraged victims. He was indifferent to the cripples, begging children, prostitutes, and Messiahs.

He was a short man, no more than five feet seven inches in height, but his bearing was that of a professional soldier. Ten years earlier, he had been a leader of men. He had worn a magnificent blue uniform cinched by a yellow belt and topped by the cockade of a trident on his cap.

In 1926, however, he was only the editor of a small Ukrainian exile newspaper. His home, which he shared with his wife and their daughter Lessia, consisted of two rooms in a fourth floor walkup on the Rue Thenarde. The sparse furnishings included a hot plate but no kitchen, so the family was forced to eat in restaurants. They frequented the Chartier because they could afford no better. Normally, they took their meals together, sometimes with a friend or two.

But on this day, Simon Petlura was to dine alone.

*****

Simon Vassilievich Petlura was born in the city of Poltava, in the Ukraine, on May 12, 1879. The son of an

impoverished Cossack cabman, he was educated, like many
other revolutionaries, at a theological seminary. Ten years
of stringent Russification had had no greater effect upon
him than upon the Ukrainian people generally, who after
two hundred years of domination by St. Petersburg and
Moscow still clung tenaciously to their own customs, ritu-
als, clothing, art, music, poetry, and history.

*Simon Petlura, one-time Holovni Ataman of the Ukrainian National
Republic, shown in uniform in 1919.* (YIVO Tcherikover Archive)

Young Petlura's heroes were Bogdan Chmielnicki, "the Ukrainian Cromwell," the "chivalrous" Ivan Mazeppa, Gregory Skovoroda (an eighteenth century philosopher who was touted by chauvinists as the equal of Diogenes, Socrates, and Rousseau), and St. Vladimir, who brought the blessings of Orthodox Christianity to Kiev in 988.

Most of all, Petlura was captivated by the life and works of Taras Shevchenko (1814-1861), the greatest of Ukrainian poets. Founder of the illegal Brotherhood of Saints Cyril and Methodius, colleague of Fyodor Dostoyevsky, Shevchenko, like Dostoyevsky, spent ten years in a Siberian army post. A passionate romantic, he remained ever loyal to the ideal of a free Ukraine dominating a pan-Slavic federation. In Shevchenko's ideal society, serfdom would be abolished along with all class privileges, and all men would live in liberty and brotherhood.

For Ukrainian nationalists, Shevchenko combined the talents of Pushkin, Goethe, and Hugo. His poem "The Dream" attacked Peter the Great and Catherine as crucifiers of the Ukraine. His "Caucasus" similarly was a call to resistance against imperial Moscow. In "Haidamaky" he chided his fellow countrymen, "The days pass by, the summer flits away. And the Ukraine is burning as you know." And in his "Testament," which came to be a national anthem for Ukrainians, he wrote:

> *Bury me and then rise boldly*
> *Break in twain your fetters*
> *And with the foul blood of foemen*
> *Sprinkle well your freedom.*[6]

Simon Petlura continued his studies in Kiev, Tiflis, Kuban, Lwow, Galicia, and Chernovitz in Bukovina. Everywhere he went, he encountered Ukrainian intellectuals who shared his ideas. Always a step ahead of the Tsarist *Okhrana*, the secret police, he joined the illegal Ukrainian Democratic

Party (founded by Mykola Mikhnovsky in Kiev in 1890).[7]
Eventually he returned to Kiev, following the abortive Russian Revolution of 1905.

For six years, Petlura published an activist paper *Slovo*
[THE WORD], until Interior Minister Peter Stolypin banned
all such publications. At that point, the thirty-two-year-old
journalist-revolutionary left Kiev for St. Petersburg, where
he served unhappily first as a bookkeeper and then as an
insurance inspector. Within a year, however, he returned to
his passion, editing a review called *Ukrainskaia Zhizn*
[UKRAINIAN LIFE], a Russian-language periodical devoted to
moderate and cautious propaganda about language rights
of the Ukrainian people. It was also in 1912 that he married
Olga Billska, a Ukrainian woman who would accompany
him to the battlefield and into exile in Paris.[8]

During the First World War, Petlura assisted in a unit
supplementing the work of the Red Cross on the Southwestern Front. When various nationalities formed their own
regiments after the March Revolution of 1917, conventions
of soldiers at Minsk and Kiev selected the politically astute
but militarily ignorant Petlura for the task of organizing a
Ukrainian brigade. Already, the Austrians were toying with
the idea of creating such a legion of captured war prisoners.

Through the turbulent days of the spring revolution, tens
of thousands of Ukrainian nationalists had taken to the
streets of Kiev, waving flags and banners calling for the
creation of troop detachments who would fight against the
Central Powers for an "autonomous" Ukraine. Petlura's
countrymen even went so far as to establish a provisional
government, the *Ukrainska Tsentralna Rada* [Ukrainian
Central Council] under the leadership of the historian
Michael Hrushevsky on March 17, 1917. It was this body
which confirmed the thirty-seven-year-old Petlura as Secretary General for Military Affairs in July of 1917.[9]

Charitable observers described Petlura's troops as Cossack units of *sans-culottes*, troops which had by January,

1918, made the Ukraine the one part of the Russian Empire where "order reigned and personal safety was assured."[10] Others criticized the Petlurist regiments as nothing more than highway robbers, bands of ex-Tsarist officers, right and left-wing Ukrainian socialists, cutthroats, adventurers, and peasant farmers from East and West Galicia. Clad in dirty-grey uniforms, some barefoot, others wearing oversized helmets, they looked ridiculous marching off to battle with shotguns, sticks, pikes, and scythes.[11] Commenting on the theatrical nature of these nationalist troops, one observer wrote, "Meeting a Haidamak [Ukrainian irregular] in the street, people rubbed their eyes and stared—was it a soldier in uniform or an actor in disguise?"[12]

To make matters worse, the army swilled vodka or any alcoholic beverage, even the antifreeze intended for tanks and trucks. Acknowledging his own personal inadequacy to deal with the crisis in discipline, Petlura appointed an old line officer, General Sherbachev, as chief of staff of this wartime army in the summer of 1917.

Periodically, Petlura issued all kinds of salutary orders to his men to remain steadfast in their support of the Allies, to "hold at any cost" against the steadily advancing Germans. When the Bolsheviks complicated matters by invading the Ukraine in January, 1918, Petlura responded by assuming personal command of his troops. Thereafter, according to his hagiographer, "constantly at the head of his troops, arms in hand, an example of sacrifice and patriotism, braving an enemy superior in number, he defended each inch of his sacred soil."[13] By the start of that year, however, circumstances had deprived the Ukrainians of mastery of their own fate.

On June 23, 1917, the Central Rada had issued a manifesto which attempted to delineate the Ukraine's relationship with Russia. Somewhat cautiously, it declared, "Let the Ukraine be free, without separating herself entirely from Russia, without severing connections with the Russian state. Let the Ukrainian people in their own land have the right to govern their own lives.''[14] Five months later, coincidental with the collapse of the Kerensky government and the war effort, the Rada issued another manifesto on November 20. Again, it reflected the uncertain movement of the nationalists toward total separation from Russia:

> On this day the Ukraine becomes the Ukrainian People's Republic. Without separating ourselves from the Russian Republic and continuing to preserve our unity, we shall firmly establish ourselves in order to assist with all our power Russia as a whole, in order that the entire Russian Republic may become a federation of free and equal peoples.[15]

For the moment, the unstable Bolshevik regime was in no position to dispute the Rada. In the middle of December, 1917, a note from the Russian government was delivered to the government of the Ukraine. It said:

> In the interests of unity and brotherhood of all the working masses who suffer from the present imperialist war, and as a result of the recognition in numerous resolutions of the organs of revolutionary democracy by councils and above all the recognition of national principles by the All Russian Convention of Councils, the Socialist Government of Russia—the Council of People's Commissars—confirms the right of all peoples oppressed by Tsarism and by the bourgeoisie of Greater Russia to a free development, *including their right to separate themselves from Russia.*
>
> *Therefore, the Council of People's Commissars recognizes the Ukrainian People's Republic and its right to full separation from Russia, as well as its right to enter into negotiations with the Russian Republic regarding mutual federation and other relations.* The demands of the Ukraine regarding the rights and independence of the Ukrainian people the Council of People's Commissars recognizes without any restriction and unconditionally.[16] [Emphasis added.]

The impression that the Bolsheviks were receptive to Ukrainian independence was reinforced by Leon Trotsky, the head of the Russian mission at the Brest-Litovsk Peace Conference. On January 10 and 12, 1918, Trotsky acknowledged the right of "every nation to self-determination" and "complete separation." He saw no reason why a Ukrainian delegation might not participate as an equal in the deliberations with the Central Powers.

Tantalized by such reassurances, the Rada declared on January 22, 1918, "On this day the Ukrainian People's Republic becomes independent, connected with no one, a free, sovereign state of the Ukrainian people."[17] That same week, Bolshevik forces under General Muraviev invaded the Ukraine. Moscow could not tolerate the loss of a region which produced three-fourths of Russia's coal, two-thirds of her iron ore, two-thirds of her salt, four-fifths of her sugar, and nine-tenths of her wheat.

The Rada was permitted to ratify the treaty of Brest-Litovsk on February 9, 1918, thereby supposedly bringing the war in the East to an end. The pact was rather beneficial to Ukrainian nationalists. The Rada gained *de jure* recognition as the government of the Ukraine from Austria-Hungary, Bulgaria, Turkey, and Germany, a price which no Allied nation seemed willing to pay at the time. Little more than a German satellite, the Ukraine received a guarantee from Chancellor von Hertling that he would order Trotsky to withdraw the Red Army.[18]

In actuality, the Ukraine was wracked by the legislative quibblings of twenty-six political parties. The Prime Minister was an ineffectual thirty-four-year-old, Vsevolod Holubovich. Incessant political discord, pogroms, the inability of the central government to cope with Bolshevik *provocateurs,* and the growing bellicosity of the *Samostiniks* (Ukrainian chauvinists) led to a loss of German patience with the Rada.[19]

On April 28, 1918, German troops under Field Marshal

Hermann von Eichhorn surrounded the building housing the Ukrainian Parliament and ordered the Rada to disband. In its place, the occupying Germans encouraged a group of conservatives and great landowners (the Society of Agriculturalists, led by Igor Kistiakovsky and Fedor Lisogub) to resurrect a *Hetmanate* or puppet government. The man selected for the role of Hetman, Paul Skoropadsky, was a descendant of Ivan Skoropadsky, chosen by Peter the Great to replace Mazeppa in 1708. The actual power rested, however, with General Eichhorn (until his assassination on July 30, 1918) and Baron Philip von Mumm of the German Foreign Office.[20]

For seven months, a relative calm settled over the Ukraine. Under the Germans, Kiev again became a boisterous city. Fortunes were made in money speculation, where Tsarist rubles, Kerenkas, Ukrainkas, German marks, Austrian kronen, dollars, and pounds sterling were all honored. Courteous German officers vied with one another for the honor of retrieving hats blown from the heads of Jewish matrons, and throughout the troubled region Jews generally welcomed the presence of the civilized Teutons.[21] Covertly, the Germans encouraged a Ukrainian Academy of Sciences, a revived University of Kiev, and Ukrainian theaters and newspapers. In the midst of relaxation and order, however, some critics of the puppet regime pointed out that the roots of Skoropadsky's name (*skoro* and *padat*) meant "quickly" and "to fall."[22]

During the reign of the Hetmanate, Simon Petlura continued to function (unenthusiastically and ineffectively) as Minister of War. Petlura recognized that the unpopular government was propped up only by German bayonets. Openly disgruntled, his loyalties became suspect, and at the end of the summer of 1918 he was imprisoned.

With Germany's defeat in November, 1918, the Hetmanate collapsed. As early as October 18, Galician nationalists in Lwow had proclaimed a separate West Ukrainian

National Republic. A few days later, Colonel Eugene Konovalets, a member of the Samostiniki National Union, proclaimed a mutiny at Belaya Tserkov, thirty miles south of Kiev. Polish troops began to move into the Ukraine. Panicked, and in desperate need of support, Skoropadsky released all enemies of his regime from prison. On November 14, he even offered to federate the Ukraine with Russia once again if only the Reds would come to his rescue.[23]

Petlura was one of those paroled, and he struck out immediately for Belaya Tserkov. Arriving there on November 16, he was hailed by his ex-comrades as Commander-in-Chief of Ukrainian Armed Forces, *Holovni Ataman,* a title he would never relinquish. Raising the standard of national insurrection, Petlura proclaimed that "for the Ukraine the hour of liberation has sounded." He ordered a general mobilization of all Ukrainians—nationalists, socialists, and Bolsheviks—in the common struggle against the Germans and their puppets.

Enumerating the crimes of Skoropadsky— "destroying the freedom of an independent Ukraine, filling the prisons, executing peasants, ruining villages, and violence against the worker"—Petlura called upon all Ukrainians to deny "the outlaw Skoropadsky" aid, food or shelter.[24] Apparently such appeals were effective, for by December 14 Kiev was in the hands of Petlura's troops. Many of Skoropadsky's officers were massacred in the takeover, but the Hetman, himself, disguised as a wounded German major, managed to flee to Berlin.

Now there was another government in Kiev, a weird melange of Rada democrats, Marxian socialists, Petlurist soldiers, ultra-nationalists, and romantic ideologues, all mystically committed to something called the Ukrainian National Republic. Its ruling executive, illustrative of the revolutionary élan of the moment, was to be known as the Directory.

The five men who originally comprised this body included Petlura (who continued to serve as commander of the armed forces), Opanas Andrievsky (a leading anti-Semitic jurist said to be more loyal to Bacchus than anyone else), Andrei Makarenko (like Andrievsky a member of the militant Ukrainian Party of Socialist Independents, a peasant who later switched loyalties to the Bolsheviks), Fedor Shvets (onetime member of the Rada, professor at the University of Kiev, commander of a battalion against the Red Army, and finally a loyal Ukrainian Communist), and Vladimir Vinnichenko (a writer and leader of the Menshevik-oriented Ukrainian Socialist Democratic Workers Party.

Although Vinnichenko was named President of the Directory, and decisions technically had to be approved by the Council of Ministers (another rubber stamp committee headed at first by Vladimir Chekhovsky), the real power in the government rested with Petlura and his troops. It was Petlura at Belaya Tserkov who issued the manifesto calling for the people to rise against Skoropadsky.

At Kasatin on December 6, 1918, Petlura warned the Germans that unless Kiev were surrendered immediately, the pitched battles which had marked the previous month would be resumed. Several days later, he entered Kiev on horseback at the head of soldiers proudly calling themselves *Petlurovtzi*.[25]

When Austrian Ambassador Eugen Fürstenberg relayed a series of wires to his government describing the events in November and December of 1918, he focused upon the activities of "Petlura's followers." He referred to the struggle as "the Petlura Rebellion" and noted that the onetime clerk was the leader of the revolutionary movement.[26]

Petlura became President of the Directory as well as *Holovni Ataman* when Vinnichenko resigned in disgust on February 6, 1919. Weeks before, Prince Fürstenberg had discounted the importance of Vinnichenko, stating that he would probably wind up in exile. But, Fürstenberg told Vienna, Petlura enjoyed the trust of the people and the faith of the army, and he possessed the necessary quality for holding the reins of government. This man, said Fürstenberg, was "fitted" for the role of military dictator.[27]

Petlura took pride in the renaissance of the Ukrainian army in 1919. On paper, at least, twelve fighting divisions, three Galician army corps, fourteen auxiliary brigades, and an unknown number of guerilla detachments were now under the Supreme Ukrainian Command. This was no longer the rabble of 1917. Nearly one hundred thousand men, possessing twenty-six airplanes, several armored cars, entire trains, and thousands of machine guns were directed by Petlura and his military adviser Lieutenant General Yunakiv, a former professor of the Imperial War Academy.[28]

Nevertheless, Petlura was forced to remove the seat of government from Kiev to Vinnitza in February, 1919, because of pressure from the Red Army. He removed it once more to Kamenetz-Podolsk in June, 1919, when the White forces of Denikin began to overrun the Ukraine. On April 21, 1920, Petlura removed it a third time, to Stanislav in the Carpathians, where he was compelled to seek an accommodation with his old enemies, the Poles. In return for Polish assistance in a new invasion of the Ukraine that year, Petlura agreed to cede to Poland the western regions of Galicia, fully a third of the Ukraine.[29]

The combined armies of Polish Marshal Pilsudski and Petlura did reach Kiev, which was in Bolshevik hands, but they were thrown back to the gates of Warsaw. Only the intervention of the French under General Weygand prevented a Red conquest of the Polish capital. In November, 1920, a battered Poland deserted Petlura, and Pilsudski concluded a separate peace with the Russians at Riga.

Petlura's continued residence in Warsaw, where he symbolized Ukrainian resistance to the Bolsheviks, became an embarrassment to the Polish government. According to Petlura's good friend and biographer Jean de Tokhary, the *Cheka* (Soviet secret police) attempted to murder Petlura in the fall of 1923 utilizing a *femme fatale*. Whether encouraged by the Poles to depart or impelled by fears for his personal safety, a disheartened Petlura fled with his family to Switzerland in 1924. In October of that year, his little band moved to Paris.[30]

Paris swarmed with Russian and Ukrainian emigres of all political leanings, and every group blamed the others for the collapse of the national dream. Democrats blamed monarchists. Monarchists blamed socialists. Petlurists blamed Galician separatists because of their ready surrender to Denikin's White Army. The Galicians countered by charging that Petlura had sold them out to the Poles.[31] And Denikin added that not only was Petlura responsible for plunging the Ukraine into a state of anarchy through his "absolute inefficiency in fighting Bolshevism," but that the Holovni Ataman was a traitor who would have concluded a separate peace with Moscow at the earliest moment and then would have turned against the White forces of "One Indivisible Russia."[32]

Despite such factionalism, Petlura still believed he could weld the dissident groups together by building upon a common hatred of the Soviet government. In Paris, he published a small tabloid, *Tryzub* [TRIDENT, named for the national emblem of the Ukraine] which preached the liberation of the fatherland. The paper was read by Ukrainians in France, Germany, the Low Countries, South America, the United States, and Australia. "The Ukraine will be restored tomorrow," he assured his countrymen. The Bolshevik tyranny would be destroyed.

In the interminable coffee house disputes about how things would be after the Leninists were expelled from the Ukraine, Petlura would counsel, "Please, gentlemen. Let the national territory be accessible to us first and then we'll talk government." According to his admirers, everything he said came from the heart, and his words of hope and comfort forged a link among the exiles.[33] A contemporary, V.

Koroliv, wrote of him:

> Really what constitutes such unlimited moral power of
> Simon Petlura? It is undoubtedly his untiring energy,
> his fanatic love to the country, his true democratic
> mind and his deep-rooted faith in the might of the
> nation, without speaking of his ideal honesty and
> absolute disinterestedness, acknowledged even by his
> enemies.[34]

Ever the chief, no matter how degraded his life may have
become, head of the Ukrainian government in exile, Petlura
clung to the fantasy of gaining recognition from the Western powers and somehow returning one day to his beloved
land as liberator. It was a dream which caused his rival
Denikin to ridicule him as a latter-day Don Quixote, "a
powerless man"[35] in pursuit of his Dulcinea.

———

Across from the Chartier restaurant, near the intersection
of the Rue Racine and the Boulevard St. Michel, a man stood
alone, shifting his weight nervously from one foot to the
other. He had been pacing aimlessly in the same general area
for nearly an hour, his eyes ever on the restaurant. Very few
took notice of this stubby figure with the well-trimmed
mustache. His nose was long, pencil thin, and accentuated
by high, almost Mongolian cheekbones. Less than five-foot-
six in height, he seemed taller because of an unruly shock of
greying light-brown hair. To attorney Regis de Trobriant,
dining on the nearby terrace of the Café Soufflet, he seemed
to be a prize-fighter. To others who saw the man named
Sholom Schwartzbard that day, he seemed no different from
any Paris department store clerk. But within his shirtfolds
he was attempting to conceal an outsized Browning
automatic pistol.

At 2:15 P.M., Petlura appeared in the doorway of the

Chartier.[36] Sholom Schwartzbard moved quickly through a group of students standing at the bookshop to intercept him in the street.

"Are you Petlura?" Schwartzbard's voice was shrill and tremulous as he accosted the former Holovni Ataman. He spat out the words in French, exposing a line of sharp, little teeth.

"Are you Petlura?" he demanded again.

The other man did not reply, but lifted his cane instead, as if moving a beggar aside.

"Defend yourself, dog!" cried Schwartzbard. The boulevard rang with the sound of five shots. "For the pogroms! For my brethren!"

Petlura's last words as he lay crumpled on the pavement were, "My God!" And then the mortally stricken man screamed something that may have been *"Assez! Assez!* [Enough! Enough!]" or simply a cry of pain—"Aiee! Aiee!"

As people ducked and scrambled in all directions, a professor of English, Reginald Smith, who had followed Petlura out of the Chartier, ran to Schwartzbard, placed his hand on his shoulder and asked, "Why did you do it?" Schwartzbard's soft, slow response was, "Because he was an assassin."

Smith recalled afterward: "He had the air of a man in a dream. Like the expression from Shakespeare: 'Your face is like a book in which men may read strange things.' I had never seen such an expression in my life and I had been to twenty-five nations. It was the expression of a man who had one idea, who was possessed, who wanted absolutely to achieve something. Truly, he had the air of an avenger, of a man who had suffered much. His figure was that of a man who seemed to know great sorrow, an immense pain."[37]

From his post on the Boulevard St. Michel, gendarme Roger Mercier heard the shots and ran directly to where Schwartzbard was still standing over Petlura. The assassin made no effort to escape. He handed over his empty revolver when the officer demanded, "Then, are you finished? Give me your gun!"

Said Schwartzbard, "I have killed a great murderer."

With the arrival of the police, a hostile crowd began to gather. "Kill him! Lynch him!" they shouted. "He's a foreigner! Tear him to pieces!"

The gendarme pushed Schwartzbard into a taxi and ordered the driver to take them to the district police station, while another officer named Munier remained with the body of Petlura. The mob, however, had grown even bolder. People pounded on the roof and sides of the auto, shouting, "Pull him out! Let's lynch him!"

"Leave him alone!" shouted Officer Mercier. "We have courts for things like this!"

As the car pulled away from the voices screaming for more blood, Mercier added another word to the mob, "Go to hell!" Then turning to Schwartzbard, he said, "That was really a wild bunch. They didn't even let me alone."

It was not yet 2:30 P.M.[38]

Notes

1. George Stewart, *The White Armies of Russia* (New York: Russell & Russell, 1933), p.421.

2. Robert S.Sullivant, *Soviet Politics and the Ukraine 1917-1957* (New York and London: Columbia University Press, 1962), pp.113-121. See also Michael Hrushevsky, *History of the Ukraine*, ed. by O.J.Frederiksen (New Haven: Yale University Press, 1941), and Demeter Doroshenko, *History of the Ukraine*, trans. Hanna Keller (Edmonton, Alberta: Institute Press, 1939).

3. For the activities of Balakhovich see *Balakhovich in Vaysrusland* and *Balakhovich Bandes in Mozirer Ro'on*, Reports of the Comité des Délégations Juives, October, 1920, File 94, Tcherikover Archive.

4. In 1920, Denikin fled from Russia to Constantinople aboard a British battleship after turning over the command of his hapless army to Baron Peter Wrangel. For contemporary newspaper reaction to the massacres of Denikin see Files 524-527, Tcherikover Archive, and Tcherikover, *Di pogromen in Ukraine*, pp.212-214. Tcherikover places the figure at 296 pogroms and 8,000 deaths caused by the White Army.

5. Anton Denikin, *The White Army*, trans. Catherine Zvegintzov (London: Jonathan Cape, 1930), p.368.

6. Elie Borschak, *La légende historique de l'Ukraine* (Paris: Institut d'Études Slaves, 1947).

7. Oleh Martowych, *Ukrainian Liberation Movement in Mod-*

ern Times (Edinburgh,Scotland: Scottish League for European Freedom, no date), pp.29-34. See also Vasyl Ivanys, *Symon Petliura—Prezydent Ukrainy* (Toronto, 1952).

8. Alain Desroches, *Le probleme ukrainien et Simon Petlura: Le feu et la cendre* (Paris: Nouvelles Editions Latines, 1962), pp. 53-58. Historians should be cautioned about the "objectivity" of Desroches' FLAME AND ASHES, which begins with an expression of "the French natural sympathy for Ukrainians," extols every attribute of the Ukraine (its people, even its mineral wealth), and introduces the reader to Petlura with the phrase, "the great Ukrainian patriot Simon Petlura who had consecrated his life to the liberation of his oppressed country, worthy successor of Bogdan Chmielnicki and of Jean Mazeppa, legendary heroes of national independence, who was cowardly assassinated in cold blood on May 25, 1926, in the Latin Quarter of Paris."

9. *Ibid.*, pp.59-61.

10. Martowych, *Ukrainian Liberation Movement*, p.42.

11. Nikolai Ostrowski, *The Making of a Hero*, trans. Alec Brown (NewYork: E.P.Dutton, 1937), pp.76 and 133-37.

12. Richard Luckett, *The White Generals: An Account of the White Movement and the Russian Civil War* (London: Longman Ltd., 1971), p.286. On the nature of these soldiers also see Konstantin Paustovsky, *The Story of a Life* (New York: Pantheon, 1964), *Years of Hope* (New York: Pantheon, 1969), and *In That Dawn* (London, 1967).

13. Desroches, *Le probleme ukrainien*, pp.63-70.

14. N.Y.Hryhorijiv, *The War and Ukrainian Democracy* (Toronto: Industrial and Educational Publishing Company, 1945), p.64.

15. *Ibid.*, p.66.

16. *Ibid.*, p.72.

17. *Ibid.*, pp.67 and 73. For the duplicity of Lenin and the Bolsheviks see Basil Dmytryshyn, *Moscow and the Ukraine, 1919-1953* (New York: Bookman Associates, 1956), pp.24-56.

18. For two dissimilar views on Brest-Litovsk, see Oleh Pidhainy, *The Formation of the Ukrainian Republic* (Toronto and New

York: New Review Books, 1966), pp.457-538; and Victor Serge, *Year One of the Russian Revolution*, trans. Peter Sedgwick (New York: Holt, Rinehart and Winston, 1930). The former, a Ukrainian nationalist, writes glowingly of Ukrainian efforts without even mentioning pogroms. The latter, who broke with Stalin by 1929, blames the Ukrainians for the failure of the great social revolution in Russia, saying they built on sand and against the proletarian revolution.

19. According to Jurij Borys, the political continuum in the Ukraine at this time included ten purely Ukrainian parties, seven more reactionary Russian affiliates, five Jewish groups, and four Polish parties. They ranged from Bolsheviks to monarchists. Borys, *The Russian Communist Party and the Sovietization of Ukraine* (Stockholm, 1960), pp.92-99.

20. W.E.D.Allen, *The Ukraine: A History* (Cambridge: University Press, 1940), p.289. For a more detailed analysis of German rule, see also Oleh Fedyshyn, *Germany's Drive to the East and the Ukrainian Revolution 1917-1918* (Brunswick, New Jersey: Rutgers University Press, 1971); Richard Pipes, *The Formation of the Soviet Union: Communism and Nationalism 1917-1923* (Cambridge: Harvard U.Press, 1964); X.J. Eudin, "The German Occupation of the Ukraine in 1918," *Russian Review*, No. 1 (1941), pp.90-103; *Materials on German Occupation in Ukraine*, File 37, Tcherikover Archives; and Tcherikover, *Di pogromen in Ukraine*, pp.1-18.

21. When the Nazis swept into the Ukraine in 1941, survivors of the pogroms calmed their brethren by reminding them of the decent treatment accorded them by Germans earlier. The result was self-deception and annihilation. As related by Anatoly Kuznetsov, "The old people had related many times how the Germans had behaved when they occupied the Ukraine in 1918. They had not troubled the Jews then but treated them fairly well; probably, some thought, because of the similarity between Yiddish and German." Kuznetsov, *Babi Yar*, trans, by Jacob Guralsky (New York: Dial Press, 1967), p.70.

22. Ilya Ehrenburg, *People and Life, 1891-1921*, trans. Anna Bostock and Yvonne Kapp (New York: Alfred A.Knopf, 1962), pp.309-310.

23. Peter Kenez, *Civil War in South Russia 1918* (Berkeley: Uni-

versity of California Press, 1971), pp.272-4; William Henry Chamberlin, *The Ukraine: A Submerged Nation* (New York: Macmillan, 1944), p. 46; and Desroches, *Le probleme ukrainien*, pp.70-73.

24. Serhii Mazlakh and Vasyl Shakhrai, *On the Current Situation in the Ukraine*, ed. Peter Potichnyj (Ann Arbor: University of Michigan Press, 1970), pp.20-21.

25. *Ukraine: A Concise Encyclopedia*, ed. Volodymyr Kubijovyc, Vol. I (Toronto: University of Toronto Press, 1963), p.766.

26. *Ereignisse in der Ukraine*, pp.102-3,120,122 and 153.

27. *Ibid.*, pp.211-12.

28. Martowych, *Ukrainian Liberation Movement*, p.54.

29. Desroches, *Le probleme ukrainien*, pp.86-90.

30. *Ibid.*, p.133.

31. John S.Reshetar, *The Ukrainian Revolution 1917-1920* (Princeton University Press, 1952). p.328. See also Borys, *The Russian Communist Party and the Sovietization of Ukraine*, pp.92-99.

32. Denikin, *The White Army*, p.285.

33. Desroches, *Le probleme ukrainien*, pp.134-142.

34. V.Koroliv, *Simon Petlura, Ukrainian Chief and Popular Hero*, trans. by Mrs. M. (Kiev and Prague: Ukrainian Editorial Co. "Chas," 1919), p.25.

35. Mazlakh and Shakhrai, *On the Current Situation in the Ukraine*, p.18.

36. The time factor is crucial. In his own memoirs, Schwartzbard records the time of assassination as nearer to 3:30. See *Inem loif fun yorn* (Chicago: M.Ceshinsky, 1933), p.183. This is accepted by Lucy Dawidowicz, editor of *The Golden Tradition: Jewish Life and Thought in Eastern Europe* (Boston: Beacon Press, 1967), p.448. In view of all testimony at the trial, it seems that 2:00 P.M. is closer to the time of assassination. The mistake may be attributed to a lapse in Schwartzbard's own memory.

37. *Revue des Grands Procès Contemporains*, No.5-6 (May,June,

1929) Librairie Générale de Droit et de Jurisprudence, XX, Soufflot, Paris. *Notes Sténographiques,* V.Bluet, Ministere Public, "Madame Veuve Petlura et M.Le Colonel Petlura (Parties Civiles) c. Schwartzbard." Fascicule 2, pp.101-103. Hereafter this source is referred to as *Notes Sténographiques.*

38. The reconstruction is based on evidence submitted by eyewitnesses at the trial, newspaper accounts and Schwartzbard's memoirs.

3.

The Meysim

FEAR, PAIN, AND DEATH were no strangers to Sholom Schwartzbard. They had been his constant companions since his birth in the *shtetl* (Jewish town) of Ismail, in Bessarabia, in 1888.

As a young boy, he was terrified by legends of the hobgoblins and watersprites that inhabited every unfamiliar patch of shadows. From medieval nightmares, the Jewish people had conjured up the *Dybbuk,* a disembodied spirit which gained possession of a man's body and soul, the *Sheydim,* creatures that drank and ate like human beings and went into the community by night to do evil, the *Estrie,* a female vampire that flitted about sucking the blood of other women, the *Mare,* which rested upon the body of a sleeping man and choked off his breath, and the *Kobold,* a double-talking devil that mimicked man to bewilder him.

For naughty children there were special monsters—the *Holda,* or lock-elf, which gobbled up children whose hair was messy, the *Rusalkeh,* the half-fish creature that lured children to their deaths in swamps, the *Shibbeta,* a strangler especially dangerous to those who did not wash their hands, and *Lilith,* the lost wife of Adam, the night-hag of the ancient Babylonians, waiting for children to wander into the forest where she might feed on them.[1]

When young Schwartzbard went to the synagogue, the

Sholom Schwartzbard. (YIVO Tcherikover Archive)

shul, and listened to the old Orthodox men, what most impressed him were tales of the *Meysim,* "the Dead Ones." Spirits of Jews recently deceased, they roamed the earth forlornly. They flickered like candles in the cemetery mists of a full moon. Or a whole army of the dead might be encountered on some deserted road, pulling wagons filled with the sins they had committed while alive. Some argued that the Dead Ones might enter the synagogue on special holidays. But others maintained that every midnight these pathetic souls, clad in tattered prayer shawls, would hold their own ghastly services. Even during the regular Friday evening service, they might hover in the shadows, waiting to pounce upon a straggler.

For little Sholom, the Dead Ones were more than fearful creatures that lurked in abandoned attics by night. They were his grandfather Moishe, a big, gentle man with a white beard and a fur overcoat, or his mother Chaia, a strict but loving woman in a plaid shawl and white apron. Like other persons he had known and loved, they had died violently in a pogrom.[2]

On the seventh day of his life, Sholom sealed his covenant with God. He was circumcised according to the rites of Judaism. Most of the townsfolk of Ismail attended this *bris*. They predicted that the baby, born on a special Sabbath, would be a joy, an avenger of his people. But the celebration was cut short by the news that all Jews in Ismail were to remove themselves once more to the restricted areas of the Pale. There were still some ten thousand Jews living in the region, and such periodic expulsions were not unusual in the time of Tsar Alexander III. Thus, under the threat of pogrom, the feast broke up and the Schwartzbard family fled fifty miles to the northeast, to the Jewish Pale of Settlement and the city of Balta.

The principal Jewish city of the Podolia region, Balta was no haven for the oppressed. Ever since the Russian government had embraced anti-Semitism as the fourth pillar of its autocracy, Balta had been the scene of some of the most barbarous acts committed against Jews. One observer, chronicling the Easter Monday pogrom of April 10, 1882, wrote:

> The houses which were not marked with a cross were invaded by the mob. Doors were beaten in, show-windows demolished, window-frames torn out. Furni-

ture was thrown out of windows, crockery smashed, house-linen torn up, with a joy in destruction both childlike and savage. The mob took untold delight in ripping open featherbeds and down-quilts and sending the contents drifting in the air like a fall of snow. In several places, the pleasure the mob took in sheer destruction overcame their rapacious instincts. Peasants who came from their villages with wagons to take away their share of booty, were repeatedly driven away by the rioters. For in certain boroughs, after the house-gear was destroyed, the houses went—floors and roofs being carried away, and nothing left standing but the bare stone walls. Not even the synagogues and cemeteries were spared by popular fury. The tombs were desecrated and the rolls of the Torah defiled. The mob naturally made first for the taverns and taprooms. Barrels were staved in; whiskey ran down the streets; men lay down in the gutters flat on their stomachs to gorge themselves with the stuff. In several localities, women, crazed with drink, gave pure spirits to swallow to infants two or three years old, that they might forever after remember these glorious days. Others brought their small children to the ruins of Jewish houses, there to bid them "remember the judgment they had seen overtake the Jews."[3]

It had just been six years since the ugly incident in Balta which left 1,250 Jewish dwellings and shops razed, fifteen thousand persons beggared, forty killed or maimed, 170 others wounded, and twenty women raped. Conditions had not changed much. The Schwartzbards came here to live with Uncle Edel and his wife but found no respite from the tension that haunted Russian Jews.

During one of the annual Easter festivities, when Christian hooligans ran amok through the Jewish sector of town, Sholom was cracked on the head by a pogromchik. His father Yitzhak, reduced to the occupation of street peddler, hoped to scrape together enough money to take everyone to America or Palestine. But when he managed to open a grocery store in a Gentile neighborhood, a fire broke out and looters sacked the store. Sholom's mother, several months pregnant, tried to halt the vandals and was mauled for her efforts. Shortly after, another son, Meir, was born. Then on Yom Kippur Eve, the night when the old Jews talked about the Dead Ones, Sholom's mother, ill since her beating, died.

The boy grew very attached to his father. Twice each week, on Mondays and Thursdays, the two of them would walk out of the city to the Jewish cemetery where the boy's mother was buried. There had been a time when husband and wife had come to the same spot, as much to breathe the freshness of the Ukrainian countryside as to pray.

"Some of this grass right here might grow on my grave," the father told his son, "because you never know where you will be buried." Father and son would pray and read silently in their Bibles, tears streaming down their faces. The elder Schwartzbard could not understand why God had brought such misfortune upon him, why He had taken away a young woman and left him with several infants he could barely support. His own brother, Edel, tried to console him, saying, "You're a Jew. It happens everywhere."

On the Sabbath, between the afternoon and evening prayers, Sholom and his father would again walk out to the vicinity of the cemetery. But as observant Jews, they would not enter the grounds of the dead on this day. As they sat on a hill, a short way off from the enclosure, Sholom would confide in his father, telling him his sorrows and asking for guidance.

Yitzhak Schwartzbard regaled the boy with tales of the Kingdom of David, when Jews' eyes were "red from wine," when their teeth were "milk-sweet white." He would point to the people working in the fields, unafraid, their neat farmhouses dotting the broad landscape, their many cows and chickens wandering about fertile land which only the very richest of Jews might purchase, and then he would say, "You see, son, that's the way we Jews lived in the olden days, on the land, by the sweat of our brow." Neither Schwartzbard could doubt that it would be so again when the Messiah came.

Eventually, the trips to the cemetery stopped. The elder Schwartzbard remarried, telling his son, "It's no good to be an orphan. I was an orphan myself." But Sholom never got along with his stepmother. She appears in his memoirs as a caricature drawn from a Grimm fairy tale, ever cursing Sholom and his brother. Once, when the older boy ripped his pants while playing on a swing, this woman scolded him bitterly until his father intervened, saying, "Let him play. I can't give him anything else."

By 1900 there were four more mouths to feed and no real place in the home for Sholom. He was sent out to work for various storekeepers in town, hawking seltzer water and lemonade. One year, he noted proudly, he managed to earn fifteen pennies. A more satisfactory arrangement was reached with a watchmaker, Israel Deck, who agreed to supply Sholom with board and the opportunity to learn a trade.

Schwartzbard recalled that life with Israel Deck was "hell on this earth." He was at once servant in the house, clerk in the store, and apprentice in the watch shop. After three years of apprenticeship, however, he knew practically nothing about watches. He could not even take one apart. Deck and his wife blamed one another for this. The man claimed that his wife took Sholom away for days to do household chores, while the woman insisted that her husband was afraid to teach the boy anything. Only in the last four months of a five year apprenticeship did Israel Deck call Sholom to the bench. And then he repeatedly chastised the clumsy, frightened youth with "Why don't you learn?"

For the first time in his life, the young Schwartzbard knew complete loneliness. Away from his father and family, unable to attend *cheder* [Hebrew school] and shunned by other boys his age, he busied himself reading the Bible. It was not enough, however. One Saturday, while on the way to temple, he encountered another lad he had met working for one of the city's storekeepers. The youth told Sholom to follow him, not too closely, out of town, and that he wouldn't regret it. Intrigued, Schwartzbard came to a ravine near a green hillock where he found several craftsmen, shop boys, students and even some actresses assembled.

The group, which called itself *Funk* [Yiddish for "Spark," doubtlessly linked in some way with Lenin's Russian journal of the same name, *Iskra*], passed the day discussing such questions as the right to vote, exploitation of the laboring man, and the need to educate the masses. When Sholom returned to Balta his blood was abroil with new ideas—republic, constitution, trade unionism. Now he had new friends and a different kind of reading material in the works of Karl Marx, Plekhanov, Liebknecht, Engels, and Lasalle. In his own way, like Simon Petlura, Sholom Schwartzbard had become a revolutionary.

Though Marx had derisively termed religion an opiate, the boy who had once amazed scholars with his piety and knowledge of the Psalms was positive that God was with the socialists. He maintained that one could believe in God (if there was one) but also be a man among men. The messianism of the prophets, Schwartzbard held, was nothing but socialism. Even the great Ferdinand Lasalle had taught that religion and the class struggle were not incompatible. But Sholom's views were so unpopular that at one meeting of *Funk*, a carpenter spit at him and stormed, "A socialist who believes in God! I don't want to talk to you any more."

By 1905, Schwartzbard's apprenticeship was finished. Seventeen years old, he set out for the *shtetl* of Kruchi, thirty miles from Balta. There he encountered several inflammatory revolutionaries from Odessa. With Comrades Grisha and Yussel the Redhead, he spent his nights distributing leaflets calling the peasants to open rebellion against the Tsar.

The young Marxists in Kruchi even went so far as to nail a proclamation demanding total equality to the door of the

house of the local *puretz* [squire]. The nobleman countered
by offering a reward for every leaflet turned in to be burned.
Illiterate peasants who hitherto had used the flyers for
sanitary purposes now scoured the countryside for the papers and even tore notebooks away from innocent students
on trains. The *puretz* also called in Cossack troops, and
Schwartzbard's comrades fled to America, where their revolutionary ardor cooled. The young watchmaker, however,
stayed where he felt he was needed, in Kruchi.

At one point, some reservists on the way to the Far East (to
fight in the insane Russo-Japanese war) decided to enjoy a
little diversion in the *shtetl*. Their drunken shouts of "Kill
the Yids!" mingled with the screams of women. It was more
than Schwartzbard could bear. According to his account, he
grabbed "a socialist cane," went out and bashed the arms
and legs of several soldiers before being knocked out by
someone wielding a larger stick.

When the "excess" was finished, and people crept back
from basements and attics where they had been hiding,
Schwartzbard was asked how he dared fight so many Gentiles. He replied, "So many Gentiles! Maybe ten! In a town
of one hundred Jews. How could you stand on the side and
be quiet?"

Pursued by local authorities who recognized him as an
agitator, and shamed by the inacton of the Jews, Schwartzbard returned once more to Balta in the summer of 1905. He
wrote later that in a sense he was sorry that he had not been
apprehended. That way he could have made some fiery
speech before departing to martyrdom in Siberia.

By October, 1905, Tsar Nicholas II could no longer put off
reform. Russian humiliation at the hands of the Japanese,
governmental corruption and inefficiency, widespread assassinations of public officials, open revolution in Poland,
strikes by workers and students, sabotage in the oil fields of
the Caucasus, and mutiny among the sailors of the Black Sea
fleet compelled the Tsar to promise a Russian parliament,
the "Duma."

In Balta, the revolutionary exhilaration was total. There was singing in the streets. Men talked of the end of religious discrimination, the cancellation of peasant debts, and the prospect for workers' councils called "soviets." But on October 17 came the chilling news that Tsarist troops had opened fire on workers in Moscow and St. Petersburg. And then came word of horrible massacres of Jews all over Russia and especially at Odessa. The reactionaries were trying to drown the revolution in a sea of Jewish blood.

Balta was only 115 miles from Odessa, where thousands of Jews lay dead. The Jews of Balta knew that any day the Black Hundreds, as the pogromchiks called themselves, would come galloping into town. Schwartzbard and his father (whom he likened to the ancient Mattathias, patriarch of the Maccabees) set about organizing a Jewish defense from the men in town who would fight. The concept was too novel for most of their brethren, who were resigned to pogroms. The Almighty would preserve them. The defense forces in Balta were able to muster only thirty or forty men.

It was on a Friday morning when Cossacks, joined by local ruffians (including the chief of police, who carried a huge picture of the Tsar), marched across town seeking a church blessing for their actions. A delegation of old Jews, hoping to placate them or buy them off, intercepted the pogromchiks. By the time the marchers reached the church of their destination, the old Jews lay dead in the streets.

The pogromchiks were certain not to strike in force before sundown, the beginning of the Jewish Sabbath. Religious Jews generally offered little or no resistance on this day. At 5:00 P.M., most Jews in Balta were on their way to synagogue, seemingly oblivious to what was about to happen. Schwartzbard's group threw wagons and barrels across four intersections near the synagogue and waited. Their kerosene-saturated bonfires glowed brilliantly in the twilight.

Cossack horsemen soon rode up and demanded to be let past the barricades "to keep order in the town." The Jews refused. Bombs were thrown and rifles went off. The few

Jews willing to fight against superior numbers eventually broke. Schwartzbard lost contact with his father, who was wounded in the melee. The last he saw of his brother Shmuel was when he was lashing out at three men with his boot. The Jewish quarter was pillaged. The elder Schwartzbard told his sons, "Yes, my children, they beat us for a while. But keep it up." On the following day, the surviving members of the Jewish defense force were thrown into jail.

Schwartzbard spent three months in prison for his part in "provoking" the Balta pogrom. Once released, he had had enough of Russia. His wanderings took him to Chernovitz in Bukovina, Lemberg (or Lwow) in Galicia, Budapest, and then Vienna. Finally, he met his brother Meir in Italy and the two of them went on to Paris in 1910. Sholom took a job in a watch factory. He met up again with many friends who were emigrants from Russia, and he fell in love with a girl from his homeland. He was a free man in a free land; yet all the while he lived with a dream that someday the Russian Jew might too lift up his head in freedom and say, "I am in heaven."[4]

As World War I drew near, Schwartzbard wrote his father begging him not to enlist but to leave the fighting to younger men. On August 25, 1914, both Sholom and his brother enlisted in the French Foreign Legion. Both were wounded at the battle of Carency in the Somme campaign and both were awarded France's highest military decoration, the Croix de Guerre. Schwartzbard was wounded by a grenade blast while on patrol in March, 1916. His lungs were riddled and at first he was given up for lost. Asked if he wanted a rabbi, he recalled having declined "in a nice way." His sergeant, commenting later on his bravery and humility, noted that when Schwartzbard was praised, he shrugged it off saying, "It was nothing. It was nothing."[5]

Schwartzbard spent fifteen days in a field hospital before being transferred to a monastery near Lyons. There he spent two pleasant months receiving diathermy treatments for his

Schwartzbard (front row, second from right) as a soldier in the French Foreign Legion. (YIVO, Thcerikover Archive)

left arm, which was virtually useless to him, and discussing history, religion, and language with the monks. In this detached, blissful, unreal atmosphere, he could reflect upon humanity and armed conflict.

Schwartzbard's memoirs are filled with passages that tell of the cruelty of war, the dehumanization even of the victors, the senselessness of infantry advances into acres of mud. One selection is especially revealing, for it conveys Schwartzbard's disenchantment with crusades and his contempt for the boorishness of his comrades in arms. A member of his unit named Mendel had marched off to war quite enthusiastic about the struggle to preserve liberty. After months in the frozen trenches, however, Mendel's idealism had disappeared, a victim of foreboding of death as much as anything. Now nicknamed "the Pessimist," he sat alone, reading Kant

59

and Nietzsche, while his companions tossed food at him, tore up his "German books," and used the *Critique of Pure Reason* for toilet paper.[6] Mendel's death, shortly after, one of millions of senseless deaths, made a lasting impression upon Schwartzbard.

In this period of convalescence, Schwartzbard reflected upon Mendel's death and the deaths of all the others in the war. There had to be some meaning to all of this. The deaths of his comrades must be a *churban,* a sacrifice to ensure that something better would come out of the conflict.

For Schwartzbard, the saga of mankind was a story of incessant warfare and oppression. Religion had been manipulated by kings, generals, patriots, and true believers to reinforce their own cause, their own tyranny. Nationality had divided men by race, language, and color. The end result had always been the suffering of mankind. Throughout the ages, chauvinism promoted by wartime profiteers had annihilated millions of the common people.

Citing Kant, he wrote, "Understanding is unity." He insisted that people know and love one another. "If a man has only one land," said Schwartzbard, "he must fight." Better to become a pacifist. He chided the Germans in particular, asking, "How many have died in the name of the Fatherland?"

If, however, man's history is one of weapons and not ploughshares, it also contains a thread of the speculative, the curious, a passion for new and fresh ideas. Clearly the dialectic is at work, argued Schwartzbard. A decaying Jewish priesthood could not destroy Jesus, nor the Romans stay the Barbarians, nor the Catholics the Protestant Reformers. When man was driven from Europe, he discovered America. When man's economic situation was sufficiently desperate, he discovered socialism.

As a good Marxian, Schwartzbard believed that each level of civilization contains within it the germ of a higher stage, an *idea* which no amount of repression can restrain. He did not assume that socialism was the ultimate stage of man's economic or political development, any more than relativity was the final word in science or pantheism the final achievement of philosophy. But socialism was the highest current stage of man's development. It was socialism that genuinely taught the people the common message of Jewish messianism and Christianity that wherever there is peace there is the fatherland. Just as it was impossible to contain the great ideas of the past, Schwartzbard reasoned, so it would be impossible to stay the generation of honor, wisdom, and good organization, a generation belonging to the family of man, born of eternal war yet choosing peace. Just as art and science knew no limits, "so in the future will mankind know no enemies, bounds, or other false ideals," he wrote.[7]

Then, in the spring of 1917, Schwartzbard learned of the overthrow of the Romanov dynasty. Intoxicated by the thought of what the democratic Provisional Government might mean for Russia, the watchmaker-soldier prepared to return to his homeland, even before his military pension had been approved by the French Government or he had been officially mustered out of the Foreign Legion. On August 5, 1917, he departed from Brest with his wife and dozens of Russian troops (who had been sent to recuperate from war wounds in 1916) aboard the paqueboat *Melbourne* bound for Archangel. Schwartzbard passed through Petrograd, as the Russian capital was now called, just after the abortive counter-coup of General Kornilov. He was moved to hear people on the streets talking of "liberty," to see passengers on trams hailing one another as "comrade," to be able to stroll in and out of the dread Petropavlovskaya (Peter and Paul Fortress), the Russian Bastille.[8]

Toward the end of September, 1917, Schwartzbard visited his father in Balta. Again there was disturbing news from Jewish communities near the rapidly disintegrating front. Schwartzbard himself had encountered some pitiful Jewish refugees from disorders in Vologda on the way to Petrograd.[9]

Again, both Schwartzbards worked to organize Jewish

defenses after appeals to local officials proved fruitless. This time, however, bands of Russian soldiers marched through Balta without incident. On every corner stood Jewish men armed with rifles. A pogrom was averted, but something was substituted in its place—Jewish cruelty. Sholom witnessed one of his men kicking a Gentile child. The sight of this, after all he had worked for, physically sickened him. The others ridiculed their squeamish leader, so he left Balta.

Schwartzbard settled in Odessa and tried to strike up a normal life as a watchmaker. In 1918, he learned that Rumania intended to capitalize on the political disorder in Russia by sending troops across the Dniester into the Crimean peninsula. Rallying ninety men in a public house with the Biblical cry, "Who is with God, come with me!", Schwartzbard set out for Tiraspol in Bessarabia. There, allied with Red Army cavalry under Kitovsky and supplied with Bolshevik cannon and ammunition, his group distinguished itself in a holding campaign. The so-called Group Rochelle (or Rasala), named for a young girl who was killed in the resistance, continued to fight for two years, from Tiraspol to Kharkov, with and without Schwartzbard, against the forces of Austria and Germany, Petlura and Denikin.[10]

In 1920, Schwartzbard, disillusioned by the willingness of his comrades to prostitute themselves and the revolution for a few rubles and horrified by the new wave of pogroms in which the Bolsheviks also participated, left Russia for the last time.

Now thirty-two years old, he opened another jewelry shop at 82 Rue Menilmontant in Paris, near the Cemetery Pere la Chise. He was active in the French and Jewish labor movements, and in 1925 he formally became a French citizen. He contributed regularly to the New York Yiddish weekly, *Di Fraye Arbayter Shtimme* [VOICE OF THE FREE WORKER] under the pseudonym "Baal Chalomoth" ["The Dreamer"]. In addition, he wrote several books in Yiddish—*Traumen un virklichkayt* [DREAMS AND POSSIBILITY, an anthology of poems], *Milchomen bilder* [personal scenes from the war] and *Fun tifen obgrund* [an effort to describe the pogroms]. All those who came into contact with him described him as an industrious worker, a good husband, and a gentle soul.[11]

But Sholom Schwartzbard was not at peace. In criss-crossing Russia, he had viewed the aftermath of the terrible carnage in 1919. In July of that year, Schwartzbard arrived in Zhidowska-Grebla two days after a pogrom had swept the town. "In the first house where I stopped, I found the shutters and doors closed in the middle of July," he recalled. "I knocked. The door remained closed and no one responded. I went to the window and cried, 'I am Jewish— open for me!' It was an *open sesame.*" What he found sickened him. Every stick of furniture had been tossed about as if in an earthquake. Two old women sat by the wall on the floor, whimpering, while lying next to them was an old man, his face bloodied, blood still running from his bandaged head. From him issued one lament, "My God, my God, why hast Thou forsaken me?"

The pogromchiks had left only cadavers, ruin, and misery in Zhidowska-Grebla. Of fifteen Jewish families in town, eight had been completely wiped out, including a mother and her six children. The woman's husband had fallen on the battlefield in defense of Russia. She had been raped and then strangled. The old ones in Zhidowska-Grebla told Schwartzbard that the pogromchiks had been Petlurists.[12]

When he came to Cherkassy, the first Jew Schwartzbard met told him, "We have just buried a thousand victims of the last pogrom. All lie in one mass grave. One gets accustomed to calamity. It is Providence."[13] In Odessa, he came into contact with more refugees fleeing the Haidamaks, the Ukrainian nationalist soldiers. He heard how 6,500 Jews were massacred and buried in a common grave at Bratskaia Mogila, how others were forced to eat their own beards or excrement, and others were buried alive. A fellow soldier in his old unit noted that "news of pogroms caused in him extreme agitation." Schwartzbard labored with a frenzy born of vengeance, succoring the aged, wounded, or orphaned as Group Rochelle moved through the country.[14]

Schwartzbard waited five years for civilization to bring the pogromchiks to justice. He waited in vain.

Then, in December, 1925, he learned that Simon Petlura was in Paris. Schwartzbard's Jewish friends were unanimous in blaming Petlura for the pogroms. He listened with horror as an acquaintance told him of two Petlurist officers who had been in a Red Cross hospital in 1919. The two men boasted that they had raped thirty-seven Jewish women in a single day and that they had killed fifteen more with their swords on the same day, all in the name of the independent Ukraine and "the little Father Petlura."[15]

Schwartzbard personally recalled coming across corpses of Jews rotting in the streets of Kiev at the end of August, 1919, victims of Petlura's advance guard. Hoodlums shouted obscenities at one grieving woman who was sobbing over the body of her lone son. "Good!" they screamed. "We'll show you damned Jews, we'll slaughter you all."[16]And Schwartzbard could not wipe from his memory the two pogroms which stained his hometown of Balta in February and March, 1919, after his departure. Ukrainian troops under Colonel Stopkievich extorted 500,000 rubles from an already impoverished Jewish community, then plundered the Jews of their personal belongings.

While frightened Christians prominently displayed icons in their windows to ward off the looters, Jews were beaten on the street or in their homes. Some were dragged away from funerals to clean out military stables. Schwartzbard could not forget that thirty of his own relatives, including his beloved father, his stepmother, his Uncle Edel, and two brothers-in-law had been butchered by soldiers calling themselves *Petlurovtzi*.[17]

Now there was no sleep. Nights he would lie awake and

cry, unable to tell his wife what prompted his tears. Visions passed before him of broken doors and windows, pictures, benches, smashed tables, burned houses, walls splattered with the blood of little children, men whose faces were distorted by insanity.

"I saw Jewish soldiers who served in Galicia or Turkey and were wounded," he wrote, "who came home to find their houses destroyed, their parents beaten, their women and children abused and shamed, people too stunned to speak. Those who could cry were fortunate. Like animals they wailed from pain and sorrow."[18]

Schwartzbard purchased the émigré journals *Les Dernières Nouvelles* and *Trident* and read of the activities of Petlura in Paris. According to Anna Schwartzbard, this only exacerbated his agonies:

> For many weeks my husband had been melancholy and nervous. I did not know the cause of it, but looking back, I remember that his depressed mood dated from the time Petlura started his Ukrainian weekly, *Trident*, in Paris. My husband read this periodical regularly and the after-effect was terrible excitement and despondency.[19]

Schwartzbard fantasized that he might be the avenger of all oppressed Jews living and dead, another Moses striking down the Egyptian overseer, a David killing Goliath. He questioned everyone about Petlura. Where could he be found? What did he look like? He made an intensive study of records in the Bibliothèque Nationale and Bibliothèque Ste. Geneviève, but the only thing he could find was a crude snapshot clipped from the *Encyclopédie Larousse*. Schwartzbard's monomania became the butt of jokes. "What will you do when you find Petlura?" his friends taunted. "Kill him? Leave his punishment to others. Don't ruin your life."

Toward the end of April, 1926, Schwartzbard's luck

turned. In the vicinity of the Cluny Museum, he encountered several persons, one of whom struck him as "very grand." He pulled out the picture of Petlura but could not be certain that it was the same man. A few days later, he encountered the same individual going into the Chartier Restaurant. Schwartzbard waited across the street for forty-five minutes, uncertain if it was Petlura, undecided what he would say or do if it were. As the man and his companions left the Chartier, Schwartzbard heard him declare in Ukrainian that he was going to buy something. The little Jewish watchmaker followed him to a residence on Rue Sommerand. He continued to follow the man for days on end, sometimes with a gun, sometimes without. "But all the time while I was following him," Schwartzbard testified later, "I wasn't sure."[20]

In the third week of May, *Les Dernières Nouvelles* published a photograph of Petlura. This picture was larger and clearer than the one which was fraying in Schwartzbard's pocket. It showed a mature man, his face lined from the strain of war, wearing a cap and heavy overcoat. Now Schwartzbard, standing watch each day as Petlura strolled arm in arm with his family or fellow Ukrainians, knew he had the right man.

On May 25, 1926, Schwartzbard rose early and donned work clothes in an effort "to fool my wife." The ruse failed, however, as Anna Schwartzbard sensed that her husband was seriously disturbed. She asked him whether he was ill, and he replied, "No, but my nerves are all gone." Anna pleaded with him to stay home, to eat something, to stay fifteen minutes, to go out after lunch. Schwartzbard refused, saying, "No, I have a very pressing affair."[21]

Later that afternoon, Anna Schwartzbard received a *pneumatique* (express letter) posted from the City Hall. It read:

> My dear Anna,
>   I am performing a duty for our poor people. I am going to avenge all the pogroms, the blood, the hatred

of the Jews. Petlura was responsible for the misfortune of our people. He must pay with his blood. As for you, conduct yourself heroically, hardily. I would never forget it if you were courageous. Accuse no one. I alone am responsible, but I could not live without avenging that great offense.

God bless you,
Sholom[22]

Notes

1. For a discussion of Jewish superstitions in Eastern Europe see Mark Zborowsky and Elizabeth Herzog, *Life is with People: The Culture of the Shtetl* (New York: Schocken Books, 1952), pp.91-92, 150-51,313-315,345-46, 349,357,359,362,376; Joshua Trachtenberg, *Jewish Magic and Superstition: A Study in Folk Religion* (New York: Atheneum, 1970 reprint of 1939 work), pp.25-43, 61-77; and Moses Gaster, *Ma'aseh Book: Book of Jewish Tales and Legends*, II (Philadelphia: Jewish Publication Society of America, 1934).

2. The information on Schwartzbard's youth is drawn from his autobiography, *Inem loif fun yoren*, pp.11-35. See also his own deposition, File 441, undated, 37651-58, Tcherikover Archive.

3. Ismar Elbogen, *A Century of Jewish Life* (Philadelphia: Jewish Publication Society of America, 1944), pp.203-204.

4. Files 904 and 905, Tcherikover Archive.

5. Letter of Tretiack to Torrès, File 427, 37060, Tcherikover Archive.

6. See Sholom Schwartzbard, *In krig mit zich aleyn* (Chicago: Ferlag Ceshinsky, 1933), pp.94-95. A French translation may be found in File 893, Tcherikover Archive.

7. Schwartzbard leaves no doubt that when he talks of a people that will lead the nations of the world to this new era, a people that carries in it the message of freedom and humanity, he is speaking of the Jews. See *In krig mit zich aleyn*, pp.256-59.

8. For Schwartzbard's view of his return to Russia, see *Inem loif fun yoren*, pp.52-57 and 61-70.

9. He refers to the spot as Volonda, probably a mistake. *Ibid.*, pp.70-79.

10. See *Leksikon fun der yiddisher literatur, presse, un filologia* (Vilna, 1929), p.527.

11. *Jewish Telegraph Agency Dispatch*, June 4, 1926, p.1.

12. *Notes Sténographiques*, fasc. 1, pp.55-56.

13. Dawidowicz, *The Golden Tradition*, p.456.

14. Deposition of Ilie Teper, December, 1926, File 469, 38978-80, Tcherikover Archive.

15. *Notes Sténographiques*, fasc. 1, p.21, and "The Schwartzbard Trial," *Jewish Chronicle*, October 21, 1927, p.26.

16. Dawidowicz, *The Golden Tradition*, p.456.

17. *The Massacres at Balta: Report to the President of the Jewish Community of Odessa* (undated), File 412, 35765-79, Tcherikover Archive.

18. Schwartzbard, *Inem loif fun yoren*, pp.211-213.

19. "Lurid Trial of Petlura's Slayer," *Literary Digest*, XCV (November 19, 1927), p.37.

20. *Notes Sténographiques*, fasc. 1, pp.23-27.

21. *Ibid.*, p.57.

22. Schwartzbard, *Inem loif fun yoren*, pp.215-16.

4.

Deification

General Petlura Is Fatally Shot in Paris
by Russian Student Seeking Revenge

THIS WAS THE TWO-COLUMN HEADLINE on the front page of the *New York Times* of May 26, 1926. The article continued: "Although called 'General,' Petlura never possessed that title; his real gift was to inspire people with faith in his plans, which were often defeated while their tradition survived."[1]

In death Simon Petlura accomplished the goal which had eluded him in life. The disunited Ukrainian exiles banded together, however briefly, in a united front. Petlura's foibles, his defeats, even his negotiations with the hated Poles over Galicia were now dismissed. The hundreds of mourners who passed by his blue and yellow draped catafalque in a Paris cathedral came to pay homage to a man whose martyrdom had elevated to the level of the great Ukrainian heroes of the seventeenth and eighteenth centuries—Chmielnicki, Doroshenko, and Mazeppa.

In Kiev, a number of his countrymen braved official condemnation to assemble in the ancient church of Saint Sophia for a memorial mass. Student proclamations were dedicated to him. Professor Serhi Yefremov (subsequently arrested and condemned in a Stalinist show trial) and Vladimir Chekhovski (onetime President of the Council of Ministers in the days of the Directory and a political foe of Petlura) went so far as to organize a series of illegal lectures praising the Holovni Ataman. These culminated in the formation of a widespread (but shortlived) nationalist conspiracy called *Soyuz Vyzvolennya Ukrainy* [Association for the Liberation of the Ukraine] composed of leading intellectuals in the Soviet-federated land.[2]

For these zealots, Simon Petlura was a sincere, cultured man who was "the great animator of all Ukrainian activity, the national hero known throughout the Ukraine, celebrated in popular songs, and summing up all the aspirations of his country." If he had been even remotely responsible for the massacres of the Jewish populace in 1919, Petlura's defenders argued, then such responsibility ought to be shared by the entire nation which followed him.

"The honor of Simon Petlura," wrote Alexander Shulgin, perpetual émigré foreign minister of the Ukrainian Republic, "is our honor, the honor of the entire nation. Our duty is to defend his great memory against all calumnies."[3]

Rue Racine, the site of the assassination, in 1926.
(YIVO Tcherikover Archive)

Ukrainian Social Democrats, at the International Congress in Brussels in the summer of 1926, went on record as identifying "completely and forever" with the policies of Petlura. "The shots, which consciously or unconsciously were directed against the revolutionary democracy, call the Ukrainian masses to further struggle for democratic liberty against Bolshevism, against Reaction." Petlura would forever remain in Ukrainian thoughts as "the fighter and martyr for the Ukrainian People's Republic."[4]

From Paris to Winnipeg, the volatile Ukrainian press commenced a campaign designed at once to absolve Petlura of guilt for what had happened to Jews during the Civil War and to paint his assassin as a Bolshevik hireling. In this, they were supported by the anti-Semitic nationalist press in Poland, *Crakow Czas, Warsaw Glos Prawdy, Kuryer Poranny,* and *Dzien Polski.*[5] In France, the Ukrainians were abetted by renascent elements of the *Action Française,* the rightist body which had all but demanded the head of Captain Dreyfus three decades earlier. Among other things, these foreign papers published editorial cartoons which portrayed Schwartzbard as a drooling maniac, clutching a dagger from which dripped "the blood of Torah."

The pogroms, it was argued, resulted from the anarchy which plagued the Ukraine in the postwar period, and the men responsible for this anarchy were "the criminals in Moscow." Russian-Bolshevik *agents provocateurs* took advantage of the "simple citizens," who were "alas, at times susceptible to abominable propaganda."[6]

It was also maintained that German occupation forces (who took their time evacuating the Ukraine after the Armistice) and French expeditionary forces in the Crimea were either "permeated with" or "soon became infected with" Bolshevism.[7] Without such subversive activity, Petlura's followers claimed, there would have been no pogroms, for the Ukrainian peasant held no deep-seated animosity against the Jews. Not the Ukrainians, but "city dwellers" or "workers imported from the North by the Tsar" had been responsible for pogroms since 1881.[8]

Moreover, the litany continued, throughout the strife-torn Ukraine in 1919 the way was open for all kinds of ambitious leaders to raise their own private armies and to operate in the name of the Directory (the Nationalist government), the Soviets, or whatever way they saw fit. Between the Rivers Dnieper and Goryn stood no less than twenty-two *batki* or "fathers," chieftains allegedly supreme in their various domains. Their bands, several thousand strong, armed with everything from machine guns to artillery, switched allegiance with the new moon, electing to fight for anyone who would subsidize them.

These "independent" warlords, supporters of Petlura claimed, were the real pogromchiks. There was *Struk,* a former schoolteacher, unsuccessful writer, and counterfeiter, who strutted about Chernobyl in a sailor's uniform, boasting of how he had drowned Jews with his own hands.[9] There was *Sokolovsky,* murderer of women and children in Brailov, Malin, Korostichev, Skiva, and Novogorod-Volinsk, a self-proclaimed Robin Hood who lived in the woods and preyed off Jews in Radomyshyl for five months in 1919, leaving that city empty of Jews.[10] There was the former carpenter *Zeleny,* butcher of Pogrebishche and Kiev.[11] There was *Angel,* the mystery man who had allegedly served as an officer in the Hetmanate army before terrorizing Bakhmach, Priluki and Chernigov.[12] There was *Volynetz,* another former schoolteacher whose men killed 340 Jews at Gaisin in May, 1919.

Tiutiunik urged on his men by exhorting them to kill their "age-old enemies"—the Great Russians and their Jewish allies.[13] *Grigoriev,* conqueror of Odessa, onetime supporter of Skoropadsky, then of the Bolsheviks, and finally of Petlura, led his men through more than fifty major massacres from Cherkassy to Elizavetgrad.[14] *Nestor Makhno,* an enlightened anarchist who liked Jews personally, did

Sleds of dead, murdered by the bands of Struk at Ivankov.

A delegation of Jews slaughtered by Kozyr-Zyrko at Ovruch.

nothing to stop the pogroms among his followers around Ekaterinoslav.[15]

Bozhko was the mad school teacher who wanted to restore the Zaporoghian Cossack Republic; he actually went about dressed in regal fashion, carrying the golden rod of his "office."[16] *Kozyr-Zyrko,* plunderer of 1,200 homes in Ovruch, was a Galician deviate who swilled vodka as he lay naked in bed and forced aged Jews to dance for his amusement.[17]

Who could blame Petlura for the more than three hundred pogroms attributed to these men or to *Lezniuk, Shepel, Blakytny, Luty, Stepovy, Mordalevich, Trepet, Sliva, Kolesnichenko,* and the countless *Doroshenkos, Triasilos,* and *Zelezniaks?*[18]

And finally there was the White Army under General Anton Denikin. In May of 1919, Denikin had found most of the Ukraine in the hands of the Soviets and their sympathizers. Petlura's troops were in rout. By September 2, however, the Whites had cleared the area of the Bolsheviks and had done extensive damage to thousands of Jews in the process. As a result, Denikin faced Petlura across a line extending through Kiev, Uman, and Birsula. Turning against the Directory, which he regarded as "a transitory stage towards Bolshevism," Denikin managed to push the Petlurists into Poland by November, 1919.

The White Army, dedicated to the supreme idea of One Indivisible Russia, distrusted the hostile Ukrainian nationalists who supposedly were working openly to cede great chunks of the Motherland to Poland. According to Denikin, the Directory, which had proven ineffective in combatting the Red Army, would have concluded a separate peace with Moscow at the first opportunity and then would have attacked his forces. Therefore, whatever actions he took against Ukrainian insurgents, Bolshevik agents, or Jews were merely precautions.[19]

For their part, the Ukrainians argued that Denikin was a

megalomaniac who betrayed them and destroyed all possibility of success against the Bolsheviks. In the course of such internecine bloodletting, especially between May and November, 1919, the Ukraine was brutalized by 625 pogroms, the greatest number in its history, a third of them attributable to Denikin's Volunteer Army.[20]

Bolsheviks, *batki*, White Russians, Poles, Asiatic deserters, German stragglers—these were the forces with which Petlura had to contend for the control of the Ukraine. Ultimately, in February, 1920, Trotsky's Bolshevik armies were to prevail. But while the civil war raged on four or five fronts, it would have been fatuous to suppose that Petlura could have suppressed all anti-Jewish outbursts. Said Foreign Minister Shulgin, "Petlura was a great man, but he was not all-powerful."[21]

The argument that Petlura was hampered in his internal policies by alien interference was developed more explicitly (if less literately) by Dr. Longin Cehelsky (then the so-called Ukrainian representative to Washington)[22] and Colonel Vladimir Kedrovsky (former chief inspector of the Ukrainian army under Petlura) in a joint communique to the *New York Times* of June 1, 1926. It was, they stated, "positively a gross mistake to connect the name of Petlura or the Ukrainian Government with these ugly outbursts of mob psychology." If the pogroms in the Ukraine were any more severe than the postwar attacks on Jews in Poland, Austria, Hungary, Rumania, or Czechoslovakia, it was because "there are living by far more Jews in the Ukraine than in all the other above mentioned countries together."[23] Not the Ukrainians but foreigners were responsible for ugly incidents:

> We Ukrainians are of the opinion that not our democratic government and not Petlura were responsible for the gruesome events, but the foreign invaders of our country—as well as the Bolsheviki, as [*sic*] the monarchistic Russians, and the Poles, financed and armed by the Allies. When we—a new revolutionary national

government—were responsible because we were not
able to maintain order in the Ukraine, the more responsible are the big powers who thoughtlessly equipped
Polish and Russian armies, which brought chaos into
our country, undermined our newly established republic and fought our army only for the benefit of
Lenin and Trotsky.[24]

According to Cehelsky and Kedrovsky, Simon Petlura
was "a real democrat . . . opposed to any religious preju-
dices." He was a general in the actual sense of the word, and
he had even been credited by French General Weygand with
inspiring the Polish defense of Lublin. As Chief Marshal of
the army, he was "like George Washington," although "not
with the same luck."[25]

A handful of Jews, including Israel Zangwill, Mark
Vishnitzer, and Arnold Margolin, described the Holovni
Ataman as virtually blameless because of the anarchic state
of affairs prevailing in the Ukraine in 1919.[26] Vladimir
Jabotinsky, founder of militant Zionism, once declared,
"The cause of the pogroms is found not in the subjective
anti-Semitism of certain persons, but in the anti-Semitism
of events. In the Ukraine, conditions of life were against
us."[27] Faced with endless citations of this statement in the
Ukrainian press, Jabotinsky publicly retracted it in October,
1927, declaring that since Petlura was the chief of the Ukrainian government and army during the worst period of
pogroms, and since Petlura never condemned the massacres
or punished the guilty, "as a consequence, he assumed
responsibility for each drop of Jewish blood spilled."[28]

Most Jews, however, echoed the sentiments of a simple
citizen of New York City, Harris Rothkowitz. Replying to
the letter of Cehelsky and Kedrovsky, Rothkowitz questioned whether it was legitimate to compare Petlura with
Pancho Villa, let alone George Washington. "If anyone
desires to find the true comparison of Petlura's type," he
added, "let him take Attila the Hun or Raisuli the Bandit."[29]

Others likened the slain Ataman to Pontius Pilate or Kaiser Wilhelm. For most Jews, there was no question that Petlura was a murderer who merited punishment. That he met his death by assassination was regrettable, but Sholom Schwartzbard was no common killer. Indeed, he was "an avenging angel," a man who had acted from an "overwhelming provocation."

Typical of this kind of reaction was the statement of Dr. Samuel Buchler, President of the Federation of Hungarian Jews in America: "The assassin Sholom Schwartzbard is no murderer at heart. He is no rogue and his record for decency leaves nothing to wish for. I look upon him as an idealist of the highest order who sacrificed himself upon the altar of human liberty and equality." Buchler, a former New York State Deputy Attorney General, added that not only should the entire civilized world rejoice that Petlura had been killed, but that it was a "pity" Denikin and the Hungarian Regent Admiral Nicholas Horthy "and others like them" were still alive.[30]

Like Petlura, Schwartzbard had become a symbol, and his people would not abandon him now. The Jewish Telegraph Agency appealed for all Jews who had participated at any time in the governments of the Ukraine during the period of the pogroms to present themselves for the trial.[31] The American Jewish Workers Alliance, while going on record to say that it did not condone murder, nevertheless volunteered to assist Schwartzbard in any possible way. In Paris, Berlin, New York, Buenos Aires, Copenhagen, Kaunas, Glasgow, and even Baghdad, impoverished Jews offered their coins to Sholom Schwartzbard Defense Committees.[32]

Often, the eagerness to be of assistance led to ludicrous situations. An example was the Jewish newspaper *Heynt* in Warsaw. Like all Yiddish papers in Eastern Europe, this journal demonstrated a passionate interest in the Schwartzbard-Petlura Affair. During the summer of 1926, *Heynt* proclaimed that it had come across documentary evidence which clearly implicated Petlura in the pogroms. Such information had come to the newspaper from an unnamed Jewish student who had befriended an unnamed Ukrainian. These two had gone before an unnamed senator from the Polish *Sejm* (parliament) in 1921 and had tried to communicate the evidence, but they had been dismissed. "Unfortunately," the story continued across four columns, the documents had been destroyed.[33]

A more reasoned analysis was presented by the great Jewish historian Simon Dubnow, who lashed out at the Ukrainian "chauvinists" who pictured Petlura as a hero. For Dubnow, the trial's significance was equal to that of the Beiliss ritual murder case fifteen years earlier. Calling the pogroms "the most horrible tragedy of Jewish history," Professor Dubnow said, "We do not desire revenge, but we must insist on revealing the terrible truth."[34]

The truth for Dubnow and his colleagues at the Jewish Historical Archives in Berlin was bound up in twelve thousand pages of reports (containing the names of at least twenty thousand Jewish dead) amassed by various commissions and welfare organizations in Eastern Europe. At least five hundred documents were said to implicate Petlura directly in the massacres.[35]

Leading the defense of Schwartzbard at the trial would be Henri Torrès, grandson of Isaiah Levaillant, the man who had founded the "League for the Defense of Human and Civil Rights" during the Dreyfus Affair. The ebullient Torrès, a native-born French Jew, was recognized as one of the most astute political lawyers in Europe. Just recently he had secured the acquittal of Germaine Berton, a young woman anarchist who had assassinated a member of the Action Française. Thirty-six years old, he had served in the First World War as an infantry sergeant, had been decorated with the Médaille Militaire, the Croix de Guerre, and a host of other ribbons. At the war's end, Torrès visited Rumania and upon returning to Paris initiated a protest campaign denouncing the barbaric treatment of Jews in Bessarabia. Balding slightly at the temples, and somewhat on the portly side, Torrès was a handsome man with a deep, sonorous voice. He was persuasive and irresistible, flawed only by a tendency to the theatrical.

The defense had eighteen months in which to prepare a case, as Schwartzbard's hearing was put off until October, 1927. During that time, the list of volunteer witnesses grew to more than 150. They included some mutilated victims of pogroms, including Etta Soschin, whose arm had been slashed away by hooligans as she witnessed the slaughter of her entire family.

Among the world's notables offering to speak on behalf of Schwartzbard and the Jews were the Comtesse de Noailles (France's leading poetess), Professor Victor Basch (President of the League of Human Rights), Mme. Severine (one of the foremost French political writers), Sinclair Lewis, H. G. Wells, Paul Dukas, Henri Bergson, Nobel Prize winner Romain Rolland, Albert Einstein, Blasco Ibáñez, Georges Weill, Max Regis, Chaim Weizmann, and even Alexander Kerensky. One of their number, Leon Blum, the head of the French Socialist party, likened Schwartzbard's agony to that of Jesus Christ and assured Mrs. Anna Schwartzbard that he was confident the accused would be acquitted in France, "a country of justice."[36]

All manner of pleadings were suggested to Torrès. Firmin Gémier (director of the Odéon Theater) proposed that if Schwartzbard should be condemned for killing Petlura, "the oppressor of the Jewish race," it ought logically to follow that all who fought for France against the Germans in the Great War should also be branded as criminals.[37]

Count Michael Karolyi, former Hungarian Prime Minister, supplied Torrès with a detailed analysis of the Jewish Problem in Central Europe and concluded that Petlura was as hypocritical about the pogroms as the anti-Semitic Hungarian Admiral Horthy.[38] The eloquent humanitarian Victor Margueritte borrowed from Victor Hugo's condemnation of Napoleon III in 1853 ("You can kill this man with impunity.") to express his feelings about Petlura. "If tomorrow in France a dictator brandishing sword or crucifix tried to exterminate our parents, our women, our children, which of us would not applaud the blow that would be delivered to this monster?[39]

Even from the Holy Land came word attesting to the evil of the pogromchiks. Pierre Bonardi (one of Torrès' associates) and Georges Suarez (editor of *Il Temps*) declared how they had been shocked by visits to Zionist colonies situated amid the malarial fens of the Jezreel Valley. In miserable camps of tents they had come across hundreds of children—ten, twelve years old—some with missing fingers or scarred foreheads. They were in Palestine ("that veritable inferno," wrote Bonardi) to work toward a golden future. They had no past. "Who are these children?" Bonardi had asked their supervisors. Invariably the response was, "They are Ukrainian orphans whose parents were massacred by Petlura."[40]

*****

Far removed from academic discussions about Petlura's responsibility for atrocities committed against children, in cell number seven of Division Five of the filthy, old Prison de la Santé, Sholom Schwartzbard waited. From the moment he had been whisked from the scene of the assassination, Schwartzbard's life had resembled that of a sleepwalker. There was an unreality about the way officers at the district police headquarters had reacted when he was brought in. Far from stirring when the word "death" was mentioned, they merely complained about such a disturbance occurring shortly before their work detail was completed. It meant more paperwork.

They did take the fundamental precautions against suicide. Schwartzbard was stripped of his belt, garters, and shoe laces, but the police seemed more interested in exchanging observations about mob violence. "People are like wild animals. If they see danger they scatter like flies. Afterward they wanted to lynch him." All the while, Schwartzbard sat quietly on a bench, his head pounding with one question. Was the man he had shot really Simon Petlura?

Nobody really seemed interested in him, not even Police Commissioner Mollard, who took his time about sitting down to interrogate the little watchmaker. Eagerly, desperately, Schwartzbard poured out a tale of historic oppression, of Haidamak massacres and thousands of Jewish dead in the Ukraine.

"All right," said Inspector Mollard, "but I want to know who this Petlura is. All that stuff about the seventeenth and eighteenth centuries is pretty old. We are now living in the twentieth century. Tell me about the murdered man. Who was he?"

As Schwartzbard tried to explain that Petlura was the equal of Haman or Chmielnicki, a gendarme came in and indicated that the victim of the assault had died at Charity Hospital. His papers identified him as Simon Petlura. At that, Schwartzbard spoke jubilantly, "Then it is right. I did not kill an honest person, only a killer." He shook the hands of those about him and added, "I'm happy I did it. I don't care what happens to me now."[41]

Later in the day, a paddy wagon took him back to his home in the Jewish quarter, ostensibly to pick up more clothes. Stupefied neighbors clustered about the handcuffed prisoner. They shouted, "Why did you have to do it? We're sorry for you." Schwartzbard seized the moment and attempted to lecture them in Yiddish, but he was cut short by accompanying officers. As the police went through the house seeking what might be relevant or incriminating material, Schwartzbard spoke to his wife and patted his dog for the last time. After a few moments, he was returned to jail.

The gendarmes had confiscated two passports, another revolver and seven bullets, and a mixed assortment of papers. The latter included working drafts of a study of the pogroms in the Ukraine, Schwartzbard's wartime memoirs, his lengthy manuscript dealing with European History from Luther through Metternich, and a copy of the Treaty of Riga.[42] Officers also found the *Dictionnaire Larousse,* with Petlura's photograph clipped from page 558, the important *pneumatique* which Schwartzbard had sent his wife that same day, and several other hastily scribbled notes which he left about the house before departing on his mission. One of them read: "Pardon me for all the sufferings that I have caused you. Eternally yours, Sholom."[43]

Though some Ukrainians were later to claim that Schwartzbard was freed on bail and flaunted his contempt for Petlura until his trial,[44] the fact was that he remained in a dank cellar for a year and one-half. It was reasoned that if he were released he would be the target of Ukrainian *revanchists.* His jailers, sympathetic to him, tried to lift his spirits. They addressed him familiarly, brought him newspapers which praised his deed, and told him not to worry because his act was correct.

But Schwartzbard was a man possessed. As he recorded it, it was practically impossible to sleep. His mind would wander into a semi-conscious state where he would visualize himself once more as a soldier at his post. Only now the battlefield was strewn with the corpses of unarmed men, women, and children.

Evening after evening, the spirit of his compatriots, other Jewish soldiers who had fallen in the line of duty, would come and excoriate him: "Go brother, go and sacrifice yourself as I did on the bloody field. Do not act like a coward or a spy. Act heroically! Let them not say that Jews are dishonest, that they buy their way out. Engrave the suffering of your brothers in your eyes. They had no place in this great world. You cannot save with your death the few who are homeless and helpless, persecuted, martyred, forgotten by God and man. But you can avenge their suffering. Go and wash out the bloody cry that has shamed and stained our people since the Middle Ages. Run and cry Hurrah! Do not ask for anything. Do not discuss it. Do not listen to your heavy heart. Go brother, go. Defend even your bitterest enemy. The time is ripe."

His guards, peering through the slot in the cell door heard an agonized Schwartzbard repeating over and over, *"Vos vill er fun mir?* What does he want of me?"[45]

Even during his waking hours in prison, Schwartzbard was beset by feelings of doubt and persecution. He was aware of the campaign of personal vilification which the Ukrainian press had mounted. He turned to the Old Testament once more for strength. "My confusion is always before me. My face is covered by shame," he wrote in his diary.

It was difficult for him to understand why people could not appreciate the significance of his deed. Reading of the killing of Agag in First Samuel, he consoled himself that he had done right: "As thy sword hath made women childless, so shall thy mother be childless among women."

And yet he doubted whether he would be given a fair trial in France. Quoting from Psalms, he wrote, "Those who hate me cover me daily with opprobrium, and those who are possessed of anger against me will judge against me." In a fit of depression, he turned to the Book of Job:

> *Tho I speak, my pain is not assuaged;*
> *And tho I forbear what am I eased? . . .*
> *Mine adversary sharpeneth his eyes upon me.*
> *They have gaped upon me with their mouth*
> *They have smitten me upon the cheek scornfully;*
> *They gather themselves together against me*
> *God delivereth me to the ungodly,*
> *And casteth me into the hands of the wicked.*[46]

To preserve his sanity, Schwartzbard busied himself writing letters to friends and relatives. He told his wife not to lament, not to lose her temper, for theirs was a minor misfortune compared with the universal sufferings of man. "Be gay, amuse yourself, take walks, and pass the time with your friends," he wrote. "I will be happy when you are calm and no longer worried."[47]

On June 6, 1926, less than two weeks after the assassination, Schwartzbard wrote to his old colleagues at the New York Yiddish weekly, *Die Fraye Arbeiter Shtimme:*

Dear Comrades of The Workers' Voice:

I am writing you from my cell and cordially greet all of you. After having served the idea of the revolution and class struggle with devotion, like a faithful soldier, for numerous years, when my life and thoughts clung to a single goal—how to ameliorate the dolorous condition of the poor and oppressed masses of humanity— I have become convinced that before being able to emancipate all mankind, one must first liberate himself, liberate the Jewish people from all persecutions and calumnies which never cease to strike this people which has been abandoned by everyone and is oppressed everywhere.

On a clear and beautiful day in the center of the metropolis of Paris, before the entire world, I performed the first act. I was too generous with this assassin, under whose command thousands, tens of thousands of Jews, children at the breast, and old men with white hair, men and women, were exterminated, under whose orders bands raped, pillaged, extorted and burned.

These same *haidamaks*, these descendants of the bandit murderer Chmielnicki, have not ceased to spill Jewish blood and bathe in it even to this day. They spared bullets; *Youpins*[48] aren't worthy of bullets; they had to slaughter them by sabre; thus were the orders of the Ataman's bandits. Well! I didn't spare bullets on this assassin; I fired five of them at his hideous body.[49]

Schwartzbard ended his angry note with a reference to the

millennia of Jewish suffering. "I have opened a new chapter in our somber and bloody history," he wrote. "Enough of slavery, enough outpouring of tears, an end to imploring, crying, bribing. Lifting our heads, sticking out our chests, we demand herewith our right: that of living equal to all!"[50]

On the same day, the prisoner wrote to the surviving members of his family, his half-brothers and sisters living on a street in Odessa named for the martyred Jewish communist heroine Rosa Luxemburg:

> I greet you, my near and dear relatives.
>
> Make it known in the cities and in the villages of Balta, Proskurov, Cherkassy, Oman, Zhitomir, Enaniev, Krivoe-Ozero, Goloskov, Kiev, Kremenchug, Poltava, Triplie, Khrestinuka, Fastov, Vassilkov, and in many other cities and towns where people have spilled the blood of Jews, pillaged their goods, defiled and outraged and burned their most sacred things. Carry the uplifting message—the angry Jew has gotten his revenge.
>
> The blood of the assassin which has fallen in the metropolis of Paris . . . will awaken the dormant universe from its somnolence and remind it of the savage crimes committed recently and again in our day against the poor and abandoned Jewish people.
>
> The ritual calumnies at Damascus, at Vienna, at Kiev, and in several other cities on this accursed terrestrial globe; the persecutions, the massacres, the devastations in old Russia, in Rumania, and in Poland at this very hour; the *numerus clausus*, the fear of ascendancy of the Jewish people, the closed doors against which Jews collide; all this ought to cease forever.
>
> We are the ones who have given the world a God, the Bible, morality. We carry in our selves the great mission of freedom, of universal emancipation.
>
> We are a people of sacred martyrs, a people that wants to free the world from slavery and decadence.
>
> We are the ones who have guarded foreign vineyards and abandoned our own.
>
> Enough. We must begin to free ourselves and liberate others afterward.

Schwartzbard closed this defiant note with a request that his relatives seek out the grave of his father in the cemetery of Ananiev and inscribe it:

> *Sleep in peace, great Jewish heart!*
> *Your son has avenged the holy and*
> *innocent blood of your Jewish brothers*
> *and of all your people, Israel.*[51]

Notes

1. *New York Times,* May 26, 1926, p.1.

2. *Russischer Kolonialismus in der Ukraine: Berichte und Dokumente* (Munich: Ukrainischer Verlag, 1962), p.77.

3. Alexander Choulguine (Shulgin), *L'Ukraine et le cauchemar rouge: les massacres en Ukraine* (Paris: Editions Jules Tallandier, 1927), p.20.

4. Resolution des Zentralkomittees der Ukrainischen Sozialdemokratischen Arbeiterpartei," June 22, 1926, File 413, 35797-804, and "Memorandum der Ukrainischen Sozialdemokratischen Arbeiterpartei an die Minderheitskommission der Sozialistischen Arbeiter-Internationale," Brussels, February 10, 1927, File 414, 35879-82, Tcherikover Archive.

5. *Jewish Telegraph Agency Dispatch,* June 11, 1926, p.1. Typical of these anti-Semitic lampoons was one appearing in a Ukrainian journal dated July 30, 1927, showing hook-nosed Jewish financiers supplanting steel-helmeted Germans as the principal threat to world peace and stability. See File 602, 52940, Tcherikover Archive.

6. Choulguine, *L'Ukraine et le cauchemar rouge,* pp.37-41 and 77.

7. Clarence A. Manning, *Twentieth Century Ukraine* (New York: Bookman, 1951), pp.54 and 64.

8. Choulguine, *L'Ukraine et le cauchemar rouge,* p.81.

9. A twenty-four-year-old peasant from Hornostaipol, Struk

loved to harangue his troops, telling them, "We are shaping history—we are building the Ukrainian state." Tcherikover maintains that no other Ataman left such a rich, wordy collection of proclamations, manifestoes and orders as Struk, who ranted against "wild foreigners, not Christians, who have come and want to take away our freedom." He charged that the Bolsheviks entered churches and spit in the face of the icons of Christ, that the Jews intended to bomb the churches. Therefore, the workers and peasants should unite in freedom and drive out the capitalist-communist might and establish the rule of the true religion in Kiev. After more than forty pogroms in the Chernobyl region, the Kiev correspondent of the Yiddish *Folkstzaytung* reported on May 10, 1920, that what Jews remained in the town were *meshugayim*, crazy people who roamed the streets aimlessly, hungry, their eyes glassy, their faces full of fear. See Tcherikover, *Di pogromen in Ukraine*, pp.225-232.

10. "Strike against the Soviet Power and Save the Faith!" "Strike against the Jews and Save the Faith!" These were the rallying cries of Sokolovsky's partisan bands. When they were finished in Radomyshyl, the city was described as like a cemetery, its main streets overgrown with grass, its stores and homes gutted, standing with open doors. See *Material of Kiev Central Committee for Help of Pogrom Victims*, collected by B. Baginski, File 48, Tcherikover Archive.

11. Tcherikover, *Di pogromen in Ukraine*, pp.225-232.

12. There seems to be no background information on this individual, who really referred to himself as *Angel Smerti* (Angel of Death). Tcherikover maintained that he was an officer in the regular Ukrainian army who was "one of the first, if not the first pogromist." Angel railed against the *Dobrovoltzi* (supporters of Denikin) and the Bolsheviks who divided the Ukrainians and sought only to rob the people, take away bread, sugar, "our entire goods." As for the Jews, they also were a guilty element who "ought to be sent to Palestine." Tcherikover, *Di pogromen in Ukraine*, pp.215-17.

13. William Henry Chamberlin, *The Russian Revolution*, II (New York: Macmillan, 1935), pp.223-225.

14. For Grigoriev's role in inciting the workers and intelligentsia to pogroms against the Jews in Elizavetgrad, Cherkassy,

Znamenka, and Kremenchug, see Tcherikover, *Di pogromen in Ukraine,* pp.303-329, and Grigoriev Pogroms, File 534, Tcherikover Archive.

15. Makhno Pogroms, File 29, Tcherikover Archive.

16. Chamberlin, *The Russian Revolution,* p.225.

17. It was Kozyr-Zyrko who was the instigator of the Ovruch pogrom in December, 1918. During the initial humiliations, rapes and beatings were common. Subsequently, the self-proclaimed liberator of the Ukraine assembled all male Jews between the ages of fifteen and forty in the village square and threatened to kill them all because of their Bolshevik sympathies. In his last days in town, this mercurial figure slaughtered thirty-two Jews, nine by his own hand, while some of them protested their loyalties with their last breaths. *Bericht funem bafulmechtikten,* S. Cohen, File 48, Tcherikover Archive.

18. According to Tcherikover, the ruffians who commanded insurgent bands frequently assumed names of historical Ukrainian leaders or names which made them sound more ferocious, and the problem of identifying the exact pogromchiks was as a result compounded. Tcherikover, *Di pogromen in Ukraine,* p.215. For a tabulation of insurgent activity, see Gergel, "The Pogroms in the Ukraine," p.244.

19. Denikin, *The White Army,* pp.234 and 285.

20. Gergel, "The Pogroms in the Ukraine," p.243, and Pogroms of Denikin, Files 524-527, Tcherikover Archives. For the pogroms of Kolchak and Yudenich, see Files 531 and 532 respectively, *loc. cit.* See also File 417, 36099-36230 and "Di ausforshung fun advokat Gruzenberg," *Heynt,* File 604, 53212, Tcherikover Archive.

21. Choulguine, *L'Ukraine et le cauchemar rouge,* p.98.

22. Cehelsky was a former member of the Austrian Parliament and later a supporter of the Skoropadsky regime. His vehement defense of Petlura was more than slightly puzzling, since he did oppose the National Union uprising which established the Directory. Moreover, Cehelsky was a bitter critic of Petlura's Galician policy.

23. This statement simply was not true, unless all of Galicia were

lumped in the Ukraine. In Poland alone there were more than 3.25 million Jews, almost as many as were found in the Russian Ukraine. Yet Polish massacres in this period by no means compared with those of the Ukraine, despite the fact that Poland also was a nation wracked by birth pangs, felt the presence of foreign troops, and was invaded by the Red Army. See *The Black Book of Polish Jewry*, ed. Jacob Apenszlak (New York: American Federation of Polish Jews, 1943), p.3.

24. *New York Times*, June 1, 1926, p.24.

25. *Ibid.*

26. As early as October, 1919, Zangwill had written to the Ukrainian government, expressing his conviction that it had taken measures ("although perhaps not all possible measures") for the suppression of crimes "for which the uncertain conditions in Russia are mostly to blame." A government which securely controlled only one-sixth of the Ukraine could hardly be blamed for what transpired in the other five-sixths, he reasoned. Vishnitzer's defense was not surprising, since he served as Secretary of the Ukrainian Mission in London during the period of the Directory. As for Margolin, Tcherikover dismissed this wealthy son of a sugar merchant as a naive person who continued to labor on behalf of the Ukrainian goverment (issuing apologetics such as "I know the government is doing everything in its power to fight pogroms—but it is powerless.") long after taking up residence in London. For the statements of those whom Sjakowski calls *Yiddishe meshorsim* (Jewish lackeys or servants), see F. Pigido, *Material Concerning Ukrainian-Jewish Relations During the Years of the Revolution (1917-1921)* (Munich: Ukrainian Information Bureau, 1956), pp.36-37. See also Tcherikover, *Di pogromen in Ukraine*, pp.188-89.

27. Choulguine, *L'Ukraine et le cauchemar rouge*, pp.136-37. It was subsequently explained that Jabotinsky's "pact with the Devil" in August, 1921, was based on a fear of new pogroms if the Slavic allies renewed their offensive in the spring of 1922. Jabotinsky allegedly flattered the Ukrainian nationalists with a view toward securing permission to organize Jewish self-defense units and thereby head off any new excesses. J. B. Schechtman, *Rebel and Statesman: The Vladimir Jabotinsky Story*, I (New York: T. Yoseloff, 1956), pp.399-415.

28. "I consider it useful to explain to that part of the Ukrainian press that it is profoundly wrong," Jabotinsky wrote in explaining his change of position. Despite his later recantation, Ukrainian apologists for Petlura have never tired of making capital of Jabotinsky's earlier statement. See *Notes Sténographiques*, fasc. 1, pp.87-89.

29. *New York Times*, June 4, 1926, p.22.

30. *New York Times*, May 30, 1926, p.10.

31. *New York Times*, August 22, 1926, II, p.7.

32. See File 506, Tcherikover Archive, for rallies throughout Europe and North America on behalf of Schwartzbard in 1926-27.

33. For this wonderful little fable, see "Shtimmung tsvishen di Ukrainer in Varshe," *Heynt*, June 10, 1926, File 604, 53205, Tcherikover Archive. Perhaps nowhere was there more interest in the trial than in Poland, where Jewish politicians and intellectuals met repeatedly through 1926-27, discussing the possible repercussions of the trial. See "Schwartzbard als Yid un als mensh," by Dr. I. M. Zelkind, *Heynt*, File 604, 53235, Tcherikover Archive; *Heynt*, June 1, 1926, p.124, 53195, File 604, Tcherikover Archive.

34. *Jewish Independent*, October 7, 1927, p.8.

35. *New York Times*, June 3, 1926, p.4.

36. Letter of Blum to Anna Schwartzbard, May 26, 1926, File 435, 37383, Tcherikover Archive.

37. Henry Torrès, *Le procès des pogromes* (Paris: Les Editions de France, 1928), p.72.

38. *Ibid.*, pp.145-55.

39. *Ibid.*, pp.189-90.

40. *Ibid.*, pp.60-63 and 247-48.

41. For a complete account of this scene at the police station, see Dawidowicz, *The Golden Tradition*, pp.449-52.

42. For this ponderous work, see File 898, Tcherikover Archive.

43. Schwartzbard, *Inem loif fun yoren*, pp.200-203; *Notes Stenographiques*, fasc. 1, pp.48-49; and Statement of Inspector Mollard, pp.18-19.

44. Pavlo Shandruk, *Arms of Valor,* trans. Roman Olesnicki (New York: Robert Speller and Sons, 1959). There is no more truth to the charge that Schwartzbard was roaming free after the assassination than to the rumor that he was publishing articles while in prison. Actually some literature was published under his name, but this consisted of essays written before the assassination. See Torrès' statement, 39011, File 471, Tcherikover Archive.

45. "Der Geist," in Schwartzbard, *Inem loif fun yoren,* pp.240-41.

46. See the heavily biased accounts issued by the Ukrainian Press Bureau in Paris, 39119-39144, File 473, Tcherikover Archive. For Schwartzbard's personal musings, see File 504, 41920-41935, Tcherikover Archive. Schwartzbard's fears that he might not receive a fair trial were shared by other Jews. See "Vos fur an urtail ervart Schwartzbard?" by Polish jurist Henryk Etinger, *Heynt,* July 7, 1926, File 604, Tcherikover Archive, 53234.

47. Letter of Schwartzbard to his wife, 39077, File 472, Tcherikover Archive.

48. Another derogatory play on the word Jew.

49. Letter of Schwartzbard to *Worker's Voice,* 39071-72, File 472, Tcherikover Archive.

50. *Ibid.*

51. Letter of Schwartzbard to relatives in Odessa, 39073-74, File 472, Tcherikover Archive.

5.

The Palace of Justice

THE SCHWARTZBARD TRIAL, which opened on October 18, 1927, provided Paris with its most sensational affair since the trial of Madame Caillaux before the war.[1] Five hundred journalists from Latin America, Australia, London, Birobidjan, New York City, and China competed for space with the more than one thousand French citizens who had clogged the streets since early morning, all hoping to gain access to the Assize Court of the Seine.

Sealed off by a high set of gates, the stately complex of grey buildings known as the Palace of Justice had witnessed many comparable sieges in its six centuries of existence. Situated on the western half of the islet in the Seine River called the Cité, the Palace had once served as the chief residence of French kings. In 1431, Charles·VI converted the halls into the chief law court or "Parlement" of Paris.[2]

Two hundred years of revolution, particularly the chaos of the Paris Commune in 1871, had taken their toll of the original structure, and little more than the stained glass splendor of Sainte Chapelle remained intact. Government renovation at the turn of the century had made the palace, together with the Prefecture of Police and the Tribunal of Commerce, an enviable tangle of marble staircases, carved pillars, and elegant courtrooms.

For the four hundred persons who succeeded in pushing

94

their way past harried ushers into a room suited for half their number, the Assize Court was a disappointment. At the front, before the judicial dais, stood the haphazardly placed tables for the press. The inadequate light from high rectangular windows fell upon the prisoner's dock and left the rest of the courtroom in relative shade. The wood-paneled galleries were stifling.

In the past, murder trials had been social occasions for the Parisian lower classes, who saturated themselves with heliotrope, packed champagne bottles and opera glasses, and assumed reserved seats to listen appreciatively to tales of

The Palace of Justice, scene of the trial, in October 1927.
(YIVO Tcherikover Archive)

poison, vitriol, or rape. This day, however, white-bearded
Orthodox Jews sat next to flappers with bobbed hair, and
the air was heavy with the scent of garlic. Above the bar
where witnesses would testify hung Bonnat's painting of
Christ, his eyes downcast, in seeming disapproval of the
unruly scene before him.

Beneath and off to the right of the high mahogany boxes
for the judges was the section reserved for the prosecution. In
this instance, civil and criminal actions against Schwartzbard were to be heard simultaneously. Thus the French
people were to be represented by Public Prosecutor Reynaud, while the parties to the civil suit (Madame Olga
Petlura and her brother-in-law Oskar) would be represented
by Albert Willm and Cesar Campinchi. Assisting them
would be Czeslaw Poznansky, an attorney from Poland, a
Jewish apostate, who had come to champion the cause of the
Ukraine against this Bolshevik assassin.

Each of the French barristers was a colorful figure in his
own right. Reynaud was a pudgy little man with a Ben
Butler mustache, whose white judicial collar draped over his
gown like an oversized bib. Willm, now fifty-nine years old,
had established his reputation as a young man while successfully defending Aristide Briand in the Cluses Affair.
Vice-president of the association of Parisian novelists, a
contributor to such radical newspapers as *Humanité* and
L'Action, Willm was regarded as one of the outstanding
figures in French law. Short, with white hair, he was hardly
the picture of benevolence. Large black eyes and thick jowls
set in a scowl seemed to accentuate his grave demeanor.

For the most part, Willm would let Campinchi conduct
the civil case. Cesar Campinchi, a forty-five year-old Corsican, was, like Defense Council Torrès, an expert in political cases. Like Torrès, he was a war hero (Verdun, 1916-17,
Médaille Militaire, Croix de Guerre). Unlike Torrès,
however, he was a reserved, calculating logician. A boxer
and fencer in his free moments, Campinchi transferred his

physical skills to the courtroom. Delicately, unemotionally, point by point, he established his arguments. Tall and angular, with elfin ears and flat dark hair parted in the center, he was popular among his peers. Still, with his long nose capped by a pince-nez, he seemed more fitted for the role of law clerk than advocate.

Near Campinchi, in another booth, sat his antagonist, Torrès, resplendent in his legal robes, bedecked with wartime medals, wearing spats. On this occasion, he would be assisted by Girard Rosenthal and a Monsieur Goudchaux.

At 12:45 P.M., black-caped gendarmes quieted the noisy crowd as the jury filed into the courtroom. These twelve men, drawn by lot from every canton in France, would decide the fate of Sholom Schwartzbard "with the impartiality and firmness becoming to an honest man of independent mind." Under French law, a simple majority would be necessary for a conviction. In keeping with the request of Prosecutor Reynaud, four extra jurors were to sit as alternates.

The extra jurors were only one example of official concern over the expedition of justice in this case. The presiding judge, Georges Flory, was attended by three assessors, one more than the usual number. Flory, sixty-nine years old, with forty-one years of legal service behind him, had appreciated the additional assessor while conducting the slander trial of Leon Daudet two years earlier.[3] A steel-jawed man, President Flory, holder of France's highest military decoration, the Legion of Honor, had also assigned two full-time interpreters to the hearings. Despite such precautions, the trial extract became a hodgepodge of misspellings of Russian, Yiddish, and Ukrainian names.

With the appearance of Sholom Schwatzbard, the crowd again became animated. The too-small assassin entered the courtroom from a door behind the prisoner's dock, followed by a single guard. Pale and nervous, he seemed worn from his long detention. He wore a dark bow tie and on his grey

coat was pinned his French War Cross. Schwartzbard would
not look at Madame Petlura, who was seated at the prosecution's bench, appropriately dressed in black.

Justice Flory frowned as the clamor which greeted the
prisoner subsided into a hum, then a whisper. "The session
is open," he declared.

Justice Flory, presiding judge in the trial.
(YIVO Tcherikover Archive)

The jurors were officially sworn. Schwartzbard was asked
him name, age and profession. Then he was informed that
he was being charged with violations of Articles 295, 296,
297, 298 and 302 of the French Penal Code (all of which
pertained to premeditated murder and all of which provided
for the death penalty). The defendant responded "Not
guilty" to the charges.

After these preliminary formalities, the court proceeded with the reading of the indictment by the clerk. This interminable document, prepared by the office of the Public Prosecutor, began not with a direct accusation against Schwartzbard, but with an elaborate defense of Simon Petlura. By means of an historical survey, counsel for the state

The reading of the indictment; Cesar Campinchi is at the right in the first row, Henri Torrès is at the extreme left. (YIVO Tcherikover Archive)

hoped to show that Petlura was not responsible for the pogroms but had in fact been a friend of the Jews and had done all in his power to protect them. The cause of those regrettable horrors lay in the state of anarchy into which the Ukraine was plunged following the Bolshevik Revolution.

"After the fall of Kerensky and the victory of Communism," read M. Willm, "the general mobilization threw onto Ukrainian territory an enormous number of men who had been freed from the army. Left without discipline and without funds, they began to pillage. *They* were the real culprits in the massacres in which both the Jewish and Christian population suffered. The Red Army and the Denikin Army were not above such practices, and no doubt the regiments of which Petlura was the official head, and which were known as Petlurians, also engaged in them. It was very difficult for the Hetman who lived far away, and whose orders were frequently disobeyed, to control these activities which were really caused by the circumstances of the moment."[4]

Petlura's supporters had steadfastly maintained that Ukrainians as a whole, and not the Jews in particular, had been victimized in this period, and the indictment reflected their views. Foreign Minister Shulgin, for example, had once said that "not a thousand or two thousand Jews, but tens of thousands, millions of Orthodox Ukrainian Christians" had died at the hands of Red Army units, White agents, or as a result of epidemics, which Shulgin termed "a pogrom of an entire country."[5]

The clerk continued: "The misfortunes and sufferings endured by the population brought to a head certain differences which had always existed between the peasant Cossacks and the Jews. It must be added that the army, having no regular supply of food, had to live on the land. The inhabitants had to provide them, willingly or unwillingly, with their supplies. The dregs of the population participated in the robberies. The peasants, exasperated by these robberies, shot at the troops, and naturally reprisals followed."[6]

According to the indictment, Petlura's every action dispelled even "theoretical responsibility" for the pogroms. With remarkable energy, it was maintained, he sought to inspire his followers with humanitarian principles. A series of formal decrees issued by him to his army clearly discouraged the organizing of pogroms, under pain of severe punishment. In the period of the Directory, Ukrainian Jews were granted extensive national autonomy beyond that enjoyed elsewhere in Europe, and much of this too could be traced to Petlura's humanitarianism. Currency notes and stamps were issued with Yiddish inscriptions. The government established a Ministry for Jewish Affairs and appointed several Jews, Margolin and Vishnitzer among them, to high-ranking judicial and diplomatic posts. Petlura had even established special commissions to investigate the pogroms, and "many" Jews, both civil and military figures, had been selected for these bodies.

Sholom Schwartzbard had killed an innocent man. The assassin could not take refuge in the argument that he was an avenger of his people, any more than he could claim that he suffered from some form of temporary insanity. The three "alienists," Drs. Marie, Turel, and Claude, who examined Schwartzbard during his long confinement over the initial protests of his counsel, were impressed by this man who read Ovid, Virgil, Renan, and Max Müller in a prison cell. They found him to be "a man of deep convictions and highly intellectual," though many of his ideas obtained through self-education were flawed. The psychiatrists noted Schwartzbard's repeated references to the Bible for justification of his act. They were also aware of the prisoner's doodlings, a mélange of boxes and bars, symbolic of his own tormented incarceration.[7]

Subsequently, Dr. Claude would testify that Schwartzbard's actions might be compared with those of an epileptic or someone in a delirious state or in mental paralysis. "There are certain acts of obsession with unconscious impulses in which there is some kind of automatic mechanism," Claude noted. "The individual cannot detach the obsessing idea from his personality, but he retains meanwhile complete control of his will."[8] Nevertheless, Schwartzbard bore no trace of nervous abnormality, inherited disease, or exceptional impulsiveness. In short, the psychiatrists testified that he was fully responsible for his actions.[9]

Far from being a deranged fanatic, the indictment went on, Schwartzbard was actually a member of a gang which had plotted the murder for some time. The basis of this charge was a deposition taken from exiled Ukrainian engineer Waldemar Koval. Professor Koval, a personal friend of Petlura, recounted how one day while dining with him and "a Pole named Levitzky" (probably a reference to Andrei Livitsky) in a little café at the Boulevard d'Auteil and Rue Denfert-Rocherau, he noticed three persons at a nearby table who seemed excessively interested in his party. They were "a dark man of Jewish type," a young man, and a well-dressed woman. Petlura bade his friends not to speak too loudly, for he had observed that he was being followed of late. When the Ukrainians left the café, Koval again noticed the two men from the café sitting in a big, black sedan. He overheard the driver say either "Jacques is there" or "Jacques, they have boarded the tram." Petlura had just taken a streetcar with Levitzky.

Professor Koval identified Schwartzbard as one of those two suspicious men dressed in black suits and hats. The only thing about which he was unsure was the color of Schwartzbard's hair. Unfortunately for the prosecution, Professor Koval had died of natural causes since offering that deposition in July, 1926. His untimely death did not prevent counsel for the public and civil parties from asserting, "Circumstances appear which do not bear out the statement of the murderer that he acted alone." Schwartzbard, it was argued, had killed Petlura "willfully" and "with malice aforethought."[10]

As the clerk read, his words were frequently drowned out by shouts of agreement or discord from spectators who threatened to disrupt the proceedings altogether. When Justice Flory attempted to have the long list of summoned witnesses read aloud, the courtroom again erupted in confusion. A temporary recess was ordered, at the end of which the President again cautioned the galleries against further interruptions. Such outbursts, Flory warned, could only contribute to an intensification of racial feeling which would be inimical to the interests of justice.

Turning to Schwartzbard, Flory said, "I am going to present you to the jurors. You can explain yourself afterward in complete freedom, but for the sake of convenience do not neglect any facts which could be useful to your defense. I recommend that you speak as loudly and distinctly as possible. It is imperative that those who judge you understand you."

The watchmaker-soldier sat stolid, almost immobile, in the prisoner's dock as Flory reviewed his background once more. When the judge came to the facts of the shooting, Schwartzbard listened intently and nodded. Asked to identify the automatic pistol which had been used to kill Petlura, he said simply, "It is mine." But when Flory asked how he had been induced to kill the Holovni Ataman, Schwartzbard required more time.

Again and again in his cell he had rehearsed this moment. In his impassioned prose, he wanted to remind the court of tyrants like Herod, Caligula, Nero, and Diocletian, all sadists who had drowned whole generations in blood, of "one long bill of accusation against humanity" in the deeds of Attila, Torquemada, Tamerlane, the religious wars of the Middle Ages, Ivan the Terrible, and the ritual murder libels. All of that was next to nothing, however, "when I recall the great sufferings which our people endured the last centuries in the Ukraine, that vale of tears."

He was going to tell the French jury how for three hundred years the Zaporoghian Cossacks drenched the soil of the Ukraine with Jewish blood, how Chmielnicki and his followers raped and killed thousands who refused to convert, how they sacked communities in Pereyaslav,

Borisovka, Piryatin, Boryslav, Dubno, and Nemirov, how the Scottish-born Krivonos ("Broken-nose") snapped people's backs like chicken wings, how Gonta and Zhelezniak puffed on pipes while their men slaughtered helpless women and children "for God and country."[11]

"Our tragedy," Schwartzbard had wanted to say, "is intensified when poets and historians glorify these grisly deeds. The barbarous epic of savage sadism commited by animals in the guise of men evokes no pity for our martyrs, no sympathy, no regrets. For these poets and historians too, the Jews are creatures without legal protection, scapegoats, animals to be driven and slaughtered with satisfaction. Historian Kostomarov, novelist Nikolai Gogol, and poet Shevchenko depicted these scenes of horror in calm tones and praised the heroes who did these things. The victims appear to them as comical creatures. The Haidamaks boasted that they were heroes because they were cruel. They were courageous because they did not shrink from killing infants in their cradles."[12]

Just as he had poured out his soul to Inspector Mollard and Magistrate Peyre, so Schwartzbard wanted to tell Flory and the world about the ghastly massacres committed by the Haidamaks of Petlura between 1918 and 1920, acts which surpassed the deeds of earlier Ukrainian heroes "in their cruelty and evil." He wanted to tell about the nightmares he had suffered and how he longed to avenge his dead brothers and sisters by killing the arch-anti-Semite Petlura. Indeed, he wished he could have had the opportunity to kill more of the Haidamak gang.

This last element may well have caused a rift between Schwartzbard and his attorney Torrès. Although Torrès was to wax historical throughout the trial, he advised Schwartzbard to stick to the facts of the twentieth century, as judge and jury might not be any more interested in "ancient history" than the police. The disagreement was just one of several which were to develop between the two men as

Schwartzbard (right) with his attorney Torrès.
(YIVO Tcherikover Archive)

Torrès labored to save Schwartzbard's life. On at least one occasion, the defendant even attempted to dismiss his counsel. As for Schwartzbard's panegyric at the opening session, it was, in the accused's own words, "the speech I did not make."[13]

Still, much of what he did say reflected that undelivered tirade. When Justice Flory asked how he knew the pogroms were organized by Petlura, Schwartzbard answered: "Petlura had taken power; he had taken command. He was the

chief of the government, the chief of the Haidamaks and
Cossacks. The Haidamaks were men lacking hearts or conscience, truly brutes, men who never attacked face to face,
who entered people's homes during their sleep because they
knew the Jewish population was defenseless. They went
into their houses, violated women before their husbands,
daughters before their fathers and brothers. They burned,
pillaged, they made a pogrom, a pogrom which is assassination, pillage, and rape. That is a pogrom."

"It wasn't the first time," Schwartzbard continued. "Such
massacres have gone on in those valleys of blood and tears
for three centuries. Petlura was the little son of a great
murderer named Chmielnicki. It was in 1648 that this great
Ataman with his Cossacks massacred the Jews and Polish
Catholics. There was a revolt against the Poles at that time
and the massacres of the Poles were carried out at the same
time as the killing of the Jews. The massacres against the
Jewish population lasted from 1648 to 1654. There were
more than five hundred thousand killed, children, women,
old people.

"A century later, there were still other Atamans, Gonta
and Zhelezniak, who organized the same carnage in the
Ukraine. They again massacred the Jewish population.
History has preserved the very painful documents about
these events. The Jews have written psalms and lamentations about these massacres. At that time again, there were
also massacres of Poles. They massacred Jews and Poles.
That was the second great massacre.

"The third time, it was Petlura, who had come in 1918. He
recommenced the same massacres. Ukrainian poets and
historians have written about these massacres. They were
always carried out against the helpless population; they
massacred women, children, the old. That was their work.
The massacres lasted forever, from the day when the tyrant
Petlura took power, that is from 1918, through 1919, 1920; all
these massacres took place under the regime of Petlura."[14]

No one tried to restrain Schwartzbard as he rambled on

emotionally. Rocking backward and forward like a Chasidic Jew at prayer, he told of villages like Zhidowska-Grebla where there were only mute witnesses to the massacres, bodies piled up as on a battlefield, lacking heads or fingers, waxen, bloodless hands outstretched in supplication, lighted houses where interrupted feasts were never eaten, blazing fireplaces that consumed the hands that lit them, wide open mouths that could never speak, glaring eyes that could not see.[15]

Thousands of men, women and children had been slaughtered by Petlurist troops, whose flags bore the inscription, "Kill the Jews and save the Ukraine." That was the order in Schwartzbard's home city, Balta, where at least 120 women, including one of seventy years, were raped. Regular Ukrainian units accused the Jews of hoarding tea and sugar. Then they sacked virtually every home, apartment, and store in Balta. Then the drunken supporters of Simon Petlura struck with machine guns. Concertinas supplied funeral music as the streets were littered with two hundred mutilated dead, some of whose ears and fingers had been torn away by looters seeking jewelry and gold. Most of the dead were the Jewish poor who had not been able to flee the village. Schwartzbard had lost two dozen relatives in the pogroms at Balta in 1919.

"When I heard that he [Petlura] was in Paris, I made up my mind to kill him. All of my compatriots, Jewish or not, could scarcely believe he was in Paris. They were unanimous in telling me, 'It isn't possible that this dog is here.'" Nevertheless, they all offered to assist me in locating him.

"I did not know Petlura. I had to procure his picture. Then I found it in the *Encyclopédie Larousse*, and a little later in the *Nouvelles Ukrainiennes*. Luck was with me. One day, in the Latin Quarter, I obtained a clue in a conversation between two Ukrainians. Afterward, I recognized him two or three times, but I spared him, because I was not sure. I was afraid of making a mistake."[16]

As he rushed along, describing the events of his final

encounter with the Holovni Ataman, Schwartzbard's voice rose to a shrill pitch. His face seemed illuminated, as if he were reliving that terrible moment. "I saw Petlura go into the café. In my pocket was a *pneumatique* to my wife telling her of my intentions, of which she was ignorant."

From his previous encounters with Petlura, Schwartzbard *knew* his victim would be in the restaurant approximately forty-five minutes. He raced across the Seine to post the letter at the City Hall, then returned to take up his vigil outside the Chartier.[17]

"I waited some minutes, and finally he came out. As Petlura came to me, I thought, 'Here's my chance.' I asked him, 'Are you Petlura?' He didn't answer. He just lifted his heavy cane. I knew it was him. I shot once! twice! three! four! five times! Yes, five times! And then two more because I could not stop! I had an automatic pistol. My aim was good. After the fifth bullet, he fell to the pavement, all sprawled out."

"Yes," interrupted Flory, "he demanded mercy and you continued to fire."

"No! When he fell, immediately he was convulsive. He didn't speak. He didn't say a word. All the time I spoke, he didn't respond. He didn't say one word. Only some cries of pain—'Aiee! Aiee!' There were cries, but no words. He fell immediately and was convulsive when he had fallen. My bullets struck well and I discharged my revolver into the soil only from a desire not to hit an innocent bystander accidentally. Then the noise of the reports drew a crowd, a policeman. He asked if I had done it and I told him, 'Yes. I have killed an assassin.'

"But a doubt plagued me. Had I been mistaken? Did I actually kill Petlura? When I was told later at the police station that it was actually Petlura I had killed with my gun, I sprang over to the policeman who came to report the news and embraced him like this."

Here, a smiling Schwartzbard turned to the gendarme in

the dock with him and clumsily demonstrated by throwing his arms about the latter's neck. A murmur of disgust rose from the crowd. It was silenced by the usher's hammer.[18]

"In a café at Boulogne-sur-Seine, then a short time after, at a tram station, you were recognized by M. Koval among a group of persons who were spying on M. Petlura," declared the President probing the defendant. "Are you the man identified by M. Koval?"

"M. Koval lies. It was not me."

"Weren't you an executioner in the service of a gang?"

"No. I acted alone."

"And the hour of your *pneumatique*?" Flory inquired, pointing out that while Schwartzbard claimed he mailed the letter at 1:35 (forty minutes *before* the killing), the express letter bore a time stamp of 2:35 P.M. (twenty minutes *after* Petlura had been shot). How could he explain the discrepancy, unless an accomplice had mailed the letter for him?

"An error of the post!" snapped Schwartzbard.

To this day, Ukrainians argue that information introduced in that first sitting more than established a circumstantial case for conspiracy against Petlura. First there was the allegation of Professor Koval about several persons (including the "Jewish type" and his female companion) trailing the Holovni Ataman. Then there was the inexplicable problem of the time stamp on the *pneumatique*.

And finally there were Schwartzbard's own words in that same express letter, instructing his wife "to accuse nobody." According to one Ukrainian historian, "It [the express letter] provides still another important piece of circumstantial evidence indicating that the assassin may have had accomplices—otherwise why would he warn his wife not to accuse anyone and stress to her that he alone was guilty"?[19]

Why Professor Koval did nothing to protect the life of his dear friend Petlura, why he did not run to the police or demand an investigation before the assassination, has never been explained. How an innocent confidence between husband and wife could be distorted into an expression of conspiracy is likewise never explained. Petlura's supporters claim only that "a scholar must be prepared to 'think the unthinkable.' "[20]

As for the problem of the time stamp on the *pneumatique*, Torrès pointed out that the letter contained still another discrepancy in time. A second relay station had received the express letter at 3:50. A third station added the time of 5:50. Common sense dictated that if it took two hours to move from Station B to Station C, then the same amount of time should have been required to move from Station A (City Hall, where Schwartzbard posted the letter) to Station B. Although French postal stations were required to advance their time stamps every five minutes, the practice of advancing a stamp a full hour to eliminate a relatively trivial task is not unknown in post offices. Thus, an over-zealous employee at the City Hall station might have stamped a letter received at 1:35 as 2:35.

Moreover, the possibility of simple human error could not be ruled out, as Torrès indicated. As proof, he produced a passport signed by the Police Commissioner of Jeumont. Dated October 11, 1936, the passport was erroneously postdated ten years. After remarking sarcastically that he did not know whether the same man would be Commissioner in Jeumont in 1936 (Torrès sincerely wished him success in future promotions), the Defense Counsel added, "Are you going to quibble with me for an error of an hour?"[21]

"In the investigation," continued Flory, "you said that Petlura was either the organizer of the pogroms or the inspiration for them."

"It amounts to the same."

"And yet," replied Flory, "former members of the Ukrainian Directory will come to testify that while he was in power, Petlura showed himself to be favorable to the Jews."

"Yes," shouted Schwartzbard, "in sending them to heaven!"

"They will say, moreover, that far from encouraging the pogroms, Petlura always strove to prohibit them by proclamations and appropriate measures, but that in those troubled times he was undone by bands of adventurers who fleeced the population indiscriminately and who indulged themselves in the worst atrocities. Some persons have even cited the fact that he had shot a Cossack chief who transgressed his given orders."

Schwartzbard was livid. Leaning over the bar of the prisoner's dock, he cried, "The pogroms were never as numerous or as atrocious as under Petlura!"

Again Flory: "An entire series of orders were issued daily to the army, all formally prohibiting pogroms. Punishment was expressly specified for the guilty. All desired, done, and signed by Petlura. And when the pogroms could not be avoided, the government went to succor the victims. In July, 1919, for example, a Jewish delegation addressed him and he affirmed his determination to do everything in his power to suppress actions against the Jews. The leader of the delegation, Rabbi Gutman, thanked him in the name of all Jewry. In a word, all who spoke with President Petlura testified to the sincerity of his efforts. He gave them all the impression that he was a man favorable to the Jews."

According to Petlura's former aide-de-camp, Alexander Dotzenko, Jews all over the Ukraine regarded Petlura as their protector, "the guardian of their rights," and whenever he would arrive in a small town in Podolia, the entire community would turn out to greet his army very cordially. The rabbis would carry their Torahs and bless him, saying, "Blessed is he who protects his people, and you are he who protects not only his people, but also ours." Thereafter, the Jews would feed Petlura's troops, quarter them, and engage in discussions over politics and religion.[22]

Schwartzbard said, "Before condemning Christ to death, Pilate also said, 'I am not at fault.' And Petlura was, like Janus, a two-faced man; none of the pogroms were stopped, and they took place under his direction, all the time."[23]

It is true that a Jewish delegation headed by Drs. Meier Kleidermann (representing the Jewish community), Alter-mann (for the Socialist parties) and Guttmann (for the workers) approached Petlura in Kamenetz-Podolsk on July 17, 1919, and pledged their allegiance to the Directory. They praised Petlura and his government for all that allegedly was being done to combat pogroms. They stated that Jews were being treated equitably by the regime. Against un-named "agitators" who were attempting to discredit the Directory in Western eyes, the Jewish representatives vowed they would stand by the cause of the independent Ukraine.[24] A similar resolution was passed by the representatives of the Jewish Socialist Democratic Party ("Bund") in Kamenetz-Podolsk a month later.[25]

The problem is, however, that from June 3 to November 7, 1919, the Directory made its provisional capital in Ka-menetz-Podolsk. The Jews of this community, survivors of Petlurist "disturbances" in May of that year when fifty-two of their number had been killed and mutilated, now found themselves directly under the barrels of the Nationalists' guns. Tension was at such a peak through those summer months that the Jews voluntarily suspended their workers' clubs for fear that these might antagonize the Ukrainians. Most remained in their homes unless it was absolutely necessary for them to venture out, well aware of the dictum among Jews that "evil spreads in proportion as the Ukrain-ian troops advance in the Province of Podolia."

It should also be noted that municipal elections were about to be held in Kamenetz when the Jewish leaders issued their unctuous statement for Petlura. The only way the Jewish parties could assure themselves a place on the ballot was by paying lip service to the Directory. Not affection, but simple survival dictated the accolades to Simon Petlura. No comparable pledge of fealty was ever obtained from a Jewish community *free* from occupation by Petlura's troops.[26]

Flory concluded his interrogation: "In sum, then, you

admit the facts. Do you admit premeditation?"

"Yes."

"You killed Petlura because you saw in him the responsibility for the pogroms."

"That is it. Exactly."

Notes

1. Joseph Caillaux was Premier of France in 1911-12. The following two years he served as Minister of Finance. At that time, Gaston Calmette, editor of *Figaro*, publicly accused him of financial irregularities. Caillaux's wife, seeking to avenge her husband's good name, shot and killed Calmette in cold blood. She was acquitted in a trial presided over with obvious partiality. In 1917, Caillaux was arrested and convicted of having collaborated with the Germans. He was imprisoned from 1920 to 1923.

2. Not to be confused with "Parliament" in England. There were thirteen of these Parlements in France, comprised of legal experts who bought their offices. With the suspension of the Estates General for 175 years, though, it can be said that they were one of the few checks on royal absolutism in the period prior to the French Revolution.

3. Leon Daudet was a Royalist at the time of the Dreyfus Affair and an extreme Nationalist following World War I. He favored, among other things, the seizure of the Ruhr. No friend of Jews, he was a director of the *Action Francaise*, and he once called Leon Blum a traitor. In November, 1923, Daudet's neurotic teen-age son committed suicide in the back seat of a cab. Daudet accused the driver, a man named Bajot, of being in league with the Surete, the Germans, and the anarchists. Bajot sued him for slander and on November 14, 1925, the same Justice Flory sentenced Daudet to five months in prison and fined him 1,500 francs. At the same time, Flory fined Joseph Dlest, manager of the Action Française, 300 francs and

sent him to prison for two months. Together, on behalf of their hatemongering newspaper, they had to pay the cabdriver an additional 2,500 francs. See Eugen Weber, *Action Française: Royalism and Reaction in Twentieth Century France* (Palo Alto: Stanford University Press, 1962), p.169.

4. "The Schwartzbard Trial: Public Prosecutor Defends Petlura," *Jewish Chronicle*, October 21, 1927, p.26.

5. Choulguine, *L'Ukraine et le cauchemar rouge*, pp.52-55.

6. *Jewish Chronicle*, October 21, 1927, p.26.

7. For these idle scribblings, see File 895, Tcherikover Archive.

8. Testimony of Dr. Claude, *Notes Stenographiques*, fasc. 4, pp.166-171.

9. Somewhat ineffectively, Torrès tried to manipulate these findings and the magistrate's statement (which referred to Schwartzbard as perfectly lucid) into an endorsement of Schwartzbard's act. See *Notes Sténographiques*, fasc. 1, pp.84-85.

10. For Professor Koval's deposition, see *Notes Sténographiques*, fasc. 1, pp.35-37; and File 451, 38077-78, Tcherikover Archive.

11. For "The Speech I Did Not Give," see Schwartzbard, *Inem loif fun yoren*, pp.308-316, and Dawidowicz, *The Golden Tradition*, pp.453-57.

12. Schwartzbard, *Inem loif fun yoren*, p.311.

13. *Ibid.*, pp.308-316. For improved relations after the trial, see File 883, 69962-70, Tcherikover Archive.

14. *Notes Sténographiques*, fasc. 1, pp.52-55.

15. For a detailed account of this melodramatic moment, see "At the Schwartzbard Trial in Paris," *Jewish Tribune*, XCI (October 18, 1927), p.5. The trial extract contains several inaccuracies, including reference to Zhidovska-Grebla as Judofskegrevia. *Notes Sténographiques*, fasc. 1, 55-56. See also "Why I killed Petlura," by Schwartzbard in *Novaia Niva*, 1926, 38829-39, File 46, Tcherikover Archive.

16. *Notes Sténographiques*, fasc. 1, p.22.

17. *Ibid.*, pp.26 and 32.

18. *Ibid.*, p.32

19. The source of the statement is an unnamed Ukrainian historian in the editorial review of this book, fall, 1973, p.5.

20. *Ibid.*, p.8.

21. Torrès, *Le procès des pogromes*, pp.33-34.

22. Testimony of Dotzenko, *Notes Stenographiques*, fasc. 5, pp.42-43.

23. *Notes Sténographiques*, fasc. 1, pp.73-76.

24. *Trudowa Hromada*, July 18, 1919, in Pigido, *Material Concerning Ukrainian-Jewish Relations*, p.61.

25. Subsequently, on August 26, 1919, the Bund in Kamenetz-Podolsk published another resolution complimenting the government for its constitutional democracy and its solicitous treatment of Jewish minorities. This statement added that the Petlura government had "energetically combatted the pogroms." *Ukraina*, September 3, 1919, in Choulguine, *L'Ukraine et le cauchemar rouge*, pp.182-3.

26. For a non-Ukrainian view of what transpired in Kamenetz-Podolsk, see Gitelman, *Jewish Nationality and Soviet Politics*, pp.170-180; Tcherikover, *Di ukrainer pogromen*, pp. 158-59; A. Gumener, *A kapitl Ukraine* (Vilna, 1921), pp.17-18; J. Schechtman, *Quelques commentaries des annexes de mémorandum de M. A. Choulguine*, unpublished report for Comité des Délégations Juives (Paris, 1927). pp.38489-93, File 459, Tcherikover Archive; and *Der pogrom in Kamenetz-Podolsk*, report for the Kiev Central Committee, 1919, 35780-83, File 412, Tcherikover Archive.

6.

Jewish Provocation

Cesar Campinchi, the Civil Prosecutor, attempted to brand the accused as a common criminal, an anarchist in league with Moscow, a sadist who reveled in his killing of an innocent man.

Campinchi began by attacking the character of the self-proclaimed avenger. In a seemingly irrelevant digression, he asked Schwartzbard to explain why he had been sentenced to prison not only in Russia, but also in Vienna (in 1908) and Budapest (in 1909).

Schwartzbard's answers were a confused tangle of misplaced dates and names. He claimed that when he fled Russia he was only a minor, wandering helplessly from country to country in quest of his daily bread. Trudging along the dusty lanes of Central Europe, he and his brother covered as much as thirty-eight kilometers in a single day. While in Vienna, a kindly innkeeper took pity on them and permitted them to sleep one night on his stoop. The next day they were arrested, charged with vagabondage, and sentenced to four months at hard labor. Later, he was arrested for suspected espionage merely because he belonged to an anarchist clique. Schwartzbard noted proudly that he had been sent to the same prison as his anarchist predecessor Bakunin. Ultimately, he made his way to Budapest where, lacking papers and stigmatized as a radical, he was arrested once more before being deported by the Austro-Hungarian authorities.[1]

Such a tale may have touched the hearts of Jewish spectators who knew the bitter and lonely taste of twenty centuries of homelessness, but it did nothing to the Prosecutor.

"A minor!" he exclaimed derisively. "You were twenty-two years old! On your arrest, you gave a false name! And you were not sentenced for vagabondage. You were condemned for burglary!"

Campinchi produced depositions and legal records from the Austrian Legation affirming that "Walsberger" (Schwartzbard) had been charged with attempted burglary not once but twice. According to court records, he had also lied about his place of birth and had tried to steal a gold bar valued at 230 kronen and a plate of unknown worth. Schwartzbard steadfastly denied that he had used the name "Walsberger," or "Weissberger" as another account had it. But Campinchi insisted that his confession also was on file. The Austrian note added that Schwartzbard frequented anarchist circles and was regarded by authorities as a dangerous revolutionary agitator.[2]

"When you returned to Russia in 1917, you went aboard the paqueboat *Melbourne*, did you not?"

"Yes."

"The officer who commanded that boat said you provoked a mutiny aboard ship. Is that true?"

That Colonel, Dukacinski by name, chief political officer aboard the *Melbourne*, had informed his superiors in September, 1917, that fourteen of the thirty-nine Russian soldiers returning from France had carried out "regrettable propaganda agitation" on the ship. Their leaders were "Djaparidze, Neisky, Schwartzbourd [sic], and Berkoutz."[3]

Schwartzbard protested that the returnees' natural exuberance about the revolution had been misinterpreted. "The revolution had taken place in my homeland. It was for that reason alone that I returned home." Certainly this was consistent with what he had told Ilie Teper in Odessa; "I could not rest at home while thousands of workers and classes of people suffer for their country."[4]

But the *Melbourne* incident became another incongruity in Schwartzbard's story. At various times he insisted he had returned to Russia as a member of an official mission sent by the French Ministry of War (on January 7, 1927, the Ministry of War informed the court that this was untrue), then in concert with the Red Cross (also untrue), and finally with his wife, carrying French and Russian passports establishing them as political refugees.

"Are you an anarchist?" Campinchi demanded.

"Yes! Yes, I am! That is why I was sentenced in Vienna. That is why I was later expelled from Budapest!"

"And that is why you returned to Russia in 1917?"

"Yes! To defend the Revolution!"

"Have you ever served in the Red Army?"

"No! In 1917 it wasn't the Red Army, but that of Kerensky."

In the next five minutes, Campinchi asked three more times whether Schwartzbard had ever joined the Red Army. And each time, an exasperated Schwartzbard responded, "Never!"[5] The prosecution was well pleased with the denial, for Schwartzbard's leadership of Group Rochelle, the unit affiliated with the Red Army which fought from the Dniester to the Donets until the middle of 1920, was well documented. Even the Jewish Telegraph Agency had written: "After the Bolshevik Revolution, he [Schwartzbard] went to Russia where he joined the Red Army and became a commander of a regiment which fought against the pogrom bands of Petlura and Denikin."[6]

Later, in his memoirs, Schwartzbard rationalized that Red Guard units in Odessa could not properly be labelled part of the Red Army because of their disparate composition and decentralized control. Life in the amorphous ranks was chaotic, discipline non-existent. Those soldiers who did not furlough themselves (as Schwartzbard himself did when he learned his father was ill) were paid, when they were paid, in French francs. And far from being a commander, Schwartzbard was merely a staff officer in the Immigrant-Anarchist Section under the command of a twenty-year-old with no military experience.[7] Had he admitted at the trial that this was an "international brigade" which fought against counter-revolutionary forces as a separate detachment of the Red Army, he might have dispelled some notions of his ties with the Kremlin.

But for the moment, Campinchi looked elsewhere, recalling Schwartzbard's glee over Petlura's death at the police station:

"Yes or no, were you glad over the death of Petlura?"

There was no response.

"You desired his death?"

"Yes."

"Then, when he was dead, were you glad?"

Schwartzbard hesitated once more. "Yes."

"Pure carelessness!" erupted Torrès, grasping the impact this line of questioning might have upon the Paris jury. "You don't mean all that. My client takes full responsibility for his act. That should be sufficient."[8]

Apparently it was not sufficient for Campinchi. He wished to emphasize that Schwartzbard's deed was totally sadistic in nature, and toward this end he called several eyewitnesses—Professor Reginald Smith, attorney Regis de Trobriant, and an Armenian named Paul Bougdadjan. Torrès was able to raise doubts about the merit of de Trobriant's testimony, noting he had viewed the encounter between Petlura and Schwartzbard from a restaurant twenty-five meters away and down a bend in the street.

Bougdadjan testified that Petlura's last words were *"Assez! Assez!"* He could not explain why the Holovni Ataman's dying gasps were in French and not in his native Ukrainian. But Torrès could not dispel one damaging piece of testimony. Even Professor Smith, rather sympathetic to Schwartzbard, conceded that the last shots had been fired into the fallen Petlura, a *coup de grace*.[9]

Such testimony could not be easily discounted, particularly when it was supported by the autopsy report of Paris Coroner Paul. This physician took the witness stand to affirm that several wounds had been inflicted upon the deceased *after* he had fallen. Petlura's body showed wounds in the shoulder, right and left abdominal regions causing perforations to the intestines, and on the right side of the face near the chin. The bullet to the chin, merely a flesh wound, had probably been the first wound. None of these, however, was the cause of death.

The "fatal" bullet had pierced both lungs and the heart, causing extensive internal hemorrhaging. From the location of the wounds and the position of recovery of the bullets, Dr. Paul concluded that all but one had been fired in a downward trajectory, while Petlura was lying helpless on the ground.[10]

Under Torrès' scrutiny, Dr. Paul held firm. Asked how he could assume that the shot to the chin was the first wound, the coroner noted that it was the only wound bearing powder burns. When Torrès suggested that all of the shots could have been fired while Petlura was at close range, tottering, the coroner again disagreed, noting that even a single shot from a powerful Browning automatic was sufficient to knock a grown man off his feet.

Nevertheless, Torrès insisted that Petlura could not have been prone when the fatal wounds were administered. All of the witnesses had testified that he had fallen in the street, with his feet toward the sidewalk and Schwartzbard. If that were so, then the bullets would have entered his body on an *upward* trajectory (*Figure 1*). For the shots to have been fired in the manner described by the coroner, Schwartzbard would have had to straddle Petlura while he was down (something none of the eyewitnesses claimed) and then shoot in an almost perpendicular direction (*Figure 2*). "People don't shoot vertically to the sun," Torrès insisted. The only way a downward trajectory could have been accomplished was if Petlura had been reeling backward (*Figure 3*).[11]

FIGURE 1   FIGURE 2   FIGURE 3

Torrès suggested that Schwartzbard had fired his last shots not at Petlura but into the ground to empty his pistol (making the last wound an accident?). The coroner shook his head in disagreement. Suddenly, Torrès pivoted and cried, "Petlura could not have been killed that way. I'll show you what happened!"

Leaping from his place at the counsel table, past his astonished colleagues, Torrès rushed the witness stand. From within the folds of his black lawyer's robes, he drew a Browning automatic pistol of the type which had killed Petlura. First he brandished it in the face of the coroner, who recoiled instinctively, then before the judge and jury. Several persons, apparently fearing a massacre, fled the courtroom. The gun gave no report. Instead, there was only the booming of Torrès' voice: "Petlura was killed by a shot as he was tottering, wounded!"[12]

Following these histrionics, Campinchi directed the jury's attention to Sholom Schwartzbard, grinning in the prisoner's dock. "There is a man who presents himself righteously before the whole world," shouted the Civil Prosecutor. "He didn't mean to shoot a man on the ground because that is cowardly. But, Schwartzbard, when you accosted Petlura, you opened fire on him. Did that take courage?"

"I told him, 'Defend yourself, dog!'"

"But you didn't give him a moment's notice to defend himself. That's all. That's sufficient."[13]

This time the theatrics of both counsels exhausted the patience of Justice Flory, who declared a fifteen minute recess. Following the break, Anna Schwartzbard was called, but with the consent of all parties she was excused without testifying. Both sides denied that they had cited "the unfortunate woman." Campinchi, for one, had no need of a desperate woman's pleadings to detract from his portrayal of Schwartzbard as a mad-dog killer. As he said, "An unuseful witness is always an unuseful witness."[14] For the defense, the decision may have been regrettable. Under oath, perhaps, Anna Schwartzbard might have revealed something to destroy the prosecution's claim of conspiracy.

For the next three days, a host of Ukrainians paraded through the witness box, all swearing that Petlura was a man of honor, a friend of the Jews, a helpless figure caught up in the anarchy of the Ukraine. The first of these, the dapper Prince Jean Tokhary (Tokarcewski-Karassowicz) had once served as an ambassador under the Directory.

Tokhary emphasized that Petlura was a great man, but not omnipotent. Neither dictator nor profiteer, Petlura had won his commission from a provisional parliament in 1918 and a worker's congress in Kiev in 1919. As President of the Directory, a position Petlura assumed only in February, 1919, upon Vinnichenko's resignation, he was hamstrung by the divisive Council of Ministers. For any piece of legislation to become operative, Petlura required the countersignature of the President of the Council, and in 1919 three different men—Chekhovsky, Martos, and Isaac Mazeppa—held this post.

Not Petlura but the Council of Ministers ultimately governed the country. Similarly, Petlura's rank as Holovni Ataman of the Ukrainian Armed Forces was little more than honorific. The military authority in 1919 rested with the

Chief of Staff, Generalissimo Ossetzki, and neither he nor Petlura had any control over the actions of battalion commanders in the field. They had moral authority, perhaps, but this was not enough.

"Simon Petlura was a man of high aims," Tokhary declared. "He led a singular life, one marked by unselfishness. I worked under his direction for two years. His integrity, his patriotism, his moral valor were above reproach, and we could not have wished for a better leader for the Ukraine. He was always a great friend of the Allies and of France. I know that the assassin wants to heap calumny

The Ukrainian witness Tokhary testifying at the bar.
(YIVO Tcherikover Archive)

upon him by pretending that he ordered or tolerated pogroms. But I was a member of his government. Petlura protected all the minorities. He was a true leader. He never was a dictator."

Torrès objected, "Wasn't he the Ataman-in-Chief, that is to say, Chief of the Ukrainian forces?"

"He was merely Commander-in-Chief of the Ukrainian Army," insisted Tokhary, "much the same way that M. Doumergue is the Commander-in-Chief of the French Army, as every head of state is."

"But as chief, he was responsible for the pogroms of 1919!"

Tokhary stood firm. "No. He repeatedly condemned the pogroms. Read his orders, his proclamations. They condemn the massacres. Our Hetman was a statesman."

"Then they truly fall under his responsibility," shouted Torrès. "He commanded. He had no parliament. No one had more authority than he. He was responsible. In Zhitomir more than eight hundred persons were killed. Were the culprits ever punished? Were they ever condemned? By whom? By what? Where are the sanctions? Where are the courts-martial?"

According to Campinchi, the answers to these leading questions lay in the more than two hundred documents which he had presented to the court. Waving a volume of orders allegedly issued by Petlura, Campinchi said, "The country was in a state of chaos. Kiev was captured and recaptured nineteen times and each time the Jews were massacred. The head of state might try in vain to prevent massacres and pillage, but he could not be everywhere at once. He could not control the actions of undisciplined troops."

"If the country was in chaos," rejoined Torrès, "why did Petlura even bother to issue any proclamations? Why did he not take summary action against the offenders when the opportunity was his? I myself," he said, tapping his chest, "have seen French soldiers shot in war after trial by court martial for lesser offenses than massacres. The jury well knows how severely French generals acted in the war when soldiers were accused of the smallest act of larceny. What of the pogrom at Proskurov in February, 1919? Hundreds of Jews were killed on one day! And what action was taken? Not a single soldier was shot, though hundreds took part in the massacre!"[15]

Campinchi foolishly chose to contest the issue of Proskurov, a Podolian city of fifty thousand, where between 1,650 and 5,000 Jews were slaughtered in the middle of February, 1919. Elements of the Zaporog Cossack Brigade of the 3rd Haidamak Regiment under the command of a twenty-three-year old neurotic named Semosenko had occupied the town in early February to head off a rumored Bolshevik coup. Sometimes described as a parvenu, a half-wit, and a degenerate sadist, Semosenko was a power-hungry man who openly boasted of having killed eight "Bolsheviks" with his own hands. In Paris, eight years after the pogrom which had occurred under Semosenko's jurisdiction, Cesar Campinchi argued that Petlura could hardly be blamed for the tragedy, as he had given orders that not a single hair of an innocent's head should fall during the occupation.

As proof, Campinchi offered the statement of M. Teresschenko, a former Ukrainian army officer who had served as Vice-President of the Directory's Council of War and who had organized a military tribunal to investigate the Proskurov atrocity. According to Colonel Teresschenko, *a score of Jews accused of the provocation had been acquitted, along with one Christian.*[16] For the next week in Paris, for the next four decades around the world, the debate would come back to what happened at Proskurov on February 15, 1919.

In the Ukrainian version of events, the Jews of Proskurov hatched a plot to seize control of the town. Relations be-

tween Jew and Gentile had not been good anyway, since,
according to the Ukrainians, the Jews had confiscated
Christian goods during an earlier Bolshevik occupation.[17]
According to Colonel Michael Shadrin, twenty-five
Podolian intriguers led by a Social Revolutionary named
Sobol and a female Cheka agent named Fanni (who sup-
posedly had killed six hundred Ukrainians at Moghilev-
Podolsk) arrived by train at Proskurov on the morning of
February 15.[18] They intended to lead 2,000 Bolshevik railway
workers, students, drifters, former Tsarists, Red Guardists,
disgruntled members of the Podolian cavalry regiments, and
members of a Jewish Fighting Organization in an uprising,
while the loyal Christian population was distracted by the
Feast of the Purification of the Virgin.

Fortunately, according to this story, Ukrainian forces
learned of the scheme from a Jewish informer, Alexei
Nabutov. When efforts on the part of a mediator named Siak
proved fruitless, the Bolsheviks and their Jewish minions
made their move. While Semosenko's troops were penned
up by machine-gun fire at the railway station, and Proskurov gendarmes remained in their barracks under orders
from some treacherous higher-up,[19] the rebels attacked the
post, telegraph, and telephone exchanges with hand
grenades.

Then at 4:00 A.M. or 6:00 A.M., depending upon the
source, Ataman Semosenko gave his men orders to stave off
the revolution. Even then, the Ukrainians moved reluc-
tantly. Lt. Colonel Alexei Boutakiv, commanding Petlurist
artillery in the Proskurov area, was ordered to open fire
against the city three times before he obeyed. Boutakiv
allegedly acquiesced in the bombardment only after being
threatened with removal and court-martial.[20]

Thereafter, Semosenko's Haidamaks, no more than three
to six hundred in number, "disciplined war heroes of pure
reputation," rapidly dispersed the Bolshevik cadres. On the
principal streets of Proskurov, where the regulars seized

control, there was no trace of brutality. Elsewhere, the situation was different. "Instinctively," "in an elementary manner," "from divine inspiration," the Tsarists and other anti-Semites turned against their own supporters.

"It was only natural," Colonel Shadrin declared, "that these troops, thoroughly demoralized by Jewish propaganda, after having adhered to the rebellion and shooting officers, would become a band of pillagers and assassins."[21]

On side streets where only later the Ukrainian regulars restored order, Jews were found murdered in bed or half-nude in the streets. Many helpless Gentiles suffered as well, including the local priest Father Kokharovsky, who was struck down at the door of his own church while bearing the crucifix and pleading for mercy. Of the slain, onetime militia officer Peter Titlouk remarked callously, "If the majority of victims were of the Jewish religion, it was that the Israelite elements were especially sympathetic with the Bolsheviks."[22]

In short, the Ukrainians claimed that a maximum of six hundred men handily routed a force at least three times as large, that their enemies were commanded by a woman who bragged of killing six hundred persons in a town which was not yet controlled by the Reds, that the frustrated revolutionaries in Proskurov turned against and slaughtered their own supporters, that all of this was excusable, for "if the revolt had succeeeded all that happened to the Jews would have happened to the Christian population."[23] The massacre of innocents was regrettable, but there would have been no killing if there had been no revolution in Proskurov.

There was a smattering of truth to the charge that someone was laying the foundation for a Bolshevik takeover in Proskurov. There were pro-Bolshevik elements in practically every city in Russia. In Proskurov, however, the two acknowledged leaders of the movement were Gentiles named Tkachuk and Dubrovnin. Even among the railway workers (who numbered only eighty able-bodied men) and the Social Revolutionaries, the leaders were non-Jews.[24]

There may have been Jews in leadership positions among other workers' and self-help units, but this was not remarkable, as Jews were represented among the intimates of Semosenko as well. A Jew named Rochman or Rochmananko was a trusted lieutenant of Semosenko. A man of low intellect, Rochmananko claimed to be a Hebrew teacher. He was especially helpful in pointing out wealthier Jews from whom money could be extorted. Later, he was to participate in the special inquiry about Proskurov along with another Jewish collaborator named Frazer. Both men were lackeys of the nationalist pogromchiks. A third Jew, known only as "the Haidamak Ballerina," supposedly entertained the Semosenkists during their stay in Proskurov.[25]

Loyalty was an elastic thing for such criminals and intriguers. There were even some Petlurists on the planning staff of the Bolsheviks, men who had penetrated the top levels of the Socialists and Bolsheviks in Proskurov. These *agents provocateurs* manipulated the revolutionary youth like marionettes, egging them on to acts of violence which would justify making a pogrom. For however much the Bolsheviks may have wanted to take power in the town in February, they were woefully unprepared for the venture.[26]

The Jewish version of events at Proskurov was radically different. On October 24, 1927, the Assize Court listened to Haia Greenberg, a survivor of the pogrom, who related her story in a barely audible whisper. Twenty-nine years old, thin, with curly black hair done in the bobbed fashion of the day, the young medical student in her trim blue suit looked more like an American stenographer. Miss Greenberg had worked as a nurse in a Danish Red Cross detachment in the Ukraine for the first six months of 1919.

The Ataman Semosenko, she charged, was "Petlura's right-hand man." On February 6, he had warned the Jewish community:

> I call on the population to cease its anarchist demonstrations for I am sufficiently strong to fight you. I especially warn the Jew of that.

> Know that you are a people disliked by all nations,
> yet you cause such trouble to Christian people. Do you
> not want to live? Have you no pity on your own people?
>   So long as you are not attacked, keep quiet.
> Wretched nation, bringing trouble on innocent
> Gentiles.[27]

Then, having demanded a "contribution" of 300,000
rubles from the Jewish community as atonement for its pro-
Bolshevik sympathies, Semosenko went to the town council
and told them that he had given orders that all Jews, adults
and children, should be killed so that "no more Bolsheviks"
would grow up.[28] When one of his own compatriots suggested that this course was extreme, Semosenko threatened
to have him shot.

Despite all warning signs, the Jews of Proskurov were
taken by surprise when the pogromchiks struck on the
Sabbath eve of February 14. A popular legend among the
people was that the "Tzaddik" [holy man] Reb Leibel had
blessed this city of peace and said that no pogromchik would
cross its threshhold. Throughout the Tsarist times of troubles, this had held true. Magically, Proskurov had never
suffered pogroms. As a result, when red-capped Haidamaks
cordoned off the Jewish quarter that Friday afternoon,
Jewish children were playing in the streets, women were
preparing the Sabbath meal, and men were at the synagogue, seemingly oblivious to the danger about them.

What followed was cold-blooded, calculated murder,
street by street, house by house. Five or ten men would enter
a house, killing all within and leaving those who tried to
bribe them clutching blood-stained currency.[29] The Cossacks burst into the synagogue and butchered all but one of
the Jews who had remained inside.[30] They even turned their
machine guns on the one hospital in town.

"I was at home, with my parents," Haia Greenberg
testified. "I had to leave on February 16, to take my examina-
tions. The pogrom broke out on February 15. Everything
had been organized. That Friday at 4:30, I was leaving the

doctor's office when I was frightened by the Haidamaks of the 3rd Regiment, with their red hats which distinguished them from other Haidamaks. Uttering savage cries, they made for the streets of Proskurov which were most populated by Jews. It was only the next day, shortly before noon, that the first victims could be recovered. The first was Mlle. Wartemberg, a friend of mine whom I had questioned about anatomy just that Friday. She had been killed by a bullet fired by a Haidamak on horseback who passed by her window."[31]

As the Cossacks roamed the streets, drinking and singing, the Jews organized makeshift hospitals. Miss Greenberg assisted Drs. Gaviev and Poldsev under the flag of the Danish Red Cross at the home of her grandparents. There, she encountered victims of the pogrom who had been left in the streets overnight. Some were so badly frostbitten that it was difficult to decide whether to treat wounds or frostbite first. Lacking decent supplies, Haia Greenberg "gave them a swallow of hot tea to revive them a little."

There were other victims, like Mlle. Kisis, a girl of nineteen whose breast wounds were so severe the doctors actually considered amputation to save her life. Eight members of the girl's family had been attacked, including a seven-year-old brother who was stabbed in the back, another brother slashed in the neck, and her mother who was one of the first fatalities.

There were the two sisters, twelve and fourteen years of age, who straggled into the "hospital" that first day. The younger one died in her sister's arms during the night. And the girl of fourteen who came with four fingers slashed away, her hand a gangrenous mess. She ended up in an insane asylum. And the terrified girl of nineteen who ran a fever for more than two weeks. Everyone, including the nurses, appeared to her to be Haidamak rapists. And the five-year-old boy who contracted meningitis from his wounds and died "in terrible suffering."

And the woman who was brought in Monday night with

her teen-aged daughter. The mother had been shot in the throat and could not swallow. She died in Nurse Greenberg's arms and her body was moved to the kitchen. The next day, the daughter flung herself hysterically over the litter of her mother. Then calmly she took her mother's coat and walked into another room saying, "Come, Mama, we will go to the synagogue. We will go to pray for you." The girl had lost her reason.

And the three-year-old boy who was always silent—his mother too had been killed in the pogrom. Miss Greenberg tried to befriend him, caress him, but he would not speak. Only after two days did he tell her how he had given a last kiss to his dead mama. And the woman who came to the house with a baby of three weeks. She told how the Ukrainians crashed through her window and lanced the little child upon a pike. Haia Greenberg tried to treat the baby, to feed it milk mixed with water, but she failed.

"The cries given out by that baby, I will never forget them. I cannot forget the little infant who always cried and whom I could not save. I was only in my first year of medicine. I was incapable of doing something useful. The baby . . . the little baby . . ." She sobbed as she repeated the word.[32]

The tales of atrocity were endless. The students Shomstein and Kulisher who were shot by Semosenko's aide Kiverchuk as they ran about the streets trying to tend to the wounded. The young girl who had been stabbed repeatedly in her buttocks. The two-month-old baby whose hands were a mass of lacerations. The five-year-old who had been pierced through and through with spears. The old man Krochak who had been pitched out of a window by his beard. The thirteen-year-old boy who became deaf as a consequence of his wounds. His brother, who received eleven wounds in his stomach and was left for dead by the side of their slain mother. The paralyzed son of a rabbi, murdered as he lay helpless in bed. The two young children who were cast alive into a fire.

Haia Greenberg, the young nurse who gave dramatic testimony on the pogrom at Proskurov.
(YIVO Tcherikover Archive)

And then there were the survivors, the endless list of survivors, whose names appeared in the reports of the Danish Red Cross with the accompanying phrases "two wounds to the head made by bayonet," "wounds to the posterior and left wrist," "contusions and bayonet wounds to the feet," and one entry which read "twenty-eight wounds in the breast, back, hands and feet."[33]

Haia Greenberg continued: "A terrible memory for me were the sleds which passed Tuesday morning and which the peasants brought to take away the cadavers from the streets where they had been since Saturday. On their return I saw the same sleds with corpses piled high, several corpses, with now a hand or a drooping breast, or a leg, or the head. The snow was red from the blood. I shall never forget the reddened snow sleds filled with the hacked bodies going to the cemetery to deposit their sad burden in a common pit."[34]

133

In fact, it was not until the first of the week that Semosenko permitted the Jews to bury their dead, although sixty peasant carts had been brought into the city the previous Thursday night by Kiverchuk specifically for such a purpose. According to reports of the Danish Red Cross, barrister A.I. Hillerson, and the Comité des Délégations Juives, the bodies lay where they had fallen and rotted in the following forty-eight-hour period. Some were even found gnawed by roving swine. Others were found with as many as thirty-six wounds, beheaded, their eyes gouged out. The bayoneted dead lay in their houses, fifteen in the house of Averbach, twenty-one in the house of Semelman, six in the house of Blechman, eight in the house of Krochak, twenty-five in the house of Kligerman, silent witnesses to pillaging which continued unabated through the weekend.

The lights which were not extinguished in Jewish homes served as beacons for the plunderers, who occasionally entered a Gentile house by mistake. When the dead were finally carted away for burial, the gaping trench which had been dug for the task near a brewery proved inadequate. Three additional pits were required as more victims were cast into nameless, common graves. The macabre procession of sleds did not end until 4:00 A.M. on Tuesday.

Even at the "cemetery," the atrocities did not cease. Peasant workmen rifled the clothes of the dead in quest of valuables. A number of corpses were found without fingers which once had borne wedding bands. Some of the dead were more than eighty years old.[35]

"Oh, no! No!" the little nurse screamed from the witness box, her shoulders shaking. "I cannot go on! They are before my eyes!"

She made a gesture as if to brush away the images of slaughter. Handkerchiefs appeared among the spectators. There was an epidemic of coughing and clearing of throats. Even the attorneys were silent. In the prisoner's dock, Schwartzbard was crying, shaking his head in a gesture of frustration.

Suddenly Miss Greenberg's grief turned to fury. "Petlura knew what Semosenko was doing!" she shrieked. "Semosenko was only the instrument who carried out Petlura's will." He had boasted that by exterminating Jews he was saving the Ukraine and would be rewarded for his efforts. "After the pogrom he was not punished. A commission was appointed to investigate, but Semosenko dispersed its members by force, saying that there was very little to make such a fuss about! He continued his terrible work!"

Under cross-examination by Public Prosecutor Reynaud, Miss Greenberg stood firm. "Petlura was responsible! Even Ukrainian officers said so! His soldiers killed our people, shouting his name. One regiment had a band and it played while knives fell on the heads of innocent babies! Petlura could have stopped it, but he wouldn't listen to our pleas!"

Still, what proof was there that Petlura had been even remotely connected with the tragedy at Proskurov?

"We hoped, all the world hoped," the witness stammered, "after the pogroms that Hetman Petlura would investigate and punish the author, namely Semosenko. Nothing was done."

Hardly conclusive evidence of culpability, insisted Reynaud.

"Personally, I never met Petlura," Miss Greenberg explained. "I never saw him. I have the conviction, and my conviction is not only that of the Jewish population which was persecuted, but also of Ukrainian officers who lodged under our roofs. Petlura was responsible. Semosenko told them himself."[36]

"You have impugned nothing in her testimony," said Torrès.

"You are wrong!" This time is was Campinchi, working in tandem with the Public Prosecutor. Torrès could bring fifty or even one hundred thousand witnesses like Miss Greenberg to tell what happened in the pogroms, but this still would not establish Petlura's involvement. On the contrary, the prosecution possessed more than four hundred

written depositions from colleagues of the Holovni Ataman
to the effect that he was a good friend of the Jews and in no
way responsible for the murders.

"I am compelled to protest against those who brand the
pogroms as the official teachings of the Ukrainian government," said Campinchi. "We all know how much the entire
population was affected, how there were victims among all
nationalities. But let me say here and now, it has *not* been
demonstrated that Petlura gave any orders directing the
pogroms. Miss Greenberg's 'proof' seems to me to be sketchy
once more."

"But the murderers were his Zaporoghian Cossacks!"
Torrès snapped. "Zaporoghian! And Haidamaks! *That*
proves it!"

Haia Greenberg reaffirmed her position. "I repeat that
the responsibility for the murders was without doubt Petlura's, personally, not only for the Jews but for all the others.
The soldiers killed and shot with the cry, 'Long live our
little father Petlura!' The least word from Petlura would
have sufficed to stop the massacres."[37]

From the welter of testimony about Proskurov, the following story emerged: On Sunday, February 16, 1919, while
the surving Jews trembled behind shuttered windows, Ataman Semosenko issued another decree to "the population of
the town and district of Proskurov." The incidents of the
previous two days he blamed on "some irresponsible men
without honor or consicence," men who, according to precise information reaching Semosenko, were "of the Jewish
nation."

The commander lamented that through their zeal to
restore order, the Cossacks had killed "many innocent persons," but "nothing can be accomplished without making
mistakes." The blood of the innocents, he charged, would
ever be a curse on the heads of "those who have acted as
provocateurs and adventurers." More, they would serve as a
deterrent to those who might attempt to bring discord to

Proskurov, to foment rebellion against the lawful authorities. "I shall stop at nothing to keep the peace," he concluded.[38]

On February 22, Semosenko again warned the populace that he knew there were many Bolshevik agitators among them. The Jews tried to forestall another pogrom by offering him additional ransom. When the veiled threats from army headquarters persisted, the leaders of the Jewish community called a public meeting to decide upon a course of action. The result was that on February 27, 1919, Semosenko issued Order Number Sixteen, dropping the pretense of a general directive and warning:

> Jews!
> Information has reached me that yesterday you wished to organize a meeting in Alexander Street to consider the question of seizing the power and that in four days you are preparing a rising similar to that which you attempted on February 14/15. I warn you that at present I have under my orders about 10,000 reliable Ukrainian men. I also have enough artillery and machine guns and the rising will be put down by a firm hand.
> I declare a state of reinforced protection in the town of Proskurov. Traffic in the town is allowed up to 6:00 P.M. only.
> Performances in theatres and cinemas are forbidden. In daytime not more than two persons may walk together and it is forbidden to stop at street corners or near your houses. Persons contravening this order will be shot without trial. I request Colonel Rogulski of the police of the town of Proskurov to send reinforced patrols all over the town at night and to arrest anybody who should disobey this order and punish him as said above.
>
> (signed) Semosenko
> Commander of the Principal
> Ataman Petlura Zaporog Cossacks
> Brigade of the Ukrainian Army[39]

Days after the pogroms, people were still fleeing in terror to Konstantinov, fifty miles away. Those who remained were afraid to look one another in the eye, ashamed that they had survived by hiding. Women roamed the streets with children who sobbed, "Where are our fathers?"[40] Though the town's Jewish leaders continually telegraphed Petlura begging his intervention, the Holovni Ataman did not respond.[41]

Finally, in desperation, the Jews gambled on the friendship of two commissioners, Verkhola and Stavinski. These men in turn contacted Vasily Maudry, chairman of the chauvinistic National Union in Proskurov. The latter needed little prompting to take action. At the height of the massacres, he had personally intervened with Semosenko without success. At one point, he was discussing the matter in Semosenko's office when a military aide named Huzar burst into the room, pale and half-dead. "Commander," Huzar cried, "have pity! They're killing innocent women and children. They're killing all the Jews. We tried to interfere, but they beat us and wanted to shoot us." Semosenko sneered, "That's all insinuation. I gave an order to destroy all Bolsheviks—and not Jews, girls, and children."[42]

Maudry appealed to the Commander of the Ukrainian Army Corps, Eugene Konovalets. Finally, an order was given through Konovalets' office not only for Semosenko to halt the violence but also to surrender his command. Lest the Ataman lose face before the Jews, however, he was given additional time to prepare his departure. On March 7, fully twenty days after the bloodiest pogrom, Semosenko left Proskurov, not under arrest, but amid great pomp with a host of valets and a trained nurse. The half-wit who had plagued the city was given a medical leave—for treatment of his venereal problems.[43]

Jewish legend held that the ghost of the town's chief rabbi, who had been killed by Semosenko, had gone to the Ataman's sickbed and pointed a bloody finger saying, "Get out of Proskurov." People said that the ghostly figure was at Semosenko's side when he left on a stretcher and that the rabbi's spirit returned to its grave once Semosenko departed for Stanislav.[44]

Seven months later, in a rare moment of candor, Julian Batchinsky, diplomatic representative of the Petlura government to the United States, would write, "I must admit that information now in my possession fully established the fact that in one case—a very severe one (Proskurov) — soldiers from the Ukrainian People's Army were the perpetrators. It was not upon the impulse of the government, nor upon a military command that they slew helpless people. It was not with the knowledge of Simon Petlura, but against his strictest orders and against the purpose of the Ukrainian People's Republic."[45]

No pogrom since Kishinev had made such an impact upon the Jews of Russia. Jewish historians agreed that Proskurov was responsible for the "Great Fear" which swept through every *shtetl* in the spring of 1919. It became a symbol for those terrible years of Jewish helplessness. It raised a barrier between the Yiddish masses and the Ukrainian people's movement. And finally, the hate generated by Proskurov was, more than anything else, responsible for a new surge of pro-Bolshevik enthusiasm among Jews, who volunteered for the Red Army "to prevent a second Proskurov."[46]

Seven years later, a Paris jury heard Colonel Teresschenko say, "A score of Jews accused of the provocation [at Proskurov] had been acquitted, along with one Christian." The man most responsible for the pogrom, Semosenko, was at liberty for more than a year following the massacre. Several thousand Jews lay dead when order was restored, but neither Semosenko nor his troops were ever punished for this crime against humanity.

It was Semosenko's hand-picked tribunal, headed by his henchman Rochmanenko, which conducted the farcical inquiry into the "provocation." Not surprisingly, this group placed the blame on the Jews.

Russian Jews were accustomed to such "justice." The Tsars had claimed Jewish provocation whenever the Black Hundreds struck at Jewish communities—provocation in the form of ritual murder, host desecration, or revolutionary activity. In 1919, Jewish provocation in the Ukraine consisted of being alive.

Notes

1. For Schwartzbard's account of what transpired in Austria, see his statement, File 460, 38560-65, Tcherikover Archive, and *Notes Sténographiques*, fasc. 1, p.94.

2. File 505, 41936 and 41937-44, and File 443, 37708 and 37710, Tcherikover Archive.

3. Deposition of Lt. Col. Dukacinski to Col. La Vergne, Sept. 4, 1917, 38089, File 451, Tcherikover Archive.

4. Deposition of Ilie Teper, December, 1926, File 469, 38978-80, Tcherikover Archive.

5. *Notes Sténographiques*, fasc. 1, pp.97,100,101,126.

6. *Jewish Independent*, June 4, 1926, p.l. A good friend, Pierre Ramus (Rudolf Grossmann) wrote Torrès that it would be wrong to equate Schwartzbard's views with those of the Bolsheviks. In a letter dated October 8, 1927, Ramus said that Schwartzbard was inspired by the ideas of Tolstoy and Peter Kropotkin. File 463, 38693-4, Tcherikover Archive.

7. For Schwartzbard's unhappy moments in the Red Guards see *In krig mit zich aleyn*, pp.76-77 and 238-39.

8. *Figaro*, October 20,1927, p.l.

9. For the accounts of the eyewitnesses, see *Notes Sténographiques*, fasc. 2, pp.90-100 (Bougdadjan), 101-111 (Smith), 115-118 (de Trobriant), 120 (Gelma) and 122 (Belat).

10. Initial reference to Dr.Paul's report appears in *Notes Sténographiques*, fasc. 1, p.50. The Coroner's complete testimony may be found in fasc. 2, pp.54-93.

11. An additional factor which may have contributed to the downward path of the bullets was that (as all witnesses testified) Schwartzbard was standing on the curb, a few inches higher than Petlura in the street. For Torrès' arguments about position, see *Notes Sténographiques*, fasc. 2, pp.60-62, 70-73, and 93.

12. The stenographic report indicated that Torrès said, "I have a gun for a demonstration." Demonstration was noted without comment. A more elaborate description appeared in *Cleveland Press*, October 19, 1927, p.15, and *The Times* of London, October 20, 1927, p.15.

13. *Figaro*, October 20, 1927, p.2.

14. *Notes Sténographiques*, fasc. 2, pp.125-7.

15. For Tokhary's complete testimony, see *Notes Sténographiques*, fasc. 2, pp.127-147. See also verbatim extracts in *Figaro*, October 20, 1927, p.2, and *The Times* of London, October 20, 1927, p.13.

16. *Jewish Chronicle*, October 21, 1927, p.27.

17. Testimony of Col. Nesterenko, *Notes Sténographiques*, fasc. 2, p.152.

18. See deposition of Col.Michael Shadrin, Jan. 31, 1927, File 449, 37843-37863, Tcherikover Archive. General Mykola Chapoval pinpointed another villain, a man named Niboutioff. Testimony of Chapoval, *Notes Sténographiques*, fasc. 2, p.178.

19. According to Officer Titlouk, the police were helpless because their own superiors were in league with the Bolsheviks. *Notes Sténographiques*, fasc. 5, p.73.

20. Deposition of Col.Boutakiv, October 18, 1927, File 488, 39779-86, Tcherikover Archive.

21. Deposition of Col.Shadrin, File 449, p.18, Tcherikover Archive.

22. Deposition of Titlouk, File 451, No. 38061-2, Tcherikover Archive.

23. Concerning the prospective Bolshevik uprising in Proskurov, see Iv. Alekseev, *Iz vospominanii levogo esera (Podpol'naia rabota na Ukraine)* (Moscow: Glavpolitprosvet, 1922), pp.34-35. As for the fantastic story of how the city was "saved"

from the Bolsheviks, see also Tcherikover, *Di ukrainer pogromen* pp.128-29.

24. Deposition of Dr.Marjan Stavinsky, September 26, 1927, File 361, 32941-32950, Tcherikover Archive.

25. A.N.Hillerson, *Postupilo uv redaktzie doklad*, Report on the Proskurov Pogrom, File 180, Tcherikover Archive.

26. *Protokol vegn Proskurov* by A.Yoffe, File 72, Tcherikover Archive. See also Report of the Proskurov *Kehilla Rat* "Tzu der idishe befelkerung," 1920, File 381, Techerikover Archive. For additional depositions, reports and documents on Proskurov, consult Files 358, 359, 360 and 416, Tcherikover Archives.

27. File 453, 38195, Tcherikover Archive.

28. "The Schwartzbard Case," *Jewish Chronicle*, October 28, 1927, p.36. See also Schechtman, *et al, The Pogroms in the Ukraine*, p.187.

29. Zofia Kossak-Szczucka, *Pozoga, wspomnienia z Wolynia, 1917-1920* (Krakow, 1927), pp.289-91.

30. Only one aged Jew, named Shlomo Rosenfeld, offered any resistance. He was immediately murdered. The sole survivor of the massacre in the synagogue was a young boy who hid in the loft. Subsequently he was beaten on the streets by the Cossacks and went mad. See Testimony of Leib Kosovoy in Tcherikover, *Di ukrainer pogromen*, p.123.

31. For Miss Greenberg's testimony, see *Notes Sténographiques*, fasc. 6, pp.74-106. She was not the first Jew to testify about Proskurov. Immediately before, Ruben Grinberg, director of a special relief committee for emigrant Jews from Russia, had testified that responsibility for the massacre, where Grinberg had lived as a child, rested with the Petlurists and their commanders. *Notes Sténographiques*, fasc. 6, pp.3-5.

32. These grotesque tales are recalled in Miss Greenberg's testimony, pp.74-84, *Notes Sténographiques*, fasc. 6. Again, the newspaper accounts add a human dimension lacking in the stenographic record. *Figaro*, October 25, 1927, p.2.

33. Reports of the Danish Red Cross and A.I.Hillerson substantiate these and other atrocities, including assaults on girls who "looked Jewish." Perhaps most disgusting was the activity of

a Dr.Skornik, who refused to supply Jews with bandages. The head of the local Red Cross was later found among the pogromists. When someone pointed out the incongruity of killing while wearing the armband of such an organization, he ripped off the marker and continued plundering. See A.I.Hillerson, *Le pogrome de Proskurov*, report to the Kiev Central Committee for the Relief of Pogrom Victims, File 466, 38862-88, Tcherikover Archives; *Les pogromes en Ukraine sous les gouvernements ukrainiens (1917-1920)* (Paris: Comité des Délégations Juives, 1927), pp.54-55; Haifetz, *The Slaughter of the Jews*, pp.202-227; Tcherikover, *Di ukrainer pogromen*, pp. 121-138; and *Pogromen in Proskurov, 1919-1924*, File 521, Tcherikover Archive. The reports of Drs. Goloubev and Hornstein for the Danish Red Cross may be found in File 407, 35340-45, Tcherikover Archive.

34. *Notes Sténographiques*, fasc. 6, p.79. See also *New York Times*, October 25, 1927, p.5.

35. See eyewitness accounts, diaries, and documents from Proskurov survivors Neiman Teplik, Sholom Bisselman, and Dr.E.F.Feinblit, File 409, Tcherikover Archive. Testified one girl, "It was a bloodbath. The whole place has been turned into a cemetery." File 411, 35682, Tcherikover Archive.

36. *Notes Sténographiques*, fasc. 6, p.85. See also *New York Times*, October 25,1927, p.5: *Jewish Chronicle*, October 28, 1927, p.36; and *Il Temps*, October 26, 1927, p.2.

37. *Notes Sténographiques*, fasc. 6, pp.88-106. See also *Figaro*, October 26, 1927, p.2; and *Il Temps*, October 26, 1927, p.2.

38. File 398, 35044, Tcherikover Archive.

39. Schechtman, *et al*, *The Pogroms in the Ukraine*, p.189.

40. Deposition of Shlomo Shreiman in Tcherikover, *Di ukrainer Pogromen*, p.128.

41. Several appeals were sent to the Holovni Ataman, who "deliberately avoided looking in on the scene." See Abraham Revutzky, *In di shvere tog ofn Ukraine* (Berlin: Judischer Literarischer Verlag, 1924) p.288.

42. Tcherikover, *Di Ukrainer Pogromen*, p.133.

43. *Les pogromes en Ukraine*, Annex, pp.51-53.

44. Zvi Zekzer, "Di toyte shtot," in Tcherikover, *Di ukrainer pogromen*, p.136.

45. The letter appeared in St.Louis, New Orleans, Ft.Worth, New York, Boston, and Philadelphia and various Jewish newspapers. See Julian Batchinsky, *et al*, *The Jewish Pogroms in Ukraine* (Washington: Friend of Ukraine, 1919), p.7.

46. Tcherikover, *Di ukrainer pogromen*, pp.158-59; Gumener, *A kapitl Ukraine*, p.31; and Solomon Goldelman, *In goles bay di Ukrainer*, p.41.

7.

The League of Human Rights

UNDER FRENCH LEGAL PROCEDURE, it was permissible for the state to call witnesses both against and for the prisoner in the interest of justice and impartiality. It was not uncommon for all manner of witnesses to be heard in criminal cases, regardless of how remote their connection with the case might be. Juries listened to personal opinions, tales of previous convictions, family histories, and even scientific theories, then retired to their chambers to haggle over a verdict.[1] On Thursday, October 21, 1927, Professor Paul Langevin of the College of France supplied the first such interlude of hearsay.

Called at his own request, Langevin was a national hero, a savant whose opinions had been sought on everything from the theory of radiation to the theory of relativity. A onetime Fellow of the Cavendish Laboratory in Cambridge, where he worked under the great physicist J. J. Thomson, Langevin was a colleague of Branly, Marconi, and Pierre Curie (whom he succeeded as director of the School of Physics and Chemistry in France in 1925). This fifty-five-year-old scholar with intense eyes, Van Dyke beard, and crew-cut hair could expostulate on the nature of ultrasonic waves, the thermodynamics of molecular motion and the ionization of gas. He also possessed a more pragmatic side, typified by his development of sonar detection devices during World War I. Moreover, he was involved with questions of human justice in his capacity as Vice President of the League of Human and Civil Rights (hereafter referred to as the League of Human Rights).

The League was founded in 1898 by Moderate Republican Senator Ludovic Trarieux, who served as its first president until 1904. Created in response to Emile Zola's article "J'Accuse," the League was instrumental in bringing the Dreyfus Affair to a just conclusion. The organization dedicated itself to the Declaration of Rights of Man, the most significant document to come out of the French Revolution. It strove toward three objectives: *laïcité* (complete separation of church and state, particularly in the field of education), *démocratie* (political rights for all men, women's suffrage, freedom of the press, the right of the laboring man to strike) and *pacifisme* (the promotion of international cooperation and good-will through the establishment of a viable League of Nations.)[2] At the time of the Schwartzbard trial, this body of idealists was just achieving its height of popularity, and it seemed logical that one of its sons should rise to speak in Schwartzbard's defense.[3] Hence the words of Professor Langevin:

"After attentive study of the public documents, I have no doubts as to the reality of the abominations which took place in the Ukraine. There is even less doubt that at least half of these pogroms were the work of regular Ukrainian troops through the orders of their chief. One should not blame only the Semosenkos. Petlura also was responsible. His proclamations notwithstanding, it must be remembered that he introduced no penalties to the guilty."[4]

Asked by Civil Prosecutor Campinchi once more to explain how he had formed such an opinion, the dapper Langevin replied, "I learned it, as I have just now said, from scrutiny of the documents which have been published in the press on the one hand, from the League of Human Rights, of which I am Vice-President, on the other. And I affirm that the investigations and opinions of the League of Human Rights are always based on the most accurate information available. And next, by the documents which have been published by the Comité des Délégations Juives at the Peace Conference, documents which were not fabricated for the moment. In any event, I have that impression because they represent the results of inquiries carried out by such organizations as the Red Cross."[5]

"Do you think, Professor," asked Campinchi, "that your documentation is sufficient for a question as complex as that which is being contested before the Jury of the Seine?" Wasn't it true, for example, that the League of Human Rights specialized in defending all kinds of men who "claimed to be innocent"?

"The League doesn't concern itself with the defense of men who *claim* to be innocent," snapped Langevin. Not Schwartzbard, but issues far transcending the guilt or innocence of the accused, were at stake here. License to kill on a grand scale, brutality as opposed to the natural rights of men, the inviolability of the individual person, human dignity, freedom from oppression, these were the real questions to be debated. If these problems were not properly resolved here, Langevin stated, he had no doubt that much greater massacres would take place in the Ukraine upon the outbreak of new disorders.

Langevin had said that more than half of the pogroms in 1919 and 1920 should be attributed to regular troops under Petlura. Didn't he know, asked the Prosecutor, that these were years of continuous defeat for the Hetman?

"I know that Petlura was part of a government called the Ukrainian Directory," Langevin replied, "that he commanded, at the service of the Ukrainian state, those troops which were considered 'regular' in the period. I suppose that he was in communication with the colonels or heads of units that comprised his army and who were responsible to him with regard to acts which they committed."

"Then according to you," Campinchi broke in again, "a chief is personally responsible for a crime of which he can also be a victim, for mutinies and pogroms carried out by the troops of his army in a country where communications are extremely difficult and roads non-existent."

"This isn't a question of mutinies. This trial concerns itself with pogroms committed under the orders of chiefs who were commanding units. It would be meaningless to say that Petlura was the supreme commander of troops if he were not in contact with their chiefs, if he weren't in the position of giving them orders or demanding accounts of them for their acts."

This was precisely the point Campinchi was trying to make. Instead of dwelling on it, however, the Civil Prosecutor chose to insult the witness. After confessing his own nervousness in the presence of such a great scientist, Campinchi wondered aloud whether Professor Langevin had not in fact superseded the bounds of science, whether he had not simply read a little about the pogroms and then volunteered an opinion much as "a man on the street," only not with the same results. Certainly Langevin's eminence in the scientific world would cloak all his opinions with respectability.

LANGEVIN: See here, I believe I am able to answer your question. What proves Petlura had control over the chiefs of the units is that there is no doubt that Semosenko ordered the pogroms and . . .

CAMPINCHI: That's settled. He was arrested and shot. He ordered the pogroms. But Petlura?

LANGEVIN: A short time after the pogroms, Semosenko demanded and obtained a sick leave, and he left town accompanied by attendants who could prove if he were ill. He received a leave which could only have come from his superiors. And the latter, knowing what had happened, simply gave it to him instead of shooting him. It was inexcusable.

CAMPINCHI: Petlura gave an order to arrest Semosenko. Have you been informed of it?

LANGEVIN: I have been informed of the fact that Semosenko was, without doubt, on leave for reasons of health immediately after those acts.

CAMPINCHI: What do you know of the orders given by Petlura to arrest Semosenko?

LANGEVIN: Nothing. I affirm that instead of being arrested, he was on leave.

CAMPINCHI: How did that happen? You have been informed of that leave?

TORRÈS: And you, you have his order of arrest?

CAMPINCHI: Yes, I have it.

TORRÈS: I would very much like to see it.

CAMPINCHI: It was a verbal order.

TORRÈS: Indeed!

CAMPINCHI: A colonel will come here to say that he received an order.

TORRÈS: And you will be harder put to produce the act of execution than to produce the order of arrest. You are reduced to the point of having to demand of Professor Langevin if he had knowledge of an order which you yourself have said was verbal.[6]

Campinchi's "Colonel," Chebotariov by name, a sadistic secret policeman who served the Poles, Ukrainians, and Bolsheviks at one time or another during the revolutionary

period, never did testify.[7] The Assize Court did have Colonel
Teresschenko's laughable testimony about Jewish "provocation" at Proskurov and a short deposition from Colonel
Boutakiv, who claimed that Semosenko had been imprisoned for a short time and "got away." But what happened to Semosenko remained muddled in the Ukrainian
telling.

Lieutenant General Pavlo Shandruk of the Ukrainian
Resistance Movement subsequently concocted a myth
where-by *he* was the saviour of the Jews of Proskurov. "The
Jews were at that time living in terror of exaggerated reports
about pogroms," he wrote in his memoirs. "They took
extremes for the average and would not believe anyone
would stand up for them." Shandruk claimed that Semosenko and his band of "exotically uniformed" followers
raided the Proskurov police station, chased the constabulary
into hiding with hand grenades then proceeded to plunder
"the entire population."

Upon receipt of orders from Colonel Andrew Melnyk of
the High Command, Shandruk hastened to Proskurov at the
head of the Zaporoghian Rifle Battalion to quell the disorders. Strangely, right after his forces entered the city, "the
bandits disappeared." What few Semosenkists could be
found were then sent "under guard" to Vinnitza for trial.
Shandruk did not explain what happened to their leader.
Afterward, the Jews of the city issued formal thanks to
Shandruk and praised Police Chief Kalenik Lessiuk (living
in Chicago after 1922 as Director of the Ukrainian Museum).
Some Jews even joined the Ukrainian Army out of
gratitude.[8]

Alexander Dotzenko, Petlura's adjutant from 1917 to 1923
and then a stone mason in Paris, credited the Holovni
Ataman himself with the rescue of the Jews of Proskurov.
According to Dotzenko's testimony, Petlura and his aides
arrived in the city at the end of February, two weeks after the
bloody pogrom. Petlura listened to a report from local

authorities and asked who was this man who had directed the massacre. When he learned it was Semosenko, Dotzenko related, Petlura "became pale, his eyes became furious." Turning to his assistants and officers, he cried, "What have you done? For all this spilled blood, the Ukraine will pay dearly! But I will settle accounts with you."[9]

Much as Petlura might have wanted to deal with Semosenko immediately, he could not. Though all of Semosenko's orders were signed "Ataman Semosenko of the Zaporog Cossack Brigade of the Army of the Ukrainian Republic," Dotzenko asserted that Semosenko was not an officer in the regular Ukrainian Army. Rather, he was a deserter from a regular detachment which had been operating on the left bank of the Dnieper River. According to Dotzenko, Semosenko crossed the river and formed a special group of Tsarist Black Hundreds and ex-convicts whom the Bolsheviks had released from jail. It was this band to which he attached the name of the First Brigade, without authorization from the government.

"At the time when Petlura came to Proskurov, there were only the men of Semosenko," said Dotzenko. "To give the order to immediately arrest Semosenko would have been the equivalent of giving the order to Semosenko to arrest himself."[10] As a result, Petlura supposedly issued a "secret order" to members of his own entourage and subsequently diverted important artillery and machine gun units from the front lines to effect Semosenko's arrest. When Semosenko learned of this, "he took flight." But he was subsequently apprehended and punished in 1919.[11]

Such expeditious action, Dotzenko insisted, was typical of Petlura. "I was with him through all his travels. I know where he went and I copied his most secret orders. I know that at the moment of the first manifestations of that revolt . . . when the Bolsheviks commenced their measures for the insurrection in Kiev and were concentrated at the arsenal, I know that it was the troops placed under the command of

Petlura who marched to attack on that arsenal. And when the arsenal was taken, and some number of Jews were found there, and when the soldiers were throbbing to attack the Jews, it was Petlura who stepped before them and with his breast protected the Jews, at the risk of being assassinated by his own soldiers."[12]

The Jews, it seems, should have raised a monument to the Holovni Ataman, who repeatedly interceded on their behalf, telling Jewish emissaries, "I have decided to have my entire army shot if it is going to drown the nascent Ukrainian Republic in Jewish blood."[13]

The Jews must have reciprocated this concern and affection, for according to Dotzenko: "Whenever the Jewish people were free, when they weren't molested, they demonstrated their eagerness in giving us aid and comfort because they knew the armies of Petlura were dedicated to the defense of their liberties. The day when the Ukraine will be free, these same sentiments, I am persuaded, will be plainly manifested and justice will be rendered to the truth."[14]

Petlura's involvement in the Proskurov pogrom was probably the most critical aspect of the trial. In September, 1926, Jewish leaders meeting with Ukrainians were informed that Semosenko had indeed been arrested at Petlura's order, but that after a short detention he had managed to escape. Ultimately, Semosenko was shot at the Yermolyntsi station for his role in the pogroms at Proskurov and Cherni-Ostrov.[15]

Ukrainian historians Michael Hrushevsky and V. Chekovsky reported quite a different tale. They claimed that Semosenko was arrested six months *after* the Proskurov massacre, and then only to provide a show trial to gain the sympathy of the West. Wrote Chekovsky: "Semosenko was, in truth, arrested, but not for the Proskurov massacre. Perhaps that was the official reason, but the guilt is elsewhere."[16]

During the spring of 1919, after the Proskurov atrocity,

Semosenko's band murdered more innocents in the towns of Felshtin and Koziatyn. When he was finally thrown into prison at Kamenetz-Podolsk, his wife implored Petlura to help her husband. According to the chief rabbi of Nemirov, Rafael Finkelstein, Petlura promised that her husband would be freed soon and that while in jail he was being treated like "a privileged character."[17] Several former employees of this prison swore that Semosenko was, in fact, "released" by 1920.[18]

That same winter, he was toasted as a Ukrainian hero at a banquet in Nemirov. A Jewish witness indicated that after several glasses of alcohol, Semosenko delivered a tirade in which he said that he had obeyed orders from "a higher power." "I with my military unit was in parts of Podolia and Volhynia to punish the Jews and stop Bolshevik uprisings." What pogroms ensued should be charged to the Jews themselves, he claimed, especially at Proskurov, for "they alone wanted the pogroms."[19]

According to Vasily Maudry, Semosenko was back in the regular Ukrainian army, serving in the ranks of General Oudovichenko, though not under his real name. Now calling himself "Doroshenko," he was blamed for several excesses committed by insurgents.[20] In May, 1920, Semosenko was arrested a second time and incarcerated in Kamenetz-Podolsk, not for pogroms, but for absconding with state moneys and various other crimes. When Petlura left for Poland at the end of the summer, Semosenko trailed along, still under arrest, in a prison car.

From that time on, according to Elia Tcherikover, "He was a slippery as water."[21] Semosenko's wife declared in her deposition that after Nemirov she never heard from him again. She did say, however, that in 1925 a friend of his informed her that Semosenko had been buried in the town of Cherni-Ostrov near Proskurov. Far from being executed as a commmon pogromchik, "He was buried with great pomp."[22]

The question of who executed Semosenko—Ukrainians, Bolsheviks, Poles—was never resolved. Semosenko himself expressed no concern over his well-being as long as he was in Ukrainian hands. During his first detention, he boasted to his jailer Colonel Sereda, "You can't execute me. I'm the voice of the Ukrainian people."[23] To another inmate, A. Chomski, a Jew from Kamenetz-Podolsk, he explained that he had been arrested not for killing eleven thousand "Yids," but because he supposedly embezzled 3,000 rubles. *"Why should I alone be made responsible* [for the pogroms]," he asked Chomski, *"when Petlura was staying in his own train at the railway station and the pogrom was also directed by Petlura's own aide-de-camp Ben?"*[24] [emphasis added]

The intimation that Petlura may have been at Proskurov during the massacres created another serious controversy. Generally, Ukrainians and most Jews agreed that the Holovni Ataman had not been to Proskurov before the end of the month of February. Ever-faithful General Alexander Oudovichenko even specified that Petlura was in Pidvolochysk on February 15.[25] He also claimed that the Zaporog Cossack Brigade which perpetrated the slaughter (and which responded to orders issued by Generals Konovalets and Mykola Shapoval) was never part of the regular army. Oudovichenko's credibility was further weakened by his own involvement in pogroms.

On March 22 and 23, 1919, the same Ataman Ben of whom Semosenko spoke, along with Colonels Zakharchuk and Kapkan of the High Command, organized another pogrom in Zhitomir. When the military censor Dobia tried to put an end to that massacre (which claimed 317 lives), he was removed from his post. While this pogrom was raging, Petlura and Colonel Oskilko (commander of the forces on the southwest front) were in the Holovni Ataman's train at the Zhitomir railway station.

A deputation of Gentiles led by M. D. Skokovsky and Mayor Pivotski pleaded with Petlura and Oskilko to put an end to the horrors. They were told that the government was sorry for what had happened and that relief would be on its way. Nevertheless, the pogrom continued for an additional forty-eight hours, until the Galician Chief of Police Bogatski, operating without orders from the Directory, intervened with his own manpower. Skokovsky's deposition on the affair noted cynically, "The supreme chief of the Ukrainian Army should have been able, in any case, to do at least as much as the chief of his gendarmerie. But he didn't."[26]

An equally callous attitude was demonstrated by the Holovni Ataman a few days later when his train was at the depot in Mamienka. To a Jewish delegation which appealed to him to stop a massacre going on in nearby Srazevedgrad, Petlura said, "Look, I don't interfere with what my army does, and I will not prevent them from doing what they judge necessary to do."[27]

Petlura was implicated in the Zhitomir and Srazevedgrad pogroms by his inaction while on the scene and through the active participation in the pogroms of his aide Ben and regular troops under his command. The same Ben was implicated in the pogrom at Proskurov, only about ninety miles from Zhitomir.

There was no doubt that Petlura visited Proskurov following the pogrom there, although the dates were confused. Moreover, in the three weeks he actually spent at Proskurov, he refused to discuss the massacres with any Jewish delegation. Nor did he visit the scene of these tragic events or issue a formal statement on the pogrom.[28]

When, during the summer of 1919, Petlura's forces occupied the city for a second time and the Holovni Ataman was staying in the home of a Jew, he did comment, shrugging off the slaughters with the cavalier statement, "It's nothing. It's simple. The Jews deserved it because they were Bolsheviks. If they would act decently, such things would not happen."[29]

Dr. Abraham Saliternik, who some claim was Jewish, treated Semosenko for a nervous disorder and "inflammation of the testicles" while the Ataman was in Proskurov. Saliternik testified in 1919 and again in 1927 that Semosenko refused to stay in bed, even though he was running a high fever.

"Semosenko responded that he couldn't stay in bed at that time since Petlura was at the Proskurov railway station and he had to get to him to make a very important report." After making this report, Dr. Saliternik noted that Semosenko was "in good humor for days." "He only said that I ought to cure him as quickly as possible since he had been named a commander in the army."[30]

A second witness, Henryk Przanowski, an attaché of the Danish Red Cross and the only foreign witness in Proskurov, indicated that Petlura arrived in town at the height of the disorders and was greeted with great pomp by Semosenko and the civil authorities at the station.

Przanowski was granted a private audience with the Holovni Ataman, during which Semosenko burst into the room shouting, "According to the order of the Head Ataman, I stopped the pogrom at 12:00 noon. Four thousand registered Jews have been massacred." Petlura reacted with great embarrassment, gave Semosenko a nasty look, and tried to shift the discussion to talk about the Bolshevik uprising in town. Standing by a table, he asked, "What did the Bolsheviks want?" Again, stupidly, Semosenko replied, "The Jews wanted nothing." Petlura dismissed Semosenko and requested that Przanowski "forget what he had heard."

A half hour later, Petlura, Semosenko, and other officers were toasting one another at a banquet. Concluded Przanowski, "I understood that Semosenko had done nothing at his own initiative."[31]

Others concurred with Saliternik and Przanowski that Petlura's role in the Proskurov pogrom was more than incidental. Leon Bienko, a Pole who was born in the

Ukraine and who held the position of top legal secretary for the Ukrainian General Staff during the pogroms, related how from his office in Proskurov he witnessed the massacre, an event that made a greater impact on him than all the years spent in combat in World War I.

On the afternoon of Friday, February 15, Bienko went out into the street and saw Jews being hacked down at Alexander Street and Pharmacy Street. Several persons came running up to him and begged his protection, and he brought them to the offices of the Tribunal of the 3rd Division. That evening, an officer named Greber entered the Tribunal and asked him, "Lt. Bienko, why have you hidden Jews here at the court? There is an order to massacre all the Jews tonight. The pogrom has already begun."

Bienko answered that he would sacrifice his own life before he would give away any of the people in the building. Lt. Greber responded, "If the Cossacks find the Jews here, they'll massacre court personnel as well." Ordered to take the people out, Bienko again pleaded that it was too cold. He finally acquiesced, taking them to the home of a rich man named Kuperwasser. During the night the house was raided and most of Bienko's supplicants were killed.

The next day, "a nice day," Bienko went out and surveyed the incredible scenes of butchery. "Bodies were lying everywhere, in apartments, ditches, courtyards," he recalled. Five pigs drew near the body of an old man and Bienko shooed them off. At that moment a Cossack appeared and shouted, "What are you doing? I direct them here and you chase them away!"

The only survivors were those who had hidden with Christians or had run away. Bienko pointed out that Semosenko extorted 300,000 rubles as a price for the Jews to bury their own dead. Not the peasants of Haia Greenberg's tale, but "courageous Jews" went out with sleds to cart the victims to five huge trenches. At the cemetery, he watched as a young woman with a child wept over the cadaver of her

murdered husband. "At that moment, several of Semosenko's Cossacks entered the cemetery and saw the Jews.
They grew enraged and hacked the woman and her child to
pieces."[32]

In talking with Cossacks and officers, Bienko, like
Przanowski, concluded that Petlura had personally given
orders for the pogrom at Proskurov, but that when he
learned how many Jews had been massacred, he became
frightened and restored order. "I am convinced," swore
Bienko, "that Petlura was the true author of the pogrom at
Proskurov and that it was he who carried all responsibility
for the massacre of thousands of innocent Jews."

"We must kill because we have sworn," the Cossacks told
Bienko. "We have sworn by him whose order is holy."

Bienko continued: "In my discussions with Officer
Bourine and with others on the General Staff, I learned that
Petlura had given the order to chastise the Jews of Proskurov. In that order it was also specified how long the
massacres would last. Only when Semosenko publicly declared that he had organized the pogroms with Petlura's
knowledge did the latter arrest and incarcerate him at
Kamenetz."[33]

Dr. Stavinski of the Proskurov Duma (assembly) and a
Ukrainian officer named Serchenko, of the Special Division,
both reported that two days before the pogrom broke out
orders had been received from Ukrainian Army Headquarters to "make a slaughter in the city out of the souls of the
Bolsheviks."[34]

Former Minister Pinchas Krasny, a Jew, claimed he had
evidence that Petlura had phoned Semosenko from
Zhmerinka, instructing him not to permit the Bolsheviks to
seize control of a vital railway link. If necessary, Semosenko
was to "massacre half of the Jewish population."[35]

Semosenko's onetime cellmate, A. Chomski, maintained
that Semosenko actually showed him telegrams and other
documents dispatched from Petlura instructing Semosenko

to suppress "the Bolshevik *Bund* in Proskurov."[36]

Zvi Zekzer, who made an official investigation for the Jewish relief committee in Kiev in May, 1919 (when Proskurov was temporarily in Bolshevik hands), claimed to have come across a packet of telegrams in the post archive. Addressed to the Ataman Semosenko and Commandant Kiverchuk, they were dated February 13, two days before the pogrom. The wires were identical in content:

> *Secret and important.* Everything indicates a Bolshevik uprising on the part of the Jewish population. Suppress absolutely with a strong armed might that no Jewish hand might rise in Podolia against the aspiring Ukraine.

The order was signed "Holovni Ataman."[37]

Leon Bienko claimed that Petlura decreed Semosenko's execution in Poland because the latter knew too much and could implicate the Holovni Ataman as the instigator of the pogroms. Traveling with Petlura's fleeing government by train, Bienko inquired of Colonel Chalaiev about the identity of a sickly prisoner. The Colonel told him that it was Semosenko. The next time he saw Semosenko, the prisoner was battered and near death. Bienko asked Chalaiev what had happened and was told that Semosenko had been turned over to a Colonel Pavlovski of Counterespionage for interrogation. Chalaiev boasted, "Whoever falls into the hands of Pavlovski disappears without a trace." Petlura wanted to ensure that Semosenko would take his secret with him to the grave.[38]

This was clear also to Colonel Hrishko Lisenko, onetime member of the Central Rada and Petlura's inner military circle. During the summer of 1920, the subject of pogroms came up while several officers were relaxing in the company of Petlura and Dotzenko. Petlura asked Lisenko who he thought was guilty and Lisenko, angry because several leading pogromchiks were still at liberty, responded, "You,

Herr Haupt-Ataman." At that, Petlura flushed, and stormed into his bedroom. Lisenko wrote that he was certain Petlura was responsible for the pogrom at Proskurov.[39]

Ukrainian apologists for Petlura argued that none of the information given above was acceptable. What kind of name was Przanowski for a representative of the Danish Red Cross? What kind of name was Bienko? What were both intriguers doing in the Ukraine at the time? Should one believe these Poles, historical enemies of Ukrainian independence? Why would Semosenko have imparted confidential information to a Jewish criminal like Chomsky?[40] Could one rely upon the testimony of the "Jewish" physician Saliternik, Rabbi Finkelstein, the head of the Jewish community in Proskurov Dr. Liser, the Jewish householder B. Wagman, the Jewish state official Lazar Goldman, the Jewish outsider Zvi Zekzer, the unstable and unpopular Pinchas Krasny? Why believe Lisenko, Maudry, Serchenko, Stavinski, Verkhola, or Sikora, Ukrainians who obviously had broken with the Holovni Ataman? Why could not the telegrams to Semosenko and Kiverchuk have originated with someone on the General Staff other than Petlura? And if these secret cables were only discovered at a time when the Bolsheviks controlled Proskurov, why could they not be forgeries? Where was there evidence other than hearsay that Petlura had been involved in any way with the Proskurov pogrom? In short, why accept any information other than that offered by Ukrainians loyal to their leader?

Evidently Professor Elia Tcherikover, of the East European Historical Archives and the YIVO Institute for Jewish Research, felt no such compunctions about Petlura. After "cautious examination" of the various witnesses' statements, Tcherikover stated that "somebody had given an order to drown the Bolshevik uprising in Proskurov in blood . . . and that somebody was Petlura."[41]

The orders originated with him. The Haidamaks were loyal only to him. He was there while the massacres raged, and he was obeyed when he commanded a halt to the proceedings. Nothing was done out in the open, but that which Petlura had desired had been accomplished. Tcherikover concluded, "The fingerprints of Petlura in the Proskurov tragedy are clear enough from the declarations of the various witnesses, Jews and non-Jews."[42]

The Prosecution could not allow such suppositions. Said Cesar Campinchi: "There is a great scholar named M. Painleve. He was Minister of War in 1917, at the time of certain troubles which compromised the unity of the French front. Being Minister of War, do you say that he was responsible for these troubles? He dealt with such men as General Nivelle, General Mangin, and the others; he saw them every day; he communicated with them by telephone. And our armies weren't in flight like those of Petlura. I ask you Mr. Langevin, excuse me once more for this nervousness which grips me, because I am before a well-known scholar. I ask you, you who belong to the elite of a civilized country. Not knowing the details of the incident, how can you naturally find that a man may be sacrificed seven or eight years after the acts which are imputed to him took place?"

SCHWARTZBARD (breaking in): France waited forty-four years to avenge the offense of 1870! I waited six years!

CAMPINCHI (horrified): You mean to say that your act was analogous to that of France in 1914?

LANGEVIN: I must reply to your question concerning Minister Painleve, sir.

CAMPINCHI: I have taken the liberty of speaking of M. Painleve who is a political figure, and as a consequence, a public figure.

TORRÈS: M. Langevin is going to tell you.

CAMPINCHI: I know that he is going to tell me. I also know quite well that *you* will tell me.

LANGEVIN: The minister could not be held responsible for mutinies which were individual acts. But he could be responsible for orders given by chiefs under his command.[43]

The Civil Prosecutor was not yet finished with Professor Langevin. How could such a logical person excuse the actions of the accused? How could he condone Schwartzbard's setting himself up as judge and jury and waiting six years to kill a man in cold blood? Dr. Langevin professed to believe in the natural rights of men. Was not Petlura entitled to those same rights? Could Langevin view this incident as "natural" or excusable?

Said the Professor: "Because we have organized law, violence is no longer possible or excusable. But, as I have said previously, it is only in the absence of organized law that individual violence may intervene. It is because there is no international law that we have wars. Wars are the consequence of the absence of international law, just as this particular act is."

Far from considering the killing "natural," Langevin protested against it. But for him, Schwartzbard was a member of a race which had been abused before the tribunes of international justice, a person who had given proof of his selflessness and sacrifice during the war. Schwartzbard had waited for such a long time because he hoped that Petlura, the symbol of Jewish affliction, the architect of the Proskurov pogrom, the symbol of his own personal sufferings, would be dealt with at the bar of international justice. When the world failed to act, Schwartzbard acted in its stead, as an instrument of humanity's conscience.

"I protest against it," declared Langevin, "but it is with all my desire that I appeal to a higher justice, to our actual conscience."[44]

Notes

1. René David and Henry P. DeVries, *The French Legal System* (New York: Oceana Publications, 1958), pp.77ff.

2. "Droits de l'Homme," *Grand Larousse Encyclopédique* (Paris: Librairie Larousse, 1962), IV.

3. By 1933 the League would number 200,000 members, including 279 Radical and Socialist members of the French National Assembly. One of its number, Leon Blum, even became premier. After World War II, however, the body disintegrated rapidly and by 1956 there were only 2,500 persons to register feeble protests against Russian intervention in Hungary and the Anglo-French escapade at Suez.

4. *Frankfurter Zeitung,* October 21, 1927, p.1.

5. *Notes Sténographiques,* fasc. 3, p.135. For Langevin's complete testimony see pp.129-140/7.

6. *Ibid.,* pp.140/1-140/3. The stenographic account has a misnumbering at page 140 for the following seven pages.

7. Deposition of Chebotariev, File 462, 386388-90, Tcherikover Archive.

8. According to one Ukrainian apologist, the forces of Semosenko "withdrew." Shandruk himself made no reference to such a magical evaporation. See Shandruk, *Arms of Valor,* pp.75-76, and Editorial Review of this manuscript, University of Tennessee Press, October, 1973, p.6.

9. Testimony of Dotzenko, *Notes Sténographiques,* fasc. 5, p.29-30.

10. *Ibid.*, pp.31-32.

11. *Ibid.*, pp.35-36.

12. *Ibid.*, pp.22-23.

13. *Ibid.*, p.25.

14. *Ibid.*, p.46

15. Abraham Revutzky was told a similar story in October, 1919, by Ukrainian Social Democrat N. Porsh. Colonel Kedrovsky, Inspector General of Ukrainian forces and later co-author of the address on behalf of Petlura which appeared in the *New York Times,* also supported this position. Tcherikover, *Di ukrainer pogromen*, pp.152-3.

16. Abraham Revutzky, *In di shvere tog ofn Ukraine*, p.290.

17. "Meldung fun Rabbi Rafael Finkelstein," October 16, 1927, Material of Schwartzbard Defense Committee, File 438, Tcherikover Archive.

18. Deposition of Trofim Atamaniouk, Daniel Shermet, and Marie Bondarev, December 1, 1926, File 398, 35045, Tcherikover Archive.

19. "Meldung fun Lemberg hilfs-komitat," in Tcherikover, *Di ukrainer pogromen*, pp.154-55.

20. Vasily Maudry, "Proskurivskii pogrom," *Kalendar Proseita* (Lwow, 1926), p. 113.

21. Tcherikover, *Di ukrainer pogromen*, p.156.

22. Deposition of Anna Shidlovski-Semosenko, October 17, 1927, File 404, 35272-75, Tcherikover Archive.

23. George Kulchycky, "Simon Petlura and the Pogroms in the Ukraine, 1917-1920," Institute of Adult Jewish Studies, Youngstown, Ohio, March 14, 1973.

24. Chomsky was an organizer of Jewish self-defense in Ourinine who had been arrested for resisting the pogromchiks. The Nationalist government condemned him to death for his actions. A. Chomsky, *Mayn protzes: In der tkufe fun der revolutzie* (Berlin, 1924), pp.261-275.

25. Letter of Oudovichenko in *En notre âme et conscience: La verite sur Simon Petlura* (Paris: Committee for the Defense of the Memory of Simon Petlura, 1958), pp.66-67.

26. Haifetz, *The Slaughter of the Jews*, p.46; Schechtman, *et al*, *The Pogroms in the Ukraine*, pp.78, 200-210; and Annex 36, p.68, in *Les pogromes en Ukraine*.

27. *Notes Sténographiques*, fasc. 7, p.26.

28. A. Revutski, *"Qui est Petlioura et quel est son rôle dans les pogromes antijuifs?"* Report, File 421, 36586-91, p.5, Tcherikover Archive.

29. "Meldung fun Alter Buchdrucker," May 25, 1927, Material of Schwartzbard Defense Committee, File 438, Tcherikover Archive.

30. Declaration of Abraham Saliternik, February 15, 1927, File 425, 36883-4, Tcherikover Archive. See also *Notes Sténographiques*, fasc. 5, pp.67-69.

31. Deposition of Henryk Przanowski, October, 1926, File 425, 36891-2 and 36896. Przanowski never testified at the trial, because Torrès waived his right to call additional witnesses after a week of hearings. For additional information on Przanowski's meeting with Petlura see Tcherikover, *Di ukrainer pogromen*, pp.146-7, and File 429, Tcherikover Archive.

32. Deposition of Leon Bienko, September 2, 1926, File 441, pp.2-5, Tcherikover Archives. See also File 425, 36841-54, Tcherikover Archive.

33. *Ibid.*, File 441, pp.5-7.

34. Tcherikover, *Di ukrainer pogromen*, pp.132-33.

35. *Proletarskaia Pravda*, Kiev, 96 and 98, 1927, later translated and published in New York's *Freiheit*, October 19 and 27, 1927.

36. A. Chomsky, *Mayn protzes*, p.261.

37. Along with the depositions of Chomsky and Przanowski, this packet of telegrams was considered the most damning evidence against Petlura by both Tcherikover and Sjakowski. See Tcherikover, *Di ukrainer pogromen*, pp.145-46, for "Meldung fun Z. Zekzer fun Lemberg tzum Farteydikungs-Komitat," April 4, 1927. Copies of the telegrams were relayed to Paris and are on deposit in File 360 of the Tcherikover Archive.

38. Deposition of Bienko, File 441, p.7, Tcherikover Archive.

39. "Meldung fun Hrishko Lisenko," October, 1927, in Tcherikover, *Di ukrainer pogromen*, p.157.

40. A better question would be why Semosenko would *not* have boasted of this feat to a doomed Jew. Chomsky explained that the Ataman was not especially popular among the prisoners and had no one else to talk with. Chomsky, *Mayn protzes*, pp.261-2.

41. Tcherikover, *Di ukrainer pogromen*, pp.149-50. For perhaps the most throrough treatment of Petlura's involvement at Proskurov, see Tcherikover's chapter in this book titled "Petlura un der Proskurover pogrom," pp.145-163.

42. *Ibid.*, p.149.

43. *Notes Sténographiques*, fasc.3, pp.140/4-140/6.

44. *Ibid.*, p.140/7.

8.

The Elusive Monsieur Volodine

WHEN ON THE AFTERNOON of Saturday, February 15, 1919, Ukrainian Commissar Taranovich sought assistance from a higher level in halting the massacres then raging at Proskurov, he turned to Ataman Semosenko's commanding officer, General Mykola Shapoval. According to Shapoval's version of what transpired, the General immediately issued a telegram to the Ukrainian troops, the receipt of which was sufficient to quiet the Zaporog Cossacks. Shapoval then, and not Petlura or Shandruk, was the deliverer of the Jews of Proskurov.

General Shapoval, the next witness for the prosecution, was a massively built Slav with a full head of stiff white hair and a black mustache. Once a "fire-eating" Social Revolutionary, he had joined with his brother Mikita Shapoval, Vinnichenko, and N.Y. Hryhorijiv in shaping the policies of the National Union, the organization of Ukrainian nationalists which paved the way for the overthrow of the pro-German Skoropadsky Hetmanate in November, 1918.

Under Petlura, Shapoval commanded more than thirty thousand troops on the Eastern Front against the Bolsheviks and White Army. Less than a brilliant military strategist, he was nevertheless credited with having successfully directed the retreat of Ukrainian forces from Kiev four hundred miles into the Galician marshlands at the end of 1919. In exile,

Shapoval served for a time as a member of the Ukrainian Institute of Sociology in Prague before coming to Paris.

For Shapoval, the source of the villainy in the Ukraine was all too clear. It was the Great Russian imperialists, both the Tsarists and their Soviet successors, who imposed a "frightful slavery upon the Ukrainian people." Noting that Russia before the war had gained a reputation as "a prison of peoples," Shapoval recited the list of Ukrainian grievances under forced Russification—the prohibition of the Ukrainian language in business, schools, and religious

Mykola Shapoval, one-time Ukrainian general and a witness for the prosecution. (YIVO Tcherikover Archive)

instruction, the suppression of Ukrainian culture, the denial of Ukrainian aspirations for national autonomy or independence. Whatever political ideology they may have followed, the Great Russians, who constituted only 43 percent of the total population of the Russian Empire, were committed to one dictum: "The Ukraine never existed. It doesn't exist. It will not exist."[1]

Jews also suffered under Russification, Shapoval conceded, and he mentioned the Pale, the Kishinev pogrom, and the more recent massacre at Brest-Litovsk in 1915 when retreating Tsarist troops destroyed practically every Jewish home in that city. Because of their misfortunes, many Jews shared the dreams of the Ukrainian nationalists.

"The Jews among whom I grew up and who were partisans as I in the Ukrainian independence, were always clearly with the Ukrainians," he said. But there were collaboraters as well. "Beside Ukrainian and Jewish partisans of independence, there were Russified Jews and Ukrainians who were the irreconcilable enemies of the Ukrainian national party. And for example Schwartzbard is the characteristic type of Russified Jew. He grew up in the Ukraine, but never was Ukrainian."[2]

Shapoval insisted that despite many provocations and temptations, none of his troops ever made pogroms. He defied anyone to find a journal or historical document where it was charged that his troops made pogroms. Why, he had even diverted badly needed troops from the front lines to deal with pogromchiks. If he had had those units in the line against the Red Army, Shapoval fantasized aloud, he might have been victorious against the enemies of the Ukraine.

As the General rambled on about his own courage and leadership, he had to be reminded by Justice Flory that the court was primarily interested in the role of Petlura. Shapoval described Petlura as "a man of humanitarian ideas," a longtime Social Democrat who was profoundly opposed to pogroms. The Holovni Ataman had issued severe orders against pogroms, and it was precisely because the regular troops "scrupulously executed his orders to the letter" that historians were forced to concede that no pogroms had been committed by regular Ukrainian forces.[3]

Far from being an anti-Semite, Shapoval insisted, Petlura might properly be called a philo-Semite. As the audience erupted with laughter, the General went on to relate how the entire Jewish community in Melnitza a *shtetl* six kilometers from Kamenetz, turned out to welcome the Holovni Ataman in May, 1919. Petlura was admitted to the home of the rabbi, and when the Ukrainian forces withdrew after two months, the same rabbi came and thanked Shapoval personally for the excellent rapport established between the two sides. As additional proof of Petlura's pro-Jewish sympathies, Shapoval cited the number of Jewish functionaries in the Ukrainian bureaucracy, Jewish soldiers and officers in the ranks of the army, even a Ministry of Jewish Affairs.[4]

"Oh!" noted Torrès, challenging the last point. "His minister, a poor clerk, a bureaucrat without importance. A man assigned to insignificant work."

"He was more," said Shapoval. "He was the agent of relief to the unhappy victims of pogroms."[5]

Supporters of Petlura made much of his Minister of Jewish Affairs. His signature appeared next to that of the President of the Council of Ministers in any proclamation affecting the status of the Jews in the Ukraine. His was the disbursing agency for funds authorized by the same council for relief of pogrom victims.

On March 23, 1919, for example, the Directory set aside 300,000 hrivni (60,000 dollars) for relief of the victims of Proskurov, a trifling amount in comparison with the damage done in that city. On April 9, 1919, the Minister of Jewish Relief was authorized to spend another 1,460,000 hrivni. And on October 29, 1919, the Petlura government pledged 20,000,000 more for relief of Jewish suffering throughout the Ukraine.[6] The Jewish community supposedly would be free to administer these funds as it saw fit according to a law of April 17, 1919, which granted Jews autonomy in all spheres—judicial, fiscal, health, and welfare. All of these measures, signed by Chepovski, were countersigned by Simon Petlura.[7]

In truth, however, the Ministry of Jewish Affairs was nothing but a facade designed for show to the Western world. The grand laws concerning Jewish autonomy were simply resurrected decrees of the democratic Rada dating back to December 2, 1917, and January 9, 1918. The amounts authorized for Jewish relief represented only a fraction of the billions of hrivni and rubles which had been extorted or stolen from the Jews. The Directory felt compelled to grant several hundred thousands of dollars for relief every few months, but according to the Kiev Central Relief Committee and the American Joint Distribution Committee, which carried out the principal relief work in the Ukraine, the Jews needed more than two million rubles (approximately one million dollars in pre-war currency) merely to clothe their naked. And according to the same sources, more than twenty million rubles per day (10,000,000 dollars) was required to feed the pogrom victims. Such sums were never forthcoming from the Ukrainian government.[8]

The idea of a Ministry for Jewish Affairs did not originate with Petlura. Under the Rada, three such positions (for Russians, Poles, and Jews) had been created by decree of July 22, 1917. Elaborate instructions drawn up by the General Secretary for Nationalities provided that the *Vitze-Sekretar* should protect the civil and political rights of the members of national minorities against judicial infringements. Each nationality was encouraged to develop its own unique national life within the overall framework of a Ukrainian society based on mutual cooperation, freedom, and democracy.[9] Jews could well have punned that the *Vitze* in the title of the Jewish Secretariat meant "joke" (*vitz* in Yiddish) rather than "deputy."

Dr. Moses Silberfarb, who served as the first Jewish Minister from November, 1917, to March, 1918, was optimistic about the role the ministry might play in building up Jewish communal and economic life. On paper, the plans looked good.[10] In the next two years, Jews would serve as Minister of Commerce, Undersecretary for Foreign Affairs, and in the press and secretariat sections of Ukrainian missions to France, Holland, and England.

Professor Mark Vishnitzer was moved to rhapsodize about the period from 1917 to 1919:

> The Jews in Ukraine have the most extended national rights. The Jewish language is officially recognized. A Jewish ministry has been able to develop its activity. Jewish congregations have been able to thrive in freedom, and now Jewish schools have grown up. In the newly founded university of Kamenetz-Podolsk, the government has established a professor's chair for Jewish History and Literature, and hereby the national rights of the Jewish people have been still more emphasized.[11]

Frustration heaped on frustration as the various nationalities vied with one another for the favor and funds of the General Secretary for Nationalities, a post which wielded total control over the others. When Silberfarb complained that Rada officials were interfering with his duties, that he was powerless to encourage autonomy for Jews, he was told to understand that nothing should be pressed as "this was the province of the central government." Convinced that the ministry was nothing but a "front" and a "help" to the Rada, and sickened by the government's inaction during the first pogroms, Silberfarb resigned in 1918.[12]

The feeling of impotence was shared by Abraham Revutzky, who took office on December 10, 1918, with the advent of the Directory. Revutzky tried to make of the Ministry something more than a small office in a hotel room. When he approached Premier Vinnichenko to obtain a clear definition of his powers, the latter made light of what he regarded as a trivial question.[13] When Revutzky brought evidence that regular army units were killing Jews in Berdichev, Ovruch, and Zhitomir, Vinnichenko promised action but again did nothing.[14]

When, on the basis of reports reaching him from Zhitomir, he asked Petlura for a strong, "unpartisan" commission to stop the pogromchiks, the Holovni Ataman offered him a commission headed by the anti-Semite Andrievski, together with Shvetz, Makarenko, General Oskilko, and Colonel Palienko, a man referred to as "the Field Marshal of pogroms."[15]

Revutzky resigned in February, 1919, either because of the Proskurov pogrom, as he claimed, or because he planned to leave office with the rest of the Vinnichenko bureaucrats anyway. Five months of this pretense, with no power, no funds, no encouragement, and no cooperation, had been enough.[16]

Concerned by world reaction to news of the pogroms, seeking the support of the mercurial "world Jewish power," and desperate for tangible assistance from the Entente, the Directory sought a replacement for Revutzky. Its dilemma was succinctly expressed by one Jewish adviser, who warned, "The democracies won't deal with you without a Jewish minister."[17]

The man who uttered this statement, Pinchas Krasny, also volunteered to take the job. A member of the small Jewish *Folkspartei*, which was generally unpopular among the Ukraine's Jews, Krasny could not even be considered a representative of that group. His own party disowned him once he became Minister of Jewish Affairs, noting that Krasny was not a member of the Central Committee of the Folkspartei and that he had been suspended from the organization for a long time for not following party discipline.[18]

In the next months, Krasny succeeded only in diminishing his stature by playing the willing lackey to Petlura. A Jewish Minister who failed even to establish one effective inquiry into the pogroms, who called on his brethren to remain loyal to a government which was underwriting massacres, who dealt in what Jews believed to be blood money consigned for relief, and who as late as August 7, 1919, issued paeans of tribute to Petlura,[19] was a sycophant who could hardly claim to represent the Jewish population of the Ukraine.

"What of the pogroms?" demanded Torrès. "What of Proskurov?"

Shapoval answered, "It was difficult to restore order everywhere. It was possible to control the regular army, but not the bands that ravaged the countryside. I myself withdrew troops from the front for the suppression of pogroms. This was one of the reasons for my retreat and defeat."

"The pogrom at Proskurov was ordered by the Ataman Semosenko," Torrès said.

"Nevertheless," interrupted Public Prosecutor Reynaud, "Petlura was not in charge."

"He was the chief Ataman," replied Torrès.

"Not chief!" shot back Reynaud.

"Chief Ataman!" Torrès insisted, his voice filling the courtroom. "Wasn't Hindenburg responsible for his troops who pillaged?"

Cesar Campinchi joined the din: "Did anyone hold Marshal Joffre or General Nivelle responsible for the mutinies in the French Army? That really makes good sense. Read *La Débâcle* of Zola and then tell us if Petlura could have suppressed the uprisings. He was one man among sixteen Ukrainian head men."

"They massacred to cries of 'Long live Petlura!'" shouted Torrès. "They massacred with rifles, with blank arms, with sabres, with rapiers—scores, hundreds, thousands of Jews! Women! Old men! Children of two years! Three years! Of four years! Of five years! Of six years! Of *all* ages! And at

Maître Reynaud, prosecuting attorney.

Proskurov did Petlura even arrest his lieutenant Semosenko?"

"He was shot," Campinchi declared.

"Much later! He left Proskurov in a special hospital train. I insist upon the word *hospital!*" Pounding his fist against the bar, Torrès fairly screamed, "Let us not forget Proskurov!" With a blow to his chest, "Let us not forget the Zaporoghian Cossacks!" And another fist onto his dossier, "Let us not forget the Haidamak Cossacks!"[20]

Throughout this exhibition, General Shapoval remained composed at the bar. He had more to offer than a mere character reference for Petlura. Where the deceased Professor Koval was only able to describe some of Schwartzbard's purported accomplices in the slaying, Shapoval could actually name one, a Monsieur Volodine.

The General had met this man at a Socialist Congress in Paris in August, 1925. After that, Volodine was a frequent visitor at Shapoval's home. Though the General remained aloof, Volodine tried to ingratiate himself, presenting himself as "a comrade." In political discussions between the two men, Volodine defended Petlura as a very humane person, a good Social Democrat. He told Shapoval that he had been imprisoned with Petlura when the Germans controlled the Ukraine.

Three weeks before the assassination, the two men were strolling in the Latin Quarter when Volodine inquired innocently if Shapoval knew where Petlura was living. Dubious of Volodine's declared intention of striking up an old friendship, Shapoval simply responded, "Somewhere in Paris."[21]

On the day of the assassination, May 25, 1926, this same Volodine made several nearly frantic appearances at Shapoval's house—at 10:00 A.M., 3:30 P.M., and at 4:00. During the last visits, the President of the Ukrainian Association in France, M. Stassif, was with Shapoval. Volodine was not free to talk, but it was evident to Shapoval that for some reason he was "clearly elated."

Later, when Shapoval went out to purchase some bread, he again encountered Volodine in the Rue du Sommerard. As they walked together to the Rue Racine, Volodine declared, "A Russian general has been shot." Before Shapoval could speak, he added, "Yes, certainly, Petlura." Shapoval was convinced that Volodine was an agent of Moscow who had been sent to ferret out information. He was certain that Volodine stood guard while Schwartzbard attacked the Ukrainian leader.

Such testimony was intriguing. Or as Defense Counsel Torrès put it, "That's it! You tie a little knot and that's it!"

Shapoval's testimony consisted of pure innuendo. If it were true, asked Torrès, why did Shapoval continue his liaison with Volodine after the assassination? Why was he

photographed in August, 1926, three months after the killing with this man he disliked and denounced? Why did
Shapoval's journal *L' Ouvrier Ukrainien* publish an article
by this same Volodine in September, 1926, four months after
the killing? Why did Mikita Shapoval's publication in
Prague accept another article by Volodine in October, 1926,
five months after the killing?

Shapoval explained: "I was from the first convinced that
Volodine was one of the accomplices in Petlura's assassination. But having not yet obtained all necessary proofs on
that subject, I decided not to break relations with him, to
continue to be on good terms, to find a means of obtaining
more precise indications."[23]

The prosecution tried to bolster Shapoval's credibility by
introducing a twenty-page letter from one Elie Dobkovsky.
This man, a Jew, warned that there was a terrorist-espionage
organization ensconced in France, part of a larger network
which extended into the colonies, the rest of Europe, and
America.

Dobkovsky claimed to have been commissioned by the
Central Muscovite Cheka, the Soviet secret police, to organize espionage and terror in Europe. For seven months following the assassination, he had held off testifying "for fear
Moscow would kill some innocents." In that time he had
undergone a political conversion. Now he was an avowed
socialist who believed in the rule of law, the rule of order,
parliamentary government, a free press, and public justice.
Conscious of his duty as a citizen and seething with anger at
the attempted deification of Schwartzbard, he had come
forward. According to Dobkovsky, Petlura was the victim of
an assassination scheme hatched in Moscow and implemented by "the anarchist Schwartzbard, the maximalist
Volodine, and by the *transfuge* [turncoat] Norich."[24]

Dobkovsky maintained that the date of the assassination
was significant. Marshal Pilsudski had just regained control
of the Polish government, and the Soviet Union feared that

he might assist his one-time ally, Petlura, in another thrust into the Ukraine. As a result, on January 9, 1926, the Comintern held a secret conclave in Moscow at which Soviet Foreign Minister Chicherin proclaimed a policy of terrorism against enemies of the International. These included high-ranking officials such as Petlura, Poincare, and Millerand, as well as capitalists and clergy. Wherever possible, *agents provocateurs* were to employ maximalists and anarchists in these devious practices.

Proof of this scheme was to be found in a message to the Comintern dated April 9, 1926, in which the South American communists indicated their refusal to abide by such a policy. Nevertheless, Dobkovsky went on, Schwartzbard had been enrolled by Moscow to carry out the execution of Petlura. The killing was to serve a dual purpose: It would remove a "dangerous" political figure whose name was synonymous with the Ukrainian liberation movement, and it would stimulate anti-Ukrainian feelings among the world's Jews, forcing a decision from the French law courts which could be manipulated against Ukrainian nationalism.[25]

As Ukrainian historians reconstructed the incident, the second point was of less significance. Petlura had to be removed because he enjoyed great esteem in Poland and France, because he alone among all the Ukrainian leaders was a symbol of resistance. As recently as March 11, 1926, Commissar Chubar of Kharkov had warned his superiors that the Moscow regime was unpopular in the Ukraine, that "many partisans" still supported Petlura. Unlike other opponents of Bolshevism, the Holvni Ataman's movement was not financially or morally bankrupt, and as such constituted a "permanent danger" to the Soviet Union.[26]

Petlura's assassination, then, was in the Kremlin's interest, not merely because it would remove the head of the Ukrainian movement, but also because it would lead to increase tension between Ukrainians and Jews. It would discredit the Ukrainian national movement in the media, especially in western liberal circles, by associating it with anti-Semitism.

According to Dobkovsky, the man assigned the specific task of liquidating Petlura was Volodine, a troublesome fellow who had been in and out of Tsarist jails for nearly a decade before the Revolution in 1917. Amnestied from a St. Petersburg jail in that year, Volodine allegedly aided the Bolsheviks by spreading their propaganda through the ranks. Later he popped up in Berlin, urging the anarchists to make common cause with the German communists. And then, in 1925, this extremist appeared at Dobkovsky's home, volunteering his services to the terrorist cell in Paris.

It was Volodine who proposed enrolling Sholom Schwartzbard in the conspiracy. Volodine had made his acquaintance through the arch-anarchist Emma Goldmann and considered Schwartzbard an excellent candidate for the role of assassin. Even Schwartzbard's weakness, his Jewish nationalism, could be manipulated by the Bolsheviks, as Ukrainians would be duped into believing that his was a hateful Jewish act of vengeance.

As Dobkovsky's deposition was read, the list of conspirators grew. Volodine. Schwartzbard. A friend of Schwartzbard's, an extreme leftist named Chreider. Norich.

Dobkovsky claimed that he himself was never intimately involved in the murder plot. In fact, at one point following the assassination, he tried to publish an article on the subject in a Czech journal. It was suppressed, he claimed, by Volodine, who had reversed roles with his onetime superior and was now Dobkovsky's watchdog. Afraid that the unreliable Dobkovsky might talk before he could be dealt with, Volodine had secured the necessary papers from the Russian consulate to return to the USSR.

Dobkovsky's deposition continued: "I demand the immediate arrest of Volodine, an anarchist and the accomplice of Schwartzbard. I demand an energetic investigation from you, Monsieur Prosecutor, to defend us against espionage and assaults. Confront me with Schwartzbard and Volodine."[27]

Confront indeed. The prosecution knew Dobkovsky's address, 5 Rue Bergere. Yet for some inexplicable reason, this vital witness was never called to testify in person at the Palace of Justice. Professor Koval's "absence" was unavoidable, but the failure to produce either Dobkovsky or the elusive Volodine could only be marked down as deliberate. Reynaud betrayed his own doubts about the statements charging Schwartzbard with conspiracy, when he said at the conclusion of the reading of Dobkovsky's deposition, "I have no other observations to make at present. I have simply introduced this document to the discussion. It is public, besides."[28]

When Schwartzbard was asked by Justice Flory to comment on the deposition, he said angrily, "The signatory of that letter had been to my house several times. I gave him assistance, as I gave assistance to everyone. He is a new Judas who plays his role as the old one played his role 1,900 years ago. There are two categories of Jews—the Christs and the Judases. He is a Judas."[20]

Now it was Dobkovsky's turn to be denounced from afar, in the deposition of Russian Social Democrat Vladimir Bourtzev. Bourtzev was a journalist who had criticized the Bolsheviks as German agents bent on destroying the morale of the Russian army during the war. Living in Paris, he had, with Gustave Herve, conducted a literary crusade against Communism. As for Dobkovsky, Bourtzev wrote that he had met the former in Paris in 1908. Though Dobkovsky tried to pass himself off as a revolutionary, he was considered "a traitor, an *agent provocateur* of the *ancien régime.*"

Loyalty was an elastic thing for Dobkovsky. Upon his return to Russia, he converted from Judaism to Orthodoxy. During the Revolution, he engaged in illegal expropriations, played both sides off against one another, and be-

trayed several companions when imprisoned. Revolution-
ary-royalist Dobkovsky served as an investigative magistrate
for Kerensky, then as an aide to Shapoval, then finally,
before coming to Paris again, as Vice-Commissar in the
Central Jewish Bolshevik Commissariat in Moscow. According to Bourtzev, Dobkovsky "has always been an extremely disagreeable and dangerous man," "a pathological
case who is not responsible for what he does."[30]

Bourtzev agreed that the Stalinist regime was involved in
foreign intrigue, but "There is no reason to admit that they
have any relation with this affair." As for Schwartzbard, he
had met him only once, in St. Petersburg, when Schwartzbard had just returned from the West "for the common
cause." Bourtzev came away with "the best impression" of
the accused and added, "All I know about his life is that he
was a very nice man and decidedly anti-Bolshevik."[31]

If Bourtzev recanted his statement about Dobkovsky following the trial, as was claimed by N. Kovalsky, Secretary of
the Simon Petlura Library in Paris,[32] such action hardly
enhanced the credibility of Dobkovsky's deposition, which
Torrès labeled the work of "the aggravated dementia of a
provocateur."

The whole idea of a Soviet plot to eliminate leading anti-
Bolsheviks was ludicrous. It presumed that the Bolsheviks,
who were able to march to the outskirts of Warsaw in 1920
when they were fighting elements of Ukrainian, Polish,
White Russian, French, Czech, Japanese, British, and American armies simultaneously, would have trembled at the
thought of a solitary Polish assault five years after consolidating their rule in the Ukraine.[33]

It presumed that Petlura, who failed to unify his countrymen before the humiliating treaty of Riga in March, 1921, a
treaty in which the Ukrainian National Movement was not
even dignified as a signatory, could have returned to the
Ukraine like some latter-day Taras Bulba and rallied the
Cossack Brotherhood against the Soviets.

It presumed that Poland, which had suffered through fourteen cabinets between 1922 and 1926, whose national parliament was torn among twenty-three political parties, whose currency was in a permanent state of decline, and whose army was riddled with mutinies, would have been interested in a "war of liberation" for the Ukrainians in 1926.

Perhaps the most serious flaw in the conspiracy theory concerned the alleged sequence of events. According to Dobkovsky, the Soviet assassination directive was issued in January, 1926, in response to Pilsudski's coup in Poland. But Pilsudski did not regain control of the Polish government until *May* of that year.

In June, 1926, the Soviet Ambassador to France, Rakovsky, made public a note to Torrès. In it, Rakovsky stated emphatically that Schwartzbard had no connection, official or otherwise, with the government of the USSR. In fact, it was reported, the accused assassin had even been denied a visa at the Soviet embassy in 1924 because he was known not to be pro-Soviet or pro-communist.[34]

Ukrainian reaction to this statement was one of undisguised mirth, as the Ukrainian Press Bureau in Paris announced it had sufficient evidence to demonstrate complicity on the part of the Soviets.[35] That evidence consisted of the word of Professor Koval, General Shapoval, Elie Dobkovsky, and the Ukrainian architect Nicholas Shumitzky, who demonstrated a classic case of paranoia at the trial, telling about "a band of suspicious men" who clustered near the hospital where Petlura was taken. "They didn't conceal their smiles," said Shumitzky.[36]

Would Moscow have bothered at all with Petlura, an exile living in poverty, when it might just as well have directed its efforts against Pilsudski, an actual power in a neighboring land? Petlura, who commanded no divisions, whose insurgent movement died out completely in 1921, was unable even to rally the forty thousand Ukrainians living on French soil, let alone the forty-five million who were under communist domination.

No such policy of terrorism existed, as the longevity of Petlura's anti-Bolshevik rivals attested. The anarchist Nestor Makhno died in bed in Paris in 1935. General Anton Denikin, criminal leader of the White Army, died of a heart attack in Ann Arbor, Michigan, in 1945, at the age of seventy-five. His successor as chief of the counter-revolutionary Rightist forces, Baron Peter Wrangel, died at the age of fifty in 1928. Paul Skoropadsky, the despised German puppet who ruled briefly as Hetman in 1918, lived to enjoy his last days under the Hitler regime in Berlin, fully twenty years after his downfall. And Marshal Pilsudski lived to the ripe age of sixty-eight, dying of natural causes in November, 1935.

The existence of a Bolshevik terrorist plot was seen in the subsequent assassinations of Eugene Konovalets, founder of the Ukrainian Military Organization, and Stephen Bandera, leader of the Organization of Ukrainian Nationalists. While there is little doubt that these two murders were ordered by Moscow, it strains credulity to suppose that they derived from Chicherin's meetings in *1926*. Petlura was killed in May of that year. But Konovalets was killed by a bomb on the streets of Rotterdam in *1938*, and Bandera was eliminated by a poison pistol in his apartment house in Munich in *1959*.[37] The same master scheme allegedly eliminated all three over the span of three decades, while Ukrainian generals such as Shapoval, Shkuro, and Shandruk ran free.

The evidence submitted to the Assize Court concerning Schwartzbard's ties with Moscow was to undergo a remarkable transformation at the hands of Ukrainian sympathizers in the next few years. If to Professor Demeter Doroshenko, Petlura's nameless killer was "more than probably" backed by Moscow,[38] then for the prestigious *Concise Encyclopedia of the Ukraine* there was no doubt. Schwartzbard flatly was "a Bolshevik agent."[39] In a single volume, Dr. Mykola

Kowalewskyj, Stephen Lenkawskyj, and Slawa Stetzko referred to Schwartzbard as "a Russian agent," "Soviet agent," "agent of Moscow," "Communist agent," "Russian communist hand," and "Jewish Communist."[40] A less than subtle libel was supplied in this devious work through the insertion of a photograph of the Rue Racine next to plates of other sites of alleged Soviet assassinations.

But the height of fantasy was concocted by General Pavlo Shandruk. According to him, the Bolsheviks kept Petlura under constant surveillance because they feared such "a very dangerous enemy." When Schwartzbard was tried in Paris, Shandruk maintains, he was "freed on bail furnished by the Bolsheviks."[41] Not a shred of new evidence was ever introduced to substantiate any of these charges.

Supporters of the slain Holovni Ataman might call Schwartzbard a Russian agent, or a Soviet spy, or a Jewish communist, but Torrès insisted, "I will not defend Schwartzbard on political issues! My client avenged his race, in which there are persons of many political beliefs. This isn't a political crime."[42]

Notes

1. *Notes Sténographiques*, fasc. 2, pp.174-180; fasc. 3, p.94.

2. *Notes Sténographiques*, fasc. 3, p.100.

3. *Ibid.*, p.111.

4. *Ibid.*, pp.91-92 and 97.

5. *Ibid.*, pp.100-107.

6. Extract of Official Journal of Laws for Territories of Ukrainian National Republic (*Vistnyk Derzhavnykh Zakoniv*), July 8, 1919, 21, p.1, 265; and August 26, 1919, 33, p.250, 490.

7. There was some question whether this was the sum total of all money set aside for relief of the pogrom victims. See *Notes Sténographiques*, fasc. 3, 109; and Pigido, *Material Concerning Ukrainian-Jewish Relations*, pp.78-102.

8. See Reports of the Kiev Central Committee for Aid to Pogrom Victims and the Joint Distribution Committee reports on Chudnov, Lukashova, Liubar and other victimized cities in Podolia Gubernia, Files 313 and 320, Tcherikover Archive. See also *Auslandishe hilfe far pogrom-gelitene*, File 564, and *Hilfe far pogrom-gelitene* File 564, Tcherikover Archive.

9. Moses Silberfarb, *Das yiddishe ministerium un di yiddishe avtanamie in Ukraine: a bletl geshichte* (Kiev: Yiddishe Folks-Farlag, 1918-19), pp.4-5. See also Oscar Janowsky, *The Jews and Minority Rights, 1898-1919*, pp.231-40; and Solomon Goldelman, *Zhydivska natsionalna autonomiia na Ukraini* (Munich: Institute for Study of USSR, 1963).

10. See *Minutes of Meetings of the Jewish National Council of the Jewish Ministry*, minutes of meetings, September, 1917, to August, 1918, File 1, Tcherikover Archive; N. Gergel, "The Jewish Ministry and the National Assembly," File 4, Tcherikover Archive; and Silberfarb, *Das yiddishe ministerium*, pp.26-39 and 80-81.

11. "Justice and Polity Demand Fair Treatment of the Jews," by Vishnitzer, in Batchinsky, *et al*, *The Jewish Pogroms in Ukraine*, p.22.

12. Whether autonomy was even feasible is discussed by Silberfarb, *Das yiddishe ministerium*, pp.39-62. Wrote Solomon Goldelman who served as Undersecretary, "It possessed no program, no shadow of independence." *Jews and Ukrainians* (Vienna, 1921), pp.24-25. For the dreary record of the Jewish Ministry see also Documents of the Jewish Ministry, Kiev, Files 5-15, Tcherikover Archive.

13. Revutzky, *In di shvere tog ofn Ukraine*, pp.99 and 140.

14. *Ibid.*, pp.144-46.

15. *Ibid.*, p.159.

16. In a telegram dated October 21, 1927, Revutzky told the Court from New York: "I ask you to lodge my categorical protest before the court against the utilization of my name during my absence in the defense of Petlura. Even as minister I have always expressed my political opposition to Petlura's conduct on pogroms. Mention my book published two years before Schwartzbard's act. Check importance, role, my resignation, February, 1919, first Minister Jewish Affairs." *Notes Sténographiques*, fasc. 4, pp.227-28.

17. Stenographic Protocol from the Trial of Ukrainian Social Revolutionaries at Kiev, 1921, in Tcherikover, *Di ukrainer pogromen*, p.185.

18. "Der yiddisher kommunist," Kharkov, April 6, 1919.

19. Choulguine, *L'Ukraine et le cauchemar rouge*, p.163. See also Krasny's statement in *Odeskia Novosti* (March 10, 1919) that "we support the Ukrainian government in the struggle against pogroms. Everything which can be done is being done. And if, despite that, there are pogroms, it is not the fault of the government."

20. *Notes Sténographiques*, fasc. 3, pp.58-67.

21. *Ibid.*, pp.114-116.

22. *Ibid.*, pp.117-118.

23. *Ibid.*, pp.121-126.

24. Deposition of Dobkovsky, *Notes Sténographiques*, fasc. 3, pp.5-6 and p.16.

25. For Dobkovsky's work, *La voix d'un Juif*, which had been narrated to Shapoval and somehow confiscated by Volodine, see File 476, 39175-99, Tcherikover Archive. For a more elaborate version, see Dobkovsky, *L'affaire Petlura-Schwartzbard* (Paris: Union Fédérative Socialiste, 1927.)

26. Choulguine, *L'Ukraine et le cauchemar rouge*, p.15.

27. *Notes Sténographiques*, fasc. 3, pp.9-10, and 24.

28. *Ibid.*, p.27.

29. *Ibid.*, p.25.

30. See Letter of Bourtsev to General Borisovich, File 430, 37131-34, Tcherikover Archive.

31. *Ibid.*

32. *En notre âme et conscience*, p.23. Because the Nazis hauled off the Petlura Library Collection during World War II, verification of this claim is difficult.

33. According to one Ukrainian source: "Stalin did promote a war scare in the summer of 1927, and Poland has always figured as an invasion route; the danger need not be from Poland alone, but from the Entente using Poland as a base. See Stalin, *Sochineniia*, Vol. IX, pp.326-27, where the British Tories, Pilsudski's Poland, and the Ukrainian emigre government all are related in Stalin's mind." Editorial report, University of Tennessee Press, fall, 1973. The comment cannot be easily refuted. One wonders, however, why neither Stalin nor the writer considered lumping American Republicans or Spanish Jesuits in the same conspiracy. History records that the Soviets made no pre-emptive strike against Poland at the time, and that later when the liberty of Poland was imperiled (in 1939) the "Entente" reacted tardily and without effectiveness.

34. *Heynt*, June 17, 1926, 53215, File 604, Tcherikover Archive.

35. File 413, 35796, May 15, 1927, Tcherikover Archive.

36. *Notes Sténographiques*, fasc. 4, p.225.

37. "Sowjetrussische Morde im Ausland and ihre Tarnungsver-suche," *Russischer Kolonialismus*, pp.343-60, and Shandruk, *Arms of Valor*, xxx. A better case might have been made for the inexplicable assassination of General Oskilko in June, 1926, in Kovno. The Ataman, who was one of Petlura's key aides, was mortally wounded in the heart as he lay asleep in bed. Police in Lithuania concluded that his assailant had been familiar with the layout of the house, but they were unable to establish any link with a Bolshevik conspiracy. The Jewish communities of Eastern Europe were well aware of the poten-tial of the Oskilko case when added to that of Petlura. See "Ver iz geven Ataman Oskilko." 53226, File 604, Tcherikover Ar-chive. See also 53225-27 in the same file.

38. Doroshenko, *History of Ukraine*, p.564.

39. *Ukraine: A Concise Encyclopedia*, ed. Volodymyr Kubijovyc (University of Toronto Press, 1963), I, p.770.

40. *Russischer Kolonialismus*, pp. 83,128,294,343,347,370.

41. "The French court freed Schwartzbard," Shandruk wrote, "and we should remember this." Shandruk, *Arms of Valor*, pp.144-145.

42. *New York Times*, October 20, 1927, p.11.

9.

Envoy to Bulgaria

THE TRIAL OF SHOLOM SCHWARTZBARD entered its fourth day. What little progress had been made met with increased criticism from impatient Paris newspapers, which brooded over the "sinister" or "mysterious" figure of the accused. Elsewhere, journalists condemned the continual excesses of both sides and hinted that perhaps a "pogrom of the witnesses" was in the making. Commented the correspondent for the *Jewish Tribune*:

> The entire case has the aspect of an open wound, pricked by too many surgical instruments—not all of them sterilized. This was especially true in the case of cross-examinations of witnesses. Too often, zealous counsels would be carried away by their own ardour and dissect their "victims." Then, like some ancient augur, they would lay out his entrails before the jury for inspection, point to some flaw in the testimony, and shout, "Liar!"[1]

Alexander Yakovich Shulgin, touted by some as the prosecution's "star" witness, was the first to testify on Friday, October 21. More than any of his predecessors on the witness stand, Shulgin had been intimately bound up in formulating government policy for the Ukraine in the postwar period. He had served the Central Rada in a minor capacity at Kiev as early as April, 1917. He was at Hrushevsky's side ten months later when the President proclaimed the independence of the Ukrainian Republic from Russia.

Shulgin had been Secretary of Nationalities for the short-lived Rada, and as such he directed the operations of the Polish, Russian and Jewish ministries. Late in 1917, the twenty-nine-year-old became acting Foreign Minister of the Republic. In the next four years, he served all Ukrainian governments loyally. Foreign Minister under the Rada, envoy to Bulgaria for Skoropadski, and representative to the Versailles Peace Conference for Petlura, he rationalized his actions by faith in the ultimate success of the Ukrainian national revolution. "A revolution," this Slavic Talleyrand had written, "is a period of illusions and disillusions, a period during which the mob dominates and the mob is an unstable element, infinitely changing."[2]

With the triumph of a Bolshevik "mob," Shulgin's dreams of a national state were dashed. He lectured on history at the University of Prague, founded the Ukrainian Academic Society in Paris, and served as Minister for External Affairs in the Ukrainian People's Republic Government In Exile. An articulate man, he should have had the answers to the terrible questions about pogroms for the Paris jury.

"I come not to defend the memory of Petlura, who was my friend and chief," he began, in a manner recalling Antony's eulogy for Caesar, "but to show that Schwartzbard has lied. He is not the avenger of the Jews but an agent of the Cheka. He was sent on the order of Moscow. I have come to that conclusion."[3]

Schwartzbard could not take refuge for his crime in the massacres of 1919, Shulgin argued, for not only Jews, but the entire Ukraine, especially the peasants, had suffered during the civil war. Poignantly, he described the uncontrollable plunder, the arbitrary confiscation of crops, the famines and starvation as wheat rotted in the fields or was despoiled by armed vandals. "It was anarchy without precedent. We can't understand it today. The pogroms took place in a special atmosophere, like the 'Great Fear' which has been described in French History."[4]

The worst pogroms took place early in 1919, "when the bandits of Denikin and Makhno terrorized the country and the Ukrainian Government was in the midst of war." That struggle was complicated by the entry of the Bolsheviks, promising the people immediate paradise. Petlura believed it was essential that the "Israelites" stand with the Ukrainian independence movement and did everything in his power to suppress the massacres. Professor Shulgin repeated this point no less than three times in the space of one minute of testimony. Petlura failed, however, because he did not hold supreme power.

"He certainly possessed military talents," said Shulgin, "and above all he knew the soul of the soldier, but he was not a soldier by profession." His rank of Ataman-in-Chief was merely a title of honor. True military authority lay with generals commanding line units. In like manner, the Ukrainian Directory bore no similarity to its French namesake. Again, real political power rested with party leaders who stayed in Kiev. Petlura was nothing but a figurehead president, ever moving about the country trying to enroll a citizen army.[5]

People had to understand, explained Shulgin, that the Bolshevik Revolution was not a simple thing. It was simultaneously an international war and a war between two distinct political and social systems. Historically, the Ukrainian peasants were "nationalist, individualist, certainly conservative." In 1919 they were also frustrated, "hypnotized by the power of revolution," and provoked by "dark forces," agitators who entered the ranks of the army with the purpose of inculcating hatred of Jews.

Jews, on the other hand, were primarily poor, humble artisans who reasoned, "To live as we do is bad; perhaps there is a better life. We want it." The alternative supposedly lay with the Bolsheviks.

"If you have some Jews who are very rich, who are very great financiers," declared Shulgin, "the majority are very poor. They live in the small towns and villages and they live miserably. They became communists."[6]

Zionists, socialists, it didn't matter. "When our Cossacks entered into battle with the Red Army, they often found at the head of the Bolshevik lines detachments composed exclusively of Jews."

One could not expect a soldier to "stop and think like an intellectual," Shulgin explained. It was impossible for Ukrainians to distinguish between Jews who fired at them and those who did not. As a result, the fury of the people against the communists was also unleased against the Jews.

"Our social struggle became a national struggle," said Shulgin. "That is why the peasants made pogroms. I swear that Petlura was not responsible. History will judge us."[7]

Historian Shulgin's testimony paralleled the thesis of his book *L'Ukraine et le cauchemar rouge (The Ukraine and the Red Nightmare)* and his memoir *Un crime mystérieux.* (The memoir was rushed into print in 1926 following Petlura's assassination.) Dedicated to the memory of "the most calumniated man of our time," these fables blamed the Bolsheviks for every wrong committed in postwar Russia. The Great Russians simply could not tolerate the independence of a once servile people, Shulgin argued. Moreover, the Ukraine provided a valuable testing ground for the Bolshevik plan of world domination and a convenient release for the energies of the Red Army, upon which the Soviet state rested. Without the Bolshevik invasion of the Ukraine in 1919, there would have been no pogroms.[8]

As for the Jews, they had brought much of their suffering upon themselves by refusing to serve in the Ukrainian army, by welcoming the Bolsheviks as deliverers, confiscating food supplies, and serving as commissars, Cheka agents, and Red Army soldiers.[9]

"A fact that seems incontestable to us," said Shulgin, "is that the workers and artisans, also some of the young Jews, whom the old Tsarist laws had prevented from receiving a good education, passed to the side of the Bolsheviks."[10] And later, with less generosity, he added, "If we study the military history of the fight against Soviet Russia, we will see that the enemy of the Ukraine found some allies in the Ukraine itself, and that it found them quite readily among the communist workers of the cities and towns. These were Jews."[11]

The specter of Bolshevism had long served to unite the Gentile population of the Ukraine against their Jewish scapegoats. For forty blood-stained years it had served the purposes of the Tsarist regime. During the German occupation, Jews in Smela, Belaya Tserkov, Verkhonieprosk, Ekaterinoslav and Kherson were charged with rumor-mongering, sedition, and circulating Bolshevik propaganda. Even the venerable *Alliance Israëlite*, which operated charitable and educational institutions in Russia, was accused of espionage on behalf of England and France.[12]

The libel endured beyond the World War. Jews were viewed as being indifferent toward what kind of government was established in the Ukraine. Jews had not proved their devotion to the republic by volunteering in droves to fight the invading Reds. They had not explicity declared their opposition to the Bolsheviks in a public declaration.

The journals *Vidrozhdennia* [RENAISSANCE], published by the Ministry of War and *Nova Rada*, the organ of the Socialist-Federalists, as well as the publications of intellectuals G. Siogobochny and A. V. Nikovski, published "reports" of Jewish women and children sniping at Ukrainian troops from the windows of synagogues, of old men betraying caches of arms to Bolshevik interlopers, of Jewish merchants who speculated with Ukrainian currency, and of

Jewish Red Guards who executed all Ukrainian prisoners simply because they were Ukrainians.[13]

As one historian put it:

> The inhabitants of South Russia knew what they had done to the Jews in the past; and they gathered that the Bolsheviks were, if not wholly Jewish, at least pro-Jewish. They therefore assumed that the Jews would support the Reds. . . . If Jews remained in the South, they obviously did so from the most dubious of motives.[14]

Ukrainians *knew* that it was the Jew Horovitz who, at the urging of Stalin, had called an All-Ukrainian Convention of Soviets on December 17, 1917, to subvert the Ukrainian independence movement.[15] They *knew* that the Cheka for the most part consisted of Jews.[16] They *knew* that many Jews were enrolling in the Bolshevik armies.[17] And they *knew* that without the communist organizations of the Jewish workers in the Ukraine, Bolshevism could not have succeeded in that region.[18]

They knew that the President of the Central Committee of the Russian Communist Party, Jacob Sverdlov, was a Jew. So were Grigorii Zinoviev (President of the Third International), A. A. Yoffe (chief Russian delegate to the peace negotiations at Brest-Litovsk), Maxim Litvinov (later Foreign Minister of the USSR), Karl Radek (propaganda chief), N. Riazanov (head of the Marx-Engels Institute in Moscow), and Leon Trotsky (founder and commander of the Red Army).[19] Ukrainians believed the rumor that Lenin himself had a Jewish mother.

Many prominent Soviet functionaries were in fact Jewish. But this no more established a Jewish-Bolshevik conspiracy against the Ukraine than the presence of the Jews Rochmananko, Frazer, and Haman in the ranks of the pogromchiks signified a united front between Ukrainian chauvinists and Semites.[20]

In the Jewish community council elections of 1917-18, elections held in 202 separate communities on the eve of the pogroms, non-socialist parties (Orthodox, Zionists, Jewish People's Party, etc.) received 65.4 percent of the vote. Only forty-six of the 125 members comprising the Jewish National Assembly in Kiev were of socialist affiliation (including such non-communist groups as the Bund and the Social Revolutionaries.)[21]

Of Communist party members and candidates canvassed as to nationality in 1922, 5.2 percent called themselves Jews. Jews comprised only 1.8 percent of the total Russian population,[22] but the party drew its main source of strength from towns and cities, urban areas where 80 percent of the Jewish people lived.[23] Of 1,773,000 Communist Party members in the Soviet Union in 1922, only 8,250 claimed to be Jews, and many of these, like Trotsky, had voluntarily renounced Judaism, even to the point of adopting Slavic names.[24]

If the Jews seemed to contribute more than their fair share of memoirs to the Bolshevik journal *Letopis Revoliutsii*, it was because literacy was almost unknown to 80 percent of the Ukrainian population. If the Jews seemed to hold a disproportionate number of high posts in the Communist regime, it was because the historic anti-Semitism and oppression in Russia had caused Jewish intellectuals to gravitate to Marxism earlier than their Gentile counterparts.

Even within the Bolshevik movement, the Jewish presence was not as formidable as one might suspect. The following chart, compiled by Solomon Schwarz, lists the number of Jews holding high office in the USSR in 1925-26. It shows that Jews were "over-represented" in only a few areas.[25]

POSITION	OFFICE HOLDERS	JEWS	PCT.
Central Committee, Soviet Union	104	11	10.6
Central Control Commission, Soviet Union	162	13	8.0
Presidium, Central Executive, Russian Republic	37	2	5.4
Council of People's Commissars, Soviet Union	12	0	0.0
Council of People's Commissars, Russian Republic	14	0	0.0
Chairmen of Communist Parties and Central Executive Committees of National Republics, and Chairman of Provincial Executive Committees	88	1	1.1
Presiding Judges of Provincial Tribunals	66	4	6.1
Provincial Public Prosecutors	66	3	4.5
Presidents of Industrial Trusts	54	4	7.4
Leading officials in central agencies and cooperatives	194	21	10.8

In response to Shulgin's rantings about the number of Jewish leaders in Moscow, Defense Counsel Torrès pointed out that *the Jews accounted for 10 percent of the Ukrainian population, while only 1.5 percent of the members of the Ukrainian Bolshevik party were Jewish.*[26]

Only 4,364 persons in the Ukraine registered as Bolsheviks in the census of July, 1918. At the height of the pogrommania, in March, 1919, the total of combined Jewish and Gentile Communist Party members was 16,363, hardly sufficient to stigmatize three million Jews as Bolshevik sympathizers.[27]

Arnold Margolin and Julian Batchinsky, both officers in the Directory, conceded that if there was pro-Russian sentiment among some Jews, it stemmed not from radicals, but from assimilationists, Jewish refugees who were strangely attached to the land which persecuted them, and from some bourgeois sympathizers of the White Armies.[28] Wrote Margolin, "The left wing and advanced parties of the left were not very numerous."[29] Most Jews were in sympathy with the ideals of Wilson and favored the establishment of a moderate socialist state.

Far from shunning the Directory, as Professor Shulgin claimed, the Jewish National Assembly in Kiev (125 delegates elected by 209,128 voters), the supreme organ of Ukrainian Jewry, "saluted" the November coup of Petlura and "the triumph of Ukrainian Democracy" in a resolution communicated to Premier Vinnichenko in December, 1918.[30] During the same month, affirmations of loyalty were received from the Jewish Democratic Union, the League of Jewish Culture, the Jewish People's University, the Ukrainian Association of Jewish Cooperative Societies, the Central Committee of the Socialist Bund, the United Socialists, and the Jewish People's Party.[31]

Though not blind to the chauvinistic tendencies of the Directory, Jews believed in the possibility of amicable relations with the government because of its much-publicized democratic base. It was not until March, 1919, as pogroms raged in every district of the Ukraine, that Jews generally boycotted elections and disdained government assistance for pogrom victims.

The question of Jewish loyalty was answered repeatedly on the battlefield, where Jewish Ukrainians fell side by side with their Gentile countrymen.[32] Jews marched together with Rada insurgents in Galicia when the Revolution broke out in March, 1917.[33]

Jews offered themselves for service in the Directory's army at Kostyshev, Romny, Cherkassy, Proskurov, Konotop, Kaharlik, and Zhitomir, but they were summarily rejected. The reason, according to Colonel Oskilko (Commander-in-Chief of the Southwest Front) and Colonel Palij (commandant of forces in Chernigov and Poltava) was that for the moment the Directory had decided not to accept *any* Jews. In 1919, it was said, "We cannot commit our national cause to Jews."[34] A more candid explanation was offered by the Ataman Zeleny, who turned down a deputation of Jews near Kiev which had come to volunteer thirty-two men to his ranks. Said Zeleny, "I don't need Jewish soldiers. I need Jewish money."[35]

There were, however, some exceptions to the policy of rejecting Jewish recruits. Ex-ministers Silberfarb and Revutzky agreed that Petlura ordered the creation of specially segregated Jewish units, *Yiddishe militer farband*. These units were sent to the most dangerous zones, where they served three functions: First, they might blunt the advance of White, Red, or Polish armies; second, they reduced the population of Jewish males; and third, they removed from the towns the men who might best be able to protect citizens from pogroms.[36]

In view of what happened at Proskurov, Felshtin, and Zhitomir, it is incredible that any Jews volunteered for service in the Ukrainian army corps. Despite the hypocrisy of the government, Ukrainian leaders would subsequently complain, "Not one single Jew reported on mobilization."[37]

It was Shulgin's contention that depressed and declassed Jews formed the nucleus of Bolshevik strength in the Ukraine, for they regarded the Reds as apocalyptic deliverers. In reality, this was not so. Brutalized in at least 196

communist massacres, especially in those regions held by
the turncoat Ukrainian Tarasha Regiment, the Jews regarded all combatants in the Civil War with terror.[38]

Vladimir Korolenko, one of Shulgin's Gentile countrymen, wrote in September, 1919, that "the poorer class of Jews
suffers most" from Bolshevik pogroms, that hundreds of
Jews lay dying in Bolshevik prisons.[39] These were Shulgin's
so-called "Cheka agents."

Finally given the opportunity to respond to all of this, a
livid Schwartzbard erupted: "I would only remind M. Shulgin, who is an historian and not a soldier—M. Shulgin has a
good memory, but he hasn't said anything of the pogroms at
Proskurov and Zhitomir. The magistrate asked him three
times if he knew of the pogroms of Zhitomir and he didn't
respond. Three times the judge asked him and he didn't
respond. *Voilà!"*

A Jewish shop in Zhitomir, January 1919.

"Are you asking him?" Justice Flory inquired.

"Yes," said Schwartzbard. "The second thing. M. Shulgin is a competent historian. He remembers what happened at Kiev in 1910-11. It was said in the capital of the Ukraine that the Jews were taking blood from Christians. Now in 1927 M. Shulgin, who is an historian, who knows well what happened in 1910 and 1911 at Kiev, cannot come here to Paris before the jury to say that Schwartzbard killed Petlura because he is a Jew. Schwartzbard killed Petlura because he is a Bolshevik! *Voilà!*"

"Because he is a Bolshevik," Shulgin repeated.

Schwartzbard then alluded to the Beiliss ritual murder libel: "Because he took blood from Christians in 1910. M. Shulgin can't say *that* because that can't be. But he says I am a Bolshevik." The defendant was on his feet, flailing the air with his clenched fists. Reporters claimed that he became incoherent, screaming, "You . . . ! You . . . !"

"Please respond," Justice Flory directed Shulgin.

"I will reply to the President, not to Schwartzbard."

Flory, with some impatience: "Respond!"

Actually, it was not the magistrate who had posed the question about Proskurov and Zhitomir; it was Schwartzbard himself during the preliminary interrogation. Shulgin had chosen to ignore the question. As for the Beiliss Affair, Shulgin argued that Schwartzbard had confused him with the anti-Semitic newspaper editor V. V. Shulgin. "I've never made anything of the ritual murder question," he said. "I was very young and opposed to the Tsarist regime."

Continuing, Shulgin said: "Schwartzbard is no avenger, but a simple Austrian house-breaker. He is not even an idealist. Schwartzbard is an agent of the Cheka, yes. Yes, that is it. But he isn't an avenger of the Jews. Perhaps he isn't a Bolshevik himself. An agent of his kind doesn't need to share the opinions of those who pay him."[40]

Schwartzbard continued to scream, "Prove it! Prove it then!"

Torrès joined the fray. "You claim to be an historian," he said. "You tell us of the preparation of a book on Voltaire and one on Jean-Jacques Rousseau. As an historian, you were in 1918, for some months, while that one [Schwartzbard] fought for us . . ."

The Defense Counsel was interrupted by Shulgin, who asked, "For you?"

"Yes," continued Torrès, his own voice showing increased irritation with the witness, "for us. This Jew fought for France. At that time, you were, you served with a good friend of France named Ferdinand of Bulgaria, as Ambassador of the Ataman Skoropadsky, another protégé of the Germans. I ask you if that is true?"

"Yes, it is true, but I am going to respond."

"Well, I am going to sit down" Torrès announced sarcastically. "Present yourself to the jury, Monsieur former Ambassador of Ataman Skoropadsky, that man imposed on the Ukraine by the Germans. *You* are going to speak about the Ukrainian national movement?"

Shulgin protested. "Will you permit me to talk? I can shout as loudly as you, but it is not with shouts that I shall reply. It is with arguments."

Directed by Flory to answer the question, Shulgin again snapped that he would not speak to Torrès but to the jury. Torrès had conjured up images of the Great War, implying that Shulgin had by his service in Bulgaria favored the cause of the Central Powers.

Moreover, Torrès implied that Shulgin had been a party to the treaty of Brest-Litovsk, which culminated in Russia's capitulation before the Central Powers in February, 1918. This was in violation of a personal pledge given three months earlier in Kiev to General Tabouis, chief of staff of General Anselme's French military mission in Odessa, that as Foreign Minister he, Shulgin, would never conclude an armistice with the Kaiser without first obtaining the consent of the Allies.[41]

Defending himself, Shulgin maintained that Brest-Litovsk had been a *fait accompli* on the part of the Bolsheviks.[42] Why the Ukraine, which had declared its independence in December, 1917, was bound by this accord, he did not say. But because Shulgin was troubled by his own role in the negotiations, he resigned his post as Foreign Minister before the actual signing of the treaty. Petlura also resigned from the Rada government about the same time.

As for laboring for Skoropadsky, Shulgin rationalized that the German puppet was only a transient ruler. The important thing was to serve the interests of the Ukrainian state, which would endure long after Skoropadsky had gone. He went to Sofia because he knew that Ferdinand was ready to quit the war and was interested in opening communications with the Allies. No one could question his pro-democratic credentials, said Shulgin, since after the war he had been warmly received in Paris by Clemenceau, Lloyd-George, and Wilson.[43]

Relentlessly, Torrès hammered at Shulgin's relations with Ferdinand, inadvertently referring to the latter at one point as "King of Rumania." With great exasperation, Shulgin again volunteered that there was a shortage of men qualified to represent the Ukraine in the diplomatic service.

"Ferdinand knew full well I was for peace," said Shulgin, "and so did the French generals who came to Bulgaria." He had even told Ferdinand, "It is necessary to end the war." And finally, "No one can say Monsieur Alexander Shulgin has not been a friend of France. I am a friend of France. I was in 1917. I was the representative of the Ukraine to the League of Nations. I was named chief of the mission to France. I have conducted relations with France and never before today, for the first time, have I ever heard it said that I am not a Francophile."[44]

On the second key point of Shulgin's testimony, Schwartzbard's alleged Bolshevik connections, Torrès lectured at length. He referred again to Langevin's testimony

and to Schwartzbard's membership in the League of Human
Rights, adding a reference here and there to Semosenko and
Ferdinand. He reminded Shulgin that Schwartzbard admit-
ted to being an anarchist, and that the anarchists and
Bolsheviks had waged bloody battles against one another in
Russia.

"Quite false!" intruded Shulgin.

"I would be obliged, monsieur, if you did not interrupt
me when I speak," said Torrès, and he asked bluntly what
proof Shulgin possessed that Schwartzbard was a Bolshevik.

"Gentlemen of the jury," Shulgin began, "when a witness who is probably dangerous for M. Torrès . . ."

"Not at all!" objected Torrès.

" . . . is presented here, they seek to compromise him
before you. But they find nothing against me about which I
have not already testified. When they see there is nothing to
be found, they repeated this same thing, in louder cries.
When one has no arguments, he shouts all the louder. But I
have arguments and I have explained very simply that
which is."

Torrès answered patiently, "I tolerate those words on the
part of M. Shulgin, but I will not tolerate them from any
other witness. I say it very clearly."

Campinchi, obviously delighted: "Are you asking protection against a witness? Indeed! You go too far!"

"I ask no protection. I am only astonished that you do not
disassociate yourself from his behavior, since this witness is
permitted to speak in such a tone to an advocate."

As the two attorneys exchanged barbs about Shulgin,
Ferdinand, and Bulgaria, the witness pleaded, "If you will
let me explain, I would like to speak."[45]

Shulgin maintained that Torrès' argument about
Schwartzbard's membership in the League of Human
Rights was irrelevant, for he knew of many agents who used
humanitarian organizations as a cover for their real beliefs.

"I can have respect for my enemy if he is a communist of

conviction," said Shulgin, "but if he is an anarchist who acts for the Bolsheviks, it is worse." Schwartzbard had been designated by Moscow to assassinate Petlura, first because the Kremlin recognized that the Ukraine was a nest of partisan activity, and second because of the return to power in 1926 of Marshal Pilsudski. "I have the absolute conviction based on information that Schwartzbard acted as an agent of the Bolsheviks."[46]

To this, Torrès snapped, "It is no proof at all, but an 'absolute conviction' about whose value and character the jurors may judge."

Shulgin remained at the bar for another hour, as the opposing counsels continued to quarrel over the true sympathies of the Ukrainian nationalists in the last days of World War I. What might have seemed a trivial point, Shulgin's mission to Bulgaria, or even Petlura's service in the Skoropadsky government, was deemed especially critical in trying to influence the French jury.

If Torrès required proof of Shulgin's or Petlura's Francophilia, Civil Prosecutor Campinchi was willing to accommodate. He produced two letters, written in May, 1927, one from General Tabouis, the other from Colonel Freydenberg of the Allied Mission to the Ukraine in 1919.

From Marrakesh, Freydenberg had written to affirm that Petlura was an "altruist," a true friend of France, who had done everything in his power to suppress pogroms.[47] This character witness, Freydenberg, was the same man who had responded with cold indifference to the revival of Black Hundreds' propaganda and pogroms when stationed at Odessa. At that time, Arnold Margolin had appealed to Freydenberg to issue a strong public statement in the name of France or the Entente condemning pogroms. Margolin also suggested that two or three battalions of French troops could secure the railway lines from Birzula to Vinnitza and from Zhmerinka to Proskurov. Freydenberg's response, which Margolin could never forget or forgive was: "The

Entente does not want to interfere with internal matters of the Ukraine."[48]

General Tabouis required more time. Before reading from his letter, Campinchi reminded the court that Tabouis had been a war hero, one of the youngest division commanders in that conflict. "He even took a German flag with his own hands."

Campinchi read from Tabouis' deposition: "I cannot forget the good relationship that I enjoyed with the Ataman and the patriotic ardor with which Petlura worked in this little office improvised by Colonel K. at forming a Ukrainian army to fight with our troops in trying to stop the breakup of Russia. . . . I understand the sorrow which you must feel in defending the memory of this man against slanders from purely political and not religious adversaries which are intended to stain his memory . . . To say that Petlura was an anti-Semite! What a joke!" The letter ended: "I have seen the dissolution of all my aspirations, which were the same as yours."[49]

Campinchi's claim that the Allied Mission was sympathetic to the Directory, let alone shared its goals, was as fatuous as Shulgin's assertion that the Ukrainian Republic had not been a party to the Treaty of Brest-Litovsk.[50] When Tabouis first approached Shulgin in November, 1917, and secured the promise that the Ukraine would not abandon the Allies through a separate peace with Germany, it was done with the understanding that the Allies could not offer immediate assistance in the form of manpower. Both Shulgin and Tabouis knew that the Ukraine stood little chance of withstanding a combined Bolshevik-German assault. When, therefore, Foreign Minister Shulgin announced a policy of "armed neutrality" on December 24, 1917, it was done in the belief that at worst the Ukraine would be occupied, like Belgium or Serbia, but would remain on the side of "civilization."

Two months after this policy was formulated, a Ukrainian delegation, not headed by Shulgin but carrying his blessing, gained legal recognition from the Central Powers at Brest-Litovsk. The free Ukraine was recognized at the cost of removing a threat of a second front against Germany, Austria, Bulgaria, and Turkey. At this point, allegedly to indicate his disapproval of the shift in policy, the Foreign Minister resigned and took the post in Sofia.[51]

The prosecution then dredged up a sixty-three-year-old chemical engineer, Albert Baudry, to testify that Simon Petlura was a man who had been most favorable to the Allied cause. The Holovni Ataman had been shot "because he was a friend of France susceptible of aiding the reconstruction of Russia by itself."[52]

Baudry had been in the Ukraine for twenty-nine years, directing an agricultural station. He had to be believed by a French jury because he was a Frenchman himself. Baudry credited Petlura with getting four hundred thousand troops into the line for the disastrous summer offensive of 1917, which, despite the outcome, tied up "seven to eight hundred thousand of the best German troops."

Baudry claimed that Petlura had opposed the defeatists Golobovich and Vinnichenko, the signers of the Brest-Litovsk accord. His attitude was always: "Down with traitors. Long live the Allies. Continue the war." When the Germans occupied the Ukraine one of their first acts was to throw Petlura into jail "because he represented the national element."

Duped by defeatists, stripped of heroes like Petlura, and enslaved anew by landholders in league with the Germans, the Ukrainian people never despaired of working against the Central Powers. Germany was compelled to station 350,000 troops in the Ukraine to maintain order, troops which could have been used against the Allies elsewhere. "I can assure you that 350,000 men were insufficient to maintain order," said Baudry.[53]

Nevertheless, Petlura accepted the post of Ataman-in-

Chief of anti-Bolshevik forces from the same defeatist Golo-bovitch in January, 1918. The following month, General Tounavich, commanding the Austro-German forces fighting the Red Army near Kiev, called upon all Ukrainians to welcome and collaborate with his troops, which included nationalist units under the command of Simon Petlura.[54] Petlura was now subject to commands of the Central Powers, although his supporters claimed he accepted this charge only to "preserve Ukrainian honor and prevent the Germans from taking Kiev."

Apparently the Holovni Ataman operated under no constraints when he unctuously wrote to the German and Austrian ambassadors in "the liberated city": "On behalf of the citizens of my country I would like to thank the powerful friends, Germany and Austria, who aided my people in realizing their national and historic ideal, which was achieved at the greatest sacrifice. I would wish that Germany and Austria, who were the first to recognize the popular Ukrainian republic as an independent state, would always remain in the heart and memory of the popular conscience, which has demonstrated a true friendship for them. I would wish that our people manifest to you its recognition for the historic services rendered to the Ukraine."[55]

The Allies never forgave the Ukrainians their duplicity in the Brest-Litovsk negotiations or their subsequent service in the Austro-German army corps. Herbette wrote in February, 1918: "The people of Kiev merit our contempt, and, if they want it, our vengeance."[56]

When the Directory sought assistance against the Bolsheviks in the spring of 1919, the French, through the very same Freydenberg who praised Shulgin and Petlura in 1927, submitted a list of punitive demands to the Ukrainian delegates. The Directory was to form an army of 300,000 men, under the Allied Command at Odessa. For the duration of the struggle against the Bolsheviks, all railroads and state finances were to be placed under French control. The matter of Ukrainian independence would be deferred and ultimately determined by the major powers in the West. And finally, the Directory would make a formal appeal to France to accept the Ukraine as a "protectorate."[57]

All of these demands were rejected by the Ukrainians as tantamount to "colonization." Even Arnold Margolin conceded that far from thinking of the Ukraine in the same sense as the nationalists, that is, as an emerging nation-state, the French were interested only in setting up another "buffer" republic in the East akin to Poland and Czechoslovakia, over which Gallic influence would be supreme.[58]

The goals of the Entente could hardly be described as "the same as" those of the Directory. And if Petlura was "at all times favorable to the Entente," as Professor Shulgin claimed, this feeling was by no means shared by Freydenberg or Tabouis. Character witnesses in Paris in 1927, the two French officers had warned Ukrainian emissaries at Odessa in 1919 that any future recognition of a Ukrainian Republic by France would be contingent upon the exclusion from the government of Directory President Vinnichenko, Council of Ministers Chairman Chekhovsky, *and* Holovni Ataman Simon Petlura.

Vinnichenko and Chekhovsky were reproached for their alleged "Bolshevism." As for Petlura, the same Colonel Freydenberg who spoke so eloquently on his behalf in 1927 told Pinchas Krasny in 1919: *"Petlura alone is a pogromchik. His army is a pogrom band. We have specific proof of this on our staff."*[59] To another member of the delegation, Dr. Ossip Nazarouk, Freydenberg added, "One does not collaborate with a leader of bandits."[60]

Notes

1. "At the Schwartzbard Trial in Paris," *Jewish Tribune*, October 21, 1927, p.5.

2. Reshetar, *The Ukrainian Revolution*, p.46.

3. Testimony of Shulgin, *Notes Sténographiques*, fasc. 4, pp.17-18.

4. *Ibid.*, pp.20-22.

5. *Ibid.*, pp.29-31.

6. *Ibid.*, pp.37-39.

7. *Ibid.*, pp.40-41. See also *Figaro*, October 22, 1927, p.2.

8. *Un crime mystérieux: Mémoire de Alexandre Choulguine* (Paris, 1926, 71 pp.), File 450, Tcherikover Archive, p.22.

9. *Ibid.*, pp.51-61. Ukrainians have made much of the charge of Solomon Goldelman that the Jewish socialists adopted a pro-Moscow orientation in the latter part of 1918. (See the recently translated *Zhydivs'ka natsional'na avtonomiia na Ukraini* by Goldelman, the last section of Chapter Six.) Ironically, little attention is paid to the explanations offered by Goldelman in his other work, *In goles bay di Ukraine*, where Moscow is viewed as a potential protector against chaos and pogroms such as the one at Proskurov. Even more ironic is the weight given to Goldelman, a minor bureaucrat, by Ukrainian historians who hastened to translate his only manuscript into Ukrainian while the works of more important figures such as Silberfarb, Revutzky, and Tcherikover, which tended to por-

tray the Holovni Ataman in an unfavorable light, remained in Yiddish.

10. Choulguine, *L'Ukraine et le cauchemar rouge*, pp.85-89.

11. *Ibid.*, p.91.

12. *Les pogromes en Ukraine*, pp.26-27.

13. Jews were simultaneously accused of being *boorzhui* and of having links with the Poles and Bolsheviks. *Les pogromes en Ukraine*, pp.23-26.

14. Richard Luckett, *The White Generals: An Account of the White Movement and the Russian Civil War* (London: Longman Ltd., 1971), pp.285-86.

15. Martowych, *Ukrainian Liberation Movement in Modern Times*, p.45.

16. Choulguine, *L'Ukraine et le cauchemar rouge*, p.90.

17. *Ibid.*, p.93.

18. The source was Moishe Rafes of the Jewish Social Democrat Bund. The energetic Rafes served as Controller of the Ukrainian Republic, then just as eagerly contributed to the development of a Soviet Ukraine. See M.G. Rafes, *Dva goda revoliutsii na Ukraine* (Moscow: Gosizdat, 1920), p.164.

19. Baron, *The Russian Jew under Tsars and Soviets*, p.202.

20. Tcherikover explains that in the midst of the storm that blew through the Ukraine, it was not remarkable to find elements of the Jewish underworld joining the pogromchiks "here and there." Tcherikover, *Di ukrainer pogromen*, pp.138 and 232.

21. Schechtman, *et al*, *The Pogroms in the Ukraine*, p.43. For an intensive analysis of Jewish participation in Bolshevik ranks, see also *Quelques commentaires des annexes du mémorandum de M. A. Choulguine* by J.Schechtman, Paris, 1927, File 459, Tcherikover Archive, pp.38482-3.

22. Solomon Schwarz, *The Jews in the Soviet Union* (Syracuse: University Press, 1951), p.261.

23. *Ibid.*, p.12.

24. Schechtman, *et al*, *The Pogroms in the Ukraine*, p.43.

25. Schwarz, *The Jews in the Soviet Union*, p.262.

26. Torrès, *Le procès des pogromes*, p.98. Dmytryshyn claimed that 6,981 of 54,818 party members in the Ukraine or 13.6 percent of the membership in April, 1922, were Jews. *Moscow and the Ukraine*, p.240. Of that number, however, only 715 were former Bundists, and 308 were former members of other Jewish parties. Only 1,887 gave Yiddish as their mother language, another indication of their estrangement from their accidental Jewish roots. See Gitelman, *Jewish Nationality and Soviet Politics*, p.220.

27. M. Yavorski, "Tzu der geshichte fun der kommunistisher partay in Ukraine," in *Di Oktober Revolutzia: Yubiley Zamlbuch* (Kharkov, 1922), pp.100-110, and M. Ravich-Cherkasi, *Istoria Kommunisticheskoi Partii (B) na Ukraine* (1923, Kiev?), p.109.

28. Batchinsky, *et al, The Jewish Pogroms in the Ukraine*, p.5 and 17.

29. *Ibid.*, p.17. Even Pidhainy concedes, "The trust the Jewish people had in the Ukrainian Rada is seen to have been great." *The Formation of the Ukrainian Republic*, p.221.

30. See *Minutes of the Meeting of the Jewish National Assembly in the Ukraine, Kiev, November,1918*, and *Minutes of Meetings of the Special Conference of the Small National Assembly, September-October, 1919*, Files 2 and 3, Tcherikover Archive.

31. Schechtman, *et al, The Pogroms in the Ukraine*, p.26, and *Les pogromes en Ukraine*, pp.29-31.

32. See *Yiddishe zelbstshutz in Ukraine*, file 566, and *Yidn in dos militar*, File 405, Tcherikover Archive.

33. *Les pogromes en Ukraine*, p.11.

34. Tcherikover, *Di ukrainer pogromen*, pp. 73-74, and Schechtman, *et al, The Pogroms in the Ukraine*, pp.53-54.

35. *Meldung fun Kaharlik*, by Yakopo Petrokovski, in Tcherikover, *Di ukrainer pogromen*, p.74.

36. Revutzky, *In di shvere tog ofn Ukraine*, p.284.

37. Vladimir Vinnitchenko,*The Renaissance of a Nation* (Kiev and Vienna: 1920), III, p.187.

38. For a survey of Bolshevik atrocities, see Gergel, "The Pogroms

in the Ukraine, 1918-1921," p.246. See also reports of the Kiev Central Relief Committee detailing Bolshevik atrocities in 1919, File 320, Tcherikover Archive, and Choulguine, *Un crime mystérieux*, p.43. For a brief resumé of Jewish volunteers in the Red Army see File 544, Tcherikover Archive.

39. *Massacres and Atrocities*, p.57.

40. *Notes Sténographiques*, fasc. 4, pp.50-52. See also newspaper account in *New York Times*, October 22, 1927, p.6.

41. Similar pledges were exchanged between Great Britain's Picton Bagge and the Council of Ministers. The Soviets contemptuously referred to these arrangements with the Allies as "piteous sell-outs," the end of which was to convert the Ukraine into a protectorate for fifty years. Serge, *Year One of the Russian Revolution*, pp.338-340.

42. Choulguine, *L'Ukraine et le cauchemar rouge*, p.28.

43. *Notes Sténographiques*, fasc. 4, pp.57-58.

44. *Ibid.*, pp.68-69.

45. *Ibid.*, pp.59-65.

46. *Ibid.*, p.71.

47. Deposition of Freydenberg, *Notes Sténographiques*, fasc. 4, pp.82-83.

48. Arnold Margolin, *Ukraina i politika antanty: Zapiski bureya i grazhdanina* (1922), p.126.

49. Deposition of Tabouis, *Notes Sténographiques*, fasc. 4, pp.76-81.

50. A claim made in Choulguine, *L'Ukraine et le cauchemar rouge*, p.28.

51. Another fantastic excuse for Shulgin's behavior was offered by Albert Baudry, who claimed that the Foreign Minister knew early in 1918 that the Germans were going to lose the war. Shulgin supposedly wanted to let Ferdinand know of this and the imminent collapse of the Skoropadsky regime. Considering the relative stability enjoyed by the Ukraine under the Hetmanate and the ability of the Germans to mount an offensive in the West that summer, this theory attributes prophetic powers to Shulgin. *Notes Sténographiques*, fasc. 5, p.93.

52. Deposition of Baudry, September 16, 1926, File 451, 38063, Tcherikover Archive.

53. Testimony of Baudry, *Notes Sténographiques*, fasc. 5, pp.76-90.

54. Report of Tounavitch, Feb. 25, 1918, *Notes Sténographiques*, fasc. 4, p.160.

55. *Ibid.*, p.153. Despite this and other forms of collaboration, the court was fairly deluged with depositions charging that (1) Petlura opposed the Treaty of Brest-Litovsk, (2) Petlura was a Social Democrat who opposed pogroms, and (3) Petlura was always a Francophile who was imprisoned for his pro-Allied beliefs after Brest-Litvosk. See Depositions of Serghi Berejni, Feb. 8, 1927, 36667-70 and A.Degtiarev, 36670-78, File 423; Vladimir Salski, November 29, 1926, 38055-6, Serge Kochora, Dec. 11, 1926, 38054, Vasily Pedalko, Feb.5, 1927, 37993-99, Leonid Martiniuk, Feb. 5, 1927, and Slavinsky, 38040, File 451, Tcherikover Archive.

56. *Temps*, Feb. 11, 1918. When Torrès attempted to read this selection, Campinchi grabbed the article from his hands and played a most undignified game of keep-away. While Torrès bleated before Justice Flory, Campinchi taunted him, "Fish! Fish! Shout! Shout!" *Notes Sténographiques*, fasc. 5, pp.126-143.

57. Yurij Borys, *The Russian Communist Party and the Sovietization of Ukraine* (Stockholm, 1960), p.217.

58. Excerpts from Margolin's *Ukraina i politika* in *Annals of the Ukrainian Academy of Arts and Sciences in the US*, VII (1959), p.1469.

59. *Proletarskaia Pravda* (Kiev), 96 and 98, 1927.

60. Ossip Nazarouk, *Une année en Grande-Ukraine, Souvenirs de le révolution ukrainienne* (Vienna, 1920), p.217.

10.

The Clans of Death

PROFESSOR SHULGIN HAD ONCE WRITTEN: "We are compelled to acknowledge that several pogroms were made by undisciplined detachments of the Ukrainian Army, either at the moment of a sudden retreat or at the moment of battle against the enemy."[1]

Petlura's supporters admitted that "several" excesses had indeed been committed by regulars in the midst of civil war anarchy. These incidents, however, by no means constituted a general policy on the part of the Directory. Many a cutthroat or bandit found temporary refuge in the nationalist ranks. That some of these hooligans were of Ukrainian descent was regrettable, but the people and government of the Ukraine could no more be held accountable for their actions than could the American people as a whole be identified with lynch mobs in the South.[2]

When the Prosecution had finished with Professor Shulgin, his place at the bar was taken by Alexander Oudovichenko, another in the seemingly endless line of onetime Ukrainian war heroes who had fallen on hard times. Now a common laborer, the thirty-nine-year-old Oudovichenko had once commanded Petlura's crack "Iron Battalion." During the summer of 1920, he led the 2nd Division, which spearheaded the thrust of Ukrainian-Polish troops to the gates of Kiev.

In France, he became the leader of the Society of Ukrainian Veterans, a position not dissimilar to that of Sholom Schwartzbard, who headed the Jewish War Veterans in that country. According to Professor Shulgin, Oudovichenko was a man well-grounded in Jewish-Ukrainian relations. Through Oudovichenko's humanitarian restraint in the face of Jewish provocation, a pogrom was averted at Kamenetz-Podolsk in the spring of 1919.[3] Such a man could truly exonerate Petlura.

Speaking in Ukrainian, Oudovichenko again affirmed that the massacres only rarely had been the work of regular elements of the Ukrainian National Army. Unwittingly, he supported Schwartzbard's contention that bigotry was endemic to the Ukraine, saying, "I believe that anti-Jewish hatred was especially strong among the Ukrainians since the Beiliss Trial in Kiev, and also because the Tsarist Government tried artificially to stimulate anti-Jewish feeling among the Ukrainian peasants."

Simon Petlura, a man who had complete respect for the rights of citizens and property, had done everything in his power to prevent pillaging. As proof, Oudovichenko cited the arrest and execution of two Cossacks who had sacked a Jewish shop. "But," he declared, "it was always very difficult for leaders to have enough influence on their troops. In the ranks there was much subversive activity." The pogroms, he concluded, were generally spontaneous outbursts on the part of enraged local populations, and very rarely the work of the Ukrainian Army.[4]

Defense Counsel Torrès was infuriated. "The deposition of the witness calls for some interest because he was himself the organizer and maker of pogroms among regular troops who fought under his command and under the supreme command of General Petlura," he said.

"No!"

"I have official documents proving that on May 24 and June 11, 1919, soldiers under your command committed pogroms in Ourinine and Shargorod!"

"That is not true!" responded Oudovichenko. "My troops were never in the places you mention." The General insisted that his units were in Austrian territory at the specified dates, not in the places mentioned by Torrès.

"An official report says they were," said Torrès. He began to read from a report of the Jewish Ministry, when he was interrupted by the witness.

"It isn't true. Quite the contrary, at Shargorod," now conceding that he had been in the disputed town, "there was simply a little pillage which was made by disorderly soldiers and this pillage was immediately stopped by the service company."

When Torrès inquired sarcastically if the one hundred Jews killed at Shargorod had committed suicide, Oudovichenko repeated, "I declare that during all my marches across the Ukraine, I don't recall a single case where a single Jew perished at the hands of the men of the 2nd Division."

Reminded of the Sanielkov pogrom perpetrated by his subordinate Colonel Shandruk, Oudovichenko conceded that the town had been bombarded in the summer of 1919 because it lay within the battle zone and because the Bolsheviks had occupied it. In the course of the barrage, Christians as well as Jews had been killed or wounded. But that was not a pogrom. "I didn't organize pogroms," Oudovichenko stated flatly.

"Yes!" shouted Torrès.

"No!"

"Yes!"

"No!"[5]

In reality, this character witness for Petlura had all he could do just to defend himself. Professor Shulgin had praised Oudovichenko as a friend of the Jews, one of those humanitarians who had prevented a pogrom at Kamenetz-Podolsk, the capital of the Directory, in the spring of 1919.

But even this was not so. Once the Bolsheviks had been dislodged from the city, General Oudovichenko had the members of the local Cheka, including its leader, the Jew Fanni, shot. He then gathered the spokesmen of the Jewish community together and admonished them for their complicity in permitting the Bolsheviks to take Kamenetz.

As he marched his soldiers through the town, firing broke out. It was unclear which side shot first, or, indeed, if there was any shooting at all from the Jewish quarter. In any case, Oudovichenko left some "trusted men" behind to maintain order. The "villains" who had fired on the Ukrainian troops were punished "without distinction as to their nationalities." The massacre of Jews which followed, and which Shulgin did not consider a pogrom, was halted only at the direct insistence of Simon Petlura himself. It would not do to have such bloodshed at the seat of the Ukrainian People's Republic.[6]

Character witness Oudovichenko might protest his own innocence, but according to the report of the All-Ukrainian Central Committee of Relief attached to the Ministry of Jewish Affairs, dated September 2, 1919, he was responsible for two separate pogroms at Ourinine in Podolia. In the first (May 21-24), his Cossacks killed sixteen Jews. In the second (June 2-11), they killed just five.

Joaniki Ivanovich Shimanovich, a Ukrainian Gentile, a peasant and a member of the All-Ukrainian Labor Congress for the district of Kamenetz, wrote to the Ministry of Jewish Affairs in July, 1919, calling for an investigation of Oudovichenko's Iron Battalion by the Holovni Ataman himself. According to Shimanovich, that unit had left the Jewish populations of Gusiatin and Chemerevtzy "utterly ruined and destitute." Damage in these areas was estimated at 796,215 rubles.[7]

According to E. I. Bograd, Acting Director of the Department of National Self-Government, the Iron Battalion, particularly those units under Colonel Pavlo Shandruk (the self-proclaimed savior of the Jews of Proskurov), had devastated the region of Moghilev in September, 1919.[8] Tongues were cut away, eyes plucked out. Hundreds were dying of starvation and at least one hundred lay dead in Shargorod as a result of the activities of Oudovichenko's *regular* troops. "At Zameikhov," where the pogromchiks ran amok on June 14 and July 7," Bograd charged, "Oudovichenko was personally in charge of the 'operation.'"[9]

Chemerevtzy, Gusiatin, Shargorod, Zameikhov, Kamenetz-Podolsk, Sanielkov, Ourinine. And still Oudovichenko could testify, "I again declare in the most formal fashion that in all the localities where my troops were located, there never were any pogroms."[10] Such incidents, he said, were rarely the work of the Ukrainian Army. The principal malefactors had to be supporters of Denikin, the anarchist Makhno, the Bolsheviks, or independent freebooters over whom Simon Petlura had no control.

This was not so, and General Oudovichenko knew it. According to the official reports of the Kiev Pogrom Relief Committee of the Russian Red Cross, 120 pogroms, or half of the massacres reported by the fall of 1919, could be attributed to "regular troops and detachments of Petlura."[11]

The Committee added: "Pogroms only commenced when the Directorate suffered defeat at the hands of the Communists who rose against them. The more decisive these defeats were, the more often the beaten Petlura troops had to carry out evacuations of territories which they had occupied, the more cruelly the defeated and irritated troops began to revenge their setbacks and hardships on the peaceful Jewish population, and the more often they began to treat the Jews as communists."[12]

At Proskurov, Semesenko commanded the regular 3rd *Haidamak Regiment and Zaporog Cossack Brigade of the Ukrainian National Army.*

The fact that the pogroms ceased upon receipt of an order from General Shapoval or someone at Military Headquarters or someone on the scene suggested that the troops were in direct contact with the High Command. Perhaps as many as 5,000 Jews were killed at Proskurov by these same units, who went on to Michaelpol and Solobkovtsy and terrorized Jews as late as July, 1919.[13]

At Gaisin, where 314 Jews were murdered, Ataman Volynetz commanded the *regular Zvenigorodka Regiment of the Ukrainian National Army*.[14] At Balta, Schwartzbard's home city, Stopkevich and Kotsura commanded the *regular Yanov Company and "Kolod Yar" Haidamaks*; several hundred Jews lost their lives at Balta. At Zhabrokichy, elements of the same *regular 2nd Infantry Division* which Oudovichenko was to command and the regular *2nd Galician Brigade* repeatedly made savage attacks upon the Jewish population from June to September, 1919, leaving hundreds dead, homeless, and diseased.[15]

In December, 1918, and January, 1919, units of the *Black Sea Regiment* and *Petlurist Republic Regiment* slaughtered Jews in the railway stations of Sarny, Bobrinskaya, and Olevsk, telling their frightened victims, "We have three days to do with the Jews what we want."[16] In February, 1919, the *regular First Regiment of the Blue Division* left fifty Jews dead at Vasilkovo.[17] Six months later, the same unit was responsible for butchering an additional 168 Jews at Pechanka.

More than a thousand were killed at Belaya Tserkov, Ananiev, and Stepantzy by the regular *Poltava Haidamaks and Shock Battalion* of Petlura under Colonel Goloub in February, 1919.[18] In March, elements of the regular *151st Regiment of Nalivaiko* tortured a number of old Jews to death at Ouchomir. A month later the *61st Gaissin Regiment* ravaged the same town.[19] At Kourilovtsy, Colonel Pavlo Shandruk commanded the regular *Haidamak Cossacks* and the regular *9th Sharpshooters Regiment*, which carried out a massacre of Jews.

Shandruk and his *9th Regiment* again massacred Jews in

Verkhovka-Bibikov, Snitkov, and Shargorod in June-July, 1919.[20] At Kopai-Gorod, the pogromchiks belonged to the *7th and 9th Regiments of the Blue Division*. At Zamokhov, in the summer of 1919, Jews were victimized again by the same units of the *Black Sea Regiment* which had distinguished itself six months earlier. At the same time, Jews in Chatov and Mourafa were brutalized by the *First Cavalry Regiment of Loubny*.

It was the *Nalivaiko Regiment* at Znamenka in January, at Korosten and Barchad in March, and Gorotchi in April. It was the regular *Vinnichenko Regiment* at Dombrovitsy on January 17. It was the *Chernobylski Regiment* at Zhourine in June, the *6th and 7th Divisions of the Zaprozhskaia Sech* at Sinkov in March, the *27th Cavalry Regiment* at Smotrich in July, and units of the *11th Dismounted Division* (former Zaporog Sech) and *11th Galician Brigade* who raped, burned, and killed in Zhabokrich late in August.[21] And when the killers passed through Vinnitza in the spring of 1919, they wore the blue and gold uniforms of Oudovichenko's regular *2nd Army Corps*.[22]

Worst of all were the *Kureni Smerti*, the special "Battalions of Death" established by the Supreme Army Command of the Ukrainian National Army in the winter of 1918-19 to deal with the problem of alleged Bolshevik sympathizers in the Jewish population. The first such Clan of Death, under the direction of Colonel Palienko, a young man in his thirties from Yaroslav, was sent to Zhitomir in January, 1919, to eliminate "a Jewish soviet."

While passing through Berdichev on January 5, Palienko's forces, some wearing helmets, some in the traditional *osedeletz* (pigtail favored by medieval Cossacks), methodically plundered the Jews of that small town for practice. The militia, comprised almost totally of Jews, was first disarmed. The men were then asked if they were Jewish or not. If the answer was in the affirmative, they were shot. In his official report to his superior officer, General Oskilko,

Palienko boasted of how he filled two wagons with corpses at the railway station. His *Kuren* even shot those who attended the funerals of their loved ones. In all his work, Palienko was protected against interference from the local constabulary by an order of General Oskilko.[23]

When he arrived in Zhitomir on January 9, Palienko demanded a sum of 80 million rubles from the Jewish community as an indemnity for their Bolshevik leanings. "All Jews are Bolsheviks, are they not?" he told the assembled elders. "I have been sent here to punish Zhitomir. I have already punished Berdichev, and Rovne, having heard of these punishments, is trembling. I shall clear Zhitomir of all factions. It shall be a clean town."[24]

Though the ransom was paid and though only nine of forty-nine workers who attempted to set up a soviet in the city had been Jews, a pogrom was authorized. The entire business district in the center of town was put to the torch, fifty-three Jews were killed (including a seven-month babe), another nineteen wounded in this, the first of many pogroms to strike Zhitomir.

The two days of pillaging were remembered as a holiday by Palienko's troops, one of whom instructed an old Jew: "I am in the service of our Ukraine. In the Ukraine, the Jews are ours. Their money is ours. We can do with you what we want."[25]

Despite the efforts of Mayor A. F. Pivotski, a Ukrainian woman named Madame Psakis, and an officer named Vozny, the pogrom raged unchecked because, an army spokesman related, "Orders have been given to massacre the Jews."[26]

Disgusted by the actions of his own countrymen against blameless Jews, one Ukrainian, N. Gladki, testified, "The Haidamaks were pogromchiks, are now pogromchiks, and will probably remain pogromchiks. Many claim to be patriots, but it is hard to say where their patriotism ends and their pogrom mood begins."[27]

On January 10, while the Zhitomir pogrom was still in progress, Vinnichenko, then the titular head of the Directory, promised Mayor D. Lipetz of Berdichev that an immediate inquiry would be held, the pogromchiks punished, and steps taken to prevent a recurrence of the atrocities.[28] A similar pledge that Palienko would be judged with severity and equity was given to Jewish Minister Revutzky by Simon Petlura.[29]

The genuine attitude of the Directory, however, was reflected in an insensitive statement of Opanas Andrievsky, the anti-Semite designated to head all commissions of inquiry. To Colonel Zolotnitski, who was supposed to investigate Zhitomir, Andrievsky said, "In general, the matter is not as serious as it would appear. There simply was an outburst of the revolt of certain Ukrainian troops against the Bolsheviks who were led by Jews, and so the pogrom happened. Moreover, those particular troops have since left Zhitomir. Their leader Palienko was even arrested. There are only small fry left. Is it worthwhile to take it so seriously?"[30]

Andrievsky proposed 25,000 rubles as a sop to the pogrom survivors. Little wonder that a commission despatched to Berdichev under Ataman Pilkevitch never sat. A subsequent one under Colonel Zolotnitski sat, but made no findings. A tribunal authorized to investigate the Ovruch pogrom was never sent. At Proskurov, Semosenko created a commission of his own men.

As for Palienko, a secret report in the Ministry of Information did blame the Colonel and his staff for "improper activity" at Zhitomir. Publicly, though, he was praised for stopping a pogrom carried out against Jews by "bandits."[31] When the order was finally given by Oskilko to detain the commander of this most infamous Clan of Death on January 17, the telegram charged Palienko and his aides Mantouliak and Nicolayev not with pogroms or killing Jews, but with "crimes against the common law," "high treason,"

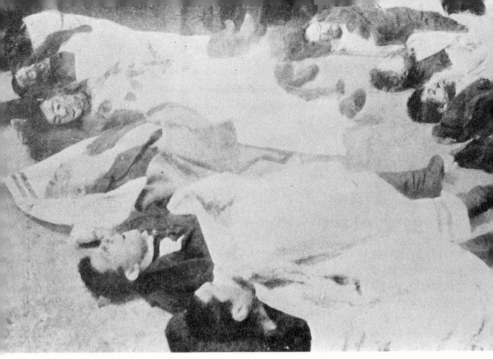

The dead at Zhitomir, wrapped in their own tallit *or prayer shawls.*

"defection to the enemy," and "pillaging." These should have been sufficient to hang Palienko, but the government, as in the case of Semosenko, was chiefly concerned about his retention of "large sums of money and stolen property."[32]

The question of what happened to Palienko supplied the Schwartzbard trial with another diverting interlude. At one point, Civil Prosecutor Campinchi, reading from Annex 22 of the documentary collection prepared by the Comité des Délégations Juives, proclaimed the "arrest" of Palienko, proof positive that the government and Petlura had no truck with pogromchiks. As Campinchi read from the document, Torrès followed him about the counsel tables and suddenly interrupted, charging Campinchi with "the supple talent of emending texts for the jury."

"Don't accuse me of suppressing evidence, Torrès!" snapped Campinchi.

"Don't force me to place in evidence your personal pedigree!" rejoined Torrès.

"If it is a personal altercation that you desire," warned the Corsican, who was a skilled fencer and boxer, "I tell you that you will have to apologize because I will have something to say about it. Do you accuse me of falsifying texts? Explain yourself."[33]

Backing off somewhat, a cooler Torrès noted that Campinchi, in telling the jury of the arrest of Palienko, had failed to refer to the subsequent content of this report, namely "the glorification" of that same Colonel Palienko.

Campinchi had neglected to tell his audience that Palienko was released from prison without trial and in February, 1919, was back in command of the same Detachment of Death at Vinnitza, the capital of the Petlura government. Irate over the sudden rehabilitation of the butcher of Zhitomir, several Jewish officials, including Revutzky, Krasny, Fania Nirenberg, G. Solodar, and I. Giterman arranged a special conference with Ukrainian military leaders in the offices of the Jewish Ministry at the Hotel Savoy.

Leading the Ukrainians was Ataman Kovenko, Chairman of the Supreme Committee of Inquiry of the Ukrainian Police, who was credited with saving Kiev from the Bolsheviks in January, 1918. The Jewish delegates could not have expected much from Kovenko, a man blamed for wholesale resignations of the Chekhovsky cabinet,[34] a man whose attitude toward pogroms had been, "Those we don't massacre today, we'll massacre tomorrow,"[35] and who now permitted Palienko to sit in full regalia at a meeting to discuss his culpability for pogroms.

When the Jewish delegates objected to Palienko's presence, Kovenko's right-hand man, a Galician Pole named Sedletzki, pointed out that the guilty ones at Zhitomir had been local Bolsheviks and that Palienko had cut them down and suppressed the pogrom. When Giterman insisted that "the name Palienko hovers over Zhitomir like a symbol of

death and blood," a young Ukrainian officer with a
pockmarked face (a man described by Revutzky as patholog-
ically criminal) countered by saying, "The Jews fight us
everywhere. Jews with great beards shot at us when we drove
the Bolsheviks out. I've killed in Berdichev and will again.
We will not stop. We are not afraid of you."[36]

When the Jews spoke of the demoralizing effect of the
pogroms upon the grand scheme of national unity, Colonel
Kovenko accused them of "sapping the idea of national
renaissance." When the Jews tried to argue that even before
the pogroms at Berdichev and Zhitomir, Ukrainian soldiers
had informed the Gentile populations of the coming violence, Colonel Kovenko interrupted again, defending the
activities of his regiment, which acted on orders against
Bolsheviks and hoarders. According to Kovenko, there had
been no pogrom in Berdichev. He offered no explanation for
the seventeen dead Jews and forty wounded in that town.

*Three Jews killed at Berdichev, one of the earliest massacres;
January 1919.*

Banging his fist on the table, Kovenko screamed, "Yes, we have killed, we are killing and we shall kill. This very night, here at Vinnitza, fifty men shall be hanged. We sent the Battalion to Zhitomir and to Berdichev and we knew why we were sending it. It is my Battalion. It is the pride of the Ukrainian Army. If Palienko had not been arrested, we would not have surrendered Kiev. Now that Palienko has been released, we will retake Kiev. I am the chief of the secret police and am not ashamed of it." Later, in discussion with I. M. Giterman, Revutzky concluded, "The pogroms were organized by Kovenko."[37]

The Clans of Death fought well; therefore they were permitted to plunder. Commandants of cities were given orders from the High Command that the *Kureni Smerti* were not to be arrested.[38] At Chemerevtzky, where a pogrom took place on July 21, the chief of the militia announced, "I have nothing against a pogrom."[39] At Mohilev-Podolsk, the Commissar of Police printed up and distributed an anti-Jewish proclamation that began, "Death to the Jews! Save the Ukraine!"[40]

Colonel Palienko was never punished. Neither was Ataman Semosenko or Colonel Kovenko. Nor was Colonel Patrov, who conceived the idea of the Clans of Death. In fact, Patrov was rewarded by being made Petlura's Minister of War. Said Premier Vinnichenko, "Today it isn't a secret to anyone in general that the officers themselves commanded the soldiers to commit the pogroms. Likewise it is no secret that none of these criminals were shot or punished by the military authorities."[41]

These incitements originated in Ukrainian Army Headquarters, where the Directory, headed by Holovni Ataman Petlura, sat in the spring of 1919. Elia Tcherikover noted sardonically, "It is hardly likely that it [the Directory] did not know what was going on under its own nose."[42]

One sector of the government did press for justice. The hapless Council of Ministers, the political facade which cloaked the dictatorship of the Directory with an aura of respectability, repeatedly passed resolutions calling for the creation of effective commissions of inquiry into the pogroms. On May 27, 1919, for example, the Council passed an elaborate twenty-four-paragraph resolution calling for the establishment of extraordinary commissions to investigate the pogroms and punish the wrongdoers.[43] This act was approved and counter-signed by Petlura and his Minister for Jewish Affairs, Pinchas Krasny, among others. It was an empty gesture, as was apparent from the fact that the Council of Ministers again petitioned Petlura on June 14 and July 17 to organize an inspector-general.[44]

Finally, on August 18, 1919, another resolution, couched in near-hysterical terms and specifically addressed to Petlura, called for the "immediate" establishment of a special governmental commission with powers to investigate and combat pogroms. The directive also called upon the Holovni Ataman to issue an "appropriate proclamation" to the people and to enforce the death penalty for "traitors" and those who committed "excesses."[45]

According to Arnold Margolin, Petlura did institute an active fight against the pogromchiks. "I had in my possession," Margolin wrote later, "documents proving that there were even death sentences carried out by order of the military tribunals against pogrom perpetrators.[46] Four persons were shot by Lt. Paliy-Sidoriansky for such offenses in the village of Vakhnovka. At the railroad junction of Khrysynivka another eighty-three were summarily executed in an action which must have resembled a pogrom. At Talnoye, Tiutiunik ordered five more pogromchiks punished. Dashenko, commander of the 4th Kiev Cavalry Regiment, and himself the instigator of January disturbances in Belaya Tserkov, had one of his own men killed in Gusiatin.[47] And in Chernovo, a soldier of the 4th Kiev Rifle Division was executed in a similar fashion.[48]

At Teofipol, the peasant Chichko combined the forces of

the nationalists and Jewish militia, to combat the Bolsheviks. The pogrom which followed in July, 1919, left seventy-six Jews dead and 176 houses gutted. In August, the Jewish community of Pogrebishche, which had lost three hundred of its people, issued a formal salute to Ukrainian commander Souprunenko, "who used all means to protect the population and succeeded." And as additional testimony to the energies of the Inspectorate, there was the letter of Mayor Mordecai Wolf Klavitzer of Ourinine, dated July 30, 1919, thanking Andre Bibikov, State Inspector, "for the energy displayed and measures taken to restore order and calm in this little locality and for having permitted no excesses."[49]

Regular Ukrainian forces reportedly put down pogroms in Korosten, Lubny, Gorodok, Gluchkov and Smotrich, always at a cost to their own men. The condemned at Khrystynivka, Vakhnovka, Gusiatin, or Kamenetz-Podolsk, where Provincial Commissar Siechinsky averted a massacre in the summer of 1919, were not, however, the Palienkos or Semosenkos who organized pogroms on a large scale. Rather, they were common soldiers who had exceeded tolerated limits of pogrom activity, looters who were sacrificed for foreign consumption. Those isolated instances of Ukrainian intervention could not be attributed to the Directory itself but to the heroism and humanitarianism which continued to flicker among a handful of regular troops, none of whom enhanced their status with the regime by their pro-Jewish actions.

As for the unctuous oaths of Jewish communal leaders, all of those cited, like the timorous declarations of the Jews in Kamenetz-Podolsk to Petlura on July 17, 1919, could be attributed more to fear of renewed persecution than to genuine appreciation for the peace-keeping efforts of nationalist officials. Not until Petlura's flight to Poland in 1920 were more of his troops punished for "crimes against the common law."[50] Professor Reshetar observed: "Although Petlura issued a number of orders during the summer and autumn of 1919 censuring the instigators of pogroms, he was unable or unwilling to have such persons apprehended and brought to justice."[51]

The vaunted state inspection was more concerned with checking out the political loyalties of officers than punishing murderers. Even in this last task, the inspectorate-general which had been sought for the relief of Jews did not function well. General Pavlo Shandruk conceded that special commissions were failures when he wrote, "Although state inspection did not perform anything worthwhile, no real harm was done, outside of a few instances of misunderstanding between commanders and inspection agents who pretended to be political commissars."[52]

It was no secret that Petlura looked with a kind eye upon the pogroms, saying, "Let the boys have some fun."[53] When the massacres began on a large scale in January, 1919, Vinnichenko scolded him, "Watch what your commanders are doing. This should be stopped!" Petlura replied, "Then why don't these accursed Jews join our army?"[54]

He used the same excuse of Jewish hostility in explaining away the Zhitomir pogrom, telling a Jewish delegation that their own people had provoked the attack by converting a synagogue into a fort and firing on Ukrainian troops sent to restore order.[55]

To a delegation of Jews from Znamenka who came to him after a vicious pogrom at Elizavetgrad had left numbers of children slain and women raped, Petlura declared, "I don't mix in the affairs of my army and I give it neither counsel nor instruction. My army does whatever it wants or pleases. I am not going to interfere with that and I forbid you from coming to me again to plead this case."[56]

When General Zhukowsky (onetime War Minister for the Central Rada) and Professor Hrushevsky rebuked him for the many massacres, Petlura said simply, "I am sorry for the pogroms, but they help maintain the discipline of the army."[57] In 1919, the time had come to decide who was friend and who was foe.[58]

As Gergel pointed out, the darkest period for Ukrainian Jews was from May to September, 1919, when the fortunes of the Directory were in decline.[59] But even before then, too many units such as the *Kureni Smerti*, Iron Battalion, Black Sea Regiment, Kosh, or Kolod Yar Haidamaks, under the direct control of Holovni Ataman Petlura, had participated in excesses. From the first pogroms along the Sarny-Zhitomir and Bakhmach-Konotop railroad lines, they were the systematic work of the War Ministry, which dispatched its troops to destroy the Bolshevik menace wherever it cropped up. Although leaders, including Petlura, frequently traveled the railroads through the beleaguered towns, little or nothing was done to succor the victims or prevent new outbreaks of pogromist activity.[60]

Said Torrès in 1927: "Ah yes, pogroms. There were some pogroms in all the armies in the Ukraine. The Bolsheviks carry responsibility for pogroms which were made by them. But General Budenny, acting like a French general, cleared his own ranks, chastising without pity the authors of pogroms. But Petlura, the Ataman General Petlura, under whose government the pogroms had been organized by the chiefs themselves, by the regiments, with their colonels in charge, by the squads with their atamans in charge, without any of these superior officers or generals being punished, without any of those who had transmitted orders for pogroms being chastened—that's the terrible and bloody responsibility of Petlura."[61]

Notes

1. Choulguine, *L'Ukraine et le cauchemar rouge*, p.75.

2. Batchinsky, *et al*, *The Jewish Pogroms in Ukraine*, p.8.

3. Choulguine, *L'Ukraine et le cauchemar rouge*, p.108.

4. Deposition of Oudovichenko, September 16, 1926, File 451, 38035-6, Tcherikover Archive. See also Testimony of Oudovichenko, *Notes Sténographiques*, fasc. 4, pp.176-219.

5. *Figaro*, October 22, 1927, p.2, and *Notes Sténographiques*, fasc. 4, pp.183-195.

6. Choulguine, *L'Ukraine et le cauchemar rouge*, p.108.

7. Report of the Kiev Central Committee for Help of Pogrom Victims, File 313, Tcherikover Archive.

8. Reports of F. Bograd to Ministry of Jewish Affairs, August 5 and September 3, 1919, File 468, 38975 and 38976, Tcherikover Archive. Shandruk later distinguished himself as an officer in the Polish Army. Taken captive in 1940, he was subsequently released and accompanied the Nazis into Russia in the uniform of the fascist Rumanian Ionescu. In his memoirs, Shandruk skims over three years in less than two pages, stating only that the Ukrainian people dicovered that the Nazis were no kinder than the Stalinists. Then in 1944, he was encouraged to form a true Ukrainian Army to fight against Bolshevism. Toward that end Shandruk received a commission from *Reichsminister* Alfred Rosenberg in March of 1945. There is nothing in his pathetic memoir, *Arms of Valor*, which indicates a germ of pro-Allied sympathies in World War II.

9. Schechtman, *et al, The Pogroms in the Ukraine,* p.218.

10. *Notes Sténographiques,* fasc. 4, p.219.

11. *Massacres and Atrocities,* p.12.

12. *Ibid.,* p.5.

13. Table of Pogroms Organized by Ukrainian Army and Insurgent Atamans who Were in League with the Ukrainian Army, December, 1918-1921, File 408, 35371-86, Tcherikover Archive.

14. Schechtman, *et al, The Pogroms in the Ukraine,* pp.229-31.

15. "Di Direktorye un di pogromen," January-October, 1919, File 522, Tcherikover Archive.

16. Appeals for Help from Jewish Villages. File 406, 35310, Bobrinskaya, Tcherikover Archive.

17. Material from pogroms in Vasilkov, Balta, Belaya Tserkov, and Teplik, File 416, Tcherikover Archive.

18. *Les pogromes en Ukraine,* pp.33 and 53-57. See also Files 298, 304, and 305, Tcherikover Archives, for original material from European YIVO on the massacres at Belaya Tserkov.

19. Table of Pogroms, File 408, Tcherikover Archive.

20. *Ibid.*

21. *Ibid.,* and also File 440, 37588-89, Tcherikover Archive.

22. "Yiddishe pogromen in Ukraine in der tzayt fun der Direktorye," Parts 5 and 6, File 518, and Attestation of residents of Emilchino, File 466, 38901-9, Tcherikover Archive.

23. Letter of G. Solodar, a member of the Berdichev Town Council, July 31, 1919, to N. Shtif in Tcherikover, *Di ukrainer pogromen,* p.84. See also "Petlura un zeyne mekurovim," by Nachman Meyzil, *Heynt,* June 2 and July 23, 1926, File 604, Tcherikover Archive.

24. See Conclusions of Commission of Inquiry into the first and second pogroms in Zhitomir, File 456, 38280-1, and Report of I. Giterman, January 25, 1919, File 457, 38297-404, Tcherikover Archive.

25. Deposition of P. Lerman, File 457, Tcherikover Archive.

26. *Les pogromes en Ukraine,* pp.38-40.

27. Deposition of N. Gladki, File 457, Tcherikover Archive. See also "Material fun der ausforschung komisia vegen Zhitomir," *loc. cit.*

28. Schechtman, *et al, The Pogroms in the Ukraine,* p.141.

29. Revutzky, *In di shvere tog ofn Ukraine,* p.285.

30. Memorandum of Mr. Gad Rosenblatt, Representative of the Ministry of Jewish Affairs, on pogroms at Zhitomir and Berdichev, June 16, 1919, p.3, File 440, 37596-37603, Tcherikover Archive.

31. Report to the Commander of the Southern District, Rovne, Feb. 20, 1919, in Tcherikover, *Di ukrainer pogromen,* p.86.

32. See Annex 22 in *Les pogromes en Ukraine,* p.38.

33. *Notes Sténographiques,* fasc. 3, pp.170-178, and fasc. 4, pp.236-240. Also see *New York Times,* October 22, 1927, p.6.

34. When he left the government, Chekcovsky complained, "We cannot work under the command of Kovenko." Revutzky, *In di shvere tog ofn Ukraine,* p.266.

35. Tcherikover, *Di ukrainer pogromen,* p.92.

36. Annex 23, in *Les pogromes en Ukraine,* pp.39-42.

37. *Ibid.* Similar opinions were expressed by A. Chomsky, who was imprisoned with Palienko and Semosenko, and by onetime Jewish Minister Krasny. Krasny went further, however, and claimed that Palienko had been instructed by Petlura personally to go and teach the Jews of Berdichev a lesson. *Proletarskaia Pravda,* Kiev, 96 and 98, 1927.

38. Haifetz, *The Slaughter of the Jews,* p.25.

39. Report of the Central Committee for Help to Pogrom Victims on Tchemerevetz, July 28, 1919, File 313, Tcherikover Archive.

40. F. Rosenblum, "A reshimeh fun di pogromirte shtet in di yoren 1919 un 1920," File 49, Tcherikover Archive.

41. Vinnitchenko, *The Renaissance of a Nation,* III, p.187.

42. Tcherikover, *Di ukrainer pogromen,* p.92.

43. This law was worked out to the finest detail, including daily pay of assistant office workers and the judicial status of members of the tribunals. See *Vistnyk Derzhavnykh Zakoniv* (JOURNAL OF STATE LAWS), July 17, 1919.

44. *Les pogromes en Ukraine*, p.76.

45. *Ukraina*, August 21, 1919.

46. Margolin, *The Jews of Eastern Europe*, p.139.

47. On January 20, 1919, Dashenko warned the Jews of Belaya Tserkov that he would hold the Jewish population responsible "if any demonstrations should take place." Such notices were generally harbingers of pogroms. J. Schechtman, *Quelques Commentaires*. pp.38494-95.

48. Fedir Pigido-Pravoberezhny, "Ukrainian-Jewish Relations, 1917-1921," *Ukrainian Review* (Munich, 1957), p.84. For similar punishments meted out to the Cossacks Shemelecki and Voroshilov, see *Notes Sténographiques*, fasc. 5, p.27.

49. *Documents sur les pogromes en Ukraine* (Paris: H. Dieval, 1924), p.133. A Ukrainian historian writes: "In the great majority of cases, the local Christian population deeply sympathized with the fate of Jews and hid them in houses. They defended them and for this very reason they sent a delegation of members of local governments and organizations to the authorities. Some people acted on their own, sometimes with great self-sacrifice. Such cases occurred in Bila Tserkva, Horodyshche, Hostomel, Korson, Cherkassy, Vepryk, Borozna, Konotop, Nizhn, Novy Mhlyn, Boryspol, Dzhuryn, and Kryvoe Ozero." N. Shtif, *Pogromy na Ukraine: Period Dobrocheskoi Armii* (Berlin, 1922), pp.24-25.

50. Dozens of documents signed by Generals Ossetzki, Melnyk, Omelianovtich-Pavlenko and others were issued tardily, in Poland. *Les pogromes en Ukraine*, pp.82-87.

51. Reshetar, *The Ukrainian Revolution*, p.255.

52. Shandruk, *Arms of Valor*, p.94.

53. Elbogen, *A Century of Jewish Life*, p.498.

54. A. Resutzky, "Petliura," *Reflex*, I (1927), p.91. The author of this article is, in all probability, the Jewish Minister Revutzky. The name problem may be attributed to a simple typographical error.

55. Schechtman, *et al, The Pogroms in the Ukraine,* p.54.

56. Deposition of L. Pechelev, October 26, 1926, File 425, 36903-4, Tcherikover Archive.

57. Deposition of Tcherikover, October 14, 1926, File 427, 37048, Tcherikover Archive, and Resutzky, "Petlura," p.91.

58. V. Timashevski, "Jews and the Ukrainian War," *Ukraina,* Jan. 22, 1919.

59. N. Gergel, "The Pogroms in the Ukraine," p.242.

60. Tcherikover, *Di ukrainer pogromen,* pp.73-75, where the author reached conclusions that "the first disorders were not from partisans but from the regular military," and p.83 where Tcherikover concluded "in military circles they realized that pogroms worked."

61. *Notes Sténographiques,* fasc. 4, pp.204-205.

11.

Order Number 131

MORRIS GOLDSTEIN, the second Jew to testify at the Schwartzbard trial, had been one of the outstanding Jewish attorneys of Tsarist Russia. During his practice in Leningrad, he had once successfully defended Leo Tolstoy.

Like Haia Greenberg, he had been an eye-witness to the devastation in the Ukraine. While residing in Kiev over the winter of 1918-19, he was selected to head a special committee of inquiry consisting of twenty-four attorneys (later expanded to forty because of the extent of the slaughter). Operating independently of the Ukrainian National Republic, these men risked their lives to amass detail reports and photographs of the pogroms. These were transmitted to Goldstein's central office in Kiev even while the massacres continued. And now, after eight years of study of the materials, Goldstein told the Paris jury, "My conviction is that the pogroms were organized."[1]

As his first reason, Goldstein cited the fact that inflammatory appeals to Ukrainian troops were always the same— "Death to the Jews! Save the Ukraine!" The adherents of Voynetz, Riashchenko, Zeleny, Semosenko, Palienko, and Angel all killed waving banners which bore identical inscriptions, identical word order. Though the Ukraine had an area of more than 225,000 square miles, though communications were disrupted, though the regiments involved were hundreds of miles from each other, remnants of these same banners were found in virtually every corner of the troubled land by Goldstein's researchers.

As his second reason, Goldstein cited official proclamations to the army calling for massacres. Like the standards, they were found all over the Ukraine. They were uniform in content, and they all originated from the government printing office. These venomous documents continued the work of the former hate sheet of the *Samostiniks, Nova Rada,* which flourished until the Central Rada's collapse in March, 1918.

When the Nationalists regained control of the government in the following November, the literary pogromchiks could scarcely keep up with the demand for material. *Ukrainskaya Stavka,* the official organ of the Ukrainian War Office, immediately launched an insidious campaign against the Jews. On December 24, 1918, the paper accused the Jews in Berdichev of helping the Germans and their puppet Skoropadsky and indicated that the Jews were "a curse on the Ukraine." On January 12, 1919, the journal carried an article which stated, "The Russian, Yiddish, and other speculators and profiteers are all enemies of the Directory."

Two days later, the Jews again were attacked as enemies of the state for failing to speak the Ukrainian language and for being in league simultaneously with the landed gentry and Bolsheviks. And again on January 19, 1919, *Ukrainskaya Stavka* lamented that there were too many "Jew children in the schools and Jew landlords in the towns," leaving little doubt that they should be expelled by force if necessary.[2]

The Information Bureau of the Army of the Ukrainian People's Republic waged a similar campaign. In December, 1918, official notices from this agency warned the Jewish "traducers" of Kremenchug that it would do them no good to remain hostile to the republic. On January 11, the Information Bureau castigated the Jews of Felshtin for "confusing the minds of the peasants." Six weeks before Semosenko ravaged that village and nearby Proskurov, the Bureau warned the area's Jews, "You will have to pay dearly. You have no one from whom to expect help."

The Information Bureau flooded the country with scores of pamphlets branding the Jews as "enemies of the Ukraine," "speculators and profiteers," "Bolsheviks," and "agitators against the Directory." More direct was the official Government Printing Works of the Volhynian Provincial Commissariat, which appealed to peasants to join Sokolovsky's brigade "to fight Russian hirelings and Jewish underlings." All of this was done with the imprimatur of the military authorities, at the head of which was Simon Petlura.[3]

Morris Goldstein had a third reason for claiming that the pogroms had been organized. The pretext for the various massacres was identical. As an example, he cited the pogrom at Proskurov: "They began by telling the Haidamaks that in a neighboring village, Felshtin, the Jews had carried off the church bells and hanged three priests. It was a lie, but it excited the soldiers. They said at Proskurov that these deeds had taken place in Felshtin. And at Felshtin, they said that they had happened at Proskurov."[4]

Goldstein's description of a typical pogrom was graphic. "A Ukrainian regiment enters a Jewish village. The ataman or his aides demand a ransom, 200,000 or 300,000 rubles, according to the wealth of the community or the fantasies of the ataman. Then they carry off all that they are able. Then the ataman says, 'It is necessary that the most powerful representatives of the Jews come to me!' The rabbis, old men with white beards, the religious ones, come. At Ovruch, there were eighteen or twenty. They were told, 'You are Bolsheviks.'"

" 'Bolsheviks? We are Jews. We are not political. We concern ourselves only with religion, with God, and with prayer.'"

"'Well, if you are not Bolsheviks, I am going to shave your beards.'"

Here, Goldstein interrupted his narrative: "It is necessary to point out that among religious Jews, among the old men, a beard is sacred. To cut it is a sacrilege. Nevertheless, the beards were cut. Then they had to dance and sing religious chants. After that, the orgy began. For the orgy, the women and daughters of these Jews, their sisters, everyone possible, were taken. These women were violated, the young girls before the eyes of their husbands, their fathers, and their brothers. And in the morning, when the orgy was finished, these unfortunates were killed. Not one was left alive."

Ovruch, the cantonal capital of Volhynia, was one of the first towns to suffer a pogrom in January, 1919. Directed by the perverted commander Kozyr-Zyrko, Ukrainian regulars terrorized the Jewish community from Christmas Day, 1918, when the meeting with the town leaders took place, until January 16, 1919, when eighty persons were murdered and 1,200 homes plundered. Telegraph wires were cut and all roads from the town blocked.

Kozyr-Zyrko, described by Abraham Revutzky as a *tunkler* (shady person) who claimed to be in the state service,[5] spent most of the time drunk and naked in bed, alternating between rape of women and torture of rabbis. The latter he ordered to flog one another and then kiss one another's wounds. Kozyr-Zyrko delighted in these games, or in forcing rabbis to make the sign of the cross, or stuffing their mouths with tobacco or lit matches. Even before the massacre at the railway station on January 16, the commander had informed the Jews assembled in the central square at Ovruch that he had a right to massacre all of them if he found just one Bolshevik in their number.[6]

If Goldstein glossed over the details of the Ovruch pogrom, it was not that he considered the matter unimportant. Rather, he was trying to establish a pattern to the massacres. When such a thing happened once or twice, perhaps it was coincidence. "But," he noted, "if it is repeated dozens of times, it evidently is a plan ordered by someone at a central position."

For Goldstein, that someone had to be Simon Petlura. To believe otherwise, one would have had to assume that there were two separate headquarters, one for war and one for pogroms. Moreover, before Petlura there had been "no" pogroms. After him, there were "none." But under Petlura's regime there had been "hundreds." Rhetorically, Goldstein asked, "What does that signify?"

The Jewish attorney even supplied the court with a character reference for Sholom Schwartzbard. In 1919 and 1920, Goldstein was Vice-President of a Committee of Relief created in Paris to assist survivors of the pogroms. In 1923, the Committee received a large sum of money from an anonymous French citizen who asked that it be used to bring forty orphans to France. The one stipulation was that the children must be placed with artisans who would rear them in the traditions of French democracy, thereby obliterating the tragic past and teaching them a trade. The committee made a general appeal to Jewish artisans in France. The first to volunteer as a foster parent was Sholom Schwartzbard.[7]

REYNAUD: I have an observation to make to the witness. He has said that there weren't any pogroms before Petlura. Did Petlura invent the pogroms? If you wish to prove too much, you prove nothing.

GOLDSTEIN: No, Petlura didn't invent the pogroms. I said in my deposition that there were some before him; but in the hundreds, as under Petlura, no, it had never been like that. I am a Russian citizen. I know what happened in Russia. Twenty-five years ago at the time of the Kishinev pogrom all of Russia was in turmoil. But under Petlura there were hundreds of pogroms. They don't compare.

CAMPINCHI: The anarchy of the war doesn't mean anything to you?

GOLDSTEIN: Before Petlura there also was war, equally so after him.

CAMPINCHI: And there were pogroms.

GOLDSTEIN: Not in the same number.

CAMPINCHI: I would like to pose a question. You have heard of the pogroms of Denikin?

GOLDSTEIN: Yes, when I was in Paris.

CAMPINCHI: They were very serious.

GOLDSTEIN: So I have read in the newspapers. I only know what I have read.

CAMPINCHI: And the pogroms of the Bolsheviks? Have you heard of them?

GOLDSTEIN: There were one or two. I was still in Kiev when they took place under the Bolshevik regime. But it is necessary to say that the regiments of Petlura had passed to the Bolshevik side and that the same regiments made one or two pogroms.

Goldstein's sense of duty apparently compelled such exaggerations, for Denikin's troops were blamed for 213 pogroms and the Bolsheviks for more than one hundred. Still, these accounted for less than one-third of all the atrocities committed in the Ukraine.[8]

CAMPINCHI: Do you know that he [Petlura] took measures to suppress the pogroms?

GOLDSTEIN: After more than 100,000 persons were killed!

CAMPINCHI: Do you mean that? 10,000!

GOLDSTEIN: Or 100,000 victims. I left Kiev June 23, 1919. I was President of the Committee for six months. I can only speak about that of which I was informed during the inquiry.

CAMPINCHI: You know the significance of my question. According to you, Petlura only took measures against the pogroms tardily.

GOLDSTEIN: Yes.

CAMPINCHI: You are sure of it?

GOLDSTEIN: I was certain of it for all the time I was still President of the Commission.

CAMPINCHI: For what period?

GOLDSTEIN: January to June, 1919.

CAMPINCHI: Don't you know that proclamations had already been issued by Petlura's government and his political allies as early as 1917?

GOLDSTEIN: In 1917, I was in Petrograd. I don't have knowledge of that.[9]

Now it was the Civil Prosecutor's turn to stretch the truth. The various manifestoes on religious liberty to which he alluded were actually products of the defunct Central Rada, in which Petlura played a subordinate role as Secretary General for Military Affairs. Typical of these obtuse proclamations of the idealistic Rada was one from the fall of 1917:

> Citizens . . . The dark forces which exploited you under the old order do not sleep . . . They are asking you to take the Cross during Easter Time and with the Cross in your hands, to rob and kill in the name of Christ who taught only to love all people. They are asking you to shed the blood of people like you, our brothers. In undermining our freedom which is so dear to us, they

are inciting you against your neighbors, calling you to
organize pogroms . . . Let us turn deaf ears to these
slogans . . . We became independent not to rob and kill,
but because we wanted to bring a better life to all our
people in our land.[10]

The declaration did not specify who the "dark forces'
were, nor did it indicate who their victims might be. The
references were understood by people in the Ukraine, who
recognized that the region was by no means the oasis of order
some had claimed.

Petlura's first official statement on pogroms dated from
November, 1917, when he told his troops, "I am asking all of
you for full support for the Central Rada and the Secretariat
General. Do not permit pogroms and disorders because if
you will permit them, you will bring infamy to the honor of
the Ukrainian Army. Pogroms should not take place on our
land."[11] Nevertheless, by December of that year, more than
sixty "scuffles," as the Ukrainians preferred to call pogroms,
had occurred in Litin, Rechitsa, Skvira, and Gaisin. Approached by J. B. Schechtman of the Zionists on November
28, 1917, Petlura promised to maintain order. Said Schechtman, "Nothing or next to nothing of the measures promised
was carried out."[12]

So much for the early proclamations of the Rada, but
Campinchi had only this day come into possession of a
volume which contained Petlura's later declarations against
pogrom activity:

CAMPINCHI: Have you knowledge of Petlura's proclamations?

GOLDSTEIN: Yes, I have said so. I have said that these proclamations found in diverse regions, a thou-
sand kilometers from one another, bore the
same official imprint.

CAMPINCHI: I don't understand. You speak of appeals for pogroms. I speak of appeals against pogroms.

GOLDSTEIN: I have never seen Petlura's appeals against pogroms.

CAMPINCHI: You say that you have seen proclamations saying, "Kill the Jews," but you have no knowledge of proclamations against pogroms?

GOLDSTEIN: Against pogroms? None at all!

CAMPINCHI: If you made an inquiry, how is it that you didn't come across the proclamations which Petlura made against the pogroms, proclamations which were so numerous, so ardent?

GOLDSTEIN: The explanation is simple. They did not exist.

CAMPINCHI: Here is one of them.

TORRÈS: What date?

CAMPINCHI: 1920.

GOLDSTEIN: In 1920 I wasn't there.

CAMPINCHI: I have seen them from 1917, 1918, 1919. I don't want to repeat myself.

TORRÈS: The witness told you: "I was there in the first half of 1919, the time that was most tragic, the time of the pogroms of Proskurov, Zhitomir . . ."

GOLDSTEIN: Ovruch . . .

TORRÈS: " . . . and I have never seen these proclamations." The witness' response was precise. It applied to a definite period.[13]

Campinchi elected to challenge Goldstein on the subject of the Ovruch pogrom. Reading from the index of the report of the Comité des Délégations Juives, he noted that even this eminent body of Jews blamed the pogrom on Ataman Kozyr-Zryko, commander of "a unit of partisans."[14] Not Petlura then, but an independent partisan was responsible for the massacre at Ovruch in January, 1919. Had the Civil Prosecutor bothered to read more than the index, however, he would have learned that Kozyr-Zyrko's unit was regarded as another Detachment of Death, that it had been sent from Korosten (the temporary capital of the Directory), and that when Bolshevik troops forced his departure from Ovruch after three blood-filled weeks, Kozyr-Zyrko led his men directly back to the sanctuary of Korosten once more.[15] Like his comrades Palienko and Kovenko in the *Kureni Smerti*, Kozyr-Zyrko was never punished.

Attorney Goldstein did not have the publication of the Comité before him. Instead, he argued that if Petlura did not personally direct the pogrom at Ovruch, it was because it was physically impossible for him to be in forty places at the same time. "It was never the commander who did the work; he commanded; the others executed."

What of proclamations dating from 1917? Said Goldstein: "I didn't even know the name Petlura in 1917." Campinchi tried to read another order from the Commander-in-Chief, but was cut short by Torrès, who objected that it again dated from 1920 and hence was beyond the scope of examination. Campinchi tried to read another order dated August 27, 1919, and again Torrès objected, pointing out that it was from the time after Goldstein had already left the Ukraine.

Frustrated, Campinchi stammered, "I will not read all the proclamations I have. But here is one taken from January 11, 1919."

Again Torrès was on his feet. "You say January 11, 1919," he exclaimed. "But on January 12, the Jewish National Assembly at Kiev protested against this proclamation, which to them seemed susceptible of stimulating pogroms!"[16]

CAMPINCHI: What! A Jewish National Assembly said this order could stimulate pogroms?

TORRÈS: Yes, because of the conditions under which that order was conceived. On January 12, the Assembly protested against this proclamation, which they thought had the effect of pouring oil on the fire, if I may use that expression.

CAMPINCHI: You are going to judge right now, gentlemen of the jury . . . You are going to see if this proclamation is capable of stirring up pogroms: "In some parts of the Ukraine, acts of violence have been committed by isolated groups. The Cossacks have been incited to commit excesses by *provocateurs* and those who call themselves Bolsheviks. These *agents provocateurs* have as an aim provoking disorders and introducing anarchy into the country to facilitate the return to power of the great landlords. Certain of these *provocateurs* have already been shot. Others are being sought. The Directory orders the Cossacks who are rendered culpable for the disorders to be arrested immediately. . . ."

Further: " . . . the Directory warns the partisans of the Hetman [that is, of Skoropadsky] . . . and all the counter-revolutionaries who hide themselves under the name of Republicans, that all of those who attempt to dishonor the army or the revolutionary workers of the Ukraine shall suffer the most severe penalty. The Directory asks the entire Jewish population to fight against their co-religionists . . . "

GOLDSTEIN: There!

CAMPINCHI: " . . . whose acts and declarations of anarchy and communism, etc. . . . " I add that another proclamation said: "The Jews have helped us, the female Jews have nursed our soldiers, Jewish children have been sacrificed . . ."

TORRÈS: That isn't from the same date.[17]

If Campinchi was guilty of amalgamating separate decrees to portray Petlura in a more favorable light before the jury, his citation of the January 11 proclamation was even more inexcusable. That appeal from the Directory was rife with untruths and provocations. At a time when the *Kureni Smerti* of the regular army were engaged in widespread slaughter, this document blamed the pogroms on "isolated groups." It singled out followers of the Hetman, Bolsheviks, and the reactionary bourgeoisie as responsible for the incidents. It rebuked "the individual Bolshevik-anarchist members of the Jewish nation" who behaved as enemies of the workers of the Ukraine and the republic. On the following day, the Jewish National Assembly reacted to this supposedly favorable decree, labeling it "absolutely unsatisfactory from the point of view of the state." Because the Directory implied that significant numbers of the Jewish population were Bolsheviks and enemies of the Ukraine, the National Assembly concluded that the appeal was *"calculated to increase and not to allay the anxiety of the Jewish population."*[18] [*Emphasis added.*]

CAMPINCHI: Will you permit me. . . . From a contemporary period of the residence of the witness in the Ukraine, April 13, 1919, here is one that I would like to read to you, gentlemen of the jury. It is a proclamation of Petlura, similar to many others: "The agents of the black bands . . ."

TORRÈS: What date?

CAMPINCHI: April 13, 1919. "The agents of the black bands, the Bolsheviks, veritable plunderers, etc., de-

stroy the country and the Jewish population
which they blame as the cause of that which is
happening in the Ukraine today. This campaign risks provoking anti-Jewish pogroms in
the Ukraine, etc. Those who want our people to
be republican ought to remember that all disorder, and the pogroms, in particular, are the
cause of these disorders, won the way for the
enemy army, that is the Bolsheviks who are
advancing from all sides . . . "

TORRÈS: By whom is it signed?

Campinchi responded tersely, "By the chief of staff of the
Army. As a consequence, it emanates from the services of
Petlura." Hurriedly, he read on into the decree of April 13:

> Remember, Cossacks, that the pogroms can diminish
> our strength, because the death of innocent persons
> weighs heavy upon us and augments the number of our
> enemies. Cossacks, the army should fight the enemy, it
> shouldn't make war on women and children. This only
> tarnishes us before the world. I order you, moreover, to
> arrest all those who carry on pogromist agitation, and
> to prosecute them immediately before a tribunal,
> etc. . . . [19]

Campinchi was astonished that Goldstein had not known
of such a democratic, humanitarian proclamation from
Petlura. In truth, astonishment should have been reserved
for those with knowledge of the source of the April 13 order
which the Civil Prosecutor had just finished reading. Torrès
had asked, "By whom is it signed?" because he knew that the
so-called Order #77 of the Ukrainian People's Republic had
been issued not by Petlura, but by Acting Ataman Andrew
Melnyk, a subordinate.[20] The order followed by a day a
proclamation of the Council of Ministers which warned that
"the Government will not tolerate any pogroms against the

Jewish population in the Ukraine, and will employ every available means for the purpose of combatting these abject criminals . . . who are disgracing our nation in the eyes of all the civilized nations of the world."[21]

For weeks, the Directory's emissary to the Allies in Odessa, Mazievich, had been badgering the High Command for exactly such a statement to counter the image of bloodthirsty Cossacks conjured up in the Western press.[22] It was only through the efforts of Pinchas Krasny and the Socialists that President Martos of the Council of Ministers forced through the resolution of April 12. Melnyk's military order the next day was an insincere imitation. Lacking the countersignature of Petlura, such decrees were stillborn. Upon the return of the Zaporog Corps from a misadventure in Rumania, pogroms broke out anew in May, 1919.

Campinchi was not through enumerating those decrees which supposedly portrayed Petlura as a friend of the Jews. He said:

> You know that he made pro-Jewish proclamations because he needed them for his policy of independence. But in certain of these proclamations he gave other reasons. It wasn't only a slogan to say, "You dishonor the Ukraine, you dishonor yourselves and our army." But he gave the Cossacks and Ukrainian peasants reasons for not making pogroms. Here, for example, is the order of August 27, 1919. It is, to be sure, a little after your period. "The Jews and namely the Bund have worked for the restoration of the independence of the Ukraine." That means the Jews are with us. "I myself know how much Jewish elements have aided our army and our republic. The enemies of the state shoot and rob the Jews." Listen, and you say if he was really a hypocrite. "It is with the greatest respect and most profound emotion that I think of the sacrifices of the Jewish population, its glorious dead, fallen at the altar of the nation." And he continued, "By communiqués I have learned that the Jewish population has cared for our sick, our wounded." Excuse me for being a little

nervous, because like Torrès, I have a deep conviction, though in an opposite sense. "National unity can only be realized if the Jews are with us." He gives the reasons. "I have learned that the Jewish population has ministered to our sick and wounded, that Jewish children in hospitals have washed the wounds of our valiant soldiers. I have been profoundly touched in seeing tears of recognition in their eyes for the care which they have received from the Jews, and I have viewed, with pleasure, some of our soldiers setting up guard before Jewish shops and warehouses to impede pillaging." Further, "Be on guard against provocators: the penalty of death ought to be applied to pogromchiks as well as to *provocateurs.*" And you recall that in another proclamation, he said, "Let not a hair of an innocent head fall."

I hardly believe that the man who wrote that and gave those reasons why one should not commit excesses—the patriotism of the Jews was incontestable, the dedicated care that the Jewish women and children gave to the soldiers—I hardly believe that this man played a double game![23]

Actually all of Campinchi's references were based on or merely repeated stock phrases contained in Order #131, issued by Petlura on August 27, 1919. While his supporters might claim that he had taken determined action against pogroms as early as July 4, 1919,[24] the fact is that Order #131 was his first official pronouncement to Directory troops on the matter of pogroms.

With the Rada, Petlura had displayed no special vigor in combatting pogroms. Through the first six months of the Directory's existence, his name was singularly missing from any decree prohibiting the killing of Jews. His July 4 communication was a cable, not a general order, to the Council of Ministers (which commanded no troops), the Minister of Jewish Affairs (who hardly needed to be reminded of the cruelty of the pogroms), and several ranking officers of the army (all of whom were aware of their chief's true feelings on the subject), not to the troops *en masse*. In this cable, Petlura went on at length on the necessity of fair treatment for the Jews, but he inserted the same backhanded references to Jewish Bolshevism which prevented the cable from being an effective deterrent.

Order #131, however, was of an entirely different nature [*emphasis added*]:

DAILY ORDER BY THE SUPREME COMMANDER TO
THE TROOPS OF THE UKRAINIAN PEOPLE'S REPUBLIC #131

August 26, 1919

This order will be read in the divisions, the brigades, the regiments, the battalions, and the companies of the armies of the Dnieper and of the Dniester *and in the detachments of the insurgents:*

> ***The sinister men of the "Black Hundred" and the "Red Hundred" are but one band. They are assiduously weaving the spider's web, provoking pogroms of the Jewish population, and *on many occasions, they have incited certain backward elements of our army to commit abominable acts.* They thus succeeded in defiling our struggle for liberty in the eyes of the world and compromise our national cause.

> Officers and Cossacks! *It is time to know* that the Jews have, like the greater part of our Ukrainian population, suffered from the horrors of the Bolshevik-Communist invasion and follow the way to the truth. The best Jewish groups, such as the "Bund," the "Unified" (United Jewish Socialists), the "Poale Zion," and the "Folks Party" (People's Party) have willingly placed themselves at the disposal of the sovereign and independent Ukraine and cooperate with us.

> It is time to learn that the peaceful population, its women and children, have been oppressed in the same way as ours and deprived of national liberty. This population has lived with us for centuries and divides our pleasures and our sorrows.

The chivalrous troops who bring fraternity, equality, and liberty to all the nationalities of Ukraine,
must not listen to the invaders and *provocateurs*
who hunger for human blood. Neither can they
remain indifferent in the face of the tragic fate of the
Jews. He who becomes an accomplice to such crimes
is a traitor and an enemy of our country, and he must
be placed beyond the pale of human society.

Officers and Cossacks! The entire world is amazed at
your heroism. Do not tarnish it, even accidentally,
by an infamous adventure and do not dishonor our
Republic in the eyes of the world. Our enemies have
exploited the pogroms against us. They affirm that
we are not worthy of an independent and sovereign
existence and that we must be enslaved once again.

Officers and Cossacks! Ensure the victory by directing your arms against the real enemy, and remember
that our pure cause necessitates clean hands. I expressly order you to drive away with your arms all
who incite you to pogroms and *bring them before
the courts as enemies of the state.* And the tribunal
will judge them for their acts and the most severe
penalties of the law will be inflicted on all those
found guilty.

The Government of the Ukrainian People's Republic has addressed an appeal to all inhabitants of
the country to resist the activities of our enemies who
provoke the pogroms of the Jewish population.

I order all troops to listen well and to retain this
appeal and to spread it as much as possible among
their comrades and among the people.

(signed) PETLURA
Commander in Chief[25]

This was truly an amazing decree. No longer was there a
denial that regular elements of the Ukrainian army made
pogroms, not just on "several," but on "many" occasions.
No longer was there a denial that Petlura controlled the
"insurgents" or partisans. No longer did Simon Petlura, as

Commander-in-Chief of the Armed Forces, require the counter-signature of the President of the Council of Ministers. The Council, especially President Martos, had been agitating for such an order to the troops since the spring. None was forthcoming. *Order #131 was issued after the fact, after 100,000 Jews lay dead or maimed, fully eight months after the beginning of the pogroms.* Only then, in August, was it "time" for the troops "to know" that pogroms were inexcusable.

Why had Petlura even bothered to issue such an order? Why did he suddenly pressure the Directory into authorizing not 25,000 but 5,730,000 rubles for Jewish relief late in August, 1919? The answers to these questions were obvious.

Chased from Kiev by the Bolsheviks in February, Petlura hoped that the pogroms might serve to unite his people against the common enemy, Jewish Bolshevism. Instead, they only increased anarchy. By May, 1919, the Soviet Ukrainian Republic was firmly entrenched at Kharkov. By the end of the summer, the Directory was being shoved completely out of the western regions of its own land.

Only the intervention of General Denikin prevented the total collapse of the National Republic at this time. Within three months, the White Army succeeded in clearing the Reds from the Ukraine. In the process, however, Denikin's reactionaries turned on the Nationalists as well, suppressing the Ukrainian language, returning large estates to great landlords, and defeating the forces of the Directory in combat. Petlura's pogrom tactic was adopted by the Tsarists and anti-Semites in Denikin's ranks.

Harried on all sides, Petlura turned to the West once more in a desperate bid for sympathy and armed support. The Ukrainian question was still before the Paris Peace Conference, but, as M. G. Sidorenko notified his superior, the Allies were horrified by reports of massacres which only too late reached them from the East. During that summer, Ukrainian ambassadors in London, Berne, Paris, and Vienna bombarded Petlura with warnings that official recognition of the regime (with all attendant material benefits) would be withheld as long as the pogroms continued.[26]

The battered Directory, which was rapidly becoming a government-in-exile, had nothing to lose in issuing delinquent proclamations such as Order #131. In a breath, it could absolve itself of responsibility for any future pogroms, cast all blame on the troops of Denikin, and emerge as the sole humanitarian force in the Ukraine.[27]

Morris Goldstein and Torrès contended that Petlura was moved by a more mercenary consideration. They charged that he hoped to secure a loan from the Rothschilds. Such a grant would have bolstered morale in Ukrainian ranks, paid the soldiers, bribed turncoats, and even covered the relief to Jews which was authorized but never paid.

Farfetched as such a Rothschild ransom may have sounded, it was very real to Ukrainians who repeatedly brought up the subject of "World Jewry" to the Allied Mission at Odessa early in 1919.[28] It was almost as if Petlura and his underlings believed the ancient canard of an international conspiracy linking all Jewish communities. Historically, Jews had proved to be excellent hostages, and a promise to end pogroms might be the leverage whereby Petlura would obtain a stable treasury and relieve pressure from "Jewish Bolsheviks" at the same time.

Whatever Petlura's motivation, orders such as #131 were not forgeries. They were, however, never circulated among the troops. Nor were they published on the dates claimed. They were written solely for foreign consumption.

CAMPINCHI: Will you permit me a very simple reply? Everybody knows the order of the day of September 6, 1914, signed Joffre: "The hour has come when we can no longer look backward." And that signed Petain: "Courage! Hold! They will be

ours." I ask if someone coming to the front
lines in France on September 12 would have
found the proclamation of Joffre? And after-
wards, the order of Pétain—if someone went to
the region of Verdun, where many of us served—would he have found that order of the
day? Orders of the day emanating from higher
levels in the ranks are read to the troops, then
disappear; they aren't read in lower units; they
are found later only in the chancelleries. I believe that I am right. I myself have never seen
either Joffre's order of the day or that of Pétain.
They were read to us and then "Au revoir." But
our troops weren't being routed, whereas those
of Petlura had been throughout the year 1919. If
you want to look for the proclamation on walls,
you will not find them.

TORRÈS: Will you permit me to make three observations?
The first is quite simple. These orders of the
day from Joffre before the Marne and Pétain at
Verdun were dedicated to deeds relevant to victory. Petlura's orders of the day also had a
dedication: the massacres of Proskurov and
Zhitomir. After Joffre's order of the day, the
French Army triumphed. After Pétain's order
of the day, the French Army liberated Verdun.
After Petlura's orders of the day, his soldiers
pillaged and massacred. That is my first response. I told you it was really quite simple.

Second, if a soldier didn't know all the orders of
the day from the high command, an investigator [Goldstein], at that time a magistrate and
historian, would have known them. And if a
Commission of Inquiry with a President like

M. Goldstein had been sent immediately after the Marne or Verdun, they [the French High Command] would certainly not have failed to supply him with the orders of the day.

Third, the proclamations, this war literature, was published only after the victory [of the Bolsheviks] to serve as a justification for a policy. It had no effect upon the troops. What is effective over soldiers is the order, the act of the leader, the sanction or penalty. And during this war, where so often men were punished to serve as examples, the leaders well knew that orders of the day weren't sufficient to put down pillaging. It was necessary to arrest the pillagers and shoot them.

In this trial, we are dealing with organized plunderers, with the chief of an army of massacre, with the atamans themselves, Petlura, Semosenko, Palienko.

No sanction was taken with regard to any of them. It is this fact which compels me to put this final question to the witness: do you, you who conducted an inquiry in the Ukraine in the cruelest period of the pogroms, from January to June, 1919, know whether Petlura took any energetic measures whatever to repress the pogroms, shoot the perpetrators, instigators, or leaders responsible?

GOLDSTEIN: Not one single time.[29]

Campinchi and Reynaud claimed that Order #131 was representative of a host of documents in their dossier, documents calling for the cessation of pogroms, documents which had been published in such diverse official journals as *Visnyk Ukrainskoi Narodnoi Respubliky* (STATE JOURNAL OF THE UKRAINIAN PEOPLE'S REPUBLIC), *Vistnyk Derzhavnykh Zakoniv* (BULLETIN OF STATE LAWS), *Ukraina, Trudowa Hromada,* and *G. Q. G. Ukrainian.*

Torrès responded: "You speak to me of the *Bulletin of Laws!* This is without doubt the most certain means by which the appeals were never made known to the troops, because I did not know that soldiers read the *Bulletin of Laws* or the *Official Journal.*"[30]

Even if these journals had been the favorites of front-line literati, one doubts that published orders would have made much difference. It was curious that in virtually every document of this kind, there was an unexplained delay between the date on which the measure was signed and when it appeared in an official gazette.

Though the Council of Ministers passed its recommendation for an immediate inquiry into the pogroms on May 27, 1919, this act was not announced publicly until July 17, seven bloody weeks later. Though the same Council of Ministers again urged Petlura to punish guilty pogromchiks according to martial law on June 14, it was not until July 4 that the Holovni Ataman issued his celebrated cable to select ministers, and this fact was not acknowledged by the official journals until July 9.[31]

And though the Council of Ministers again urged him to establish a special government panel to investigate pogroms on August 18, it was not until mid-September that the Ukrainian Foreign Secretary V. Temnitzki cabled such an invitation to Menachem Ussishkin (President of the Jewish National Assembly in Kiev and one of the leading Zionists in the world), Asher Ginzberg (better known as "Ahad ha-Am"), Dr. D. Jochelman and Israel Zangwill of London, and Leon Motzkin (General Secretary of the Comité des Délégations Juives, the umbrella organization of Jewish delegations at Versailles) to proceed to the Ukraine to conduct such an inquiry.[32]

Even granting that delays in publishing anti-pogrom edicts or other decrees affecting Ukrainian-Jewish relations might have been caused, in part, by normal bureaucratic sloth or mechanical printing problems, there was no accounting for the dearth of such decrees before the late summer of 1919. Campinchi could produce his sheaf of documents which testified to a genuine humanitarianism on the part of Petlura, but for the most part these emanated from the hideaway in Poland and were dated after December, 1919.[33]

At the time when the Directory represented the supreme authority in the Ukraine, that is from December, 1918, through March, 1919, and even later when it still commanded the loyalty of great numbers of soldiers, no 'order denouncing pogroms was issued to the ranks. No placards, no posters comparable to those calling for massacres were distributed across the Ukraine warning pogromchiks of impending punishment. Petlura waited eight months too long, after thousands of innocent people had been killed or mutilated, to issue Order #131, which became a landmark of human hypocrisy.

Notes

1. For Goldstein's testimony, see *Notes Sténographiques*, 6, pp.8-72, and Torrès, *Le procès des pogromes*, pp.75-126. See also Deposition of M. Goldstein, File 427, 37052, Tcherikover Archive.

2. *Di ukrainishe presse un di pogromen,* December 16, 1918-March 15, 1919, File 523, Tcherikover Archive.

3. *Notes Sténographiques,* fasc. 6, pp.8-11, and *Les pogromes en Ukraine,* pp.31-32.

4. *Bericht fun Hillerson,* Testimony of T. Verkhola, Testimony of V. Schneider, Report of the student L. Beyzer, Files 409-10, Tcherikover Archive. See also *Notes Sténographiques,* fasc. 6, p.12, and Tcherikover, *Di ukrainer pogromen,* pp.138-142.

5. Revutzky described the fear and feeling of impotence of Jews who knew that orders had been given at Kiev for the extermination of Bolsheviks. This was regarded as a prelude to greater misfortunes. *In di shvere tog ofn Ukraine,* pp.137-38.

6. *"The Pogrom at Ovroutch,"* by A. I. Hillerson, 4 pp., File 440, and Ahron Dubenski, "Di blutike teg in Ovruch," (1926), File 453, Tcherikover Archive.

7. *Notes Sténographiques,* fasc. 6, pp.17-18.

8. Elbogen, *A Century of Jewish Life,* p.499.

9. *Notes Sténographiques,* fasc. 6, pp.20-21.

10. Joseph Lichten, "A Study of Ukrainian-Jewish Relations," *Annals of the Ukrainian Academy of Arts and Sciences in the United States,* V (Winter-Spring, 1956), p.1165.

11. *Ibid.,* p.1166.

12. Schechtman, *et al, The Pogroms in the Ukraine,* pp.9-11; and

Report of J. B. Schechtman on Pogroms in Small Rada, File 440, 37596-603, Tcherikover Archive.

13. Torrès, *Le procès des pogromes*, pp.87-88.

14. Schechtman, *et al, The Pogroms in the Ukraine*, p.283.

15. *Ibid.*, p.39 and 140.

16. Schechtman, *et al, The Pogroms in the Ukraine*, p.100. The appeal read:

In certain parts of the Ukraine isolated groups of Cossacks are committing acts of violence against Jews. It has been ascertained that the Cossacks have been instigated to this by provocators—followers of the Hetman, volunteers, and persons calling themselves "Bolsheviks." This has been done in order to stain the fair name of the Ukrainian Republican Army, in order to excite hatred against the Ukrainian Cossacks, in order to provoke disorder and crime, and through these methods to reinstate the old Empire of the landlords and the bourgeois. Some of these provocators and pogrom-mongers have already been arrested and shot; others will be tried by court-martial. The Directory calls upon the Cossacks of the People's Army and upon all honest citizens to arrest any such provocators and all those who incite to violence and to bring them immediately before a court-martial. At the same time, the Directory warns all the Hetman's counter-revolutionaries who hide under the mask of "Republicans" that anybody daring to lift his hand against the honor of the army of the Ukrainian laboring revolutionary people will be punished most severely. The Directory calls upon the whole of democratic Jewry to fight energetically those individual Bolshevik-anarchist members of the Jewish nation who behave as enemies of the working people of the Ukraine and of the State. For it is these elements who enable the Hetman's men and their provocators to carry on a demagogic agitation against the mass of Jewry which is non-Bolshevik and who involve the Ukrainians, the true defenders of all workers, in grave misunderstandings with the Jewish democracy, which is not anarchist or bolshevist, and is true to the Ukrainian State democracy.

(signed) The President of the Directory
V. Vinnichenko

Members: Makarenko, Shvetz,
Petlura, Andrievski

17. Torrès, *Le procès des pogromes,* pp.94-97.

18. *Minutes of Jewish National Assembly,* File 2, Tcherikover Archives.

19. *Notes Sténographiques,* fasc. 6, pp.38-39. See also *Di Direktorye un di pogromen,* January-October, 1919, File 522, Tcherikover Archive.

20. Melnyk, a loyal Galician Ukrainian, succeeded Konovalets as head of the OUN in 1938 and died in 1960. In 1919, however, he was a subordinate whose actions required the countersignature of Petlura. This was absent from the April decrees. For a debate on his signing powers, see *Notes Sténographiques,* fasc. 3, pp.72-79.

21. Pigido, *Material Concerning Ukrainian-Jewish Relations,* p.52.

22. "Di ukrainishe forshteyers in Odes un di pogromen," in Tcherikover, *Di ukrainer pogromen,* p.185.

23. *Notes Sténographiques,* fasc. 6, p.46.

24. Choulguine, *L'Ukraine et le cauchemar rouge,* pp.157-59.

25. *The Jewish Pogroms in the Ukraine* (Washington: Friends of the Ukraine, 1919), pp.15-16. Interestingly enough, the Editorial Board of the Ukrainian Information Bureau, which published F. Pigido's documentary study, deleted the first two paragraphs, which indicated Petlura's control over the insurgents. Pigido, *Material Concerning Ukrainian-Jewish Relations,* pp.68-69.

26. For these panicky letters, see Files 140, 373-74-75, Tcherikover Archive.

27. A similar logic lay behind Himmler's order to stay the extermination of Jews in the last days of World War II. With the war lost, it was hoped that such "humanitarian" acts would earn some forgiveness and possibly even preferential treatment for the executioners from the Allies.

28. See Tcherikover, *Di ukrainer pogromen,* pp.184-85, for reference to "Velt-Yidntum" at Odessa conferences between the Ukrainians and the Allies.

29. *Notes Sténographiques,* fasc. 6, pp.59-63.

30. Torrès, *Le procès des pogromes*, p.121.

31. *The Directory and Petlura's Government*, File 34, Tcherikover Archives.

32. *Ibid.*, and also Schechtman, *et al*, *The Pogroms in the Ukraine*, pp.92-93, and p.251.

33. See orders in *Petlura's Headquarters*, File 30, and *The Directory and Petlura's Government*, File 34, Tcherikover Archive and *Les pogromes en Ukraine*, pp.82-87.

12.

The Mobilization of Israel

THROUGHOUT THE COURSE OF THE TRIAL, supporters of Petlura insisted that their heroic leader had been slain by a fanatic. Then his memory had been slandered by an entire people merely because the assassin belonged to their "race." Jewish outrage, the Ukrainians believed, was illegitimate, indecent in view of the cold-blooded nature of Schwartzbard's mercenary crime.

The Prosecution apparently agreed, for as early as the second day Willm raised eyebrows when he commented: "Israel has mobilized for this affair. They don't speak to us of the slaughtered Christians, of all the armies which set upon that rich and unhappy Ukraine, the battleground of Europe for some years."[1]

To a generation of Frenchmen nurtured on the *Protocols of the Elders of Zion*, such words rang true. How else could one explain the creation of Schwartzbard Defense Committees from Shanghai to Chicago? It was obvious that Jewish bankers had mobilized all their forces to procure witnesses who would prostitute themselves for Jewish gold.

More rational men might be puzzled that these unnamed capitalists would work so strenuously in concert with a "Bolshevik conspiracy." No matter. The Jews sought to divert the press, public opinion, and world attention from the real issue, the killing of an unarmed innocent, to Jewish history, Jewish suffering, and Jewish deaths.

Thus far, the court had heard from nurse Greenberg and attorney Goldstein. Both testimonies might be discounted as the emotional responses of hypersensitive people, but the Prosecutors knew that more victims and eyewitnesses would follow in an effort to damn Petlura. The Prosecution therefore sought out objective Jews, such as the three mentioned by Professor Shulgin: Drs. Sliosberg, Tiomkin, and Tcherikover.

The first of these, Dr. Heinrich B. Sliosberg, was one of the most renowned jurists of Tsarist Russia. He had been with the defense in several important anti-Jewish trials, including the Beiliss Ritual Murder case. During the Ukraine's time of troubles, Sliosberg was living in Petrograd, where he headed the Central Committee for Relief of Victims of the War and Pogroms. This organization had been established in 1916 to aid the Jews of Poland who had been ravaged as German, Austrian, and Russian troops criss-crossed the Eastern Front.

The Petrograd committee was never out of touch with developments in the Ukraine, and by the end of 1918 it was in possession of the first accounts of organized pogroms uncovered by Sliosberg's fellow barrister, A.I. Hillerson. Nine years later, the sixty-four-year-old Sliosberg, an imposing figure with long grey hair and a Clemenceau mustache, described to his French audience the contents of Hillerson's communiqués.[2]

"These reports truly overwhelmed us," he began nervously. "We were stupefied because never in the long and sad history of Jewish massacres in Russia had such horrors been committed." Not even the tragic pogroms of Kishinev, Gomel, and 275 other places in 1905 and 1906 could compare with what Dr. Sliosberg termed "real pogroms."

"There had been some brawls, some little pogroms between different sides, and some general pogroms which were caused by the war," said Sliosberg, using "pogrom" in its general meaning of riot or incident. "We always classed those victims as victims of the war. But if a pogrom occurred where the Jews alone were victims, a pogrom specifically against the Jews, we then classed the victims as victims of pogroms.

"We know by experience that if a government doesn't want to allow pogroms, there won't be any. We know by experience that when a government telegraphs a chief of police, 'You will be prosecuted in a court of law if a pogrom is made,' pogroms don't take place." As proof of this, Sliosberg cited his own intervention on behalf of the Jews of Romny in 1906. Following an appeal to Minister of Interior Pierre Durnovo, Romny Police Chief Ivanov, instigator of the slaughter, was warned that he would be brought before a magistrate unless the killing stopped. Meekly, Ivanov quelled all disturbances in the town.[3]

The Jews of Petrograd were shocked by reports of the pogroms, but "more striking was the fact that they were systematic, that the pogroms followed, so to speak, the movements of the Petluran Army." Supporters of the Ataman blamed the massacres on anarchy, but this was indefensible. For Dr. Sliosberg, the Directory was responsible for everything that transpired under it. In this, he echoed the sentiments of a Jewish delegation headed by Drs. M. S. Schwarzman, M. B. Kleinman, and G. Hindes to Odessa on February 22, 1919. In a note to Minister of Foreign Affairs Matzievich (Shulgin's successor), the Jews protested against the Directory's failure to suppress the pogroms:

> We definitely declare that the responsibility devolves upon the authorities, whoever they are, and whatever the conditions of their tenure of power. We cannot stop to consider whether this authority is strong or weak. If the authorities have an "address" we direct our protest to that address; our sole demand is that there shall not be any more pogroms.[4]

For Sliosberg, as for Revutzky, Schechtman, Goldstein, and all other Jewish leaders, there could be no doubt that officially the "address" of the government in the Ukraine in 1919 was the seat of government of the Directory and Simon Petlura. Regardless of whether it was located at Kiev, Kamenetz-Podolsk, Vinnitza, or in a moving railway coach, this was the government to which Jews appealed for help and for which, on rare occasions, they issued sycophantic testimonials.

Germany, Austria-Hungary, Turkey, and Bulgaria had recognized the independence of the Ukrainian National Republic in the treaty of Brest-Litovsk. Though the treaty had supposedly been invalidated by the defeat of the Central Powers, official notes of the People's Commissariat of the Soviet Republic and Red Army chieftain Leon Trotsky (at least on paper) continued to indicate that the Ukraine had severed itself from Russia. Finland recognized the Directory in 1918. Poland and Latvia followed in 1920. Even Great Britain and France cloaked the regime with trappings of sovereignty until the departure of their military missions from the Crimea in the spring of 1919. Sliosberg argued that the Directory had been recognized *de jure* by most of the important countries of the world. Having established this, it ought logically to have followed that the Directory was the *de facto* government as well.

Once more, Sliosberg pointed out that Simon Petlura was the chief of the Ukrainian Directory. He was Ataman-in-Chief of the army. He maintained ministers and legations abroad. He was represented at the Paris Peace Conference by Temnitzki, Shulgin, and Margolin. Ultimately, therefore, he had to bear responsibility for the policies of his government.

In his army, where a colonel one day might be a general of a brigade the next and a general of a division on the day following, the problem of supplies was critical. The pogroms afforded Petlurist divisions a convenient opportunity to secure food, clothing, and ammunition at no cost. The killing of "Bolshevik Jews" was done before Petlura's very eyes. Said Sliosberg, "I cannot deny that Petlura was a man of honor, but he knew very well what was happening." In this knowledge, Petlura should have emulated his Jewish ministers and resigned from the government in 1919.

There had been proclamations against pogroms, Sliosberg conceded. "But has anyone presented a single judgment of a court-martial condemning the authors of these massacres?" Petlura may well have been "a man of character," "a man of will," a Social Democrat who was no anti-Semite in the ordinary sense of the word, but he took no action against the leading pogromchiks. Despite his dilatory decrees, the Jews would ever hold him responsible. "It was necessary to act," said Sliosberg. "He didn't. He talked."[5]

"That is our opinion. I say our, that is to say, mine and all my friends. And having had the misfortune or good fortune of representing Israel in Russia for close to forty years (and this was not an easy thing), I can say that it was the feeling of most Jews about what happened, about what we had seen, what had drained our hearts, and which we would never forget. No, we will not be able to forget it. It is impossible."

According to the record, Sliosberg trembled as he cried out, "Gentlemen of the jury, a Roman General conquered Judaea, had the Temple of the Jews burned. Titus was surnamed 'Delight of Humanity' by the Romans. He was, perhaps, a brave man, but for us he was the destroyer of our Temple, the cause of all our misfortune for two thousand years. And we cannot forget Titus.

"We are friends of the Ukrainians. We have lived on good terms. We have been good neighbors. The old Tsarist governments tolerated, or ordered, the pogroms in little villages. They were forgotten the next day. After the pogroms of Kishinev, the Jewish population lived on better terms with the peasants and understood that their executioners were uncouth tools. You know what the cultural level in Russia, Bessarabia, and even the Ukraine could be.[6] There were always some elements attempting to seize the goods of others. From time to time, the pogrom was for them a little festival.

"But the pogroms of Petlura were not like the others. These we will never forget. We will not reproach the Ukrainian people for them because they were at war. But we may reproach and will reproach Petlura for them, because his government tolerated the greatest tragedies in Jewish history, a history which is filled with martyrs."[7]

Sliosberg had said that Petlura was under a moral obligation to resign his post rather than continue to head an anti-Jewish government. And yet, Civil Prosecutor Campinchi interrupted, another Jew, State Controller Moishe Rafes, had written recently:

> One of the thoughts dearest to Petlura as well as to numerous Ukrainian nationalists had always been the idea of the union of Ukrainian democracy with Jewish democracy. He spoke of his passionate desire to realize the union. He spoke only of that.[8]

Should such a patriot have resigned in the face of adversity? Dr. Sliosberg's answer more than dignified the question. In the first place, he was personally acquainted with Rafes but had not read his book. Sliosberg regarded Rafes, a former official in the Ukrainian Republic, as a turncoat. Once a member of the Jewish Bund and later a Bolshevik, Rafes had made the fantastic allegation that his people, the Jews, were responsible for the success of the Soviets in the Ukraine. He thus hoped to ingratiate himself with his new overlords.[9] "Rafes," said Sliosberg, "was a prejudiced man who caused many unpleasantries for the Jews."

As for Petlura, "I don't deny that he was animated by grand sentiments. He was a great Ukrainian patriot. But I question whether he was the sole liberator of the Ukraine. I myself have known some Ukrainian patriots, equally great, who were as capable and perhaps even more capable than

Petlura of being the leaders of the government. If, therefore, Petlura imagined that passing power to another's hands would have meant that the cause of Ukrainian freedom would be lost, it was an immodest thought. I assure you, gentlemen of the jury, that even among the witnesses that you have heard before me, there were some persons as capable as Petlura of liberating the Ukraine and doing it, perhaps, without pogroms!"[10]

Campinchi returned to the attack: "You have said just now that certain pogroms were made under Petlura's own eyes. Do you forget, Mr. Sliosberg, that Petlura's government, at one particular moment, was reduced to holding its deliberations in a railway coach? In January, 1919, namely, he and his minister were so destitute in everything that they were obliged to help the train's engineer put coal and water into the engine. Some months later, in a period not contemporary with these deeds, do you know that Petlura's government was reduced to a thin band of territory at Kamenetz, not even a sixth of the Ukraine?"[11]

"It was enough to make pogroms," Sliosberg replied. The Hetman may not have been responsible for massacres east of the Dnieper River, from Odessa to Ekaterinoslav, which were the work of independent renegade bands, "but the pogroms of Proskurov, Berdichev, Ovruch, Felshtin, all those horrors were produced at his command. Those pogroms were carried out as one makes war. The general said, 'Mobilize. Fire. Do this. Do that.' That is how the pogroms took place in this region. Not the populace, not disorganized bands, but the army organized by Petlura, of which he was the leader, committed the pogroms."[12]

What of Schwartzbard? Would he, Sliosberg, a moderate, have come forth to testify in such a trial if he knew that the accused was an agent of the Cheka, a Bolshevik? Campinchi's question was double-edged. Not only did it place Dr. Sliosberg, once accused of being a "monarchist," a supporter of the Russian Tsar, and hence a foe of Ukrainian independence, in the position of apologizing for a Bolshevik, but it also implied that the Professor was coming forth merely to aid a fellow Jew. The insinuation ignored the fact that it was the prosecution which had summoned Sliosberg.

"I am able to swear," said Sliosberg, "that Schwartzbard acted not as an agent or under any instigation of the Bolsheviks." The accused had spent his years in Paris as if under a glass bell, for the entire world to see. Like Goldstein before him, Dr. Sliosberg recounted how Schwartzbard had volunteered to aid in settling orphans of the pogroms in France. It was Sliosberg who introduced the testimony of M. Bourtzev, clearing Schwartzbard of any connection with the *agent provocateur* Dobkovski. In fact, charged Sliosberg, the entire tale about Schwartzbard's sinister dealings with Moscow had been fabricated by leaders of the Ukrainian exiles.

Speaking of discussions which he had held with Ukrainians, Sliosberg said, "In our conversations, the Ukrainians insisted, and especially M. Shulgin, that it would even be very desirable to insert this theory that Schwartzbard was an agent of the Bolsheviks into the debate. It wouldn't upset the Communists; it wouldn't affect the others concerned; it would be better for all parties. I replied to him, 'We cannot acknowledge a fact that isn't true.' "

Sliosberg claimed that he had tried to reason with Professor Shulgin and the others, tried to show that such a slander would cause irreparable harm to all Jews who had paid sufficiently in "taxes of blood."[13]

As for the suggestion by the Prosecution that he was merely part of the so-called "Jewish mobilization," Sliosberg said angrily, "If you speak of the mobilization of Israel, we take offense at that. You don't want to admit that among fifteen million Jews in the world there was one, who having been an eyewitness to all these misfortunes, concealed a desire for vengeance in his heart.

"I am an old jurist. I don't approve sentiments of hate. But I have had the good fortune of being spared the sight of rivulets of Jewish blood. But for one who had seen them, they were sufficient motive to commit an act of frenzy.

"We don't approve it, but we Jews, we understand it, and the Ukrainians don't want to understand it! They give evidence based on nothing. They say that Schwartzbard is an agent of the Bolsheviks. That is what provokes us. That is what mobilizes us, as if to say, in a completely metaphorical sense, that we are compelled to shake with indignation.

"Someone has spoken of 'the mobilization of Israel.' He should have looked into the synagogues on October 18, when the trial began. That was the day when the dead were remembered. In all the synagogues prayers were said for the tranquility of the martyrs who had perished in the Ukrainian pogroms. You should have seen all the Jews, what tears, what cries, what lamentations in all the synagogues! *That was the mobilization of Israel!* We mobilize ourselves every year, the anniversary date of the destruction of the Temple! We fall to the ground. We mourn. That is our Jewish mobilization!"[14]

All very touching, the Civil Prosecutor conceded. As a Corsican, as a member of a small people which had fought for its liberty over the centuries, which had succeeded in averting enslavement by the Romans, Campinchi could sympathize with people who mourned the destruction of their sacred city. It was true that Jews were oppressed everywhere, martyred everywhere. But this was not the question. The question was whether the tears which fell after the pogroms were due to anti-Jewish orders "of a man called Petlura," who was slain without defense on the Boulevard Saint-Michel.

CAMPINCHI: When you tell me of all that you have suffered in the course of history and that, alas, you still suffer, I agree with you. But so far as proof of that which you are trying to say—Petlura was a murderer—I demand that you supply a document, that you say—at such a place, at such a time, he gave orders, at such a moment his apparent philo-Semitism was only hypocrisy. That you cannot do. You cannot try. You will not do it.

SLIOSBERG: I would reply only that we have no more proof that Titus himself burned the Temple.

CAMPINCHI: You are being unfair in your comparison.

SLIOSBERG: You know that he (Titus) was the chief of the army that destroyed and burned the Temple.

CAMPINCHI: Would you permit me, since we are in an historical controversy . . .

TORRÈS: That's settled! That's your point of view: Petlura wasn't responsible for acts which his troops and his generals committed. Don't review it. Everybody has understood. We agree, it's settled. That's your point of view.

CAMPINCHI: Your client has spoken of Haman and of Ahashuerus. M. Sliosberg has likewise spoken of Titus. But that was a matter of a Roman Emperor who had his troops under control. Roman discipline has never been equalled in history. If a Roman soldier committed an act against that discipline, one hundred of them were executed. I can understand how one such general should be responsible when it is a matter of Roman civilization advancing like a steam roller. (You understand what I want to say.) But when one speaks to me of a man who was delegated responsibility, an improvised general who commanded an army in the process of organization, which M. Torrès termed the "rascal army," you clearly must recognize that the responsibility isn't the same.

TORRÈS: An army of rascals.

CAMPINCHI: [*ignoring him*] Titus, yes, because he was a
               Roman and his discipline was of iron; Petlura,
               no, because he wasn't able to be at all the
               breaches of the rampart when they destroyed,
               when they slaughtered, when they burned,
               when they disemboweled. You are aware of my
               point of view and how the situations differ
               historically.

SLIOSBERG: I don't want to return to the question of Pet-
               lura's responsibility because I have clearly ex-
               pressed myself.

TORRÈS: The witness has replied that he considered
               Petlura responsible and he said why.

CAMPINCHI: Morally . . .

SLIOSBERG: . . . and politically. I rest on that ground and do
               not change my opinion.[15]

Sliosberg went on to describe Petlura's newspaper in
Paris, *Trident*. He agreed with Schwartzbard that *Trident's*
contents were provocative and potentially dangerous to
Jews remaining in the Ukraine. And Schwartzbard had
shouted, in the midst of one exchange with Campinchi:
"The Trident was the symbol of the Devil in Hell, the
symbol that the Petlurians carried. The Trident was above
the flags of those who massacred the Jews and were under
the direction of Petlura. I recognized the significance of the
Trident symbol. It indicated to me that it was indeed a
matter of Petlura."[16] Sliosberg concurred, telling the court,
"This journal was expressly anti-Semitic and the moving
force of a collaborator of this journal [Petlura] was himself
an anti-Semite."[17]

Other witnesses, specially Ukrainians, would not allow *Trident* to be labelled anti-Semitic or provocative. Viacheslav Prokopovich, Education Minister for the Directory and in 1927 editor-in-chief of the newspaper, indignantly rejected Schwartzbard's claim that the journal had made anti-Jewish statements which threatened new pogroms.

"That is a lie," Prokopovich testified. "The principal aim of our publication is the fight for the independence of the Ukraine." And while Petlura may have contributed an article or two, the substance of which was always "nationalist and anti-Soviet," Prokopovich claimed, "As editor I bear responsibility for every article."[18]

Court interpreter Magron testified that he had researched available copies of *Trident*, seeking out the incendiary articles mentioned by Schwartzbard, but could find none.[19] This prompted Civil Prosecutor Campinchi to declare that Schwartzbard's outrage over *Trident* was nothing more than a fraud. Said Campinchi, "There is no indication that Petlura signed an article in which he declared himself a partisan of pogroms or tried to renew the massacres."[20]

Most damaging to Schwartzbard's case against *Trident* seemed to be the claim of Ilarian Kosenko, another contributing editor, who charged that Schwartzbard could not even read Ukrainian. Thus he could not have read *Trident* and could not have been provoked by anything. Kosenko, who endorsed the Bolshevik conspiracy idea, continued: "At my request the magistrate presented Schwartzbard a Ukrainian text, a page of *Trident*. He looked at it and understood nothing."

Schwartzbard protested lamely that he did not have his glasses at the time and that his Ukrainian was a bit rusty. For a moment it seemed as if the defendant's credibility was about to collapse. After some dispute between opposing counsel, however, Schwartzbard submitted to a verbal examination at the hands of the court interpreter. Apparently he responded well enough for Magron to proclaim, "He speaks Ukrainian as one speaks it in the region of Balta."[21]

The other points in favor of *Trident* were also disposed of. Torrès referred Magron to specific articles, dated February 7, March 7, March 27, April 2, April 18, and May 2, 1926, one of which was definitely signed Petlura.[22] They all related to a Soviet plan, enunciated by the All-Ukrainian Central Executive Committee on October 11, 1924, to settle Jewish families on Ukrainian soil as farmers in collectives. The measure affected 3,000 families, numbering 15,000 persons, at 200 collectives.

These people were not being imported from White Russia, as *Trident* implied. The proposed resettlement was completely legitimate, since among the Ukrainian estates confiscated by the Bolsheviks there was some land belonging to Jews. Sliosberg himself had owned some land, for which he received no compensation when it was "nationalized."

The concept of agrarian colonies was not new to Russia. Tsarist governments had toyed with the idea of removing urban populations to the wilds of Siberia for more than fifty years, but the responsible agency had been a dismal failure. Faced with a mass of indigent Jews, impoverished and demoralized by pogroms, the Soviets set aside 80,000 hectares of land in the Ukraine, approximately 200,000 acres of land, for Jewish collectives.

As Sliosberg pointed out, a single Jewish family, that of Baron Joseph Ginzburg, held 50,000 hectares (125,000 acres) before the Revolution.[23] By the end of 1925, less than this amount of land had been converted to use by Jews.[24] One could hardly object to returning a pittance of Jewish land to Jewish colonists, but this was precisely what Petlura and *Trident* had done. For the nationalist leader, the trickle of Jewish agriculturalists (who were to number no more than 1.06 percent of all those employed in farming in the Ukraine by 1929[25]) was potentially a dangerous flood against which the Ukrainian peasants were entitled to protect themselves at whatever cost.

On February 7, 1926, *Trident* published "A Letter from the Ukraine." Signed by Petlura, it read:

> Our countrymen are very excited because of the Jewish colonization in the Ukraine. It is only in the Ukraine, especially on the right bank, where there is a paucity of arable land, where many people are thinking of emigrating to Siberia. Tens of thousands of the best lands in the region of Ekaterinoslav, Kherson, and Tauride have been distributed to the Jews. Such a policy instead of making national hatred disappear will increase it.[26]

On March 7, *Trident's* editors lashed out sarcastically against what they termed "the New Palestine":

> One must say that the word of the Old Testament addressed to the Jewish people is being realized: "You will receive a vast and beautiful land which was not created by you, and plain and opulent houses which were not constructed by you."[27]

Again, on March 27, 1926, the editors of *Trident* wrote:

> The Ukrainian sea will never accept the new Jewish stream and these intruders will never be at rest. The divergence of opposing interests is further accentuated by economic conflict. While the indigenous Ukrainian population lacks land and is forced to emigrate from its native land to far off Siberia, Ukrainian land is distributed to newcomers. Discontent grows now and forever. Now and forever this discontent begins to take the form of a severe protest. *We know, perhaps, what the severe character of these protests against these newcomers will be.* The news of the skirmish in the region of Krivoi-Rog between the Ukrainian population and the Jewish colonists is an unquieting sympton. *This little fact is a menacing forewarning of the future.*[28] [*Emphasis added.*]

And on April 12, 1926:

> It was not surprising that the peasants of the district of
> Krivoi Rog did not permit the Jews to do agricultural
> work in that spring. This was why anti-Semitism in the
> Ukraine emerged suddenly. This was altogether nor-
> mal. As for anti-Jewish feeling in the army, there was as
> much as one looked for.[29]

Torrès returned repeatedly to the phrase "altogether normal" (*mais bein comme il faut*). Prokopovich defended the
Ukrainian position, generously conceding that Jews had a
right to live in Ukraine, but that even the Zionist Jabotinsky
had opposed the Soviets' colonization scheme. Ignoring
Jabotinsky's reasons, Prokopovich rambled on: "It was in
the interest of the Ukrainian population, of the entire
population, Christian and Jew, that I fought and I will
always fight the Jewish colonization of Ukrainian land. It
was the Soviets who took the land of Ukrainians to profit the
Jews, to make there a Jewish national nucleus. Then, they
would create a Jewish republic on Ukrainian land. That I
fought and always will fight. Is that anti-Semitism?"[30]

Sliosberg had proven to be anything but a favorable
witness for the prosecution. He concluded: "If a Ukrainian
journal is permitted to say that this [the colonization of a few
Jews] is a cause for future pogroms, it justifies the pogroms
in advance and commits an instigation for pogroms."[31]

Notes

1. *Notes Sténographiques*, fasc. 2, p.156.

2. For Sliosberg's deposition, see File 427, 37039, Tcherikover Archive. For his testimony at the Schwartzbard Trial, see *Notes Sténographiques*, fasc. 6, pp.114-159, and Torrès, *Le procès des pogromes*, pp.207-246.

3. *Notes Sténographiques*, fasc. 6, pp.114-118.

4. Schechtman, *et al*, *The Pogroms in the Ukraine*, pp.67-68.

5. *Notes Sténographiques*, fasc. 6, pp.118-122.

6. In 1917, more than 83 percent of the Ukrainian population could neither read nor write. Baron, *The Jews in Russia under Soviets and Tsars*, p.217.

7. *Notes Sténographiques*, fasc. 6, pp.123-4.

8. Rafes, *Dva goda revoliutsii na Ukraine*, p.133.

9. *Ibid.*, p.164.

10. On Rafes, see *Notes Sténographiques*, fasc. 6, p.126. For Sliosberg's opinions of Petlura see p.128. *loc.cit.*

11. *Ibid.*, p.129.

12. *Ibid.*, p.130.

13. Sliosberg refused to lie about Schwartzbard when his life in Paris was an open book. It would have been unfair to the accused, who had lived through three generations of bloodshed. *Notes Sténographiques*, fasc. 6, pp.149-50. For another

meeting along the same lines and with the same purpose see the report of the magistrate on the meeting of Goldstein, Prokopovitch, and Koval, July 20, 1926, File 427, 37056, Tcherikover Archive.

14. *Notes Sténographiques*, fasc. 6, p.151.

15. *Ibid.*, pp.154-55.

16. *Notes Sténographiques*, fasc. 4, p.6.

17. *Notes Sténographiques*, fasc. 6, pp.157-59.

18. An argumentative witness who refused to "be insulted" by Counsel Torres, Prokopovitch blamed the Bolsheviks for most of the pogroms and "could not say" who was responsible for pogroms at Proskurov, Felshtin, and Zhitomir. See *Notes Sténographiques*, fasc. 3, pp.146-47.

19. *Notes Sténographiques*, fasc. 2, p.21. A day later, the overworked interpreter reported to the court that he still had not had time to review the materials.

20. *Notes Sténographiques*, fasc. 4, p.16.

21. For this dramatic moment, see *Notes Sténographiques*, fasc. 5, pp.151-54. Kosenko's deposition claimed that a Ukrainian friend named Loubenetz was informed by another Ukrainian named Nesterenko that one of Schwartzbard's aides in the conspiracy, named Norsgowski or Sougoff, had been seen following Petlura. Such was the chain of proof. Deposition of Kosenko, June 29, 1926, File 451, Tcherikover Archive.

22. *Notes Sténographiques*, fasc. 2, p.21. For copies of *Trident*, see Files 454 and 471, Tcherikover Archive. For some of Petlura's articles in exile, see Simon Petlura, *Statti, lysty, dokumenty* (Petlura Memorial Committee in America and Ukrainian Academy of Arts and Sciences in U.S., 1956), pp.287-388.

23. Baron Joseph Ginzburg, a leader of the St. Petersburg community, accumulated great wealth in the nineteenth century through banking, railroad, and Siberian gold mining enterprises. Honored with the title of Duke of Hesse-Darmstadt, he eventually settled in Paris. His sons, Horace and David, continued his philanthropic and educational work until their deaths in 1910. The latter was a leading force in the establishment of the Institute of Jewish Studies in St. Petersburg. Sliosberg was intimate with the family, having written a history of the Ginzburgs.

24. By the end of 1919, only 24,300 desiatins (approximately 56,000 acres) had been reserved for the Jews. In the next six years, the government added another 45,000 desiatins, a total far less than that which had been promised and which had been stolen from Jewish landlords. See Gregor Aronson, "Soviet Russia," in *The Jewish People: Past and Present, II* (New York: Central Yiddish Culture Organization, 1948), p.56.

25. In 1927, the total Jewish farm population numbered 107,500. See Vlas. Ya. Chubar, *Do novykh peremoh* (Kharkov: Proletarii), pp.36-37, and Dmytryshyn, *Moscow and the Ukraine*, p.81.

26. See *Notes Sténographiques*, fasc. 3, pp.148-49, and File 471, 39061, Tcherikover Archive.

27. *Notes Sténographiques*, fasc. 3, p.149, and File 471, 39062, Tcherikover Archive.

28. *Notes Sténographiques*, fasc. 3, pp.150-51, and File 471, 39063, Tcherikover Archive.

29. *Notes Sténographiques*, fasc. 3, p.149, and p.159.

30. *Ibid.*, pp.160-63.

31. *Notes Sténographiques*, fasc. 6, p.159.

13.

We Have Pleaded Too Much

On Tuesday, October 25, 1927, the trial of Sholom Schwartzbard was only into its second week; yet it seemed as if it had been dragging on forever. Perhaps it had. Perhaps there was nothing new in the saga of Jewish suffering. These same tales had echoed in Roman villas where patricians gorged themselves on squid and truffles, in darkened medieval hamlets where the Devil Incarnate roamed the lanes claiming men's souls, and even in the mirrored halls of an "Enlightened" Europe where periwigged grandees concluded grand alliances. Inquisitor, baron, and *muzhik* heard the sobs of a ravaged people and were not moved.

On this day, the Jury of the Seine would listen again to such tales from Jewish witnesses called by the Prosecution. The writings of Vladimir Tiomkin and Elia Tcherikover, as well as their conversations with Ukrainian leaders, left little doubt that they would absolve Petlura of complicity in the pogroms.

Engineer Tiomkin, another venerable gentleman with a long salt-and-pepper beard, had been one of Theodor Herzl's earliest supporters. A participant at the first Zionist Congress in August, 1897, he had also served in the ill-fated All-Russian Constituent Assembly twenty years later. From the position of President of the Jewish community of Eliz-

282

avetgrad, he had risen to Town President (no mean feat for a Jew in Tsarist Russia), then to President of the Jewish National Secretariat in Kiev. During the epoch of pogroms, the sixty-six-year-old Tiomkin came to be regarded as the unofficial spokesman of Ukrainian Jewry.

Like so many of his countrymen, Tiomkin had fled the Ukraine because of the Bolshevik takeover. In 1921, he prepared an authoritative report on the pogroms for the Conference of Jewish Organizations at Karlsbad. In it, he accused the Volunteer Army of General Denikin of the most horrible massacres in the Ukraine. "The new administration," he wrote of Denikin's regime, "brought with it a pronounced official anti-Semitism." Even the commanders

Dr. Vladimir Tiomkin, one-time leader of the Ukrainian Jewish community and a witness at the trial. (YIVO Tcherikover Archive)

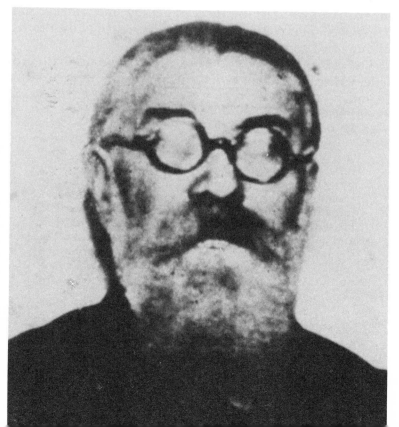

reflected this, as one White General had said, "We have come not to fight the Bolsheviks, but to make war on the Jews."

According to Tiomkin, Denikin's army expelled all Jewish officers from its ranks, dismissed Jewish representatives from rural and urban councils, resurrected the Jewish quota in education, denied Jewish wounded admission to hospitals because of "insufficient space" and operated in direct concert with notoriously anti-Jewish organs which had their roots in the Tsarist Black Hundreds.

While the counter-revolutionary press, sympathetic to Denikin, openly agitated against "Jewish Bolshevism," and "Jewish provocation," all reference to pogroms at Fastov, Ekaterinoslav, Odessa, Novorossisk, and two hundred other places was ruthlessly suppressed. Jews were flayed or burned alive by units of the Volunteer Army. Then, Denikin's military tribunals, unlike those of Petlura, met quickly and dispatched their victims (usually Jews accused of the deaths of unnamed persons) within the hour.[1]

The sadism of this Volunteer Army was immortalized in a letter written by a member of General Andrei Shkuro's staff.[2] It read:

> My dear Kostia:
> Come to our rooms this evening at seven to have a cup of tea with us. We intend to show you something very interesting. Denis has picked up a small Jewish boy who he calls "the Commissar" and with whom he intends to have great fun this evening. He has prepared something in the nature of a crown and a bamboo stick. He will place the crown on the head of the little Jew and will press it down with the stick until the skull of the Jew bursts. Is this not entertaining? I can imagine how the Jewboy will cup up! By the way, Irina Petrovna and Anna Nikolaievna will also be present. I count on you . . .[3]

So in 1921 Dr. Tiomkin considered Denikin the greatest villain in the Ukraine.[4] Six years later, he clarified that position. Hands resting on a cane, Tiomkin declared, "I believe General Denikin shared the responsibility for the massacres, but Petlura had the greater prestige, so his was the prime responsibility."[5]

Apologizing in advance for what he might say, as he was "very old, near the door of my tomb," the onetime sage strayed far afield in his testimony, now recounting his love of country, now telling of his school days in Petrograd. One thing was clear, however, and that was the exuberance he had felt as a result of the spring revolution in 1917. Like many others, he returned to Kiev to participate in the new era for Jew and Ukrainian alike. Tiomkin even asserted that the concept of Jewish autonomy, favored by the Kerensky regime, had originated with the Ukrainian nationalists.

What soured him on the prospects for genuine bi-nationalism in the south were the events of 1918-19. Tiomkin refused to collaborate with the newly proclaimed Directory because it was "laced with Bolshevism." He was further upset by the unwillingness of nationalist leaders to do anything about pogroms. When he complained to Eugene Konovalets about looting in the village of Brovari on December 20, 1918, Tiomkin was told, "It stems from the fact that we don't have a regular commissariat. We don't even have a department to furnish rations to our troops and that is why the troops procure for themselves."

When Tiomkin pressed his complaint concerning physical violence committed by regular troops, he was told by Konovalets, "Address yourself to Petlura. That's his department."[6] When he appealed to Vinnichenko about the incidents at Sarny, Ovruch, and Bakhmach, he was again referred to Petlura. And when he ultimately secured an audience with Petlura, a man he had heard was favorable toward Jews, to complain about Palienko, Kovenko, Andrievsky, Semosenko, and Angel, Tiomkin was promised, "Yes, we will take measures. We will stop them."[7]

"I have always been a just man and would not tarnish the memory of a man if I were not sure about things," said

Tiomkin. "I have already said and I repeat that I do not consider the Ukrainian people responsible for the pogroms. The only man who had the power, the prestige over the troops, was Petlura, and this is why I consider him responsible for the pogroms."

Reynaud, interrupting: "You were not always of that opinion. At the Zionist Congress at Karlsbad, you said the worst pogroms were committed by Denikin!"

The old man lost his composure and stammered something about not being able to remember so well after all these years. Then he went on to claim that Denikin was "a prisoner of his army," before Justice Flory gavelled a temporary halt to the proceedings.[8] When the sessions resumed, Tiomkin offered another excuse, explaining that he meant to say that Petlura and Denikin were equally responsible, and that his remarks about Denikin being a prisoner to his own troops had been poorly translated.

Civil Prosecutor Campinchi reminded Tiomkin how Arnold Margolin had quoted extensively from the Karlsbad report, blaming Denikin almost to the exclusion of any other leader. Tiomkin passed it off, calling Margolin "a weak man." When Campinchi persisted, Tiomkin said angrily, "Margolin wasn't present at Karlsbad when I made my report. He wrote his book based on press summaries. As soon as this book appeared, I wrote Margolin to reproach him. He responded in an insulting letter. I repeat, he is a weak man."

Campinchi, seeking to "check the veracity" of the witness: "Did you not say at Karlsbad that Denikin 'annulled civil and national equality which had been extended to the Jews by the Revolution'?"

Torrès interrupted: "If you want to plead the case against Denikin, I would join with you. But it has no relevance here."

"Are you testifying for the witness?" Campinchi asked. "He [Tiomkin] said that Denikin made pogroms, that he carries responsibility for Jewish blood that stained the streams of the Ukraine.''

Finally able to make himself heard above the voices of opposing counsel, Tiomkin explained that his problems with Margolin dated back to 1919 and the Ukrainian mission to the West. Though Margolin had participated eagerly, Tiomkin, as the leading figure in the Ukrainian Jewish community, would have nothing to do with the mission. Neither Zionists nor victims of pogroms found Jewish participation in the diplomatic efforts of a government of pogromists acceptable.

Tiomkin repeated that the Ukrainian civil party headed by the writer Vinnichenko wanted to fight the pogroms, but they were not strong enough to prevail. While military authorities could have stopped the massacres if they had desired, they showed not the slightest inclination. The leader of the military was Simon Petlura, who was no prisoner to his soldiers. He simply did not wish to act until August, 1919, when he felt menaced by the growing power of Denikin, who faced him across the Kiev-Uman-Birsula line. Concluded Tiomkin, "All the Jews who served Petlura resigned because of this."[9]

Campinchi, somewhat disgusted by Tiomkin's convenient emendations, could have attempted to write off his testimony as that of an unstable old man, a man who, having broken with the moderate Zionists, had become a militant Revisionist. He could have attacked Tiomkin as an embittered dotard seeking only blind revenge, who had broken his covenant with the Ukrainians who trusted him in the months leading up to the trial. But Campinchi could not deny that Tiomkin and Sliosberg both had implicated Petlura in the pogroms.

Next on the witness stand was Elia Tcherikover, the third of Professor Shulgin's "objective" Jews. Tcherikover was Director of the East European Jewish Historical Archives in Berlin. In his earlier writings, he had blamed the

Bolsheviks for most of the disturbances. In 1923, for example, he wrote: "The participants in the pogroms were not Ukrainians by origin, or at least only a few of them were; in general, they were Russian soldiers."[10]

Tcherikover was actually referring here to the initial pogroms committed in 1917-18 by the defeated Russian armies fleeing Galicia. But supporters of Petlura tried to use this passage to exculpate their leader. As a further example of Bolshevik responsibility in 1919, they cited the following, a letter from Volhynia a year earlier:

> Men dressed as soldiers loot, plunder and burn. It is impossible to describe the terror. The soldiers stationed in those localities call themselves "Bolsheviks." They spread terror and intensify the anarchy. These soldiers say, "These are not our people. We are not Ukrainians."[11]

If portions of Tcherikover's manuscript were perverted by Ukrainian nationalists to encompass the pogroms of 1919 (something the author never intended), the Jewish historian nevertheless was guilty of several errors of judgment. He described Petlura's puppet Jewish Minister Pinchas Krasny as an important figure in combatting the pogroms.[12] Tcherikover suggested that the Jews themselves were responsible in large measure for their troubles since often they occupied important posts in the Bolshevik hierarchy and were energetic supporters of Moscow dictates. And while they were originally sympathetic toward the concept of Ukrainian autonomy, the Jews, Tcherikover wrote in 1923, opposed complete independence:

> It should be admitted that the idea of an independent Ukraine, although it was supported by Jewish political parties, did not penetrate the masses of the Jewish population, which approached the question with a lack of confidence that was especially noticeable in their ridicule of the Ukrainian language and in their

passive resistance to Ukrainianization in general. The Jewish masses feared the idea of Ukrainian independence, which was alien to them; and despite all their suffering of recent years, they still believed in the Russian state and culture. . . .

Those Jewish political parties that gave their support to the Ukrainian cause undoubtedly became separated from the Jewish masses . . . while a certain number of Jewish workers joined the Red Guards, they did not contribute one single volunteer to the Ukrainian Army.[13]

Thus, in 1923, Tcherikover could rationalize the pogroms as a result of "the morbid militarized psychology of masses who had become familiar with guns," the rebellious traditions of peasants, the demoralization of the war and revolution, the Bolsheviks and Denikin,[14] and the failure of the Jewish people to break away from allegiance to Moscow (whether the rulers in the Russian capital were Reds or Whites).[15]

Before the Jury of the Seine, Tcherikover told another story. Now he had no doubt that Petlura was the architect of the pogroms. Having served with the Comité des Délégations Juives, having supplied Defense Counsel Torrès with many of the invaluable documents on later pogroms from the East European Jewish Archives, he was certain that Petlura had done nothing to prevent the massacres. Said Tcherikover, "Based on documents collected by me and on facts to which I was personally witness in Ukraine, I have arrived at the deep conviction that responsibility for the pogroms which were accomplished in the Ukraine falls upon Petlura."[16]

Tcherikover went on to explain his conclusion. Petlura was the head of the army from November, 1918, when he became Holovni Ataman. He was at the head of the military party which held power while Ukrainian nationalists struggled for independence. Petlura was the head of the Directory, so dominating the Council of Ministers that one member of that body (Chekhovsky) did not even know of the declaration of war against the Soviets in January, 1919, until he read it in the newspapers.

It was Petlura who demoted Oskilko from his command on the Southwest Front and ordered the Ataman Balabachan, commander of the Army of the Right Bank of the Dnieper, to be shot for disobeying his orders. It was Petlura who forbade the Workers' Congress of June, 1919, to institute a commission of control. It was Petlura again who declined to assist the Jews of Pogrebishche and other towns in setting up self-defense units.

Conversely, it was Petlura who granted promotions to the pogromchiks Patrov, Shepel, Volynetz, and Struk. It was Petlura who conducted diplomatic negotiations abroad, sending missions, concluding treaties, issuing tardy appeals against pogroms. Tcherikover observed sarcastically, "Petlura's appeals were comparable to a physician's medicine administered after the death of the patient."[17]

It was Petlura, moreover, who interfered with the efforts of Vinnichenko and other ministers to have the Ataman Angel punished for his role in pogroms in January, 1919. Said Tcherikover, "Petlura did not want this, and it was not done."[18]

The reference to Angel, commander of a partisan unit of some twelve thousand men, was not to pass unchallenged. Here the Prosecution saw an opportunity to dispute Petlura's alleged responsibility for atrocities committed by the many autonomous or seemingly autonomous chieftains in the Ukraine.

"This Ataman was not under Petlura's command!" exclaimed the Civil Prosecutor. "He commanded a band of insurgents."[19]

Whenever such bandits as Angel, Kozyr-Zyrko, Struk, or Zeleny raised the blue and gold standard of the Trident, their loyalty had been purchased for the minute through several million paper rubles, much liquor, some arms, and an elaborate certificate from the Directory acknowledging the formation of a detachment. Once the money, ammunition, and liquor ran out (usually before a pogrom), the insurgents turned again to the nearest, if not the highest, bidder. Of questionable loyalty, their fighting ability was even more in doubt.[20]

Under such circumstances, the Prosecution argued, it was ludicrous to blame the Directory for the misdeeds of profligates who might serve three masters (the Directory, the Bolsheviks, and Denikin) all within the space of a week. For Campinchi, Simon Petlura was an unfortunate, a man compelled by the nature of things to fight alongside reprobates, just as Lazare Carnot, the military genius of the French Revolution, had been forced to accept aid and counsel from royalist generals in the struggle against the First Coalition.[21]

Nothing could have been further from the truth. The man who called himself Angel (*Angel Smerti*, the Angel of Death) appeared at Chernigov in December, 1918, claiming to war against the White Russians and Bolsheviks. He specifically warned the Jewish population, "Sooner or later, the Directory will triumph. We will write down the names of those who set us against ourselves, rob, take our bread and sugar, our entire goods away to Moscow, for future reference."[22]

Lieutenant Angel commanded the Cossacks of Petlura's Black Sea "Kosh" brigade at Bakhmach in January, 1919.[23] Though Vinnichenko and others demanded his arrest and execution, Petlura never complied. Instead, after several months in hiding, *Captain* Angel reappeared in April, 1919, at the head of the "Left Ukrainian Battalion of Death on the Left Bank of the Dnieper." In June, his troops made more pogroms in Priluki and Ichnia.[24] On July 17, 1919, a "secret" order from Directory Headquarters (numbered 751) notified "*Ataman* Angel of insurgent troops of the government of

Chernigov" that regular Ukrainian forces would commence an offensive against the Bolsheviks in Kiev the next day. Angel's troops were to strike south as part of a three-pronged attack linking up with insurgents Sokolovsky from Radomyshyl and Zeleny from Poltava. "Our partisans must give assistance to our army," was the cryptic command to Angel.[25]

Writing later in his *Annals of the Ukrainian Revolution,* Petlura's aide Alexander Dotzenko noted, "The Ataman Angel was always uniquely subordinated to the High Command of the People's Ukrainian Republic and only received orders from it."[26]

If there was any question of his connections with the Directory, it should have been dispelled by a message from Angel to Petlura, dated September 18, 1919, which appeared in the official Ukrainian Information Bulletin of November 18, 1919: "We, the partisans of the Poltava and Chernigov counties, hail thee, the constant defender of Ukrainian liberty, thee and thy army which make our country free." For six months, said Angel, his men had struggled against the Bolsheviks who attempted to occupy and batter the homeland. "Defend thou our cause before the civilized nations of the whole world," he encouraged Petlura. *"For us, thy word is law."*[27] [*Emphasis added.*]

That Petlura regarded the partisan atamans as an extension of his own army was evidenced by a host of statements drawn from official Ukrainian sources during 1919. In May, a letter issued in Petlura's capital, Kamenetz-Podolsk, noted that "the Commander-in-Chief Petlura succeeded in establishing contact with all of them" (here referring to Sokolovsky with 10,000 troops, Struk with 6,000, Gonchar-Batrak with 8,000, Karmeliuk with 10,000, Angel, and Zeleny) "in preparing a joint offensive."

On June 23, 1919, Foreign Minister Vladimir Temnitzky wrote in the Official Bulletin: "The committees of these groups are subordinated to the Directory and are in close contact with President Petlura."[28] Dotzenko also noted that in the summer of 1919 "organic connection" was made between the Directory and headquarters of Zeleny, Mordalevich, Sokolovsky, Angel and Zakusilo.[29]

In October, 1919, the Ukrainian paper *Vpered* (published in Lwow) quoted "a well-informed Ukrainian" to the effect that "all the groups of partisans are in close contact with Petlura's headquarters, even those carrying on at the rear of Denikin's and Bolshevik troops."[30]

Petlura's chief military aides, Generals Mikhailo Omelianovich-Pavlenko, George Tiutiunik, and Oudovichenko all were engaged in coordinating some aspect of partisan activity. Indeed, the Directory appointed General Malolitko commander-in-chief of all partisans in July, 1919, and replaced him with General Volok in September of that year. Petlura's anti-pogrom orders of the summer of 1919 were plainly addressed to "insurgents" as well as to regular forces.

The Holovni Ataman himself claimed authority, when he told the State Council on October 25: "All the Ukrainian armies march in unity against the common enemy of the Ukraine. The popular uprisings which have multiplied contribute a vigorous aid to the army; all these efforts are united by a sense of confidence in the Ukrainian Directory as the common center."[31]

If Ukrainians subsequently denied that the Directory was the common center for partisan activity, there were many who believed otherwise. British and French missions at Odessa referred to the perpetrator of the Bakhmach pogrom as "Ukrainian Partisan Angel," who with Shpel and several others were directly under the command of Petlura.[32] The atamans themselves considered the Directory as "the common center." Angel would withdraw under Petlura's wing for four months, then re-emerge with a promotion.

The Ataman Zeleny, accused of forty pogroms, was given a solemn reception by officials of the Ukrainian National

Republic when he arrived at Kamenetz-Podolsk on September 14, 1919. Zeleny, the "butcher of Tripolye," was hailed as "the doughty champion of our country's cause."[33]

An even greater tribute was reserved for the Ataman Sokolovsky, who followed to the letter the instructions of the Official Government Printing Office in Zhitomir to war against "Yid officials."[34] When this man who left thousands of women and children dead in Skiva, Brailov, Malin, Korostichev, Yustingrad, Novgorod Volinsk, and Radomyshyl, was slain in the summer of 1919, the official newspaper in Kamenetz-Podolsk could scarcely restrain its grief. *Trudowa Hromada* lamented the loss of "the honorable warrior for Land and Liberty, the defender of peasant rights, the famed Ataman Sokolovsky." The tragic news could not pass without special observances: "We are very sad, without joy. Come with your Cossacks to the funeral. Let us make a memorial."[35]

The Ataman Lazniuk, who ravaged Chabne and Ivankov, forced the Jews of the latter community to their knees, boasting that he was "subordinate only to the Directory and followed its orders."[36] Similar vows of fealty came from the Ataman Struk, instigator of what *Trudowa Hromada* called "people's risings" at Chernobyl and Mezhigorie. This political chameleon avowed, "I have never been, nor will I ever be an enemy of the Fatherland. For me, the Ukraine is under the yellow and blue, under the rule of Petlura. I would do anything he asks."[37] Nine months after the collapse of the Petlura regime, possessing an order binding him obediently to the Ataman Petlura, Struk declared, *"For my work, I am responsible to my government who gave me my appointment and instructions."*[38]

Zabolotny, Koslowsky, Shepel, Mordalevich, Romachko, Kasakov, Ogorodnikov, Sokol, Klimenko, Goly, Golub, Kolesnichenko, Diakov, and all the other insurgent warlords with the exception of Makhno, had visited Petlura at one time in his capital, were acclaimed as Ukrainian pa-

The Jewish quarter of Boguslav, ravaged, May 1919.

triots, received commissions, and then swore allegiance to the colors of the Republic and "the little father" Petlura.[39]

This alliance between the Directory and the "insurgents" had been forged at least as early as the spring of 1919. The Vinnitza Relief Committee complained in May, 1919: "The position now is that almost every town occupied by Ukrainian regulars has been placed under the orders of a former partisan ataman who is terrorizing the Jewish population; so it was, for instance at Yanov and at Litin."[40]

So it was at Gaisin, Litin, and Yanov where Volynets and Shepel slaughtered one thousand Jews between May 12 and July 11, 1919. So it was at Tulchine, Bratslav and Pechura between July 13 and 31, when the troops of Liakhovich left another five hundred Jews dead.[41] So it was at Volodarka and Golovanevsk between July 9 and August 4 when

Sokolov's haidamaks killed three hundred Jews, at Dubovo in the same period when Kazakov's men massacred another eight hundred, at Bobrovisy where Romachko left fifty-six dead, at Pogrebishche and Yustingrad-Sokolovka where Zeleny murdered another six hundred Jews.[42]

The period when the Directory sat at Kamenetz-Podolsk, between June 3 and November 17, 1919, had generally been regarded as the "quietest" as far as pogrom activity was concerned. In fact, while there may have been nothing on the scale of Proskurov during this period, there were more than four hundred pogroms committed by regular Ukrainian troops along with the insurgents.[43] For some observers, the torture, rape, deliberate maiming of children, and general bestiality of that summer exceeded even the horrors of February.[44]

Yet it was not until June, 1920, that Petlura called upon his irregulars to disband. At that time, he commanded "the separate detachments" (which had been formed "to fight our oppressors" and which his defenders later said were not his to command) to report to Polish or Ukrainian battalions to be incorporated into regular army units. "I absolutely forbid the continued existence of separate detachments which are a waste of our forces and a crime against the country," he wrote.[45]

The partisans fought as Cossacks had always fought—as guerrilla bands in the service of the Holy Ukraine. Bound to Chmielnicki against the Poles in the seventeenth century, to Stalin (none too willingly) against the Nazis later in the twentieth century, in 1919 they followed Petlura. It was he who gave them their inspiration, their ideology, their artillery, and their orders. Said Elia Tcherikover, "If the Atamans were directly connected with Petlura's staff and worked according to their instructions, and if they belonged to the Ukrainian Socialist Party, who bears responsibility for their deeds?"[46]

After the debacle, the Directory supplied a convenient

escape route for deposed atamans. By 1921, no fewer than four (Shepel, Oskilko, Angel, and Struk) were safely in exile in Constantinople.[47] None of the insurgent pogromchiks was punished for his role in the massacre of Jews.

"*Salus rei publicae suprema lex,*" Campinchi declared. "The good of the nation is the supreme law." This was the rationalization of Petlura's association with such rabble. In the Ukraine, where the Jews comprised one-twelfth of the total population, their sufferings were the regrettable pangs attendant to the birth of a nation.

"A country which savored the prize of innocent victims is not worthy of praise!" boomed Torrès. Then, borrowing a page from Campinchi's abridged history of the French Revolution, he added, "You would excuse Danton of the September Massacres when the army of Brunswick was marching on Paris and the country was in danger."[48]

"No! I am only defending the memory of an innocent man who was struck down, murdered, in the street."

"That is not the question. Now it is which Hetman was an assassin. And we contend it was Petlura!"[49]

"I killed him!" shouted Schwartzbard with defiance. "I killed him because he was responsible for the massacres. He led the army. The guilt was his. You don't have to believe me. I am a murderer. But can't you believe the witnesses, distinguished men, who one after another, testify to his guilt?"[50]

The Prosecution called one last witness, Jacob Zafran, a poor shopkeeper from Kiev. Now a resident of Vienna, the forty-six-year-old Zafran testified that he had lost his sixteen-year-old son in the pogroms. On August 30, 1919, Petlura's troops recaptured the ancient capital of the Ukraine from the Bolsheviks. According to the nationalists, their brief occupation of Kiev was practically harmless. "There were no casualties unless you count a wrecked ice-cream cart on Vladimir Hill and one ear knocked by a shell-splinter off the plaster statue of either St. Methodius or St.

Cyril," wrote Paustovsky.[51] Zafran's story, based on his own experiences and those recounted to him by Morris Tormov, another survivor of the incident, was quite different.

On August 31, thirty-five members of the newly formed Jewish self-defense unit, mainly young students, including Zafran's son, were called to the Hotel François by Petlurist chief Levka. They hoped to obtain certificates legitimating their militia. Instead, the Jews were disarmed in Zhilianski Street and marched out of the city. For these captives, who were now branded as "Bolsheviks," the beatings with horse-whips and sticks only presaged more terrible sufferings. That evening at a military academy, a pair of Ukrainian officers conducted an examination of papers and physiog-nomy. Those Jews who "looked Christian" and had the presence of mind to claim such identity were released. Thirty of their comrades were murdered.[52]

At first the elder Zafran did not think much of the delay in his son's return. After four hours, however, he trudged the seven kilometers out to the academy. When he arrived, he asked where were the young men who had been arrested. The Ukrainians mockingly replied, "In the celestial head-quarters of heaven."

Zafran himself was then subjected to an interrogation. Was he Jewish? "I said I was with the Norwegian Consul-ate." He carried a document of the consulate, but his in-quisitors persisted, wanting to know if he was a Jewish diplomat. They held him aside, for as Zafran testified, "It was obvious they wanted to kill me." Fortunately, a cavalry officer arrived and prevailed upon his compatriots to release the prisoner, since "it wasn't necessary to have an interna-tional incident."

Zafran considered it a miracle that he was able to get home alive. He then formed a committee of relatives of the young men to find out what had happened. Said Zafran, "It was fourteen days later that we were able to discover the cadavers of these young people, gnawed by dogs, lying about like filth." Even then, the Jews who tried to reclaim the bodies

were menaced anew by Petlurist soldiers. This time Zafran
was protected by a set of Red Cross papers. Ultimately
twenty-nine of thirty bodies were recovered. The thirtieth, a
victim of the forced march, had been interred at the academy
before the "selection" began.[53]

It was only later that Zafran learned from survivors what
had transpired at the school. "Some of them were practically
children," said Zafran. "They were asked, 'Are you Youpin
[Yid] or no?' Those who had a little courage said they
weren't and were taken to another side. My son had the right,
more than the others to say he wasn't Jewish because we are
of Karaite origin.[54] He didn't want to do it, because he didn't
want to abandon his friends."[55]

Jacob Zafran's son had not been a Bolshevik. In fact, his
group had been warned by the Bolsheviks that they would be
destroyed unless they disbanded. They had welcomed the
return of nationalist Ukrainian troops to Kiev. They had
hoped to fight alongside them. And yet within forty-eight
hours they were annihilated by the very soldiers they had
considered liberators.

The massacre was carried out in the major city of the
Ukraine, the ancient capital. According to eyewitnesses, it
was carried out by regular troops. *And it happened less than
five days after Petlura's infamous Order #131 was issued on
August 26, 1919, commanding the troops to desist from
making pogroms.*

"Are you completely with Schwartzbard then?" asked
Torrès. "Did you not in fact intend to kill Petlura yourself?"

Zafran answered, "I followed Petlura. I wanted not to kill
him as Schwartzbard did. That would have been too quick
for him. But I wanted to inflict such a vengeance upon him
that he would remember all his life."

Then Zafran turned to the jury: "Here they say Petlura
was not responsible for the pogroms. But those who know
the truth and say that are concealing like rats, since he was
the one responsible."[56]

At this point Torrès informed the court: "For seven days

witnesses for the prosecution have been heard. By an extraordinary accident, those who have appeared in the last two
days have been extremely favorable to the defense. I originally cited eighty-two witnesses, among whom were fifteen
soldiers who could testify to Schwartzbard's bravery at the
French front during the World War. I will, however, give up
all these witnesses. I believe the jury has already made up its
mind. I am ready for summation."

Campinchi apparently agreed, although he was not especially pleased that Torrès had presumed to speak for him.
Nor could he avoid a last minute argument over how much
time should be allotted for final summations. But Campinchi had consulted with his colleague and they had agreed
that at the current rate of hearing two or three witnesses per
day they would all be in court past Christmas.

Ukrainians have always been suspicious of the prosecution's response to Torrès. They have contended that in
consenting to Torrès' proposal to terminate testimony,
Campinchi acted arbitrarily and harmed the prosecution's
case.[57]

But the skeptics neglect to mention that all the remaining
witnesses were to appear for the Defense. Torrès was prepared to summon French war heroes who would testify to
Schwartzbard's valorous service, neighbors who would
swear to his good character, and numerous survivors and
chroniclers of pogroms, among them Henryk Przanowski,
Dr. Moses Silberfarb, N. Gergel, Herz Zekzer, and I. Guiter-
man. Further testimony could not possibly help the Ukrainian cause.

"We have pleaded too much," Campinchi said wisely,
"too much to our grief and the grief of the jury. Tomorrow
we will speak more briefly."[58]

Notes

1. Margolin, *The Jews of Eastern Europe*, pp.146-151.

2. Shkuro's life was fascinating. As Denikin's lieutenant in the North Caucasus, he distinguished himself for his cruelty and banditry. After the defeat of the White Army, he fled to Western Europe, where he worked for a time as a horseback rider in a circus. During World War II, Shkuro assisted the Nazis in operations against the Soviets. Eventually he was captured by the British and was delivered up to be hanged in his own homeland.

3. *Dokumente über die Massnahmen der ukrainischen Regierung im Kampfe mit den Pogromen:Die Briefe Nikowskjys an die jüdischen Führer,* September, 1919, p.18, File 434, Tcherikover Archive.

4. By his own admission, Denikin refused to cooperate with the Directory because it was hostile, inefficient, and contrary to the idea of One Indivisible Russia. He accused the leaders of the regime of being sympathetic to the Bolsheviks and blamed them for the pogroms, saying, "The anti-Jewish pogroms during the period of the Directory were particularly fierce and sanguinary." Denikin, *The White Army,* p.234.

5. Testimony of Tiomkin, *Notes Sténographiques,* fasc. 6, p.181. For his deposition, see File 427, 37050-1, Tcherikover Archive.

6. *Notes Sténographiques,* fasc. 6, p.170.

7. *Ibid.,* p.173

8. *Ibid.,* p.181, and *Notes Sténographiques,* fasc. 7, pp.2-3.

301

9. *Notes Sténographiques*, fasc. 7, pp.3-19, and *Il Temps*, October 27, 1927, p.4. On September 2, 1919, Denikin and his aide General Schilling launched an attack against his former allies, the Ukrainians. Though outnumbered, at least on paper, by October of that year Denikin succeeded in routing Petlura's forces. Denikin, *The White Army*, pp.284-6. See also George Brinkley, *The Volunteer Army and Allied Intervention in South Russia, 1917-1921*, (South Bend: University of Notre Dame Press, 1966), pp.200-203.

10. Elias Tcherikover, *Antisemitism and the Pogroms in the Ukraine 1917-1918* (Berlin: Ostjüdisches historiches Archiv, 1923), p.50. Writing further, Tcherikover specifically said of Petlura: "No one can doubt the good faith of the Secretary General who took all possible precautions to preserve the country against the savageries and pillages," p.190.

11. Report of the Jewish Association in Sudylkiv, in Tcherikover, *Antisemitism and the Pogroms in the Ukraine*, p.52.

12. *Ibid.*, pp.94-95.

13. *Ibid.*, pp.115-116.

14. *Ibid.*, pp.25-26.

15. *Ibid.*, p.68.

16. Testimony of Tcherikover, *Notes Sténographiques*, fasc. 7, pp.21-23.

17. *Ibid.*, p.29

18. *Ibid.*, p.25.

19. *Ibid.*, pp.72-73.

20. Paustovsky, *In That Dawn*, p.132.

21. *Notes Sténographiques*, fasc. 7, pp. 87-88. Carnot was a member of the dread Committee of Public Safety, which was headed by Robespierre at the time of the Great Terror. Following the rout of the small and ineffectual French Army at Lille in 1791 (as much the fault of mutiny and disloyalty as anything else), Carnot set about reorganizing an effective fighting machine. By 1793 his troops had fought the Austrians, Spanish, and English to a standoff. Unlike Petlura, however, Carnot went personally among his soldiers, punishing them,

not only for looting but also for drunkenness. When Robespierre chided him for shielding aristocrats in the army, Carnot said he needed suitable leaders, regardless of their background. A popular libel that sprang up later was that he sacrificed Generals Kellermann and Hoche to the Terror to save his own life. See J. Mills Whitham, *A Biographical History of the French Revolution* (New York: Viking Press, 1933), pp.306-331.

22. Report of Ukrainian Commissariat for Secret Affairs to Press Bureau, June 10, 1919, File 48, Materials on Character of Insurgents and Pogrom Activities in Villages, Tcherikover Archives.

23. Report of Visit with Vinnichenko, Jan.10, 1919, N. Gergel, File 48, Tcherikover Archive.

24. S. Segalowitch, "The Tragedy of the Left Bank of the Dnieper," File 53, Tcherikover Archive.

25. C. Rakovski, *Izvestia*, August 14, 1919, and *Les pogromes en Ukraine*, pp.93-95.

26. Alexander Dotzenko, *Annals of the Ukrainian Revolution*, V (Lwow, 1924), p.100.

27. *Bureau Ukrainien de la Presse*, 79, Paris, September 18, 1919.

28. Schechtman, *et al*, *The Pogroms in the Ukraine*, pp.116-17.

29. Dotzenko, *Annals of the Ukrainian Revolution*, IV, p.37.

30. Schechtman, *et al*, *The Pogroms in the Ukraine*, p.115.

31. *Information Bulletin* 80, November 19, 1919. File 452, Tcherikover Archive.

32. Tcherikover, *Di ukrainer pogromen*, pp.217-18.

33. Schechtman, *et al*, *The Pogroms in the Ukraine*. p.116.

34. B. Livshitz, Material on Zhitomir Pogroms, Report on Second Pogrom, File 457, Tcherikover Archives.

35. *Trudowa Hromada*, August 21, 1919. See Tcherikover, *Di ukrainer pogromen*, p.224.

36. Communication to Jewish National Secretariat about Lazniuk and Struk, Jan. 21, 1919, File 6, Tcherikover Archive.

37. *Volia*, September 25, 1920, p.554, for letters from Struk to General Galkin, July, 1920; Tcherikover, *Di ukrainer pogromen*, pp.235-36; and Schechtman, *et al*, *The Pogroms in the Ukraine*, p.116.

38. *Bulletin of Information*, Ukrainian Press Bureau, 37, June 30, 1919, File 452, Tcherikover Archive.

39. *Les pogromes en Ukraine*, pp.97-99.

40. *Ibid.*, pp.90-93.

41. Material on pogroms in Belaya Tserkov, Berdichev, Bershad, and Bratslav, File 305, Tcherikover Archives.

42. Material on pogroms in cities and rural areas, File 419, Tcherikover Archives.

43. Gergel, "The Pogroms in the Ukraine," p.243.

44. A. Guimener, *A kapitl in geshichte fun Ukraine*, p.53.

45. *Les Dernières Nouvelles*, June 2, 1920.

46. "Petliura et les Partisans," File 456, Tcherikover Archive.

47. A representative of the Jewish Committee in Constantinople claimed to have identified Angel, Shepel, Struk, and Oskilko in that city. The Ukrainian Ambassador in Turkey disagreed, saying that "Angel" was in reality an innocent man named Vasily Shkotin. At the same time, a *provocateur* named Semionov charged that the Zionists planned to kill off all leaders of pogroms. See *Novoi Vremia* (Belgrade), July 7, 1921, in Tcherikover, *Di Ukrainer pogromen*, pp.217-19.

48. Danton, one of the three great radicals in the Terror, is held responsible for the murders of 1500 "counter-revolutionaries" during the period of the "Little Terror" (August 10 to September 21, 1792), when the Duke of Brunswick menaced France with an army composed of Austrians, Prussians, and French émigrés.

49. *Notes Sténographiques*, fasc. 7, pp.92-94 and *Figaro*, October 26, 1927, p.3.

50. *Notes Sténographiques*, fasc. 7, pp.16-17, and *New York Times*, October 26, 1927, p.7.

51. Paustovsky, *In That Dawn*, p.174.

52. Annex 44 in *Les pogromes en Ukraine*, pp.79-81.

53. Testimony of Zafran, *Notes Sténographiques*, fasc. 7, pp.155-158 and *Figaro*, October 26, 1927, p.3.

54. Karaite Jews were an endogamous sect dating from the Middle Ages. Fundamentalist in belief, they rejected the Talmud and other oral traditions, keeping to themselves and considering themselves superior to the mainstream of Jewish life. To Gentiles, Karaites, whether of Tatar or Semitic origin, were still Jews, and Mr. Zafran's comments were illogical.

55. *Notes Sténographiques*, fasc. 7, p.159.

56. *Ibid.*, pp.160-61.

57. Editorial Report, University of Tennessee Press, 1973, p.10.

58. *Notes Sténographiques*, fasc. 7, pp.162-65.

14.

Five Questions

"THE HEARING IS RESUMED. Gentlemen of the jury, would you sit down."

Thus, a fatigued Justice Flory opened the final session in court after noon on Wednesday, October 26. Then, to the captain of the guard, he said, "I give you a formal order if there are disturbers, expel them immediately. I hope that we will never come to that extremity and that the public understands that it must have a proper and decent attitude toward justice."[1]

Despite the numerous tactical blunders committed by the Prosecution in its examination of Jewish witnesses, it was the consensus of the eight hundred persons who jammed the Hall of Justice that Sholom Schwartzbard would be found guilty of murder. In part, this was due to the influence of the Paris journals which attempted to fan public outrage over the deed and Schwartzbard's own unwillingness to recant. One foreign observer noted that only the leftist papers refrained from whitewashing Petlura or clamoring for the punishment of what others termed "an ordinary murder."[2]

The writings of *Figaro's* Georges Claretier were typical. This journalist described Civil Prosecutor Campinchi as a paragon of logic, while Defense Counsel Torrès was likened to an ever-running automobile, now chugging "Zaporoghian!" now "Haidamak!"[3]

Justice Flory addressed to the jury five questions to be decided at the end of the day's summations. The questions were arranged in ascending order of seriousness:

1. Was the accused, Sholom Schwartzbard, guilty of voluntarily striking blows which caused injuries to Mr. Simon Petlura on May 25, 1926?

2. Had the said blows and injuries, thus inflicted, caused the death of Simon Petlura?

3. Had the said Schwartzbard the intention of causing death to Simon Petlura?

4. Had the said Schwartzbard acted with premeditation?

5. Had the said Schwartzbard acted from ambush?[4]

All of these questions had been answered repeatedly by Schwartzbard himself. With the exception of the final one, the answers had always been Yes.

At 1:00 P.M., Albert Willm began his review of the case for the Prosecution. With the possible exception of Simon Petlura himself, no one had been more tainted by this affair than this aging jurist. Originally hired as Chief Counsel for the Civil Parties, he had largely abdicated his duties to his younger assistant Campinchi. On those occasions when Willm did elect to speak, he did his cause more harm than good. On the second day, while Torrès and Campinchi were arguing about the responsibility of a chief of state for the acts of military subordinates, Willm blurred the issue by pointing out that Christians as well as Jews had been killed in the massacres.[5] Master of the non sequitur, Willm was also responsible for the unfortunate references to "the mobilization of Israel," which antagonized so many Jewish leaders, including Dr. Sliosberg.

At the termination of the long interrogation of Morris Goldstein, Willm attempted to read several passages condemning Denikin from the volume by Arnold Margolin. Flory ordered him to "sit down." The proud barrister was then mocked by Henri Torrès, who asked, "You reproach Schwartzbard for not having killed Denikin?"[6]

Willm sat down, vowing that he would give his opinions and proofs of Petlura's innocence and Schwartzbard's guilt "at the appropriate hour."[7] Apparently that time was now.

"It was May 25, 1927," Willm began. "In a little chapel near the Place d'Italie, decorated with funereal crepe paper upon which were attached the colors of the Ukrainian Republic, that a ceremony commemorating the death of the Ataman Petlura was held. And mingling with the voices of the admirable Ukrainian choir were the moving, poignant sobs of the crowd in the chapel.

"And alone at the foot of the altar, standing apart from the benches reserved for the crowd, holding a lighted candle in her hand, the kind of candle which is given to everyone in funeral ceremonies of the Orthodox Church, was a young girl, draped in the vestments of mourning, stoically struggling against tears. She was the only daughter of the Ataman Petlura."[8]

Willm's purpose in recalling this scene was to emphasize that bereavement was not solely a Jewish prerogative, that all Ukrainian émigrés had suffered a loss in the death of this "indomitable fighter," this "heroic descendant of past centuries." If the Defense chose to slander the memory of this symbol of freedom, neither the Prosecution nor the Ukrainians would dignify such a "second assassination" with a reply. Yet this is precisely what Willm proceeded to do.

For three years, he argued, Petlura, having only a disorganized army behind him, tried to bring peace and security to the Ukraine. The Holovni Ataman had to combat pillagers, demobilized Russian troops, the Bolsheviks, and the Whites. "This man, obliged to face all these difficulties, occupying Kiev, chased from Kiev, re-entering Kiev, not having a minute to free himself, still tried to organize his country in the face of complete anarchy." If his proclamations against pogroms proved nothing, why did one hundred thousand Jews beg his protection following the signing of the Treaty of Riga and the flight of White General Wrangel in 1920-21?[9]

No, said Willm, "The only witness you have heard who is worthy of confidence, because he is neither a White Russian, nor a Bolshevik, nor a Jew, was the French engineer Albert Baudry." This agronomist, who had spent nearly thirty years in the Ukraine, had sworn that "Petlura was hostile to the pogroms." In several conversations with the Holovni Ataman, he had gained the impression that everything possible was being done to discourage the killings.

"I affirm that in the state of anarchy in which the Ukraine found itself, no government could have been able to suppress the pogroms," said Baudry. If the Jews sought villains, let them blame Makhno, Grigoriev, Denikin, and the Poles.[10]

Willm appealed to French vanity to reject every witness except another Frenchman. Of all the witnesses, Ukrainian as well as Jewish, Baudry alone testified that the pogroms before 1914 had been more frequent and more severe than those in the period of the Directory. Baudry alone testified that the Germans were unable to restore order to the Ukraine between April and November, 1918. And Baudry admitted that he was indebted to Petlura for having saved his life when the Bolsheviks took Kiev.

Baudry said very little about the suffering of human beings in the pogroms. Instead, he carried on at length about the fate of his precious farm projects: "I told all the plunderers, the Jews, the Bolsheviks, the Reds, 'Take but do not destroy.' But they did destroy. All of my cultivations were ruined. All of my horses were killed, all my cattle had their throats slit by these agents of destruction."[11]

Willm persevered. "No history is crueler than that of the Jews, no people have been marked more by repression and extermination," he said. "We indignantly protest against the massacres of Jews, against the Jewish pogroms, but we add that we feel the same contempt, the same indignation, the same desperation about the massacres of Christians. If our witnesses had been here to the end, we would have made this point with precision. And we add that it should be recognized that very often in different situations, it was the very attitude of the Jews which provoked the pogromist movements."

Willm returned repeatedly to the claim of Jewish provocation. "The Bolsheviks invading the Ukraine had the greatest talent for sending Jewish functionaries as *agents provocateurs*, people's commissars, and chiefs of the Chekas. Among these secret police chiefs there were some women, very often crueler than the men. Inevitably, when the Bolsheviks had to fight in retreat, the populations which had been exposed to all the violence, to all the cruelty, to all the infamies that occurred, held the Jewish people responsible.

"Note that on this point we have testimony from our adversaries themselves. We have very clear, incontestable testimonies. We have the writings of M. Margolin and M. Tcherikover, writings which have acknowledged that for a very long time, for the entire epoch of Ukrainian history in these last years, the Jewish population had a tendency to rally to the Bolsheviks and not take a position favorable to the National Ukrainian Movement."[12]

Again, Willm referred to "the mobilization of the Jewish people" to save Schwartzbard, to make of him a national hero. "So be it," he declared. "Each race, each people chooses its national heroes. It pleases the Israelites to choose Schwartzbard. I am afraid that this will not be a choice destined to carry blessings for Israel."[13]

Having slandered an entire people, the Counsel for the Civil Parties proceeded to defame Schwartzbard personally. From the start, the defendant was not what he pretended to be—an isolated man, acting without plan, aid or approval of others.

"Strange faces were seen in the vicinity of the Boulevard St.-Michel at the spot of the shooting on the day it happened," Willm intoned ominously. "Schwartzbard fired in obedience to define orders at the prescribed hour."

The defendant was no avenger of his race, but an agent of the Cheka. His association with the Bolshevik camp was established in five ways:

First, there was the matter of Monsieur Volodine (Mykola Shapoval's mysterious Red spy, who was never produced). Second, there was Professor Koval's deposition, identifying Schwartzbard as one of a gang of suspicious characters who had trailed Petlura. Third, there was the inexplicable error in the time stamp on the *pneumatique* sent by Schwartzbard to his wife, proving he must have had an accomplice. Fourth, there was Soviet Foreign Minister Chicherin's directive on assassinations in 1926, followed too closely by the liquidation of one of Moscow's most formidable enemies. And fifth, there was Schwartzbard's own life history, a tangle of anarchist associations, service in the Red Army, and friendship of thirty years with Emma Goldmann and other "radicals" in the United States.[14]

Only the Bolsheviks stood to benefit from this "odious crime," Willm said. He reminded the jury that France had offered its protection to Petlura after his loss of power.

"Schwartzbard hasn't the right to stain this community by such an abominable crime. We must shut France to assassins who choose our streets for their bloody vengeance. You must remind them that there are other countries where they can try to muster courage to commit assassinations. You must especially demonstrate to them that it is repug-

nant for us to have them come to France, commit abominable crime with impunity, then rely upon our sweetness,
benevolence, and indulgence. Let us abandon the assassins
to those who claim them and want to transform them into
national heroes."[15]

Willm's monologue consumed the better part of two
hours. Although some journalists applauded his fiery delivery, his harangue had been merely the last vapid gasp of a
once vigorous dragon. Even in summation, Willm was
upstaged by the younger Civil Prosecutor Cesar Campinchi,

The Corsican's statement was brief, lasting barely thirty
minutes. His review of the anarchy which beset the Ukraine
was more succinct than his predecessor's. And when Campinchi had finished, he did not leave his listeners with the
distasteful notion that "some of his best friends" might be
Jews. A man destined for greatness,[16] Campinchi fought the
good fight for what he saw as the truth.

Where Willm had drummed on the alleged "mobilization
of Israel," Campinchi deftly expressed his admiration for
Jewish solidarity. "Yes, I admire the fact that a blow struck
at Proskurov or at Zhitomir has its sad impact on London,
Berlin, or Copenhagen," he said. "It is a grand example that
the Jewish race gives to all others. And I would be well
pleased if all Frenchmen would show as much fraternity and
devotion to themselves and their history."[17]

"I condemn the pogroms," Campinchi added. "I consider
the Jews a noble race who have suffered from the time of the
Babylonians right up to the time of the Russian Tsars. But
Schwartzbard in his desire to avenge the pogroms mis-
takenly killed an innocent man."[18]

For Campinchi and for Ukrainians around the world,
Simon Petlura was a legendary figure. He was, said the Civil
Prosecutor, "the idol of the Ukrainian people," a man
whose life and memory were equated with the very honor
and history of the entire Ukraine.

"This man conceived a great idea; he was identified with

it; it was of liberating a people of forty million persons from the grip of Moscow. That idea dominated his militant and patriotic life. But he knew that he could not realize it without establishing beforehand a communion of peoples, whoever they might be, Jews or Ukrainians. To free a people is a great task. It cannot be accomplished without unity."

"Numerous witnesses have come here, some Jewish historians or victims. Countless documents have been introduced in the discussions. No one meanwhile has been able to supply a shadow of a proof which could stain the pure memory of the deceased.

"No! Petlura was not responsible for the pogroms. And if not one line has been introduced establishing that he ordered them, here is a book of more than three hundred pages containing the orders, proclamations, decisions, acts by which his anti-pogrom action is constantly manifested."

Could anyone fully appreciate Petlura's problems? Could anyone even comprehend the true nature of his authority? Prestige and power were two different things, and it would be insanity to judge Petlura by standards applied to French generals of the Thirty Years War like Turenne, Conde, Villare, Catinat, or Luxembourg, or the Napoleonic general Duc Elchingen.

"Do not, therefore, seek to judge Simon Petlura," Campinchi admonished the jury. "But a man has been murdered. That is a fact."[19]

And what was the motive for this murder? When Schwartzbard was interrogated, he responded, "I killed Petlura because I dreaded new pogroms. I am the avenger of my race. That man was an assassin. I have killed, not only for past massacres, but to prevent those which might occur in the future."

All rubbish, insisted Campinchi. Turning to the defendant, the Prosecutor spoke in anger:

"You should have brought proof that Petlura was responsible for the pogroms, and you have not done so. You pretend to have killed because he was a hangman. But in reality, you killed because he was a national chief desiring the independence of his country. He was a good man, just and courageous, who desired the respect of the minorities, notably of the Jewish minority. His declarations constantly establish this.

"And you, Schwartzbard, who are you? Your hands, are they clean? An idealistic anarchist, someone has said. Perhaps. But your idealism started with burglary and ended with assassination."[20]

Campinchi asked, "Do you believe you have rendered a service to your co-religionists? I don't think so, and I am not the only one who has that opinion." The Civil Prosecutor then cited the findings of the Twentieth Assembly of the American Jewish Committee on November 19, 1926. At that time, AJC leader Louis Marshall had warned:

> It seems that the recent assassination of Simon Petlura, former chief of the Ukrainian party, by a Jew of Paris, might create difficulties for Jews in Ukraine, among people where Petlura is held in great esteem.

> The Ukrainians are irritated by attempts which have been made to prove that Petlura was not only personally, but also officially responsible for the pogroms, and by the attitude of Jews of different countries who have regarded the act of the assassination as that of national heroism.

> That attitude is not only dangerous, but also incorrect. It is a grave error and an injustice to try to influence the decision of a French tribunal which is deliberating the extent of Petlura's responsibility in the massacres.

> Although we can understand how a man who continually dreams of wrongs and crimes against humanity and whose relatives were victims of pogroms is compelled to commit such a desperate act, there is no excuse to make of him a national hero and to justify the murder which was committed as a private punishment for the alleged wrongs. Nor should the Jewish people assume responsibility for his action.

We hope that the agitation which is following such directives will cease.

His [Schwartzbard's] defense ought to be found in the realm of mental responsibility and not in that of justification.[21]

The sentiments of the AJC were similar to those of Dr. Tiomkin, who said practically the same thing to another Jewish group in 1927.[22] But Campinchi neglected to tell the jury all that the American Jewish Committee had said.

Shortly after Marshall's report of November 14 was made public, the Executive of the AJC issued a strong follow-up, castigating those who might distort the meaning of the report. The declaration protested against "certain Ukrainian elements" who were conducting a campaign against all Jews and who were attempting to make of Petlura a saint. Neither Schwartzbard nor Petlura merited canonization.

The important point in this affair, the American Jewish Committee emphasized, was justice: "We declare our sole interest in the Schwartzbard affair is that justice be done, that the true motives which forced Schwartzbard to commit his act be clearly revealed and that the world be clear about the terrible tragedy of pogroms in the Ukraine."[23]

Said Campinchi, "The hour has come, Schwartzbard, not for vengeance, but for justice, and justice for men as well as for ideas."

It was now incumbent upon the French jury, the Prosecutor declared, to let the world know what price it attached to human life. If Schwartzbard were acquitted, there would be hundreds of persons ready to hoist him onto their shoulders and carry him out of the courtroom in glory. And Petlura's soul would leave the courtroom by a hidden door, alone, silenced, crushed under the weight of public damnation. Such a perversion of justice could not be tolerated.

Campinchi again warned the jury: "If Schwartzbard is acquitted by you, what will prevent your successors from acquitting this young man," pointing to Petlura's brother Oskar who sat nearby, "if he were to track down Schwartzbard and shoot him in vengeance? Gentlemen, I say this to you with the greatest respect, with the deference that I have for jurors before whom I have so often pleaded. There is only one alternative—on the one side serene justice, on the other blind fanaticism."[24]

The last of the prosecution advocates to make a summation was Public Prosecutor Reynaud. He repeated that if the jury acquitted Schwartzbard, another jury would probably set free Oskar Petlura if he later went out and shot his brother's assassin. The result would be a return to primitive blood feuds and vendettas. A France based on the ethics of the Bible, the philosophy of the Greeks, the law of the Romans, could not tolerate such a turn of events.[25]

That there were pogroms under Petlura, just as before his time and after, Reynaud did not deny. "When one studies the reports which have been given us here, he has only one thought—to lift his eyes to heaven. But alas! Heaven remains quiet and God does not respond."

Still, the question was one of responsibility, and the burden of proof concerning Petlura's guilt rested with Schwartzbard. All he had brought to date were individuals who had been victimized by the pogroms, whose testimonies said only, "We don't have direct proof. We declare Petlura responsible because the massacres took place before his eyes, because he was the chief." Proof of this kind was no proof at all.

The Prosecution, on the other hand, did possess evidence of Petlura's sincere regard for Jews. His legislation granted autonomy to minorities, including Jews. (Reynaud was most impressed that the Holovni Ataman permitted the Jews to collect their own taxes.) He established commissions of general inquiry after the pogroms (and he allegedly executed such organizers as Semosenko, Romachko, and Kasakov—the last two, incidentally, punished by the Bolsheviks). He authorized expenditures to bring relief "at the occasion of every important pogrom." He established the Jewish Ministry and encouraged the creation of a Jewish gendarmerie. He issued daily orders labeling pogroms "crimes against humanity." He published general decrees drafted in language of "Napoleonic inspiration" after August, 1919, in Kamenetz-Podolsk, Stavka, and elsewhere, pointing out the good done by Jews and warning that all who abused them would be punished.

All Ukrainians testified that Petlura enjoyed "cordial relations, amicable relations, excellent relations" with the Jews. The Jews themselves, at Kamenetz-Podolsk, in July, 1919, the Social Democratic Bund in September, 1919,[26] and in the writings of Vladimir Jabotinsky, Elia Tcherikover, and Heinrich Sliosberg (previous to their undergoing "singular evolutions in thought"), had testified that Petlura's basic policy was the creation of a viable state uniting Christians and Jews in the Ukraine.

Finally, Reynaud drew the jury's attention to the note written by Petlura in September, 1919, to the Comité des Délégations Juives in Paris. It read:

> I have had enough of these calumnies and imputations. I want to bring it out into the open. I place myself at your disposition. Name a commission. It will be under my protection. It will have all the power to act. It will be composed exclusively of men independent of me, that is to say, of Jews.[27]

Of the Jews Petlura had in mind, none were able to accept the invitation. Achad Ha-Am, the peaceful Jewish poet of the Ukraine, declined because of poor health. The others—Menachem Ussishkin, Leon Motzkin, and Dr. D. Jochelman—submitted the communication to the assembly of Jews in Paris. On September 12, 1919, the Ukrainian delegate in Paris, Count Tyshkevich, was notified that the Comité had agreed to select members for an inquiry. This invitation coincided with Petlura's defeat at the hands of Denikin's forces, when Petlura could not have guaranteed the safety of any investigators.

Testifying in Paris, Motzkin said: "We were ready to go. We waited. How to go? Where to go? Remember 1919. It was really impossible because we didn't have a definite invitation. We only had an invitation of principle. We knew that Petlura didn't hold much territory, that the Ukraine was lost. In those circumstances, where could we go?"

Motzkin recognized that the invitation was a charade. Jews like Israel Zangwill, who indicated a willingness to serve on the impossible commission, played along, issuing statements lauding the Holovni Ataman, but only to mitigate the suffering of their brethren.

As for Petlura, Motzkin declared, "Petlura believed that if he allowed an inquiry commission to come into the country, what could it do? There had been others, and you know the outcome of those inqueries."[28]

For Prosecutor Reynaud, Simon Petlura was a man of great insight and political acumen, a man who preached the fraternity of two peoples. But he was also a victim of chaos in his country, his government, and his army. Petlura was powerless to stop the slaughter of the Orthodox or Roman Catholics, much less the Jews. He was powerless to suppress marauders in invading armies or even in his own army, for he was "no dictator, no generalissimo." His orders had to be countersigned by a minister. The real authority rested with Generalissimo Ossetzky and a host of independent atamans. Only "theoretically" was Petlura the chief of the Ukraine.

Earlier in the week, Reynaud had charged, "Schwartzbard could have killed Petlura in Warsaw, but he knew that Polish justice was too severe; he was afraid to risk his neck there. At Paris, he felt he could hope for an acquittal."

It was not the first time that the prosecution had emphasized the choice of site and victim. Campinchi, too, had chided Schwartzbard for not trying to kill Denikin or Lenin, both equally responsible for massacres of Jews. Willm also had wondered why Schwartzbard did not try to kill the well armed and well protected Petlura when both were in the same general area of the Ukraine.

Schwartzbard's reply was, "I was in Odessa when the country was occupied by them [the Ukrainian nationalists]. They controlled the railroads. They refused passports. It wasn't easy to return and seek out the great culprits, especially Petlura."[29]

As for why Schwartzbard had not trekked to Warsaw after the wars to kill Petlura, his counsel Torrès asked in amazement, "Should he have left France for Galicia? Reynaud reproaches Schwartzbard for killing Petlura *too late!* That is a singular reproach. French justice notes that you killed too late."[30]

Reynaud responded: "We tell you non-Frenchmen, 'Yes, French hospitality is great. But leave us out of your crimes. Go commit them elsewhere, in foreign countries. You will find courts martial there which are not so merciful and which do not have the tolerance, humanity, which grace the French jury—a toleration and humanity which at the same time constitutes a distinct danger for France.'

"You have a female ancestor, Schwartzbard, who has given you an elegant lesson in courage—Judith—who, wanting to kill Holofernes, penetrated his camp, and killed him in the midst of his guards, in the midst of his soldiers. That was, perhaps, more worthy of indulgence than what you did here in France with regard to an unarmed Petlura."

"One must not shed blood with impunity!" the Public Prosecutor cried. "Vengeance, though a proper defense, should not be represented as virtue before all juries. The role of regicide, the role of judge, the role of Brutus and Cassius is hardly befitting of you or your decorum, Schwartzbard. Brutus and Cassius were honorable men. You are a disgraceful housebreaker who hid under the name of Walsberger, who erred left and right, who was tracked down by all the police not for your political opinions (I would not reproach you for this) but for your offenses against the common law. And it is that for which I reproach you. It is because your story of revenge does not seduce me and does not move me."

"If you are an avenging angel and a savior, then reclaim the cross and the crown of thorns and accept the halo of condemnation."

"Schwartzbard had no excuse for what he did," Reynaud told the jury. "He must be punished for willful murder, and the sentence for that is death. If you find any extenuating circumstances, the sentence should be penal servitude or isolation."[31]

Notes

1. *Notes Sténographiques*, fasc. 8, p.1.

2. *Frankfurter Zeitung*, October 27, 1927, p.1.

3. *Figaro*, October 26, 1927, p.3.

4. *Notes Sténographiques*, fasc. 8, p.1.

5. *Figaro*, October 20, 1927, p.2.

6. Torrès, *Le procès des pogromes*, p.126. See also the dispute in the midst of Oudovichenko's testimony, *Notes Sténographiques*, fasc. 4, pp.208-209.

7. Torres, *Le proces des pogromes*, pp.128,228.

8. *Notes Sténographiques*, fasc. 8, p.3.

9. *Ibid.*, pp.8-9

10. Testimony of Baudry, *Notes Sténographiques*, fasc. 5, pp.76-143. See especially pp.95-101.

11. *Ibid.*, p.111.

12. *Notes Sténographiques*, fasc. 8, pp.4-10, and *En notre âme*, pp.58-59.

13. *Notes Sténographiques*, fasc. 8, pp.4-5.

14. *Ibid.*, pp.26-39.

15. *Ibid.*, pp.60-62.

16. Elected to the National Assembly as a Radical Socialist from Bastia in 1932 and 1936, Campinchi established his prestige in

321

a party which Phillipe Henriot once called the most conservative and bourgeois of all French parties. On June 23, 1937,
Campinchi became Minister of Marine, and as such was
responsible for rebuilding the French fleet. The battleships
Clemenceau and *Richelieu* were built and naval bases at Mers
el-Kebir and D'Aspreto enlarged in his ministry. Campinchi
was to serve as Navy Minister in the War Cabinet of Paul
Reynaud. In this capacity, he was criticized by General
Weygand and Paul Baudoin, who claimed he suggested the
resignation of the Reynaud cabinet to facilitate the French
capitulation before the Nazis in 1940. In reality, Campinchi
resigned his post on June 16, 1940, and fled to North Africa,
hoping to urge his countrymen to continue the war. Known to
collaborators as "the most dangerous minister," he was placed
under house arrest in Casablanca and returned to Marseilles.
There he died in a clinic on February 22, 1941. See Paul
Reynaud, *In the Thick of the Fight*, trans. James Lambert
(New York: Simon and Schuster, 1951), pp.390-96, and 587;
and *Dictionnaire de Biographie Française* (Paris: Librairie
Letouzey et Ane, 1956), VII, 999.

17. *Notes Sténographiques*, fasc. 9, p.10.

18. *Ibid.*, p.1.

19. *Ibid.*, pp.2-5.

20. Desroches, *Le problème ukrainien*, pp.203-206.

21. *Notes Sténographiques*, fasc. 9, pp.16-18.

22. Said Tiomkin, "We don't want to make Schwartzbard a hero,
but we want to tell the world what crimes have been committed against us. We have done no harm to anybody. We have
touched nobody. Jews do not wish to deprive Ukrainians of
their independence. We want them to know and remember
that they cannot seek their freedom by shedding Jewish
blood." See speech of Tiomkin, File 453, 38188, Tcherikover
Archive.

23. Declaration of American Jewish Committee, File 466,
38920-21, Tcherikover Archive.

24. *Notes Sténographiques*, fasc. 9, p.20.

25. Pleading of Reynaud, *Notes Sténographiques*, fasc. 10,
pp.1-4.

26. See the unctuous statement of the Bund declaring that Jewish and Ukrainian democracy are one, that the government is energetically combatting pogroms, and generally commending the Directory for its many concessions to Jewish autonomy. *Notes Sténographiques*, fasc. 7, p.127.

27. Petlura's feigned indignation was illegitimate for several reasons. He neither assisted nor convened earlier inquiries by Jewish bodies in Kiev or Petrograd. And while he said he was willing to have the Jews name anyone as an investigator, his communication nonetheless outlined what he expected and from whom. Schechtman, *et. al, The Pogroms in the Ukraine*, p.251.

28. *Notes Sténographiques*, fasc. 7, p.114 and 125. Motzkin was taken to task by Cesar Campinchi, who noted that in his deposition he had stated that he "did not believe Petlura ordered the pogroms." Motzkin stated that further investigation demonstrated to him that the pogroms were indeed the responsibility of Petlura. In reality, he needn't have bothered with such a flimsy excuse. The deposition also said that Petlura "tolerated" the pogroms for five or six months. For Motzkin's Deposition, July 17, 1926, see File 427, 37037, Tcherikover Archive. For Motzkin's testimony, which echoed that of Goldstein, Sliosberg, Tiomkin, and Tcherikover, see *Notes Sténographiques*, fasc. 7, pp.98-128.

29. *Notes Sténographiques*, fasc. 5, pp.5-6.

30. *Ibid.*, pp.7-10.

31. *Notes Sténographiques*, fasc. 10, pp.42-43.

15.

Torrès

Shortly before 5:00 p.m., Defense Counsel Henri Torrès rose to deliver his rebuttal.

"Gentlemen of the court, gentlemen of the jury," he began, "yesterday I engaged myself almost completely in an act of faith toward you. I took the unheard of step of renouncing close to eighty witnesses whom I had cited for the defense, that is to say, persons who represent the highest, the brightest French genius in every field, persons who had suffered pogroms in the flesh and who would have come to you and listed the specific personal responsibilities of the Ataman General Petlura, and finally fifteen of Schwartzbard's comrades, Jews voluntarily involved in the Great War, who would have told you that this naturalized citizen paid the price of his naturalization with his freely spilled blood, that he fought at Arras, at Carency, in the Argonne, at Vosges, at La Chapelote, an admirable hero like all French soldiers, without distinction of origin or religious confession. I took this responsibility and I do not guarantee your successors that this precedent will always be followed by those who come after me.[1]

"I have taken the responsibility of renouncing the depositions of these admirable men and women who promised me they would have come, the ailing,[2] the most illustrious French poetess of this age—Madame la Comtesse de

Noailles,[3] others who have come from America, North America and South America, to tell you who made the pogroms and how members of their families were killed by ferocious Haidamaks or Zaporoghians to the repeated cries: 'Long live *Batko* Petlura!' 'Long live little father Petlura!'

"I have taken this responsibility and do not regret it, members of the jury. And if in a similar case, where I might carry the cross of so many unfortunates who had suffered so much and awaited a judgment of redemption from you, if you did not listen to me, I would ask that I be struck by this bar and never recover again.

Maître Henri Torrès, Schwartzbard's defense counsel.
(YIVO Tcherikover Archive)

"I have taken this responsibility, gentlemen of the jury, without your knowledge, and without asking myself if you are of the Right or of the Left, if you are reactionaries or socialists, radicals or moderate Republicans, readers of *Echo du Paris, Figaro, Gaulois, Oeuvre, Quotidien,* or *Populaire.*[4] I have not posed this question. Why? Because I know that in France even the most different and antagonistic groups join together in condemning and censuring brutal massacres.

"I recall that the supreme Pontiff, Pope Benedict XV, denounced the crime of pogroms in an admirable Encyclical, where he equated anti-Semitism with crimes against Christianity.

"I recall that after the abominable pogroms of 1882, in a protest committee which was headed by Victor Hugo and which also included Carnot, a relative of this Lazare Carnot about whom you told us yesterday, M. Campinchi, beside Carnot, beside de Lesseps, beside Emile Deschanel, beside Gambetta, there also figured the Archbishop Cardinal of Paris, that is, the highest ecclesiastical authority of this country.

"And I recall that at the time of the pogrom of 1905 at Kishinev, when a French committee was organized not only to lament the horror of the pogroms but to specify the responsibility of Tsarism, which had desired the pogrom and did not interfere with it, as Petlura later desired the pogroms and did not interfere with them, in this committee beside Anatole France, beside Octave Mirbeau, figured, of all persons, a great novelist of chivalry, the Comte Albert de Mun, the noble figure of the Catholic Party and one of the nation's leading conservatives.

"And finally, I recall that in 1887 when the Court of Parlement concerned itself with pogroms even more terrible than those in which the Jews were massacred, the pogroms of the Turkish government against the Armenians, M. Denys-Cochin took the platform and said, 'There are certain crimes which are for me, a man of principle, a man of order, a man of justice, revolting. Thus the dastardly or cowardly assassination of a defenseless population by fanatic Turkish soldiers.'

For Torrès, French tradition was bound up in the challenge of Ambassador Cambon, who sheilded many refugees from the Turkish holocaust. The Grand Vizir would pay with his head, Cambon had warned, if mobs about the French Consulate harmed a single Armenian under his protection.[5]

Regarding the five questions of the indictment, Torrès emphasized that only the first question—was Sholom Schwartzbard guilty of voluntarily striking blows and causing wounds to Simon Petlura—was significant. And here the question was not *did* Schwartzbard strike and wound Petlura, but was he *guilty* of having wounded him. "To this first question, the only one which I count," said Torrès, "the question of responsibility, I expect from you gentlemen for the honor of our country, a unanimous verdict, the response —*No.*"

A verdict of acquittal would not make of Schwartzbard a national hero, for "killing a man, even legitimately, is a great misfortune." Nor could Schwartzbard be regarded as a hero of the Jewish people or nation, since there was neither for Schwartzbard nor Torrès nor for any others a Jewish nation. Schwartzbard knew only one nation, France, and there was no chance that his deed would be considered an act of courage here. These things recalled, Torrès proceeded to an examination of the accused's life history.

"Schwartzbard, gentlemen of the jury, is from Smolensk, but he was raised almost all his life as a child and adolescent in Balta, where he returned still later at the end of the war. Balta is a city which has always been decimated by pogroms, by those pogroms of which I have just now spoken to you— the pogrom of 1882, the abominable pogrom of 1905 on the subject of which a very honorable man from the monarchist benches in the Duma, Prince Oroussov, rose to denounce the Tsar's responsibility, despite a very simple and ridiculous alibi which the government took in printing scraps of proclamations without effect and in making a few distributions to succor Jewish communities which had been ravaged by the most vast and premeditated of pillages.

"In 1882 a pogrom at Balta. In 1905 Balta again was attacked. In 1917 at Balta a new pogrom. And in 1919 more pogroms at Balta, three particularly violent ones in the first half of the year, when, to some extent, the pogromist activity of the troops of Ataman General Petlura was greatest."

Wherever Schwartzbard lived, Torrès continued, in Balta, in Podolia, he was shadowed by the specter of the pogroms. In 1905 he had felt the exuberance common to those revolutionaries who opposed the Tsar. But after the defeat of the hope of parliamentary government, the Tsarist regime instituted another ruthless suppression of the leaders of the democratic movement. Many Jews were forced to flee Russia without passports or identity papers. Among them was Schwartzbard.

"Ah, the papers, the identity papers! Who would have given them any? The Tsarist government refused them. They roamed, outlaws, crossing Europe. The police of the Hapsburg and Hohenzollern monarchies, together with the Tsarist police, the *Okhrana*, tracked them down without mercy. It was necessary to go from city to city, country to country."[6]

Certainly Schwartzbard had been condemned in Vienna. But he was a young man, no more than twenty. He had no means to sustain himself. That was why he turned to housebreaking. He had erred, but this crime had been erased by a life dedicated to good deeds and generosity. Even more, the legal convictions had been erased by French amnesty law, and the Prosecution was unfair in dredging them up at this time.

Schwartzbard's ideological leanings? Torrès pointed out that in the Prosecution's summations, the defendant had been accused of simultaneously being an anarchist and a Bolshevik, "two terms representing the most opposite poles of political activity in Russia." Whereas the Bolsheviks adhered to the Leninist teaching of a state dictatorship of the proletariat guided by an elite party, the anarchists rebelled at all authority and all concept of state. This was the basis of the terrible quarrel between Bakhunin and Marx in the Second International. Throughout the Russian Revolution, the two groups remained at odds, politically and militarily. With the Bolshevik victory, the anarchists were one of the first groups earmarked for annihilation. And yet Willm called Schwartzbard "Bolshevik" while Campinchi labelled him "anarchist." He could not be both.

"Yes," said Torrès, "he was an anarchist, but an ideological, idealistic, theoretical anarchist, what one might term, on the whole, a Tolstoyan. Tolstoy once asked Maurice Barrès, who had been one himself, 'Who isn't a little anarchistic at twenty?' People are occasionally also socialistic. Schwartzbard was like those who gave up anarchism, like some who have given up socialism. An anarchist, but not a terrorist of direct action. On the contrary, he led the calmest, the most peaceful life.

"This man became an artisan, then a little merchant, enjoyed good relations with all who mattered in his neighborhood. It is established by documents which I will show you presently, gentlemen of the jury, namely a touching petition signed by close to two thousand of his neighbors, residents of the Menilmontant quarter who aren't Jews, signed by decent people among us who pay homage to the integrity and virtue of this man.

"And when he was arrested, gentlemen of the jury, what was found on him? A card of the League of Human Rights, which is not, I suppose, a nest of anarchists, but a great democratic organization which always aspires to lift the great voice of our people's profound justice above the brawls of court proceedings and party strife.

"And when the police made their investigations, when

they reported that he did not belong to a political party, that he was not seen associating with some group, that he didn't attend any public gathering regularly, then what did they discover, gentlemen of the jury? They found that in addition to the League of Human Rights, he is a member, a diligent, fervent, passionate member of an association where he goes every day, to which he reports on several matters.

"What association? The Committee of Relief to the pogrom victims, where he meets not only men belonging to the most moderate democratic parties but also a man like M. Sliosberg, the great Russian lawyer you heard the day before yesterday, a notable adversary of the Bolshevik regime, who represented the right in Russian political life, the Cadet [Constitutional Democratic] Party.

"Those are his relationships. That is his life. I add, gentlemen of the jury, that he was an admirable husband, ever a true friend, always a devoted comrade. In this regard we could have heard the greatest assortment of witnesses, customers, neighbors, his work companions, who could have told you what a decent and honest man you have before you."[7]

When the World War erupted in August, 1914, Schwartzbard was one of the first to volunteer—for the infantry in the Foreign Legion. Now Torrès went over that record once more.

"Among all the testimony, there was that of Captain Rousset, today an attorney at Marseilles, a captain of the 363rd Infantry Regiment during the war. He addressed a letter, which is in my dossier, to one of Schwartzbard's comrades and ended with these words: 'Wish good courage to Schwartzbard on the part of Captain Rousset, that he may endure the distressing hours he is going through with the memory of the little group of volunteer Russian comrades like him in the French army, whose valor and heroism I was personally able to appreciate in the battles of the Somme in 1916.'

"He [Schwartzbard] didn't fight next to his Jewish brothers of days gone by," Torrès said emphatically. "He fought beside his French brothers of today, to whom he has become an equal in valor and sacrifice. He was wounded, a wound piercing his lung and fracturing the shoulder plate. I have his certificate on the source of the wound and I shall call that admirable citation to your mind in order for you to review it in your chamber of deliberations: 'Excellent soldier, always a volunteer for the dangerous posts. On the first of March, 1916, at La Chapelote, while a sentinel at the extremity of an advanced forward trench, was gravely wounded at the moment he threw some grenades.'

"After the wound and convalescence, he was discharged and even given his liberty. He left for Russia. Some have said it was a mission; others have said it wasn't. Who knows? This is certain. At the moment when he arrived, he rapidly enrolled in the Russian Army, the army of Kerensky. Some days after, there was the debacle. The military units were dispersed. Schwartzbard left for Odessa.[8]

"You know what he did at Odessa, gentlemen, and how he worked patiently at his trade of watchmaker. To Odessa, however, came numerous victims of the pogroms. Just now, in the most discreet terms possible, my friend M. Campinchi set out the picture of the pogroms for you. I will not review that. I do not want to abuse the horror of this case, no more than I would abuse the hundreds and hundreds of photographs that I have of it, taken after the pogroms of Zhitomir, Ovruch, and Proskurov. In one of these photographs you will recognize the unfortunate young girl that you heard testify the day before yesterday. She is stooped over a wounded child. I will not show them to you. I will not paint a picture of these horrors. You know them.

"But I want to tell you, although you may know it already, that it was to Odessa that the panicked victims flocked, fleeing the horror of those tragic nights when the Cossacks came, devastating everything, with those dreadful scenes, as for example, in that pogrom perpetrated by the soldiers of Kozyr-Zyrko, one of Petlura's subordinate atamans, commander of regular Petlurist troops with the infamous 'Clans of Death.'

"During this pogrom the unfortunate Jews who were massacred displayed the terrible passivity of that sort of Ukrainian Jew, who, crouched in his ghetto waiting for the Messiah and I don't know what kind of mystical deliverance, never lifted an arm for an arm, never possessed a will to resist, a will to kill. These unfortunate Jews were gathered about the village square. They [the Cossacks] made them sing—out of derision. They cut the old men's beards. They forced the women to undress. Then the Cossacks struck into the lot, shouting, 'Glory to the Ataman Kozyr-Zyrko!' And the unfortunate wounded, who didn't want to be finished off in this horrible massacre, also raised their trembling arms and, hoping to arouse the pity of their executioners, cried with their death rattles, 'Glory to the Ataman Kozyr-Zyrko!' to one who had killed them."[9]

According to Torrès, the survivors all fled by rail and by boat to Odessa, hoping to leave the country. Schwartzbard, working as a volunteer aide in a surgical hospital, heard their tales and could do nothing. In 1920, he returned to France, where he again tasted freedom.

"I spoke just now of the passivity of Jews who never organized this gendarmerie of which Petlura only began to speak after there were dozens and dozens of thousands of deaths among this people, murdered by Petlura's soldiers because no one had ever seen a Jew lift a stick to defend himself. In such a manner had that race, submissive to an ancestral domination, been accustomed to the organization of terror. Well! I say that when one becomes a French citizen like Schwartzbard, when one has felt the vibrant freedom of the Paris crowd, when a French soldier has felt cold steel in the trenches, I say that a new spirit, trembling and ardent, awakes, and that one strikes out for justice.

"Ah yes, he waited. You have heard it, Schwartzbard. You have been reproached for having waited. He waited, and why? Because when one returns to Paris in 1920, one is taken up again by the kind of sweet and smiling ease of life among us. Because one rediscovers the hearth, family, habits, work, friends, committees, meetings, gossip. Because one speaks of organizing relief for the pogrom victims instead of thinking about striking at the person responsible for these crimes. And Schwartzbard would have grown used to spending his life at the side of the poor woman for whom he is all life, as she is for him all family, if one day he had not read that Petlura had reappeared."[10]

Torrès himself had assisted in the Relief Committee working to rescue orphans of the pogroms. He had planned to call to the witness stand Joseph Kessel, a celebrated author, Georges Suarez, editor of *Temps*, and Pierre Bonardi, one of Campinchi's countrymen "from that passionate and wild little island" of Corsica. These men had visited eight hundred such orphans in the Jezreel Valley in Palestine, had seen their physical scars, had listened to stories of Jewish mothers in Russia chiding their unhappy children to fall asleep with the words, "Hurry to sleep, or Petlura will come and get you."[11]

Sholom Schwartzbard had taken in one such child, an escapee from the Petlurist hordes. When he read what he considered to be inflammatory propaganda issuing from Petlura's *Trident*, propaganda which was tempered only by the possibility of censorship on the part of French authorities, his quiet life came to an end. As examining psychiatrist Dr. Claude had said, "Schwartzbard's implacable obsession with the cursed name of Petlura pierced his soul like a flaming arrow."

"As soon as I knew he was there," Torrès continued, giving voice to Schwartzbard's thoughts, "I resolved to kill him by myself. Ah, yes, all alone!"

Was it necessary to explain that a man with such an

obesssion did not need any accomplices? Was it necessary to
point out that Koval's two depositions, taken five days apart,
first described Schwartzbard as one of three persons who
trailed Petlura, then simply as accompanied by a woman?
Was it necessary to review the matter of the *pneumatique*
once more to prove that no French official was infallible,
that the time stamp was simply a clerical error?

Torrès insisted that Schwartzbard's actions, from the
moment of his apprehension, answered these questions. He
could have pleaded the customary excuses, temporary insanity, irresistible impulse, but he did not. In accepting flat
responsibility for his act, Schwartzbard displayed a rare
degree of honesty and frankness. This should have sufficed
to dispel any notions of a Bolshevik plot directed against
Petlura.

"For the dignity of this debate," Torrès added, "I leave
Koval in his tomb, Shapoval among the witnesses, Volodine
and Dobkowski where they are or where they ought to be."[12]

The Defense Counsel noted that many courts in other
lands had acquitted assassins for comparable acts. In 1924,
for example, the White Russian Conradi tried to kill Bolshevik Foreign Minister Chicherin when the latter was in
Switzerland. Instead, he had to settle for Chicherin's aide
Vorovsky. Conradi told the court at Lausanne, "I polished
my bullets because they might make more painful, more
surely fatal wounds in case they penetrated the abdomen."
The Swiss acquitted Conradi.

Three years earlier, in Berlin, a young Armenian student
named Teilirian murdered the former Grand Vizir of Turkey Talaat Bey, to avenge the terrible massacres done to his
people. General Liman von Sanders, replete with *Stahlhelm*
and spurs, came to testify that Talaat Bey had been a staunch
ally of the Germans in World War I, that he had denied the
French and British transit on Turkish railway lines.
Teilirian, like Schwartzbard, openly exclaimed, "I am happy that I did what I did. I have avenged my people. I have

killed an assassin!" And the German jury acquitted Teilirian of killing a former ally in cold blood.

Why then could not a French jury acquit Schwartzbard, a man who killed not to avenge a people in the "national" sense, but who killed to avenge people who were dear to him, two brothers-in-law, an uncle, his mother, his stepmother, twelve cousins, all of whom had been murdered in the pogroms?[13]

"Enough talk of you, Schwartzbard," said Torrès, pausing. "I must speak of the victim, Simon Petlura. I shall not, to be sure, systematically malign the memory of this man. I shall not question the generosity that motivated Petlura in 1917, when the revolution spread over Russia like a great liberating breath. But perhaps promoted too rapidly to a destiny too great for him, Petlura found himself locked in a frightful historical dilemma, which he solved by the worst of demagogies, that is, by the demagogy of murder.

"The explanations? I am seeking them because Petlura the democrat and Petlura the pogromchik—that is a terrible contradiction! In order to resolve it, perhaps one might limit oneself by saying that if Petlura was a bad democrat, he was a good pogromchik. Well! I believe that Petlura was prompted to tolerate and encourage the pogroms, to assure them an impunity which was a veritable encouragement to resume, because it was impossible to realize his own policy."

On the previous day, Torrès had read from a statement dated May 3, 1918, in which Petlura thanked his "powerful friends and allies" Germany and Austria for permitting the Ukraine to achieve statehood. It was Torrès' contention that the Ukrainian Nationalist Movement was inexorably bound up with the German cause, that once Germany was defeated, this movement was doomed. Demoralized, bankrupt, and now subjugated by foreign troops of all religious and political beliefs, the Directory sought every artifice by which it could cling to a delusion of independence. Pogroms seemed the most convenient.[14] In effect, Torrès charged Petlura with directing a Ukrainian *Götterdämmerung.*

The Defense Counsel's interpretation of history was a bit shaky, since the Nationalists had been violently opposed to the puppet Hetmanate of Skoropadsky. But the center of Torrès' argument was his view of Petlura's responsibility as chief of state: "A chief answers for his soldiers, for their crimes as well as their exploits," Torrès insisted. "Etymologically, 'chief' comes from *caput*, 'head.'" For Torrès, one could not attempt a distinction between the active and passive responsibility of a man whose troops flaunted his name in fire and blood, whose Cossacks killed better than fifty thousand Jews in the name of the "little father."

"A singular 'little father!' One whose name terrified Jewish children . . . Little Father, Ataman General, exercising his authority and prestige over the army, Commander-in-Chief of the Ukraine, that is sufficient to condemn Petlura.[15]

"That is my case, gentlemen of the jury. Ah, the friends and partisans of the Ataman Petlura tell me, it is necessary to choose, was he a hangman or a great chief? I tell you, he was the chief of the hangmen, or if you want, the chief hangman. We are in a country where it is understood that the brain causes action, and that leaders are responsible.[16]

"It is impossible, gentlemen of the jury, to warp the instinct of a people. Instinct is a passionate thing, vigorous, indomitable, like blood in a man's arteries. It is also called tradition, but I prefer its true name, because it carries in it a force and a generosity which is more natural, more French. Well, gentlemen of the jury, the instinct of the French people has always been a sensual and emotional one. It has always recognized liberty, justice, courage, the dignity of men, all men, and consequently of Jews as well. And it is this, gentlemen of the jury, that the case of Schwartzbard, possessing an intensity and resonance which it could not have anywhere else but within these walls, blends with the purer French instinct, since it concerns ideas of that Great

Revolution of which no man living cannot say that he is, more or less, a son."[17]

According to Torrès, the French nation had spoken out against oppression of the Jews 138 years before, at the first meeting of the National Assembly. The Abbé Gregoire advocated national autonomy for those who had suffered throughout history. The Protestant pastor, Rabaud Saint-Etienne, the Count de Clermont-Tonnerre, and Honoré Gabriel Riquetti (Count de Mirabeau) all advocated civil rights for "the most generous and most unfortunate of peoples." In creating a world free of blight, the men of the Revolution sought total emancipation for the Jews. In turn, the Jews, through Adolph Cremieux, attempted to repay their debt of gratitude to humanity by emancipating Negro slaves in French possessions in March, 1848.[18]

"I am done, gentlemen of the jury," said Torrès. "It is now the solemn moment when once again the voice of France will be raised, free and just, in you. The forces of our country, its profound forces, its eternal forces, the force of our past and of heaven, those forces which were voiced 130 years ago by the fathers of the Revolution, the voices of the most distinguished ministers of the priesthood, of our inspired poets, of our most brilliant magistrates, of all those who are noble, generous, and friendly to France, those forces should not leave this audience diminished or belittled.

"No, it is no longer Schwartzbard who is at issue here. It is the pogroms. Gentlemen of the jury, to condemn yesterday's pogroms is to prevent the pogroms of tomorrow. This is not simply Schwartzbard's advocate who is speaking. With him are the thousands and thousands of tortured, and with them the voices of the Abbé Gregoire, Rabaud Saint-Etienne, Mirabeau, Gambetta, Victor Hugo, all those dead and all those living, who entreat you that he should be acquitted, that this man who carries all the tragedies of a people on his forehead like a terrible mark should go free.

"Gentlemen of the jury, I am done. Reply No to the first

question. Acquit Schwartzbard because you have compassion. Gentlemen, today you are responsible for the prestige of our nation and of the thousands of human lives that depend on the verdict of France."[19]

Notes

1. For complete summation see Pleading of Torrès, File 496, Tcherikover Archive, and Torrès, *Le procès des pogromes*, pp.1-54.

2. Torrès referred here to Mme. Severine, Pierre Mille, and Firmin Gemier, all of whom were suffering from the grippe or bronchitis this chilly October.

3. It is doubtful that the poetess could have contributed much to the discussions save a personal endorsement of the accused. The fact that she was to be called at all should be written off as another cheap appeal to French glory.

4. Campinchi had held that readers of the Left papers would be for acquittal and those on the Right for conviction.

5. Pleading of Torrès, pp.1-11.

6. *Ibid.*, pp.13-14.

7. *Ibid.*, pp.16-18.

8. *Ibid.*, pp.18-20.

9. *Ibid.*, pp.20-21.

10. *Ibid.*, pp.21-22.

11. *Ibid.*, pp.24.

12. *Ibid.*, pp.26-28.

13. *Ibid.*, pp.29-31.

14. *Ibid.*, p.32.

15. *Ibid.*, p.33.

16. *Ibid.*, p.34.

17. *Ibid.*, pp.34-35.

18. *Ibid.*, pp.35-37.

19. *Ibid.*, p.38.

16.

The Verdict of Civilization

THE JURY WENT OUT at 5:40 P.M. A few moments later, Schwartzbard was led out of the prisoner's dock to a nearby cell.

At the prosecutor's table, Campinchi and Willm were confidently reassuring Mme. Petlura and her brother-in-law Oskar that justice would be done. Defense Counsel Torrès could be seen conferring with aides, perhaps envisioning an appeal.

Three squads of special police in black and red uniforms warily eyed the restive crowd of Ukrainians, Jews, and supposedly impartial Frenchmen who had shoved their way into the courtroom. General Mykola Shapoval, the man who had accused Schwartzbard of being in league with the Bolshevik conspirator Volodine, was there. Leon Motzkin, Secretary of the Comité des Délégations Juives, was there, one of many Jewish witnesses who had branded Petlura a pogromchik. And Anna Schwartzbard, the assassin's frail wife who had nearly suffered a nervous collapse during Sholom's incarceration, was there, surrounded by friends in the stifling atmosphere of the Court of Assizes.

In the corridors, more gendarmes linked arms to hold back the hundreds who, regardless of motive, wanted to be present for the moment of judgment. The mob extended several hundred yards from the Palace of Justice as far as the old Pont Neuf and the Boulevard St. Michel.

They waited.

At 6:05 P.M., the bell above the door of the jury room rang twice. The sound was repeated forthwith by another bell placed over the main entrance to the courtroom. The jury was coming back. Their deliberations had consumed so little time that Schwartzbard was not even in his place when they returned.

Cries of "Sit down! Sit down!" filled the hall, as the usher called for silence. Justice Flory took his seat at the high bench and cautioned, "Whatever the verdict of the jury may be, I must insist on the public keeping strict silence. I shall not hesitate to have anyone who presumes to applaud brought up before the court."

Turning to his right, he said, "Mr. Foreman, be so good as to acquaint the court with the result of your deliberations."

To the first of the five questions posed by the Prosecution (was Schwartzbard guilty of having struck blows which caused injuries to Simon Petlura on May 25, 1926), the Foreman of the Jury of the Seine replied, "On my honor and my conscience, before God and before man, the verdict of the jury is *not guilty.*" The first answer dispelled the necessity of inquiring into the other four questions.

Flory's admonition to silence notwithstanding, the courtroom erupted in cheers, screams, and laughter. Hardened foreign journalists joined the other spectators in shouting, "Long live France! Long live the French jury!"

Down in the main lobby of the Palace, the demonstration was even more boisterous. Hats flew into the air, and bearded East Europeans embraced one another in jubilation. Runners carried the news to the Jewish quarter of the city. Soon people were filling the streets to sing and dance.

In the courtroom, an attempted riot by several Ukrainian partisans was squelched by guards after an initial exchange of blows from fists and canes. Petlura's sympathizers continued to struggle as they were escorted from the hall, down the corridors, and out into the street, where they again set upon the police and the Jews. Through the furor, Mykola Shapoval, defender of the Directory, made his way over to Leon Motzkin and told him, "Now that the trial is ended, let Jews and Ukrainians live in peace together."[1]

Sholom Schwartzbard learned of the verdict from the Associated Press correspondent as he was being led back into the courtroom. His face lit up when he heard the roar of the spectators.

"Am I acquitted?" he asked eagerly, trying to suppress a grin. The cheers of his supporters were too much for him. Tears welled up in his eyes and he almost toppled over as he saw his wife weeping joyously.[2]

At this moment, Henri Torrès rushed toward him and the two embraced. Not many knew of the serious personal differences between Schwartzbard and his counsel. All was forgotten in the flush of victory. The two men smiled warmly; then Schwartzbard was handed on to Assistant Defense Counsel Rosenthal (a young man whom Schwartzbard preferred to Torrès) and to the other aide Goudchaux. At last his wife and friends were allowed to come forward. He had not held Anna in his arms for eighteen months.

An obviously delighted Justice Flory patiently attempted to restore a semblance of order. He had the clerk read the verdict to Schwartzbard. Then, in his most solemn voice, he added, "We, President of the Court of Assizes, by virtue of the powers with which we are invested by the law, having received the verdict of the jury to the effect that the prisoner at the bar is not guilty of the acts imputed to him, do now declare him acquitted of the charge laid against him, and we order that he be forthwith released, if he not be required on another charge."

French law, however, compelled Flory to elicit some kind of compensation by way of civil damages. As a result, Schwartzbard was fined two francs, one each for Madame Petlura and Oskar Petlura.[3]

The trial was over.

******

Congratulatory messages poured into Paris from every corner of the globe. From Kazan, Saratov, Dniepropetrovsk, Beirut, Shanghai, Buenos Aires, Kishinev, Montevideo, Brussels, Warsaw, Detroit, Lublin, Bratislava, London, Amsterdam, Rio de Janeiro, Berlin, Odessa, Dresden, Chicago, Bordeaux, Kaunas, Geneva, Asuncion, Madison, San Juan, Grenoble, Jerusalem, Vienna, Bogota, Jaffa, Lyons, Vera Cruz, Malmo, Capetown, Montreal, New York, La Chaux-de-fonds, and Johannesburg, the telegrams came. Perhaps the most significant was the following:

> The Jewish Congregation of Moscow expresses its admiration to the French nation whose conscience has condemned the massacres organized by Petlura. *French justice, by its historic judgment, has become the eloquent interpreter of the sentiment of all civilized nations against the makers of pogroms. [Emphasis added.]*
>
> (signed) Fuchs Anken, Advocat, President
> Dr. Wermel, Dr. Urisson, Members, Dir.[4]

Understandably, the Jewish communities of the world hailed the verdict as a sign of a new willingness on the part of Gentiles to acknowledge the hideous wrongs done to Ukrainian Jews (and to their brethren in a dozen other lands). But Jews also were eager to read into the acquittal of Schwartzbard something that was not there—a pledge that the civilized world would never again permit the mass murder of Jews, never again tolerate pogroms.

"A sign of an awakening world conscience, a greater sensitiveness in noting, and possibly righting, the age-old indignities, hatreds and persecutions," gushed the *American Hebrew*. "Schwartzbard's acquittal will mean that through the medium of the French Court of Assizes, Europe condemns the brutal Jewish massacres of which Simon Petlura was, let us hope, the last of the instigators. Schwartzbard is a symbol of the indignation coursing through the whole world at the cold-blooded program of murder and rapine planned and executed by a super-hooligan. His name does not matter. It is his type that will ultimately be exterminated, not by the crude and indefensible counter-violence of murder, but by the devastating force of enlightened public opinion. To France, through the Schwartzbard trial, is given the opportunity of helping the progress of civilization to higher spiritual levels."[5]

France was similarly acclaimed in the New York Yiddish dailies, *Freiheit, Der Tog* and the *Morning Journal.* Even the staid *Jewish Tribune* praised the nation which now served as spokesman for the civilized world against "super-hooligans":

> The acquittal of Solomon [*sic*] Schwartzbard was in the spirit of the supreme gesture of France. Here was a nation which for almost half a century had known the dread of oppression and which had harbored the pangs of hate. All those years she planned and lived for the hour when she might strike down the foe. And strike she did.[6]

Such lavish praise was misspent on France, where the leading newspapers unanimously condemned the verdict. Claretier, writing in *Figaro,* complained: "Nowadays one can kill with impunity in salons or bedrooms or even in the streets. Thus goes the world. The pogrom on individual morality has begun."[7]

The conservative *Echo du Paris* commented angrily: "This incomprehensible verdict is made more intolerable by the applause, cries, and shouts with which it was received. It is extraordinary that on behalf of the dignity of French justice not a single word was pronounced to put a stop to this scandal."

The *Temps* wished to disassociate itself from the verdict

by relegating the story to the last page; previously, the trial
had been covered extensively on pages 2 and 3.

The Socialist *Oeuvre* noted glumly that following the
emotional testimonies of Mlle. Greenberg and Jacob Zafran,
acquittal was "only to be expected."[8]

The impact of Torrès' appeal to French "instinct" was
ephemeral. Immediately after the trial, Schwartzbard had to
go into hiding for several days in fear for his life. The danger
of retaliation made it impossible for Schwartzbard again to
become "the humble and industrious watchmaker he was
before he fired those fateful revolver shots."[9] For weeks after
the trial, rumors persisted in Paris and other European
capitals that exiled Ukrainian officers had contacted Oskar
Petlura for the purpose of arranging Schwartzbard's
execution.[10]

Some Jewish leaders urged him to emigrate to America,
and finally in March, 1928, Schwartzbard made known his
plans to leave the country which had rendered civilization's
verdict against pogroms. His decision was symptomatic of a
greater sickness in France.

On December 9, 1927, not six weeks after Schwartzbard's
acquittal, anti-Jewish elements of the Right congregated in
Paris to form the League of Order, an organization whose
prime purpose was "to free France from Jewish high finance
and freemasonry."

In the next decade, the seven hundred thousand members
of Francois de la Rocque's *Croix de Feu*, the hooded klans-
men of *La Cagoule*, Charles Maurras' xenophobic *Action
Française*, René Coty's *Solidarité Française*, Fernand de
Brinon's *Comité France-Allemagne*, Jacques Doriot's *Parti
Populaire Français*, Pierre Taittinger's *Jeunesses Patriotes*,
and a host of proto-fascist splinter groups headed by Marcel
Deat, Georges Valois, Gaston Bergery, and Henri Dorgeres
worked to undermine the unstable Third Republic.

France may have been the mouthpiece of civilization in
1927, but in 1939 another French jury would convict

Herschel Grynzspan, an eighteen-year-old Jewish youth living in Paris, of the murder of Ernst von Rath, Assistant Secretary to the German Embassy. The fact that the Nazi regime had earlier expelled eighteen thousand Polish-born Jews from its boundaries (including Grynzspan's parents, residents of Germany for thirty years) to a stateless limbo, living in boxcars or ditches, shunted back and forth across Eastern Europe's borders, and the fact that Grynzspan was half-crazed with grief made little difference to the France of 1939. Not only was the boy imprisoned, but with the advent of the puppet Vichy regime in 1940, Herschel Grynzspan would be "transported" eastward with one hundred fifty thousand stateless Jews from France.

Grynzspan's attorney, a Deputy in the French National Assembly from 1932 to 1936, would flee to safety in the United States. Although he was a native-born Frenchman, he was forced to flee because he was a Jew. His name was Henri Torrès.[11]

If France learned little from the Schwartzbard trial, what could be said for the newly created "republic" of Poland and the other East European chauvinist tyrannies born of World War I (Lithuania, Latvia, Estonia, Hungary, and Rumania)?

Poland had festered with pogroms—at Kielce, Lwow, Vilna—since January of 1919, from the very moment of that country's birth. Only the harsh rebuke from Poland's "god-father," Clemenceau, had forced the government to grant the three million Polish Jews some respite. Thus, when Defense Counsel Torrès received congratulatory messages from Jewish leaders in Warsaw and Lublin, they expressed the hope that Polish Jewry had seen the last of the massacres.[12]

Not until 1931 did Poland remove from the Jews the last of the restrictions inherited from Tsarist times. Even then, discrimination was continued in a variety of ways—an official Jewish quota for schools and the professions, passage of obligatory Sunday closing laws, a ban on ritual slaughtering of animals, boycotts of Jewish merchants, the establishment of state monopolies in certain industries (salt, liquor, tobacco) along with a denial to Jews of work in these fields, and the official program of encouraging Jewish emigration to Madagascar, Palestine, anywhere, out of Poland.

On June 4, 1936, Premier Skladkowski, while claiming to reject violence, defended the economic struggle against the Jews. The Polish Cardinal Hlond echoed this argument in a national radio broadcast. Polish pogromchiks proceeded to distinguish themselves in a new wave of terror in Minsk, Czestochowa, Brest, and a host of other towns.[13]

Schwartzbard had killed, he claimed, so that Jews might live in dignity. But by 1939, the name of Schwartzbard meant as little to the doomed Jews of Poland as the empty platitudes about "world conscience" and "justice." Pale-faced children playing in rags, masses of persons stricken with typhus, women fighting over rotten potatoes considered unfit for consumption by army troops, three million declassed, depressed, despised souls, these were Poland's Jews *before* Hitler.[14] By 1945 more than ninety percent of their number would be murdered, less than two decades after civilization supposedly had given a final No to pogroms.

In the United States, most observers did not see the Schwartzbard trial as a triumph of enlightened conscience. The *New York World* grumbled that Petlura had been tried posthumously. The *Brooklyn Eagle*, mindful of a heavy circulation among the various nationalities in metropolitan New York, tried to appease them all by saying, "Petlura may not have ordered the pogroms, but he did nothing to stop them." The *New York Herald-Tribune*, wondering editorially if the verdict was just, mused: "No, it is not justice. But it is the Parisians' acknowledgment of the imperfections, the hatreds, the stubborn primitiveness of human beings and the difficulty of cloaking them in the formal outlines of institutions." The *New York Times* did not deem the verdict worthy of editorial comment.

Schwartzbard never did emigrate to America. Moreover, the American Jewish Congress decided to withdraw an invitation which had been sent to Henri Torrès to speak at its convention because "unfortunate misunderstandings would undoubtedly have followed."[15]

The United States proved to be less concerned with the "world's conscience" than with the preservation of her own pristine neutrality. In 1938 and 1939, ships laden with refugees fleeing the impending European Holocaust were turned away from America's shores. The land of the refugee, whose Statue of Liberty was inscribed with the words of an immigrant Jewish poetess, was unable or unwilling to rescue European Jews on the eve of their destruction.

In 1938, a half-hearted international conference at Evian came to naught. Before December, 1941, fear of a Nazi-inspired fifth column precluded any rescue efforts. In 1943, an inconsequential and insincere refugee conference was held at Bermuda. The "world's conscience" had no money, no transport, and, above all, no room for the doomed Jews.

Even after the war's end, 60 percent of Americans polled argued that the nation's doors should remain closed to the most undesirable of all European refugees, the Jews. Congressional sentiment, as expressed in postwar restrictionist legislation favoring Balts, Ukrainians, anti-communists, and "proven agriculturalists," reflected the prevailing American hypocrisy.[16]

In England, the *London Times* ho-hummed the acquittal of Schwartzbard, saying; "In view of the habitual leniency of French juries in the face of pleas of justification, the verdict was not unexpected."[17]

Five months afterward, in March, 1928, Schwartzbard applied to the British authorities in the Middle East for a visa to go to Palestine. Repeatedly through the next decade, in correspondence with the Jewish Agency in Jerusalem,

with the World Zionist Organization in Geneva, in letters to
Dr. Jacob Blaustein in Tel Aviv, he expressed his desire to
settle in Palestine and become part of the thriving Jewish
settlement there.[18] At one point, with the accession of the
socialist Labor government of MacDonald and Webb,
Schwartzbard's hopes grew high. But his application to emigrate to Palestine still was denied. The Colonial Office
approved the decision of the Mandatory Government. No
statement was ever issued, no reason given.[19] By January,
1935, Schwartzbard wrote to Blaustein, "I am certain that the
doors of Palestine will always remain closed to me."[20]

Perhaps the British saw in Schwartzbard the kind of
provocative personality who might upset the delicate balance of non-peace which they were trying to maintain in the
Middle East. Even without Schwartzbard, however, 246
persons were killed in the Wailing Wall riots of 1929 and
some three thousand more between 1936 and 1939.

In May of 1939, Great Britain, the nation which in 1917
had promised the Jews a homeland in Palestine, which
championed all oppressed peoples during World War II,
delivered its own interpretation of the "world's conscience."
The infamous "White Paper on Palestine" issued in that
month restricted Jewish immigration to the Holy Land to a
maximum of 75,000. While Jews died in Auschwitz and
Maidanek, while 25,000 of their number fought for the
Allies at Alamein and Tobruk, other British forces turned
back steamers packed with Jews clinging desperately to life.
The refugee ships S. S. *Struma, Patria, Liesel,* and *El
Salvador,* sank because of the British blockade of Palestine.[21]

The world need not have worried that Sholom Schwartzbard would be deified by the Jews of Palestine or anywhere
else. Most respectable Jewish leaders repudiated the assassination as an act of vengeance. The venerable *Jewish
Chronicle* editorialized in London on October 28, 1927:

> Nonetheless, the idea underlying his [Schwartzbard's]
> deed surely calls for the strongest reprehension. To

excuse it, still more to justify it, seems to introduce nothing short of social chaos where the law of the jungle prevails. However aggrieved and however altruistically, no man has the right to take the law into his own hands and deal as he wishes with any life, however despicable.[22]

It was shocking, noted the *Chronicle,* that some Jews had entered Schwartzbard's name in the Golden Book of the Jewish National Fund, among the honored names of those who had served the national cause and striven for the rebirth of a Jewish state in Palestine: "What a mark of respect to the other names contained in the Golden Book! What good taste! What a sense of the fitness of things! And above all, as Carlyle would have put it, how significant of much!" Not thus was the Jewish battle to be won, not by revenge or violence and the negation of all that Judaism teaches. This was not only "unmoral," but dangerous in the highest degree.[23]

Ironically, one of the most jubilant commentaries on the Schwartzbard trial was published in Germany. *"Schwartzbard Freigesprochen!"* exclaimed the gothic headline on the front page of the *Frankfurter Zeitung* on October 27, 1927. "Schwartzbard Acquitted!" Journalist Friedrich Sieburg could scarcely restrain himself:

> For twenty centuries, they [the Gentiles] have tyrannized over the Jewish people; for twenty centuries, from the days of Titus to those of Torquemada, they have pressed the lively brains of this race beneath their heels. *And lo, at long last, one of them hits back* [original italics], and after the Petluras of all lands have been commiting outrages for two thousand years. A Jew has pulled a trigger! The whole world is agape, and when it gets its breath again, it acquits him to the cry of "Vive la Republique!"
>
> Schwartzbard possessed the moral courage which we may search for in vain among the annals of German History. He was a Jew, a saviour of his people, no fair-

haired conspiratorial youngster, not a cunning murderer, who would fain not have committed the murder,
or would have acted at the behest of another, an unknown, who would not have remembered how he had
come to do such a thing; he was no faint-hearted traitor
walking casually through the Brandenburg Gate just
as the *putsch*-troops marched in. No, this man declared
quite frankly: "I killed him deliberately and I am glad I
did so."[24]

Six years later, the German people were to chant *"Sieg
Heil!"* before the most monstrous pogromchik of all.

Sholom Schwartzbard had tried to rouse the "world's
conscience." Civilization had, in fact, passed judgment
upon pogroms. God, fate, chance, or destiny had given
mankind an eleventh hour reprieve, an opportunity to
repudiate genocide and race hatred. No longer could anyone's sadistic curiosity be piqued by the wonderment at how
much pressure was required to crush the skull of an infant of
six months or how many times a woman could be raped
before she went mad.

The world knew what would happen if another Petlura
came to power. Yet it did nothing to prevent the rise of
Hitler or to rebuff him before he plunged humanity into the
End of Days.

The year Adolf Hitler came to power in Germany,
Schwartzbard warned against nationalism, especially German chauvinism and of the dreadful sacrifice which another
war would bring. He encouraged mankind to take a lesson
from the Jewish people, to love the entire world as its own.
An optimistic Schwartzbard wrote confidently of a better
future of freedom and humanity.[25]

For the next five years, the onetime soldier-poet-anarch-
ist-watchmaker-assassin criss-crossed the globe from Cal-
gary to Chicago and Seattle, laboring toward those goals.
On March 3, 1938, while Pastor Niemöller was being brutalized in a Nazi concentration camp, while Stalin's purges

raged in Moscow, while Spain still bled beneath the heel of Fascist intervention, while the Japanese tramped through Shansi province, Sholom Schwartzbard was on a journalistic assignment in Capetown, South Africa, where, at the age of forty-nine, he died.[26]

A year later, a Ukrainian apologia published in Great Britain fantasized that Schwartzbard, "a Soviet agent," was "now back in the USSR."[27] Whether because of slanders such as this or because of the imminent horrors awaiting Europe's Jews, just the deification that more sedate Jewish leaders had feared came to Schwartzbard after his death. The Lithuanian poet Jacob Gottlieb, soon to perish in the Nazi Holocaust, composed the following Yiddish dirge:

SHOLOM SCHWARTZBARD

Blessings upon your strong hand
That took vengeance for our shame.
You sounded a mighty trumpet-call.
And it was like thunder and flame.

Not a drop of blood that is spilt is lost.
For that is why you came,
Like a bow and arrow, like the storm
To avenge our shame.

Avenger of our blood that was spilt,
Now you lie dead.
Great heart that revolted against our shame,
Your life has fled.

But your deed remains our destiny,
A flame generations will see.[28]

Notes

1. *Jewish Telegraph Agency Dispatch*, November 4, 1927, p.1.

2. "Lurid Trial of Petlura's Slayer," *Literary Digest*, p.38.

3. *London Times*, October 27, 1927, p.11.

4. See Schwartzbard's correspondence with former co-legionnaires, File 880, Tcherikover Archive, and Torrès, *Le procès des pogromes*, p.263.

5. "Schwartzbard's Acquittal—The World's Conscience," *American Hebrew*, CXXI (1927), p.891.

6. "The Schwartzbard Trial," *Jewish Tribune*, XCI (November 4, 1927), p.23.

7. *Figaro*, October 27, 1927, p.1.

8. *New York Times*, October 27, 1927, p.6.

9. *Jewish Tribune*, November 11, 1927, p.8.

10. See letter from Paul Grunbaum to Moses Waldmann, November 15, 1927, File 430, Tcherikover Archives.

11. At the war's end, Torrès, who had served as editor-in-chief of *La Voix de France* in the USA and later as a professor of law at the Universities of Rio de Janeiro and Sao Paulo, returned to his homeland. He was elected to the French Senate and later did extensive work in the national radio and television system.

12. *Jewish Independent*, October 28, 1927, p.1. For the reaction of Jews in Eastern Europe, see "Shvartzbard Freigeshprochen," *Di yiddishe shtimme*, Kovno, October 27, 1927, p.1, File 506, Tcherikover Archive.

13. Bernard Weinryb, *et al*, *The Jews in the Soviet Satellites* (Syracuse: University Press, 1953), pp. 208-10.

14. Pierre van Paassen, *The Forgotten Ally* (New York: Dial Press, 1943), pp.18-19. See also Milton Hindus and Lionel Reiss, *A World at Twilight: A Portrait of the Jewish Communities of Eastern Europe before the Holocaust* (New York: Macmillan, 1971).

15. "Torrès and Schwartzbard," *Jewish Tribune*, XCI (November 11, 1927), p.8. Schwartzbard did succeed in making several tours of America between 1933 and 1935. He was sponsored by Workmen's Circles who hoped to underwrite publication and publicity expenses for his books. See Files 876 and 889, Tcherikover Archive.

16. See Arthur Morse, *While Six Million Died* (New York: Random House, 1968); David Wyman, *Paper Walls: America and the Refugee Crisis, 1938-1941* (Amherst: University of Massachusetts Press, 1968); Henry Feingold, *The Politics of Rescue* (New Brunswick: Rutgers University Press, 1970); and Saul S. Friedman, *No Haven for the Oppressed* (Detroit: Wayne State University Press, 1973).

17. *London Times*, October 27, 1927, p.11.

18. File 881, Tcherikover Archive.

19. *New York Times*, March 11, 1928, p.6.

20. Letter of Schwartzbard to Blaustein, January 7, 1935, File 878, 69817, Tcherikover Archive. For his comments on the MacDonald government and his frustrations with the Zionists in Geneva see this file and File 881.

21. The classic work describing the agonies of the Jewish refugee bound for Palestine is Arieh Tarkakower and Kurt Grossmann, *The Jewish Refugee* (New York: Institute of Jewish Affairs of the World Jewish Congress and the American Jewish Congress, 1944).

22. "The Schwartzbard Case," *Jewish Chronicle*, October 28, 1927, pp.7-8.

23. *Ibid.*, p.8. Similar disapproval was expressed by the *Jewish Tribune*, November 16, 1926, p.6, and *The American Jewish Year Book*, Vol. XXIX (Jewish Publication Society of America, 1927), pp.427-28.

24. *Frankfurter Zeitung,* October 27, 1927, p.1.

25. Schwartzbard, *In krig mit zich aleyn,* pp.257-58. By 1935, Schwartzbard had made copies of his memoirs available to the Sorbonne Library and the Musée de la Guerre, which accepted the writings formally but without much enthusiasm. See File 877, Tcherikover Archive.

26. *New York Times,* March 4, 1938, p.23. See also File 879, Tcherikover Archive.

27. Yeats-Brown, *The European Jungle* (London: Eyre and Spottiswoods, 1939), p.51.

28. *The Golden Peacock: An Anthology of Yiddish Poetry,* ed. Joseph Leftwich (New York and London: T. Yoseloff, 1961), p.492.

17.

Simon Petlura

IN OCTOBER, 1927, the literary deity of the Bolsheviks, Maxim Gorki, wrote to Torrès that anti-Semitism was a feeling alien to the populations of Russia. Ignoring the historical facts of six centuries, Gorki blamed Tsarist absolutism for the pogroms. Not the Ukrainian people, but its leaders, like Petlura, nurtured in Tsarist hatred, were to be held responsible for the carnage, said Gorki.[1]

This was precisely the attitude of many Jews. "We should now hold guilty not the entire Ukrainian people," wrote the *Jewish Tribune,* "but those who misled them by their lies and calumnies."[2] And from a statement issued by the Federation of Ukrainian Jews in the United States on November 4, 1927:

> From now on it will be known. *Petlura was guilty in the pogroms, not the Ukrainian people.* We Ukrainian Jews have always asserted that were it not for the inexcusable inciting of the followers of Petlura, Denikin, and the others, the Ukrainian people would not have committed the pogroms, and peace between the Jews and Ukrainians would never have been disturbed. We are satisfied with the verdict and we are convinced that the Ukrainian people will now recognize that not the Jews are their enemies, but those who incited them to pogroms against the Jews.[3] [*Emphasis added.*]

Thus also the Yiddish-language *Tog* of New York:

> The significance of Schwartzbard's acquittal lies not so
> much in the personal freedom of the defendant who
> had taken his life in his own hands, thus showing that
> he sets little store by comfort and security, as in the
> public and irrevocable acknowledgment of Petlura's
> guilt for the torrents of innocent Jewish blood spilled
> in pogroms in Ukraine during Petlura's regime. *For
> the verdict of "not guilty" for Schwartzbard means
> exactly a verdict of "guilty" for Petlura who now stands
> condemned before the public opinion of the world.*[4]
> [*Emphasis added.*]

From the beginning, Ukrainian nationalist spokesmen
rejected any thought that Simon Petlura could have been
connected with the massacres. On February 26, 1918, Ukrainian Social Democrats pressed the moribund Second International in Zurich for a resolution which delcared, "Petlura
never fomented nor organized pogroms against Jews and
could not be accused personally."[5]

For more than thirty years, Ukrainian writers and sympathizers insisted that an injustice had been committed at
the Court of Assizes. Then on February 28, 1958, the French
television series "En Votre Ame et Conscience" devoted a
program to the Schwartzbard Affair, calling upon many of
the principals involved with the trial, including Torrès.
Ukrainian reaction to this "one-sided presentation," which
blamed Petlura for the pogroms, was immediate. Protests
against "flagrant lies" were sent to Radio-Television
France, the Foreign Ministry, and French Embassies abroad
from Orthodox Metropolite Nikanor Abramovich (Western
Europe), Metropolite Jean Theodorovich (United States),
Archbishop Jean Boutchko (Rome), Alexander Shulgin,
Vladimir Janiv (President of the Christian Ukrainian Move-
ment), Alexander Kulchytsky (Professor of the Free University of the Ukraine in Munich), the National Ukrainian
Council in Munich, the General Secretary for Foreign Af-

fairs of the Ukrainian Council for the Liberation of the Ukraine in New York, the Central Committee of the Anti-Bolshevik Bloc of Peoples, the Organization of National Ukrainians, the Union of Liberation for the Ukraine, and a dozen other committees in a dozen different lands.[6]

Why was it necessary to attack "the grand champion of Ukrainian liberation," a man akin to Bolivar or Garibaldi? Why weren't Ukrainian witnesses such as Shulgin, General Oudovichenko, and the Engineer Choumitzki, all living in Paris at the time of the broadcast, asked to appear? And if the goal of the program was to stimulate the soul and conscience of France, why not devote the hour to the sufferings of Ukrainian Metropolite Slipy (then in exile) or Metropolite Lipkivsky (who struggled on behalf of his people through the famines of the early 1930's)?

When no answers were forthcoming to these questions, more than two hundred persons gathered in the Paris cemetery where a dark marker bearing the Ukrainian Trident and the name Petlura stood. There, on March 2, 1958, many of Petlura's old comrades-in-arms listened as the sixty-eight-year-old Shulgin delivered yet another eulogy to Simon Petlura, "the national hero."[7]

An American emissary sent to investigate the Ukrainian pogroms in September, 1919, had said, "Proof was not furnished that the actions were concerted or that any one man was responsible for a large number of deaths."[8] This was precisely the position of the nationalist Ukrainians. It was precisely incorrect.

Historians generally attribute the massacres to four inter-related causes: (1) historic antipathy of the Ukrainian peasant for the Jew, (2) identification of the Jew with the Bolshevik movement, (3) continuous fighting in the area, and (4) absence of central government. It is necessary to examine each of these, if only briefly, in order to comprehend Simon Petlura's culpability.

1. Historic antipathy of the Ukrainian peasant for the

Jew. According to the Ukrainians, there never was such a thing as organized anti-Semitism with its genocidal overtones in the Ukraine. There was no trace of bias in the folklore or popular songs, in the literature or political life of the people. "Organized and systematic anti-Semitism in [the] Ukraine has never existed," wrote journalist Lev Shankovsky, "unless it was introduced by the foreign powers occupying and oppressing [the] Ukraine."[9] From the middle of the nineteenth century forward, that oppressor was the Tsarist government, whose reactionary internal policy was based on "the state monopoly of alchol production and overt anti-Semitism."[10]

Fifty years of repression of the revolutionary ardor of the peasants, together with the concerted diversion of these passions toward acts of violence against Jews, mentally prepared Ukrainians for the pogroms of 1919. As Arnold Margolin put it, some Ukrainians "got the pogrom habit."[11] Bolshevik Moscow's unwarranted intrustion into Ukrainian affairs merely supplied "the torch to the powder magazine."[12]

Such an explanation of the general participation of the population in pogroms for generations is too simplistic. As Princeton's John Reshetar has said: "Anti-Semitism in Eastern Europe can be understood only when viewed in the historical context which is rooted in profound social, economic, and religious differences."[13]

Whether in Rumania, Hungary, Lithuania, or the Ukraine, over the course of centuries the Jew had always been identified as the Christ-killer, the unassimilable Cain, who looked different, dressed differently, spoke differently, and even smelled different from his Gentile neighbors. After the sixteenth century, this pariah came to be regarded as the economic oppressor of the illiterate, superstitious peasants. Polonized landowners on the right bank of the Dnieper employed Jewish "stewards" to manage their estates, collect taxes, even control the keys to Ukrainian churches. The end result was that all Jews, rich and poor alike, were massacred by Cossacks after 1648. In the towns, relations between the two peoples deteriorated as more peasants became personally indebted to Jewish merchants, whom they considered to be unscrupulous and greedy.

The canard of Bolshevism merely supplied the final catalyst to a brew of racism endemic to the Ukraine for centuries. This was conceded by Petlura's predecessor as President of the Directory, Vladimir Vinnichenko, who said, "Sons of shopkeepers, *kulaks*, priests, and Christians, they [the Ukrainians] had from childhood been infected with the spirit of anti-Semitism."[14]

For Jews in the Ukraine, the threat of rape and riot was constant, and few of those safely away from that region now recall the Ukraine with any fondness. The civil war merely afforded an opportunity for Ukrainians, Gypsies, Rumanians, and Russians, all blurred as Ukrainians in the eyes of Jews, to join the vanguard of murderers and thugs. Men, women, and children of all ages swooped down on ruined Jewish communities after the Haidamaks departed, to haggle over, confiscate, and plunder Jewish goods. The absence of basic human compassion during those times is well-documented. Jews could only conclude that if not all Gentiles in the Ukraine were pogromchiks, very few of them were not overtly anti-Semitic and hence silent partners in the devastation of the Jewish people.

2. Identification of the Jew with the Bolshevik movement. The Ataman Zeleny's motto was "Death to the Jews and down with the Bolsheviks!" Struk's was the same. Yatsenko announced, "The Jews are all Communists! They defile our churches and change them into stables!"[15] Many peasants who lost their grain to Bolshevik commanders of Jewish parentage believed that the movement was a Jewish phenomenon.

This idea seemed to be corroborated by the fact that

poorer Jews in the cities often supported the Bolsheviks in the hope of securing political and economic freedom. Jews did flee their homes at the approach of hoodlums who strutted about calling themselves the Ukrainian Nationalist Army. They did return with the advance of the Bolshevik forces. This ebb and flow of populations could scarcely go unnoticed by Ukrainians.

Nevertheless, no more than 1½ percent of all the Jews in the Ukraine belonged to the Communist Party. Of those so-called "Jewish Bolsheviks," Professor Simon Dubnow had this to say: "They appear under Russian pseudonyms because they are ashamed of their Jewish origins. But it would be better to say that their Jewish names are pseudonyms; they are not rooted in our people."[16]

This the Ukrainians could not see. Nor could they appreciate the fact that Jews were victimized by the same Bolsheviks of whom they were supposedly the leaders. When, for example, another of those endless deputations of Jews appealed to Leon Trotsky, as one of their own, to give them succor from massacre, Trotsky responded: "Go home to your Jews and tell them I'm not a Jew and don't care about the Jews or what happens to them."[17]

3. Continuous fighting in the area. The disaster in the Ukraine dates from the time when deserters and disgruntled soldiers of the Provisional Government first sacked the Galician towns of Tarnopol and Kalush in 1917. "During the first years of the Revolution, 1917-20," wrote Fedir Pigido-Pravoberezhny, "the Ukraine was the battlefield of the Germans and Austrians against the Red Russians, of the Ukrainians against the Red Russians, of the Ukrainians against the White Russians, of the White Russians against the Red Russians, and of the Poles against the Red Russians, concurrently."[18] The author did not even mention Haller's Polish legions which belabored the Ukrainians, the rival West and East Ukrainian armies, and the various

Allied Expeditionary Forces which were present in the Crimea.

Each new day found the Jews held as hostages of a new band of pogromchiks. Men, having been baptized in the ritual of war, became "dazzled by blood," as Professor Shulgin put it.[19] In such circumstances, the Jew, easily identifiable as an "alien," was brutalized. To the Whites, he was a Bolshevik. To the Bolsheviks, he was a White. To the Ukrainians, he was a Jew.

Though there is no question that the Ukraine was a constant battlefield, it is significant that in the period of the greatest ascendancy of the Directory and Petlura, from May to September, 1919, the number of pogroms each month more than doubled. Whereas as many as fifty or sixty such incidents had been recorded in the first months of the year, 148 were registered in May, ninety-five in June, 138 in July, 159 in August, and eighty-five in September. In addition, several major pogromchiks, Grigoriev and Makhno among them, had either been routed from the Ukraine or were operating at reduced strength by the end of that summer.[20] Denikin's forces accounted for only a third of the number of pogroms, and then only at the end of summer.

After September, 1919, after the Petlurists had been driven from Russia, there were only 108 pogroms recorded in a twelve-month period. The period from May to September, 1919, regarded as the high point of the Ukrainian national renaissance, saw 625 pogroms committed against the Jewish people, more than half the total for all the years between 1917 and 1921. Not ironically did N.Gergel conclude, "The main center of pogroms was on the right bank. The Petlura movement which accounted for the largest number of Jewish victims in the Ukraine had its roots here."[21]

4. Absence of central government. This argument, a favorite of the prosecution during the Schwartzbard trial, has some foundation in fact. According to Professor

Reshetar, "The real cause [of the anarchy] was the failure of the Directory to establish contacts between the capital and local authorities."[22] This was in part due to poor communications[23] and inadequate railroads.[24]

As a result, it was not surprising that men like Zeleny, Struk, Angel, Shuba, Makhno, and Grigoriev ruled as "veritable satraps" over portions of the land. By the spring of 1919, said Vinnichenko, the independent military commanders rather than the Directory constituted whatever government there was in the Ukraine. Arnold Margolin agreed. The Directory was so concerned with issues of national self-determination and independence in the first three months of 1919 that it accepted all kinds of recruits into its large army. Commissions were bought and sold. Faced with the immediate task of repulsing the Red Army, the Directory, hampered by poor lines of communication, could ill afford time to deal with such problems as pogroms, which were of a purely "internal" nature. What pogroms took place in that first quarter of 1919, then, should have been attributed to the debauchery of individual commanders.[25]

For Margolin, there was no question that Petlura tried everything in his power to suppress the pogroms, but he could not be everywhere at once. It was tragic that the West expected more of a "bookkeeper" like Petlura than a soldier like Denikin. Denikin was the real villain in the Ukraine, said Margolin. His army included the worst pogromchiks of all, the Great Russians, Don Cossacks, and the Chechens from the Caucasus.

"News of even the remotest connection between the regular Ukrainian Army and the irregular bands of Struk and the others," wrote Margolin, "would plunge me personally into utter despair and precipitate my resignation from the Ukrainian delegation at the Peace Conference in Paris."[26] It apparently did just that, for Margolin resigned in March, 1919, after waiting in vain for the Directory to do something about the fifty-five pogroms which had taken place during the two previous months.

Historic antipathy, identification with Bolshevism, continuous fighting, anarchy—these were supposedly the factors that contributed to the plight of the Jews in the Ukraine. But there was one more—direct encouragement from the National Ukrainian Government itself.

"Whereas the old pogroms were committed with the connivance of the government," read the report of the Russian Red Cross on the 1919 massacres, "the newest pogroms were actually organized and directed by those who held the administrative power in places where the Jewish population was, for days, weeks, and even months, at their mercy, without the slightest prospect of relief from anyone."[27]

The tides of pogroms followed a general pattern, ebbing as the Directory gained victories over the Bolsheviks and rising whenever it was put to rout. If the Haidamaks could not defeat the Red Army in battle, they could give vent to their frustrations by killing Jews, all of whom were Bolsheviks anyhow. Eventually followers of Petlura were to bear the guilt for no fewer than *493* separate massacres.[28]

Unofficially, the attitude of the Directory toward pogroms was well known. When Petlura entered Kiev astride a white horse in December, 1918, military officials quipped, "Tell the Jews that we will get even with them. We know your speeches; we will dispose of you and your associates."[29]

Later, Jews who protested the initial slaughters of 1919 were told, "One cannot make omelets without breaking eggs."[30] And when the government prepared to flee westward from Kiev in February, 1919, a high official warned, "Wait, we haven't played our main trump. Before anti-Semitism, no Bolshevism will stand."[31]

The official position of the Directory on pogroms was also evident. Said the Comité des Délégations Juives in Paris in 1919:

> The Directory did not even see its way to express an unqualified and clear condemnation of the pogroms, but in all its announcements and conversations with Jewish representatives it systematically made an implied defense of the pogroms by charging the whole of Jewry with pro-Bolshevism and ill-will towards the Ukrainian People's Republic.[32]

What then might be said of Simon Vassilievich Petlura, the man who had written in the forward of Evgeny Chirikov's 1907 play, *The Jews*:

> The suffering of Nachman [a character] will evoke deep compassion from everybody, even from those who do not belong to that nationality which was fated to bear such a heavy burden of oppression and persecution. . . . The importance of this drama lies in the fact that it creates in the hearts of the audience warm feelings for the oppressed nationality and sincere sympathy for their sufferings, at the same time provoking wrath and hatred for the regime under which such savage atrocities toward innocent victims are possible.[33]

For Vladimir Vinnichenko, Petlura was "a pogrom man," an ordinary small townsman who had been imbued with a heritage of anti-Semitism, but who was ready "in principle" to concede that Jews were human beings entitled to legal equality. A man of very gentle character, moderate intelligence, weak will, but of a nervous ambition which guided all his actions, this was how Vinnichenko in 1926 described his former rival and colleague. "Petlura had neither the moral nor technical authority to be chief, but merely play-acted at it," he declared.[34]

Vinnichenko painted a far different picture of the Holovni Ataman from that presented by other Ukrainian émigrés. He recalled that Petlura had never been elected to any position by the Ukrainian people. Before the Revolution, Petlura had only been a trooper, a man not especially active or important in the Social Democrat Party or National Union movement. He was a functionary in uniform, a man who claimed the distinction of designing the headgear worn by the cossacks. The Rada at one point even discussed revoking his commission.

According to Vinnichenko, Petlura created his own myth as the great anti-Bolshevik protector of the Ukraine, trotting about on a white horse in a village occupied and protected by the Germans. The Bolsheviks themselves contributed to his undeserved notoriety, referring to him as their most dangerous enemy and a friend of the Germans. All of this, Vinnichenko argued, was a sham, because the Soviets actually welcomed an opponent with the limited ability of Petlura.[35]

Continuing his deposition, Vinnichenko declared that the military clique that was responsible for the destruction of democracy and parliamentary government in the Ukraine elevated Petlura to a position he did not deserve. Although he was not a dictator, Petlura was responsible for the pogroms because he violated the directives of the Council of Ministers, because he supported the "free atamans" and declined to punish those wild elements, because he deliberately supplied false information to the Directory when Vinnichenko was its President, because he supported the thesis that all Jews were enemies of the state and Bolshevik sympathizers, and because he believed it to be expedient policy to "let the boys have a good time" with the Jews. Said Vinnichenko, "Responsibility for anti-social acts rests not only with the perpetrators of the acts, but equally with the forces which assumed defense of the interests of society, that is, the state and its government."[36]

According to Vinnichenko, Petlura's power-hungry junta shamed the Ukraine with "its barbaric chauvinism, suppression of free speech, and violation of all the liberties and rights of Jews, Poles, Russians, and Ukrainian workers and peasants."[37] Petlura was not a Ukrainian Garibaldi or Napoleon. His partisans had no right to identify the Ukrainian people with Petlura's government.[38]

When Schwartzbard struck, Petlura was a pathetic figure, living in poverty, in exile, destined for oblivion, commanding the allegiance of only a handful of friends. Said Abraham Revutzky, "Schwartzbard should not have interfered with this natural process of political decay. He should not have surrounded Petlura with the halo of a martyr, of whom *no aut nihil, aut bene* could be said."[39]

Was Simon Petlura responsible for the pogroms? Ukrainian apologists argue that no orders leading to pogroms can be attributed to him, that there is no documentary evidence of any incitement to pogroms by government agencies, that anti-Semitic remarks attributed to the Holovni Ataman constitute hearsay, that Petlura lacked the power to stop pogroms. According to one Ukrainian source, the attempt to paint Petlura as a pogromchik was the purest piece of slander.[40]

On the serious question of complicity, however, Ukrainians have likened the alleged crucifixion of Petlura to the trial of General Yamashita, commander of Japanese armed forces in the Philippines between October, 1944 and September, 1945. After the war, Yamashita went before a regular war crimes tribunal, which charged that he had "unlawfully disregarded and failed to discharge his duty as commander to control the operations of the members of his command, permitting them to commit brutal atrocities and other high crimes against the people of the United States and of its allies and dependencies, particularly the Philippines, and that he thereby violated the laws of war."[41]

According to the revisionist view of the Yamashita trial, which has gained currency in pro-Petlurist circles, the defendant was railroaded in the emotional aftermath of the war. Today, it is argued, the view of dissenting Justices Murphy and Rutledge would probably prevail.

Though the Yamashita case may seem remote from the Schwartzbard-Petlura affair, the issues raised are similar. Justice Murphy might well have been writing about Petlura when he declared:

> He was not charged with personally participating in the acts of atrocity or with ordering or condoning their commission. Not even knowledge of these crimes was attributed to him. It was simply alleged that he unlawfully disregarded and failed to discharge his duty as commander to control the operations of the members of his command, permitting them to commit the acts of atrocity. The recorded annals of warfare and the established principles of international law afford not the slightest precedent for such a charge. This indictment, in effect, permitted the military commission to make the crime whatever it willed, dependent upon its biased view as to the petitioner's duties and his disregard thereof, a practice reminiscent of that pursued in certain less respected nations in recent years.[42]

And further on:

> If we are ever to develop an orderly international community based upon a recognition of human dignity, it is of the utmost importance that the necessary punishment of those guilty of atrocities be as free as possible from the ugly stigma of revenge and vindictiveness. Justice must be tempered by compassion rather than by vengeance.[43]

And finally:

> International law makes no attempt to define the duties of a commander of an army under constant and overwhelming assault; nor does it impose liability under such circumstances for failure to meet the ordinary responsibilities of command. The omission is understandable. Duties, as well as ability to control troops,

vary according to the nature and intensity of the particular battle. To find an unlawful deviation from duty under battle conditions requires difficult and speculative calculations.[44]

In rendering his opinion in the Yamashita case, Justice Murphy said, "Had there been some element of knowledge or direct connection with the atrocities, the problem would have been entirely different."[45]

That was precisely the point with Petlura. It cannot be said that Petlura did not know what was happening in the Ukraine between 1917 and 1920. Nor could he take refuge in the favorite excuse of Nazis at Nuremberg. Petlura was not merely "following orders." Too many eyewitnesses claimed that he was at Proskurov, Zhitomir, or Smerenka when those towns were put to the torch.[46] Petlura was the actual power in the Ukrainian Directory. The marauding troops called themselves *Petlurovtzi*.

The Holovni Ataman could have done something to stop the bloodshed. He could have withheld financial assistance from "independent" *batki*. He could have withheld military supplies from his own regular troops or punished the pogromchiks to set an example. Or, failing that, he could have resigned his post, like any honorable man. The true test of a war criminal, Sir Hartley Schawcross argued at Nuremberg, was the moral decision to serve or not serve the criminal state.[47] For some Ukrainians, at least, Petlura's resignation was unthinkable. Wrote Professor Shulgin:

> The Captain always stays at his post despite the danger. He does all that is in his power, and if he is carried away by the waves, he cannot be accused. He has accomplished his duty. In the ocean of the Ukraine, the Ukrainian government and its supreme chief Simon Petlura stayed at their posts and they accomplished their duty.[48]

But Petlura did not do everything in his power to suppress the pogroms. If his was not a sin of commission (as no one can single out an instance where he personally killed a Jew), then it most certainly was a sin of omission. He did nothing to prevent the killing of Jews, even when it was within his province to do so.

After four years of continual military service and command, Petlura must have been familiar with the Hague Convention of 1907 on Land Warfare. Among other things, this compact prohibited "all needless cruelty and needless destruction of human life or property." Similarly, the Convention commanded that "peaceful inhabitants are to be spared in person and property during hostilities, so far as military necessity and the conduct of such inhabitants will permit."[49] As the titular or real head of the independent Ukraine, Simon Petlura was obligated to implement the terms of the Hague Convention. He did not.

Colonel Nikowskjy, blaming both Petlura and Denikin, charged that "guilt rests with reactionary and anti-Semitic men and their cronies who did nothing."[50] Topelberg-Ovcharenko stated flatly, "If Petlura had wanted, he could have put down the massacres. He did nothing."[51] And Elia Tcherikover noted, "One thing is clear, and that is that Petlura held authority in the region and did not react against the pogroms with a single word."[52]

Petlura issued no statement on the sufferings of Ukrainian Jewry until nine months after the first incidents at the railway depots in Bakhmach, Sarny, and Olevsk. In December, 1918, Petlura had not been so laconic. His secret circular to Ukrainian nationalist troops commanded the inspection of all papers at railway stations to prevent possible sabotage. If people were "not of Ukrainian appearance," they were to be "turned over to the military authorities."[53] That marked the onslaught of the crusade against the Jews.

Five years later, the feelings of this so-called philo-Semite were again made manifest. To the Archangel Nicholas Solovei, a Ukrainian priest, Petlura declared in Paris in 1924: *"The Jews are a pest, and when I am returned to Russia, it will be necessary to slaughter (égorger) all the*

Jews. Only then will calm prevail in Russia."[54]

In 1950, the International Law Commission reported to the United Nations General Assembly that complicity in the commission of a crime against peace, a war crime, or a crime against humanity is a crime under international law. The fact that a person committed such an act as head of state does not relieve him of responsibility. "Leaders, organizers, instigators and accomplices participating in the formulation or execution of a common plan or conspiracy to commit any of the foregoing crimes are responsible for all acts performed by any persons in the execution of such a plan."[55]

By these standards, Simon Petlura was responsible for the pogroms. The following conclusions are inescapable:

1. Simon Petlura was Chief of State, Ataman-in-Chief, with real power to act when he so desired. No Ukrainian leader enjoyed comparable respect, allegiance or authority. His orders of August, 1919 (against pogroms) and of October, 1920 (calling for the dissolution of partisan bands) indicate that he required no ministerial countersignature for action.

2. Units of the Ukrainian Army directly under his supervision (the Clans of Death) committed numerous atrocities. Instead of being punished, the leaders of these units (Oudovichenko, Palienko, Angel, Patrov, Shandruk) received promotions. *(See Chapter X.)*

3. Insurgents dependent upon Petlura for financial support and war material commited pogroms in his name. Petlura maintained a special office to coordinate the activities of these partisans. Rather than punishing them, he received their leaders with honors in his capital. Some even fled with him to Stanislaviv in the Western Ukraine. *(See Chapter XIII.)*

4. Official organs of the Ukrainian War Office, the Government Printing Works, and the Information Bureau of the

National Army incited pogroms by vicious anti-Semitic propaganda. This was done with Petlura's acquiescence. *(See Chapter XI.)*

5. Petlura reneged on promises made to Jews as early as November,1917, that effective inquiries would be made into pogroms. Though the Council of Ministers requested this of him on three specific occasion in 1919, it was never done. *(See Chapter X.)*

6. There is good reason to believe that Petlura may have ordered pogroms in Proskurov and Zhitomir in the early months of 1919, and that the Holovni Ataman was in the immediate vicinity of these towns when pogroms were raging. Yet he did nothing to intervene personally; nor did he command the expeditious punishment of the major pogromchiks. *(See Chapters VI and VII.)*

7. Petlura's famous orders of August 26 and 27, 1919, forbidding pogroms, were issued eight months too late, at a time when the Holovni Ataman had no real power. They were designed specifically for foreign consumption. A truer reading of his attitude toward pogroms may be found in his remarks to Vinnichenko, Revutzky, Krasny, Wagman, and Buchdrucker approving the excesses. *(See Chapter XI.)*

8. What funds were authorized for the relief of pogrom victims were a trifle compared with how much was needed and how much had been stolen from the Jews. Like Petlura's famed orders, they were too little and too late. *(See Chapter VIII.)*

9. Petlura's Jewish Ministry was a mere facade and his last minister, Pinchas Krasny, a sycophant, totally out of touch with his own community, reviled by the Jews. Other paper concessions to the Jews, such as the printing of money in Yiddish, granting autonony, opening Jewish schools, and the like, were expedient carry-overs from the days of the democratic Rada. *(See Chapter VIII.)*

10. Even from afar, in Paris, Petlura conducted a program which infuriated Jewish exiles. The patriotic campaign in *Trident* was interpreted by many as a new provocation against the Jews still resident in the Ukraine. *(See Chapter XII.)*

Perhaps it was too much to hope for moral leadership from the Holovni Ataman, who was, in the words of Revutzky, "a man of mediocre attainments," a man whose only outstanding quality was "an enormous ambition, an almost maniacal obsession concerning his role in the historical destiny of his nation."[56]

No *spiritus rector* of Ukrainian independence this, no Gandhi or Masaryk, but a middling man with delusions of grandeur. "Petlura really believes he is king," said Nikolai Vassilko, onetime Ukrainian minister to Switzerland.[57] "A brute," said Archangel Solovei.[58]

Like Adolf Eichmann and others, Petlura was thrust by history into a situation where he was the source of orders which ultimately led to the slaughter of thousands of innocent people.

There was an unhappy postscript to the life of Simon Petlura. During the first three days of July 1941, the "Nightingale Battalion," composed almost entirely of Ukrainians under the direction of the Gestapo, slaughtered seven thousand Jews in the vicinity of Lwow (Lemberg). Before their executions, Jewish professors, lawyers, and doctors were made to lick all the steps of four-story buildings and to carry garbage in their mouths from house to house. Then, forced to run a gauntlet of men who wore blue and gold armbands (coincidentally the colors of the Petlurist Republic), they were bayonetted to death in what was officially termed *Aktion Petlura*.[59]

A year later, in the same district, Ukrainian *Einsatzgruppen* again distinguished themselves in mass executions of Jews. These were the same villages and towns, the same victims, the same murder as in 1919. To this date there has been no denunciation by Ukrainian nationalists of the atrocities in World War II or of the voluntary assistance afforded the Nazi death machine by Ukrainians in Warsaw, Paris, or in the death camps of the Holocaust.[60]

Notes

1. Gorki to Torrès, October 16, 1927, in *Le procès des pogromes,* pp.127-131.

2. "The Schwartzbard Case Opens," *Jewish Tribune,* XCI (October 21, 1927),p.8.

3. *Jewish Independent,* November 4, 1927, p.5.

4. "Lurid Trial of Petlura's Slayer," p.42

5. The Committee of Minorities headed by M. De Broukere of Belgium delivered the report, a product of studies by Broukere, Otto Bauer (Austria), Abramovich (Russia), and Fedenko and Mazeppa (Ukraine). With such composition, it was not surprising that the report exonerated Petlura. See "Memorandum der Ukrainischen Sozialdemokratischen Arbeiterpartei an die Minderheitskommission der sozialistischen Arbeiter-Internationale in Brüssel," File 414, Tcherikover Archives.

6. *En Notre Ame et Conscience,* pp.5,10,11,12,14,16,19,20,23,38.

7. *Ibid.,* p.30 Alexander Shulgin died on March 4, 1960, at the age of seventy. A prolific writer after the Schwartzbard trial, he continued to blame the Soviets for all that had gone awry in his native land. He was especially concerned with the lot of the millions of Ukrainians who starved in what he considered deliberately staged famines in the 1930s.

8. *Massacres and Atrocities,* p.38

9. Lev Shankowsky, "Russia, the Jews, and the Ukrainian Liber-

ation Movement," *The Ukrainian Quarterly*, Vol. XVI (Spring, 1960), p.156.

10. Pigido-Pravoberezhny, "Ukrainian-Jewish Relations," p.86.

11. Margolin, "The Jews in the Ukraine," in *The Jewish Pogroms in Ukraine*, p.20.

12. Pigido-Pravoberezhny, "Ukrainian-Jewish Relations," p.97.

13. Reshetar, *The Ukrainian Revolution*, p.253.

14. Arthur E. Adams, *Bolsheviks in the Ukraine* (New Haven: Yale University Press, 1963), p.235. See also discussions in Hugh Seton-Watson, *Eastern Europe between the Wars, 1918-1941* (New York: Harper, 1967), pp.288-96, and generally Heinrich Graetz, *History of the Jews*, Vol.V, and Simon Dubnow, *History of the Jews in Russia and Poland*, Vol. IV. For the culpability of the Orthodox Church, see John Shelton Curtiss, *The Russian Church and the Soviet State, 1917-1950* (Boston: Beacon Press, 1953).

15. Haifetz, *The Slaughter of the Jews*, p.66.

16. *Nationalism and History: Essays on Old and New Judaism by Simon Dubnow,*, ed. Koppel Pinson (Philadelphia: Jewish Publication Society of America, 1958), p.26.

17. Norman Cohn, *Warrant for Genocide: The Myth of the Jewish World Conspiracy and the Protocols of the Elders of Zion* (New York and Evanston: Harper and Row, 1966), p.121.

18. Pigido-Pravoberezhny, "Ukrainian-Jewish Relations," p.88.

19. Choulguine, *L'Ukraine et le cauchemar rouge*, p.58.

20. See Documents on Grigoriev, Files 74-75 and 534, and Makhno Pogroms, File 29, Tcherikover Archives.

21. Gergel, "The Pogroms in the Ukraine," pp.238-242.

22. Reshetar, *The Ukrainian Revolution*, p.253.

23. *The Ukraine* (London: Handbooks prepared under the Historical Section of the Foreign Office, 52, 1920), p.58.

24. *Ibid.*, p.65.

25. Margolin, *The Jews of Eastern Europe*, p.136.

26. *Ibid.*, p.133.

27. *Massacres and Atrocities*, p.5. It has been suggested that an additional element in the pogrom atmosphere of 1919 was the "Russophilism" of the Jewish masses. Editorial Report, University of Tennessee Press, fall, 1973, p.10. Considering the constant persecution engineered by the Tsars, the reluctance of Jews to attend "Russian" schools or to list "Russian" as their native tongue, it is impossible to understand the basis of this canard. Apparently the Jews, already indicted by Ukrainians for mass paranoia, should also be faulted for masochism and love of their Russian tormenters.

28. Elbogen, *A Century of Jewish Life*, p.498.

29. Haifetz, *The Slaughter of the Jews*, p.17.

30. Schechtman, *et al*, *The Pogroms in the Ukraine*, p.46. The remark did not originate with Petlura. It was supposedly first uttered by the Count of Artois (brother of Louis XVI and later King of France under the name Charles X) when the Royalist reactionaries were trying to stay the French Revolution in the summer of 1789.

31. Chamberlin, *The Russian Revolution*, p.229.

32. Schechtman, *et al*, *The Pogroms in the Ukraine*, pp.44-45.

33. Pigido-Pravoberezhny, "Ukrainian-Jewish Relations," pp. 84-85.

34. See Statement of Vinnichenko, File 432, 37245-66, Tcherikover Archive, p.19. Also "Vinnichenko vegn Petliren," File 428, 37075-82, Tcherikover Archive.

35. Statement of Vinnichenko, File 432, Tcherikover Archive, pp.12-15.

36. *Ibid.*, pp.18-21 and p.5.

37. *Ibid.*, p.10.

38. *Ibid.*, p.18. Vinnichenko claimed that Petlura's supporters would sacrifice the honor and interests of all Ukrainians to preserve the honor of their little clique and its leader.

39. Resutzky, "Petliura," p.92.

40. Testimony of Kosenko, *Notes Sténographiques*, fasc. 5, p.154.

41. *In Re Yamashita*, 327 U.S.1. See *The Case of General*

Yamashita by A. Frank Reel (University of Chicago Press, 1949), p.261.

42. *Ibid.*, p.274.

43. *Ibid.*, p.275.

44. *Ibid.*, p.281. It should be noted that Justice Stone, writing for the majority, did take cognizance of a special military commission which explored the various problems which General Yamashita faced. Here too there were similarities with the problems faced by Petlura, including "the swift and overpowering advance" of the enemy, "errors of predecessors, weakness in organization, equipment, supply . . . training, communication, discipline, and morale of his troops" and "the tactical situation, the character, training, and capacity of staff officers and subordinate commanders as well as the traits of character of his troops." The Court held that violations of the law of war triable before a military tribunal need not be stated with the precision of a common law indictment, p.264.

45. *Ibid.*, p.285.

46. For the sworn statement of an eyewitness who claimed to have seen Petlura idling in the burning village of Smerenka, see Deposition of Jacob Klein, File 426, 36995, Tcherikover Archive.

47. John Appleman, *Military Tribunals and International Crimes* (Westport, Conn.: Greenwood Press,1954), p.56.

48. Choulguine, *L'Ukraine et le cauchemar rouge*, p.95.

49. *Crimes of War*, ed. Richard Falk, Gabriel Kolko, Robert Lifton (New York: Random House, 1971), pp.35-40, and Appleman, pp.29-35. Such phraseology was subsequently adopted and ignored by the signatories to the Geneva Convention of 1929 and the Genocide Convention of 1949.

50. Report of Nikowskjy for the Jewish Commission, September, 1919, File 434, Tcherikover Archive, p.30.

51. Topelberg-Ovcharenko, "A Personal History," File 461, Tcherikover Archive, p.61. Topelberg-Ovcharenko agreed with Vinnichenko that Petlura was a "nobody" before the war.

52. Tcherikover, *Di ukrainer pogromen*, p.184. For Tcherikover's

retraction of pro-Petlura statements see Files 458 (Yiddish) and 459 (French), Tcherikover Archive.

53. Revutzky, *In di shvere tog ofn Ukraine*, p.156, and Tcherikover, *Di ukrainer pogromen*, p.98.

54. Deposition of Solovei from Montevideo, File 455, 38215-65, July 15, 1927, p.10, Tcherikover Archive.

55. *International Criminal Law*, ed. Gerhard Mueller and Edward Wise (London: Street and Maxwell, and New York: New York Univerity Press, 1965), pp.280-88. In like manner, the United States Army Field Manual of 1956 states in Section 501: "The commander is also responsible if he has actual knowledge or should have knowledge, through reports received by him or through other means, that troops or other persons subject to his control are about to commit or have commited a war crime and if he fails to take the necessary and reasonable steps to insure compliance with the law of war or to punish violators thereof." See Falk, etc., *Crimes of War*, p.68.

56. Resutzky, "Petliura," p.88.

57. Statement of Vassilko, Nov. 30, 1926, File 456, 38276, Tcherikover Archive, pp.8-9. Vassilko, who was married to a Jew, referred to Petlura as a little peasant who had no idea of what a national policy should be.

58. Deposition of Solovei, File 455, Tcherikover Archive, p.10.

59. See Aleksander Drozdzynski and Jan Zborowski, *Oberlaender: A Study in German East Politics* (Warsaw: Wydwanictwo Zachodnie, 1960), pp.86-89, and Gerald Reitlinger, *The Final Solution* (New York: Beechhurst Press, 1953), p.229. Incredibly, some Ukrainians have tried to soften the severity of what happened at Lwow in 1941 by offering reference to another *Aktion Petlura*, that which destroyed the Petlura Library in Paris during World War II. Editorial Report, University of Tennessee Press, fall, 1973, p.11. Such an attempt to equate the slaughter of human beings with the loss of Ukrainian records reflects upon the character of the one who raises the comparison.

60. For Ukrainian contributions to the Nazi cause, see *The Black Book of Polish Jewry*, p.100; Raul Hilberg, *The Destruction of the European Jews* (Chicago: Quadrangle Press, 1961),

pp.192, 204, 223, 225, 236, 240, 252, 295-6, 329-30, and 343; and Nora Levin, *The Holocaust* (New York: Thomas Crowell, 1968), pp.263-64, 280.

Afterword

On Assassination

SIMON PETLURA WAS DEAD. A man had been killed in cold blood, and his slayer was set free. Some considered this a mockery of justice.

Pointing to the outcome of the Grynszpan trial a decade later, where pressure from a powerful Nazi Germany compelled punishment of the Jewish assassin, Ukrainian apologists argued that Schwartzbard also would have been condemned if there had been an internationally recognized Ukrainian state in 1927. France would not have dared to risk impairing diplomatic and trade relations with a free Ukraine over the action of a fanatic. Or, failing that, if the killing had occurred in another era, as after 1945 when the villainy of international communism was at last fully appreciated, then too Schwartzbard would have been condemned. Or, finally, if the trial had taken place anywhere but France, where men's heads were easily turned by emotional appeals and hearsay, some form of retribution would have been exacted.

Sholom Schwartzbard had committed murder, and no code of laws formally condones such an act. Legislators have excused killings done by crazed persons, or those who acted out of "irresistible impulse" (a vague medical-legal term which, like insanity, continues to defy definition), or those who acted to "avenge outraged honor," or those who acted

"in self-defense," but lawgivers have been silent about political assassins.

Assassination has been found in every society since the
first caveman decided to club his chief and usurp leadership
of the clan. The twentieth century fairly redounds with
incidents of political murder:

President McKinley at Buffalo in September, 1901. King
Alexander and Queen Draga of Serbia in 1903. Pettkov of
Bulgaria and Delyannis of Greece in 1907. King Carlos
of Portugal the following year. Egyptian Prime Minister
Butrus Pasha Gali in 1910. President Caceres of the Domin-
ican Republic in 1911. Francisco Madero of Mexico in 1913.
The Archduke Franz Ferdinand and Jaures in the summer of
1914. Rasputin in Petrograd in 1916. Karl Liebknecht, Rosa
Luxemburg and Emiliano Zapata, all in 1919. Erzberger.
Paasche. Gareis. Weimar's Foreign Minister Rathenau in
Berlin in 1922. Gabriel Narutowicz, Poland's first constitu-
tional president, and Irish Prime Minister Michael Collins
killed in the same year. Count Stambolisky in Bulgaria in
1923. Matteoti in Rome, Sir Lee Stack in Cairo, in 1924.
Petlura. Obregon of Mexico in 1928. President Paul
Doumier of France in 1932. Duca in Bucharest in 1933.
Anton Cermak in Miami the same year. French Foreign
Minister Barthou in Marseilles in 1934. King Alexander of
Yugoslavia. Dollfuss of Austria. Admiral Francois Darlan of
Vichy on Christmas Day, 1942. King Boris of Bulgaria, nine
months later.

All were victims of murder prompted by personal gain,
diplomacy, internal reasons of state, religious motives, or
ugly chauvinism. And there were many others.[1]

The seventeeth century Swedish jurist Hugo Grotius once
wrote: "No one can justly be killed by design, except by way
of legal punishment or to defend our lives and property
when it cannot be effected without his destruction."[2] *Vim vi
repellere cuique lict* (it is permissible to repel force by force)
has been an established principle of the law of nations.

The sixteenth-century theorists Duplessis-Mornay, George Buchanan, and Juan de Mariana all advocated punishment of a temporal ruler if his objectives did not correspond to the welfare of the people. Justifications for rebellion and tyrannicide may be found in the writings of Coluccio Salutati, William of Occam, Marsilius of Padua, Machiavelli, John Locke, John Knox, Robert Bellarmine, Theodorus Beza, and Francisco Suarez.

Perhaps the most eloquent defense of tyrannicide came from the pen of Giuseppe Mazzini. To Daniele Manin in 1865, Mazzini wrote:

> When justice is extinguished and the terror of a single tyrant denies and obliterates the conscience of the people and God, who wished them free, and when a man unblemished by hatred and base passion, solely for the Fatherland and for the external right incarnate in him rises against the tyrant and exclaims: "You torture millions of my brothers, you withhold from them that which God has decreed theirs, you destroy their bodies and corrupt their souls; through you my country is dying a lingering death; you are the keystone of an entire edifice of slavery, dishonor and vice; I overthrow that edifice by destroying you." I recognize in that manifestation of the tremendous equality between the master of millions and a single individual, the finger of God. Many feel in their hearts as I do, and I express it.[3]

It is because tyrannicide is closely connected with the legitimate principles of killing in self-defense, war, and revolution, that it has been the refuge of every self-seeking scoundrel in history, that it has been claimed as a defense by religious zealots, Jacobins, and fascists. This has been especially true in the past blood-stained decade, since work commenced on this study a few months before the assassination of President John F. Kennedy.

For American Professors Oscar Jaszi and John D. Lewis, tyrannicide is "an act of conscience," a harmonious blend of "love" and "reason," "our feeling of unity with the moral order, with the pattern of values that religious men call God or philosophers the good life."[4] Thus, the killing of a tyrant has even higher dignity than individual self-defense, for the assassin has totally disregarded his personal safety to accomplish something for the good of the entire people, where the all-pervading tyrannical power makes collective action hopeless.[5]

The same criterion of "the public good" is vital to the thinking of Professors Feliks Gross and Edward Hyams. Gross argues that resistance to domestic autocracy and foreign conquerors is justified, but he disapproves of incitements by "militants in a self-governing and democratic community."[6] For Hyams, who actually endorses the concept of an international Assassination Commando under the jurisdiction of the Secretary General of the United Nations, the controls are very similar to those advocated by Jaszi and Lewis. Murder for personal gain is repugnant, but assassination supported by the "consensus of decent opinion" must be retained by the people "at all costs." Hyams adds: "It ought to be clearly understood that assassination, to be useful and meaningful, must be based on principles and on reason and not on a state of unwholesome excitement."[7]

By no stretch of the imagination can one fix the concepts of "love," "reason," "the good life," "God," or "the public good" upon a Hitler, an Oswald, or a Sirhan, any more than the idea of an "all-pervading tyrannical power" applies to their victims—the frightened Jews of Europe or President Kennedy and his brother. Lofty expressions of humanitarianism do not, however, solve the problem of tyrannicide. Fanatics have always deluded themselves that their madness is consonant with the divine music of love and reason. Taken to the extreme, practically any political leader may be perceived as a tyrant by someone. As Hyams admits, "One man's tyrant is another man's hero."

Should it happen that the "tyrant" is not chastened in some manner, either at the polls or in a dungeon, then the true believer might be tempted to act as the conscience of mankind. The question remains, who is a tyrant? Eichmann? Stalin? Franco? Unquestionably. But what of an Admiral Horthy, who sacrificed some lives in World War II for the good of the greater number of Hungarians? Or Pierre Laval, who traded off 160,000 Jewish aliens in France for the safety of his own Jewish countrymen? What of those who believed that Lyndon Johnson was ultimately responsible for My Lai?

More than thirty years ago, Emil Ludwig, an historian-biographer of some repute, made an exhaustive study of political assassinations. Utilizing admittedly arbitrary standards, Ludwig compiled a list of twenty-eight assassins who were "persons of magnanimous and noble disposition" and who apparently were justified in their assaults. "Almost all of them" he wrote, "from Brutus (extolled by Plutarch) to the Russian fanatics of the last half-century, were sensitive, were self-sacrificing, were men and women into whose hands a weapon was pressed by an exacting sense of honour."[8] In this category, Ludwig included Sholom Schwartzbard.

Ludwig found that six factors distinguished these individuals from the gangs of terrorists and free-booters which have punctuated the twentieth century with political murder. Each of his idealistic assassins, "champions of liberty" as he called them, operated singly, in a public street, mindless of witnesses, stared his victim in the face, did not attempt to flee, and felt his deed was right.[10] Sholom Schwartzbard satisfied each of Ludwig's criteria.

To the eminent legal scholar Hans Kelsen, these points would still be insufficient. Schwartzbard's act, based on the primitive "eye for an eye" principle, boils down to retribution pure and simple, and retribution is not justice. Retribution merely reacts to evil with evil.[11]

But there was an additional element in Schwartzbard's actions which must not be overlooked. Sholom Schwartzbard was a Jew.

His was a people possessed of a unique history of tragedy heaped upon tragedy, a people that had seen a million of its number slaughtered and enslaved by the Romans in the first century and another million massacred by the same Romans a century later, half a million slain by Persians, Byzantines, and Arabs in their contests for domination of the Middle East during Europe's Dark Ages, another hundred thousand murdered by Crusaders, fifty thousand by the Inquisition, a quarter of a million as a result of sham trials for "ritual murder" and other charges, and then as many as half a million in the Cossack Deluge of the seventeenth century.[12] His was a rootless people, expelled from every land, still retaining unending belief in the goodness of man and traditionally shunning counter-violence. Only rarely did frustration prompt one of its number to emulate Judith or Pinchas, the grandson of Aaron, who struck out at the principal tormentors of the Jews.

This is the condition, then, which distinguishes the Jewish tyrannicide from the Arab terrorist, for example. The Jewish tyrannicide is an aberration. His act is not overwhelmingly approved by Jewish communities around the world, nor is he transformed into a colorful "freedom fighter" who may live out his days in a comfortable villa (like the surviving perpetrators of the 1972 Munich Massacre or the 1973 Athens Airport slaughter). Unlike the Arab "Black Septembrist," who lived for a quarter of a century on the welfare of the international community while being manipulated by his kinsmen in eighteen neighboring Arab lands and by Stalinists in the Soviet Union, the Jewish tyrannicide knew no international charity or goodwill, no haven from oppression for twenty centuries. His people were massacred daily, without any hope of deliverance.

Unlike the Black Septembrist, the rare Jewish tyrannicide

struck not against athletes or school children or humanitarians like Robert Kennedy, but against the uniformed leader of a regime directly responsible for the murder of his people. His act was not the product of an internationally financed cabal like the slaughter of thirty-two innocents at the Rome and Athens Airports in 1973 which was underwritten by the Libyan government. The Jewish tyrannicide did not hire surrogate kamikazes to commit mass murder, as in the case of the Japanese anarchists who machine-gunned Puerto Rican pilgrims at Lod Airport in June, 1972. The Jewish tyrannicide did not conceal his face beneath a hangman's hood; nor did he seize innocent hostages. And unlike the psychopathic murderers who have sought to destroy Jews wherever they may be, the Jewish tyrannicide did not preach destruction of all members of the opposing group— genocide.

Neither is it fair to equate the act of Sirhan Sirhan, operating alone, with that of Sholom Schwartzbard. According to Thomas Greening, one may measure an assassin's degree of contact with reality through the extent to which he (1) correctly selects his victim, who is in fact the enemy of his cause, (2) correctly predicts that his enemy's death will advance his cause, and (3) correctly perceives that as an assassin he will be affirming the wishes and values of the group he claims to represent.[13]

Unlike Schwartzbard, who resisted the Ukrainian nationalists on the battlefield until it was impossible for him to fight on, Sirhan never joined the Jordanian or Egyptian Army or even Al Fatah in order to face his enemies on the field of combat. Unlike Schwartzbard, who focused upon Petlura, the onetime leader of a government charged with the slaughter of one hundred thousand of his people, Sirhan arbitrarily selected Bobby Kennedy as his victim because the Senator was known to be friendly toward Israel and had advocated sending arms to that country. How Kennedy's death advanced the Palestinian cause has yet to be determined, but the assassination of Simon Petlura fixed world attention, at least for a moment, upon the suffering of the Jews. Said Greening:

> Assassins and murderers such as Sirhan, Lee Harvey Oswald, James Earl Ray, Leopold and Loeb, Benny Smith, Dick Hickock, Penny Smith, Richard Speck, and Charles Whitman were strangers, loners, odd and unique individuals, sick in their own way and quite independent of our society.[14]

Such individuals were generally products of disturbed childhoods, suffering poor ego image, physical inferiority, inadequacy, and sexual inhibition. The "typical" assassin has been described by Dr. Lawrence Z. Freedman, a psychiatrist and consultant to the President's Commission on Violence, as "a moral masochist whose capacity for social adaptation was seriously defective."[15] Sirhan's life, for example, was a steady history of childish tantrums, unrealistic goals, preoccupation with vindictive thoughts, schizoid withdrawal, fanatical religiosity, and persistent refusal to accept or adjust to reality.[16] He had lost a sister to leukemia, suffered a serious head injury himself, flunked out of college, and lost his job as a delivery boy all within two years of his murder of Senator Kennedy. By way of contrast, Sholom Schwartzbard was happily married, a successful craftsman, a joiner, popular with his comrades-in-arms in the Soviet Union and the French Foreign Legion, a union leader, active in welfare for children, popular among his neighbors and friends, able to adjust to societies as diverse as the Russian, Austrian, French, and American.

According to the psychiatrists who examined him at Paris, Schwartzbard possessed rare qualities—absence of ego and complete self-effacement—in contrast with the narcissist personality represented by Dr. Freedman's typical assassin.[17] Schwartzbard was said to be extraordinarily kind, generous, truthful, and incapable of doing bad things.[18] In this too he differed radically from the common assassin.

According to Greening, assassins are usually paranoid schizophrenics or paranoid personalities with psychotic episodes. Richard Lawrence who attacked Andrew Jackson in 1835, John Schrank who attempted to kill Theodore Roosevelt in 1912, Leon Czolgosz, John Guiteau, Joseph Zangara, John Wilkes Booth, and Lee Harvey Oswald all suffered from mental disorders.

This was true also of Sirhan Sirhan. All but one of the many psychologists and psychiatrists who testified at the Palestinian's trial concluded that the assassin suffered from pronounced paranoid characteristics. Seven defense psychiatrists called him a "paranoid schizophrenic." The prosecution referred to him as a "paranoid borderline schizophrenic." And Dr.Olinger, the only one who would not certify him as suffering from a clinical malady, indicated that he was suffering from "pseudoneurotic schizophrenia."

If there is a parallel in history to the Arab terrorists, it is not the Jewish tyrannicides but the Semosenkos and Palienkos, the Petluras. Like the pogromchiks of old, the Arab assassins act with the connivance and blessing of ruling officials. Their targets are the Jewish people and friends of Jews, no longer chastised for their alleged "Bolshevism," but for "cosmopolitanism," "imperialism," "capitalism," and "fascism."

Labels change, but it is still the Jew who is the singular obstacle to the liberation of the fatherland by fanatic chauvinists. The Jew must be removed by force. And when he is, the terrorists revel in their massacres and are hailed as national heroes. And none of these sociopaths is ever punished.

Section 46 of the Grisons Code of Switzerland states: "Self-defense may be pleaded by one who has to avert an illegal onslaught on his own or another's life and limb, health, property, liberty or honor, *in circumstances when no adequate appeal to the help of the authorities is possible.*"[19] [*Emphasis added.*]

Unlike the Palestinians, who are welcome in the United Nations and supported by the oil powers, the "nonaligned" nations, and the Soviet bloc, the Jews of the Ukraine, Jews everywhere, had no one to whom they could make "adequate appeal" for tanks, rockets, or justice in 1648, 1881, 1905, 1919, or any other time of pogroms. Sholom Schwartzbard's actions were indeed outside the law, but as a Jew he was part of a spiritual nation which had been forced to live outside the protection of international law for two millennia.

"The calamity of the rightless," says Hannah Arendt, "is not that they are deprived of life, liberty, and the pursuit of happiness, or of equality before the law and freedom of opinion—formulas which were designed to solve problems within given communities—but that they no longer belong to any community whatever. Their plight is not that they are not equal before the law, but that no law exists for them."[20]

It was ironic that a Gentile world which had slaughtered Jews in every epoch, exiled them from every land, deprived them of basic political and social rights, turned a deaf ear to all lamentations while eleven million Jews perished at the hands of the Tenth Legion, Visigoths, Almohades, Crusaders, the *Chern,* and the SS, should even consider branding a Jew an "outlaw." The Jew waited for liberties promised him by the Enlightenment. He waited for the world's conscience to be truly awakened. He waited in vain. The slaughtered thousands of Ukrainian Jews cried out in 1919 and their cries went unheeded by the Christ of Versailles. To whom could Sholom Schwartzbard have appealed in 1926? Calvin Coolidge?

"I am no partisan of terror," Maxim Gorki wrote, "but I am not able to refuse a man the right to defend himself. It seems to me that a murder can be committed for fear of seeing the past repeated, and by the natural desire to prevent the possibility of greater horrors."[21]

No one can be certain whether Schwartzbard actually

believed he could prevent renewed pogroms against his kinsmen in the Ukraine by assassinating Petlura. If this was a part of his motivation, it was a failure. His murder did not bring the one hundred thousand victims of pogroms back to life; nor did it preserve the six million from the wrath of Hitler. To "the years of Haman," the years when Jews especially suffered—1096, 1348, 1492, 1648, 1881, 1903, 1919—were added 1939, 1940, 1941, 1942, 1943, 1944, 1945. To the names Mainz, Madrid, Kishinev, Balta, Proskurov, Torquemada, Chmielnicki, Plehve, and Petlura were added Auschwitz, Maidanek, Janowska, Babi Yar, Heydrich, Ohlendorf, and *Aktion Petlura.*

"A sea of blood storms and tosses, a sea of tears for which the nation has no revenge." Thus wrote the Jewish poet Nadson of the pogroms.[22] There could be no vengeance for the Ukrainian Jews massacred in 1919 any more than for the millions slaughtered by the Nazis twenty-five years later. Each of them, separately, was a human being, entitled to life with all its passions, good and bad, and the killing of one man who had helped engineer the slaughter could not compensate for their unfair deaths. Not even the elaborately staged trial of Adolf Eichmann could provide the catharsis that Jews sought in erasing the memories of the twentieth century.[23]

Was Schwartzbard's act justified? Perhaps no one will ever know. Grotius wrote: "To justify a punishment of that kind [killing an enemy] the person put to death must have committed a crime, and such a crime, too, as every equitable judge would deem worthy of death."[24]

The Nuremberg War Crimes Tribunals stated that the penalty for pogromchiks is death. The place for such criminals to be punished, however, is not on the streets but in the courtroom. As Simon Wiesenthal, Director of the Nazi War Crimes Documentation Center in Vienna, put it: "Jews don't need a balance. Just because Germans once killed Jews, no Jews kill Germans. If so, future generations will keep the accounts open. We need trials in German and Austrian courts.[25] The problem for Sholom Schwartzbard was that no one was interested in such trials in 1926.

None of this, not Proskurov, not Felshtin, not the Rue Racine, not Auschwitz, not Nuremberg, can ever be permitted to happen again. No longer can one people stand by, apathetic witnesses to the extermination of another. No longer can moral bankruptcy, active or passive, be excused.

The aged Simon Dubnow, himself the victim of a murderer's bullet in 1941, supplied an answer to Elia Tcherikover in a letter written in 1939. Said Dubnow: "When the knife is at the throat, we must hasten to stay the hand of the murderer and save the victim. We must create a world organization to combat this band of murderers, and we must also set up organizations to find emigration lands for the exiles and refugees."[26]

Dubnow was talking about Jews, but he might just as well have been talking of the unfortunates in Juba, Dar es-Salaam, Lagos, Calcutta, or Saigon. Not by procrastination, nor by retribution, nor by adherence to an empty godhead of relativism, but by an active commitment to justice and love would a better world be forged.

The observation of *The American Hebrew* in 1927 rings bromidic. It nonetheless remains true: "Petlura is gone, but the Petluras will live on until the whole world is ready to answer in response to the old query, 'Am I my brother's keeper?' a fervent 'I am and I never forget that he is my brother.' "[27]

Notes

1. See Murray Clark Havens, Carl Leiden, and Karl M.Schmitt, *The Politics of Assassination* (Englewood Cliffs, N.J.: Prentice-Hall, 1970), pp.161-68.

2. Hugo Grotius, *The Rights of War and Peace*, trans. A.C.Campbell (Washington and London: M. Walter Dunne), p.359.

3. Edward Hyams, *Killing No Murder: A Study of Assassination as a Political Means* (London: Thos. Nelson and Sons Ltd., 1969), pp.17-18.

4. Oscar Jaszi and John B.Lewis, *Against the Tyrant: The Tradition and Theory of Tyrannicide* (Glencoe, Illinois: The Free Press,1957), p.238.

5. *Ibid.*, p.237.

6. Feliks Gross, "Political Violence and Terror in Nineteenth and Twentieth Century Russia and Eastern Europe," p.422, in *Assassination and Political Violence*, ed. James Kirkham, Sheldon Levy and William Crotty, Vol.8 (Washington: Government Printing Office, 1969). While this epic makes reference to assassinations in Japan, France, Germany, China, Austria, and Canada, and Gross specifies assassins among Russians, Armenians, Serbs, Poles, Macedonians, and Rumanians, there is no appreciation in the commission's study of the special condition of Jewish assassins or the suffering of the Jewish people. Crotty's *Assassination and the Political Order* (New York: Harper and Row, 1971) is of little more use.

7. Hyams, *Killing No Murder*, pp.220-225.

8. Emil Ludwig, *The Davos Murder*, trans. Eden and Cedar Paul (New York: Viking Press, 1936), p.86.

9. Ludwig, *The Davos Murder*, p.87.

10. *Ibid.*

11. Hans Kelsen, *What Is Justice?* (Berkeley and Los Angeles: California Press, 1957), pp.14 and 312.

12. These figures are estimates based on the best records available from contemporary sources as balanced by historians such as Graetz, Grayzel, Ausubel, Baron, and Abram Sachar. The figures include deaths by brutal action as well as those which may have resulted indirectly through starvation or disease brought on by the massacres. Such estimates may actually fall short of the real numbers. Catholic historian Malcolm Hay has written: "No people has ever had to pay so fearful a price for freedom—the uncounted, unrecorded dead: an exceeding great army. Only a remnant has escaped from the contempt and hatred, from the toleration and patronage of the Western World." Hay, *Thy Brother's Blood* (New York: Hart, 1975).

13. Thomas C.Greening, "The Psychological Study of Assassins," in Crotty, *Assassination and the Political Order*, p.233.

14. *Ibid.*, p.224.

15. Dr. Lawrence Z.Freedman, "The Psychology of the Assassins," in Crotty, *Assassination and the Political Order*, p.152. An equally cogent and disparaging analysis of the "typical" assassin is offered by Albert Ellis and John Gullo, *Murder and Assassination* (New York: Lyle Stuart, Inc., 1971), pp.190-239.

16. Among his other fantasies was the wish that a lightning bolt might strike Moshe Dayan. See Ellis and Gullo, *op. cit.*, pp.230-31.

17. Freedman, "The Psychology of the Assassins," p.152. Freedman also argues that the assassin feels no personal involvement with his victim; nor does he operate under irresistible impulse. Neither statement applies to Schwartzbard, who believed Petlura to be personally responsible for the deaths of

his family in the Ukraine and who was likened on more than one occasion to a man moving as if in a somnambulent state.

18. Deposition of D. Dawidoff, Professor of Anatomy, Université de Perm, Faculté Secours de Paris, December, 1926, File 427, 37041, Tcherikover Archive, and signatures of neighbors of Schwartzbard, File 508, 42052-83, Tcherikover Archive.

19. Ludwig, *The Davos Murder*, p.91.

20. Hannah Arendt, *The Origins of Totalitarianism* (Cleveland and New York: World Publishing Company, 1962) pp.295-6.

21. Torrès, *Le procès des pogromes*, p.131.

22. From the poem "What has Amalek Done to Us?" in Dubnow, *Nationalism and History*, p.200.

23. See Arendt's strained comparison between Eichmann and Schwartzbard in *Eichmann in Jerusalem: A Report on the Banality of Evil* (New York: Viking Press, 1971), pp.265-67.

24. Wiesenthal made these comments in an interview with Dick Cavett, June 14, 1973, over ABC Television.

25. Grotius, *The Rights of War and Peace*, p.360.

26. Dubnow, *Nationalism and History*, p.355. On the night of December 7-8, 1941, the Nazis liquidated the Riga Ghetto. The eighty-one-year-old Simon Dubnow, suffering from a fever, apparently moved too slowly for a Latvian militia man. The greatest Jewish historian of the twentieth century was shot in the back and killed.

27. "Schwartzbard's Acquittal: The World's Conscience," *American Hebrew*, XXV (November 4,1927), p.891.

Index

Index

Saul S. Friedman is Associate Professor of Near Eastern and Jewish History at Youngstown State University, Youngstown, Ohio. He received his Ph.D. from Ohio State University in 1969, writing a dissertation on Jewish refugees of the Holocaust.

In addition to *Pogromchik,* Dr. Friedman has written a book entitled *No Haven for the Oppressed: Official U.S. Policy toward European Jewish Refugees, 1938-1945,* which was published by Wayne State University Press in 1973. He has also written articles appearing in *Midstream, Jewish Frontier,* and *Chronicle Review,* among others. Dr. Friedman is currently at work on two books, one on the blood libel in America, the other based on oral testimonies of 36 survivors of the Holocaust.

The 39-year-old professor lives with his wife Nancy and their children, Jonathan and Molly, in Youngstown.